COMMUNITY LIBRARY
LIS 133.5815 RUD
The astrology of person...nd philosophy.
Rudhyar, Dane,

3 2301 00045543 0

D1179878

for Refer...

Not to be taken from this room

THE ASTROLOGY OF PERSONALITY

Other books by
Dane Rudhyar

-:-

THE REBIRTH OF HINDU MUSIC
(Theosophical Publishing House, Madras, 1929)

ART AS RELEASE OF POWER
(Harbison and Harbison, 1930)

NEW MANSIONS FOR NEW MEN
(Lucis Publishing Co., N. Y.-1938)

THE FAITH THAT GIVES MEANING TO VICTORY
(Foundation for Human Integration, 1942)

THE PULSE OF LIFE
First edition, Mackay, 1943
Second edition, 1963 (Servire, The Hague)

THE MOON
The Cycles and Fortunes of Life
Mackay, 1945

MODERN MAN'S CONFLICTS
The creative challenge of a global society
(Philosophical Library, N. Y. 1948)

GIFTS OF THE SPIRIT
(New Age Publishing Co. 1956)

THE WAY THROUGH
(Seed Publications, 1961)

THE
ASTROLOGY
OF
PERSONALITY

A Re-formulation of Astrological Concepts
and Ideals, in Terms of Contemporary
Psychology and Philosophy

by

Dane Rudhyar

SERVIRE/THE HAGUE

COPYRIGHT, 1936 BY LUCIS PUBLISHING CO.
COPYRIGHT, 1963 BY DANE RUDHYAR

MANUFACTURED IN THE NETHERLANDS

42,658

GIFT SEPT. 05

LIS
133.5B15
RUD

PREFACE
to the second edition
(1963)

"THE Astrology of Personality" was first published in the
fall of 1936 by the Lucis Publishing Co., New York. It
had been written mainly during the summers of 1934 and 1935
on a beautiful ranch in New Mexico, near the Rio Grande and
within view of the mountain site which, a few years later, was
to attain world fame as the birth-place of the atom bomb, Los
Alamos. Some of the material in the book had been printed,
in a less coherent and philosophical form, as articles written
for Paul G. Clancy's magazine, "American Astrology", since
its inception in 1932-'33. Thirty years, therefore, have passed
since the basic attitude and the concepts formulated in this book
came to the attention of the American and English people.

Naturally, there are quite a few points in this volume which
I would express differently today. In thirty years and after producing a continuous stream of monthly articles for several astrological magazines in the United States, one is bound to modify, if not one's basic attitude, at least the manner in which it
establishes and deepens itself through multiple correlations with
other modes of thinking and through a great variety of personal
experiences. But it would be impossible to change a few paragraphs here and there without running into all sorts of problems; besides, the only way it was possible in the present
circumstances to re-publish this book has been through an
"offset" process which made changes practically impossible,
particularly as it was reprinted in Holland where the old type
was not available. American and English publishers had been
unwilling to assume the financial responsibility of a new edition,

even though there had been a constant public demand for copies of the book.

The main change in my astrological outlook concerns the matter of the "houses". For a time, when I began to study in deep earnest the meaning of all the tools used in astrology, I accepted the then widely-used idea according to which the houses are produced by the daily rotation of the earth-globe; thus, the natal horizon is seen moving every day around the zodiac and the rotation of the globe around its axis defines the houses, just as the earth's revolution around the sun defines the signs of the zodiac. Everything is in movement; and astrology deals with time values, with cycles.

This is true, as far as it goes; yet, there is also space; and there is, I believe, that which, in every human being, remains a constant. Every person is *inherently* an individual self, with a particular rhythm (or "tone") of being and with an orientation to space which defines what I call now his "individuality", the "seed pattern" of his individual being. This is his "place in space", the way he becomes aware of his own self and of his capacity for relationship with other selves. Every human being is born at the center of *his own space;* and it is that space to which the circle of houses refers. Fundamentally it *is* a circle. The circle, of course, turns in time, and we can speak of the "wheel of houses". But there is a fundamental space-orientation which remains as a permanent "Image" of individual selfhood, and this is the most important factor in an astro-psychology which deals, not primarily with external events, but with the *innate potential of individual existence* in every human being. The purpose of this astro-psychology is to help the person to actualize this innate potential, to bring what is only *possible* to an, at least, relatively complete state of fulfillment. It is clear that the vast majority of human beings, not only do not experience such a state of fulfillment, but remain in nearly total ignorance of what one may call, using a phrase popularized by Zen Buddhism, their "fundamental nature".

The reader will find such ideas expressed in this book, but perhaps not as clearly as should be. Their reference to the houses is important, for now I conceive the houses most definitely as 30-degree sections of the space surrounding the natal act of individualization, i.e., the first breath which establishes the individual rhythm of the newborn. The houses are not *in* the zodiac; but it is the signs of the zodiac and all celestial bodies which find their location in this or that house. As a result, the Placidus system of house-determination, which is still mostly in use, does not fit in with such an approach, for it is based on a time-factor. The Campanus system, on the other hand, is a space-based method of calculating the longitude of the cusps of the house, and I am therefore using it and finding it more and more revealing in astro-psychological practice.

Quite a few other points could be mentioned if space permitted. I might say that my thinking in the years immediately following 1933 was deeply impressed by some of the psychological ideas of C. G. Jung; indeed, it was in order to integrate the old concepts and symbols of astrology (to which Marc Edmund Jones had just begun to give a deeper meaning) with the ideas of C. G. Jung, that I started writing a series of articles for Paul Clancy's magazine in the fall of 1933. I had begun to study astrology and to erect charts in 1920, while living near the headquarters of the Theosophical Society in Hollywood, but it was only after reading Marc Jones and Carl Jung (and also General Smuts' "Holism and Evolution") that I realized the possibilities of astrology as a practical application of the concepts of cyclic process and *gestalt* which had developed within my mind since I wrote my first book, "Claude Debussy and the cycle of musical civilization", at the age of 16.

Though, in 1936, I was already questioning quite critically the presentday validity and applicability of many of the premises, ideas and feeling-responses derived from a transcendentalistic and so-called "occult" (or esoteric) tradition, the reader will find in this book many places in which this point of view is implied or expressed in one form or another. In recent years, I have increasingly looked at man, life and the universe from the point of view of what I might call a "cyclic existentialism"; I have also coined the term "eonics" to differentiate my approach from what is usually called metaphysics. This approach, without any reference to astrology, has been condensed in a book written in French in 1961 and called, "Existence, Rhythm and Symbol"; and I hope to be able to develop the material it contains in a series of volumes in English. This kind of existentialism is, of course, fundamentally different from the religious irrationalism of Kierkegaard, or the atheistic pessimism of Sartre. It is an existentialism which integrates the immediate experience of change (and the spontaneity of an open response to life and relationship) with a basic realization of the structured order in all processes of existence, cosmic and personal.

There are a great many possible approaches to astrology; and I have very little doubt that sooner or later a new science will be built which will deal with cosmic electro-magnetic fields, cosmic vibrations and their effect upon the earth's biosphere. It may be that some of the younger astrologers who try so hard to be "scientific" are working toward such a goal, but I do not think that when such a science is established it will be any more what has been traditionally known as "astrology" than modern chemistry is alchemy. A truly "sidereal" and scientific astrology would be one which takes the whole galaxy as its frame of reference and which, for instance, deals with the ever changing relationship between the earth-equatorial plane and the plane of the galaxy. It would substitute actual star-groups and their relative motions to the old type of zodiacal mythology which relies solely on pictorial and symbolic man-made constellations. We may learn, of course, from the archaic past of humanity; but it should be *the whole* of humanity, including, for instance, the Chinese and the Mayan cultures. Above all, I believe in a "twentieth century astrology" which meets adequately the psychological need of modern men, women and children.

To me, the basic message of astrology is a message of order in a disordered society, or (as in the days of primitive man) in a jungle environment which seemed to reveal but chaos, caprice of "fate", danger and fear. Modern man may have conquered much of the physical jungle, but he cannot yet feed adequately two-thirds of an insanely proliferating earth-population. He had learned to use nuclear forces, but he coldly juggles with calculations of tens of millions of deaths in all-out war; and modern psyches are often reminiscent of jungles. Everywhere, at every moment, the great tides of change sweep over all existences; yet there is foreseeable repetition; there are patterns of transformations, cyclic processes at work. There is order, as well as change; nay, more, there is an order *immanent* in all changes. It is an existential order; and we need no longer see it as something utterly transcendent, and/or exterior to existential processes.

Astrology was the first human expression of an awareness of order. That there was order and structure of existence seemed such a wonderful and supernatural thing that, for primitive man, this could only be the work of gods, or God. Whether it is or not is largely a matter of semantics, of defining carefully one's terms. I shall close this Preface by repeating what I wrote, in the FOREWORD to the first edition, concerning "personality":

"Personality, in the largest sense, is the organic whole in which the physiological and the psychomental natures of man are progressively integrated. Therefore it represents the wholeness of the human being as a microcosm: man as a complete image of the celestial order of the skies; man as a whole solar system operating on the background of, and in constant relationship to the zodiac or the galaxy ... Astrology ... is an art of life-interpretation and it provides us with a technique for the development and fulfillment of "personality". Its aim is to transform chaotic human nature into a microcosm. When man becomes truly a microcosm, he demonstrates personality to the fullest extent and manifests as a living Person, or as a great Personage ... The goal of astrology is the alchemy of personality. It is to transform chaos into cosmos, collective human nature into individual and creative personality."

D. R.

Table of Contents

xiii

PROLOGUE

Prelude to a History of Astrology

THE history of astrology is the history of the successive transformations of man's attitude to Nature:—external nature, perceived through sense-impressions; and as well, internal or "human" nature, the sum total of those physiological and psychological phenomena which somehow man calls his own; saying, "my" body, "my" soul, "my" mind.

What today is usually called astrology is the result of a particular phase of this relationship between man's conscious ego and Nature. Though this phase may have lasted hundreds and thousands of years, it was preceded by other phases of perhaps greater significance; and the purpose of this book is to show that a new phase is just now beginning. Mankind is changing radically its outlook upon external nature—witness the startlingly new concepts of modern science concerning space, time, matter, and the universe. The psychological outlook is being just as fundamentally transformed. Man is meeting "life," within and without, on new terms. Astrology reflects the quality of this meeting, interprets it in functions of actual behavior, gives it significance in both a very fundamental and a very practical way. Astrology is the most significant index to man's practical philosophy of living. Philosophy *per se* speculates about life and man. But astrology, in every age, characterizes, directly or indirectly, the deepest quality of man's actual response to life.

Philosophies have succeeded philosophies. Likewise the astrology bequeathed to *us* by the nineteenth century was but one of the many astrologies which man has projected out of his need for a practical understanding of and adjustment to

3

life. Moreover, as various types of philosophy have always existed simultaneously in man's effort to interpret reality at various levels of thought and intuitive perception, so in every period—at any rate during historical times—astrology has been divided into more exoteric and more esoteric systems. This division must not, however, blind us to the fact that "esoteric" and "exoteric" represent merely two ways of expressing, at any time, the basic keynote of an epoch. It is more important to know what the keynote is than to find out whether it is expressed exoterically or esoterically.

The astrology which is in vogue today originated almost entirely in the work of the Alexandrian astrologer, Claudius Ptolemy: *Tetrabiblos* (or *Four Books on the Influence of the Stars*). According to Temple Hungad: "Ptolemy was born at Pelusium, Egypt, in the first century A.D. He gathered the written observations left by the students of importance who preceded him, and enriched and augmented them after many years of personal research. These facts are set forth in his *Great Construction*, consisting of thirteen books containing the sum total of the knowledge on the phenomena of the world and the universe in general. This was the first complete and comprehensive document on the economy of the world, and the ideas therein demonstrated are often referred to as the 'Ptolemaic System.' Just as did the *Great Construction* contain the geographical and astronomical, so did Ptolemy's *Tetrabiblos* embrace the astrological knowledge to be acquired; and, although written in Asia during the first century, this work became the cornerstone of astrology in Europe after intellectual light had begun to dawn there." (*A Brief History of Astrology*—by Temple Hungad).

We shall return later to the subject of medieval astrology in Europe, which has in some of its aspects greater depths than that derived from Ptolemy; but our first task is to understand the position occupied by this writer. In order to do this we must extend our inquiry and note that at certain periods of the world-history great upheavals come which transform the very essence of civilization. We may call them "Dark Ages." At any rate, they are periods of transition separating from each other two ages. And it is interesting to realize that at the very beginning of these periods, before the "Dark Age" really sets in, men always appear who, as it were, sum up and focalize the knowledge of the then closing cycle in writings (or monuments) which become the very seed and foundation of the culture which arises later, as the "Dark Age" becomes illumined by a new spiritual-mental vitality.

Such men become then the channels through which the old is conveyed to the new. Their works contain all that the new will probably ever know of the old; which—and this is important—does not mean, however, the total wisdom of the old, not even the best of the old, but only what the new will be able to assimilate of the old. Numerous examples can be given. Confucius is the typical one, summing up as he does archaic China. Archaic China is known almost solely through what Confucius preserved of it. But, let us not forget, it is archaic China *as Confucius understood it.* Likewise very little is known of Pythagoras' musical ideas, save as they were transmitted to us by his distant follower, Boetius, in the late Roman Empire. For a long time Plato and Aristotle meant for Europe almost the whole of Greek learning. The Spanish Kabbalists of the eighth and ninth centuries have given us, as Kabbala, what they knew and understood of the old Hebrew mystery-knowledge. And in every case we know the archaic wisdom and living philosophy only through the minds of men who, being the end-products of a civilization, necessarily had lost the *feeling* of what this living philosophy and practical wisdom meant for the men who were the originators of this civilization.

It is not our purpose to discuss such matters at length; but it is nevertheless imperative for anyone who cares to understand the vital meaning of astrology to grasp the above-mentioned facts. For thus only can be avoided the tragic mistake of believing that the astrology presented to Europe by an intellectual *Alexandrian* was the astrology which measured the very pulse of ancient mankind. Ptolemaic astrology is the end-product of the East Mediterranean-Greek culture, and can only be understood in function of the intellectualism of this culture. This intellectualism has moulded the mind of Europe in nearly all its aspects. Aristotelianism and Ptolemaism are the results of this Greek era after it had lost the living contact with the spiritual tradition of the Orphic period and even of Pythagorean philosophy after it had turned away from the soil whence archaic man drew power and instinctive wisdom. If we want to understand the living essence of astrology we must forget Ptolemy and the type of medieval astrology from which present-day astrology is mostly derived, and reach to the earthly vital depths of archaic mankind.

A very remarkable series of articles by R. Berthelot, *L'Astrobiologie et la Pensée de l'Asie* in the *Revue de Métaphysique et de Morale*, 1932-1933, which we recently came across, is to our knowledge the best, if not the only study which has been made of the vital origins of astrology. It is not made from the astrologer's standpoint, but from that of the development of human civilization and human attitudes to life in general. Hence its great significance; for it is absolutely useless to try to grasp the meaning of ancient astrology unless one places astrology at the very center of the culture of the times. The so-called "Histories of Astrology" today available in print are rather useless; are in fact quite misleading. They enumerate a few disconnected facts and names without giving any idea of the living reality of astrology. No wonder, then, that the cultured man of today shrinks from considering seriously such a pseudo-science!

The following pages should not in any way be taken as a history of astrology, years of research by specialists being needed before the scant data which are scattered in many books, often untranslated into any European language, could be critically examined, compared and correlated. What we wish to do is merely to present a sort of historical background, very general in its outlines, which will help the reader to get a new approach to astrology, and thus to be better able to grasp the meanng of our re-interpretation of the basic meaning of astrology as a living and practical philosophy of psychological fulfillment and integration. What the ordinary astrologer offers to our present generation is not only far from coming up to the mental level of the intelligent thinker; it is, moreover, often decidedly nefarious and psychologically disintegrating. The living astrology of all times can, however, be said to have as a basic keynote: *integration*. And we claim that any astrology which does not bring to man a message of integration is an adulteration and a perversion of true astrology.

The Animistic Stage

Primitive man lives still in the womb of Nature. His entire life is an experience which is at the same time psychological and physiological, because he is as yet hardly able to differentiate the outer world from the inner, the objective from the subjective. He is so completely one with Nature that he constantly finds himself dissolved into natural phenomena, now projecting his infant selfhood into them, then building them into his psyche as states of consciousness which by a process of unconscious identification he calls his own. Levy Bruhl has used the term "*participation mystique*" to describe this or a similar process of psychological identification with objects.*
It corresponds to an attitude to life which can also be designated by the word *animism*.

Animism makes of all material objects "spirits," and materializes psychic facts into objective entities. Everything is animated by a spirit, whether it be a tree, a mountain, the sun,

---

* Levy Bruhl, *Les Fonctions mentales dans les Sociétés inferieures* (Paris, 1912).

a star, or even instruments made by men, as for instance a sword, a house. On the other hand, every inner feeling or emotion is an "astral" entity, which has come into the soul, and which can be expelled from it by appropriate magical practices.

Nature, inner as well as outer (both being one to the primitive), is thus a chaos of entities, acting and reacting in the most awe-inspiring confusion. It is a vast jungle in which the only law is that of self-preservation and survival. Where physical strength fails, cunning steps in; or intimidation. Soon, however, a certain sense of causality arises in man. He realizes that certain facts always follow others. He begins to "name" not only things, but relations between things. The only relation he knows personally is that of blood-kinship. Thus a crude mythology is created, where natural forces and elements mate and bear progeny.

All the while, however, the dominating emotion in primitive man is that universal emotion of the jungle—fear. What one fears is called "evil." Evil entities must be propitiated, or overcome by ruse, or restrained by magic. The main principle of magic is that of "sympathetic action." By acting, behaving and appearing as a bear the magician identifies himself with the bear; or rather he brings to a focus the identity which exists psychologically between himself and the bear. Being one with the bear, the magician can thus use the "bear spirit" to his advantage and gain ascendancy (through this transfusion of instinct, as it were) over any bear. Moreover, he also comes to know the "name" of the "bear spirit" and thus works magic in two ways. First, by uttering wilfully the name of the bear he gains control over the bear. Also this control is enhanced by the fact that generations of tribesmen have used this name magically, and when it is uttered the combined power of those tribesmen (very much alive as ghosts or spirits) backs up, as it were, the magician's power.

At the animistic stage of development, man refers everything to himself and to his fears or his desires. He projects his reactions to things into the things themselves, which become personified images of his impressions. If he is moved, there must be a mover whose very nature is to move him in this way. That which causes fear must needs be a fearful being; that which gives joy must be a bounteous entity. In this sense the whole life of man is psychological, for he lives in a world peopled by the very projections of his own reactions; but these reactions are almost solely physiological and biological. Thus psychology here means really an extension of physiological reactions; the psyche being but a diffuse aura around the biological human entity, an emanation thereof.

The Sun and the Moon are known as the givers of light. Light and life become inseparable, for darkness and night but too often mean death. Sunlight dispels fear, brings to the senses a clearer perception of objects. Thus the Sun is the great life-giver. As to the Moon, it hides a mystery. It waxes and wanes. Its light surrounds the jungle with an uncanny glow. It is changeable, mysterious, like woman. Yet its phases are soon noted down. The sense of periodicity and time is aroused by its cycles. "Spirits" are best evoked under its light, which light excites man's imagination. The Moon becomes the power of magic, the power of all mysterious operations.

With the Sun and the Moon, and probably later with the brilliant stars, man also feels a vague identity. He feels them, tries to become ever more one with them, to become instinct with their essence. Sun, Moon, stars are "great spirits." Some stars scintillate with a strange glow. They seem ominous, evil, as they rise—like the eyes of tigers and panthers seen through the forest. Stars are like eyes of fantastic animals in the dark jungle of the sky. There are men who feel strangely attracted to some particular stars. Perhaps they were born as those rose or stood high overhead. And we come down to ancient Chaldea, or perhaps even before in Atlantis, when men lay upon the ground, facing the stars, absorbing into their souls the rays of a particular star, identifying themselves with it, to know its essence and feel its exalted life. This star-worship (or rather star-identification) parallels the cult of the *totems*. Totems are mostly animals, like the bear, the eagle, the deer—but may also be stars, and even clouds and mountains. Totemism is still alive among many so-called primitive races, even among the American Indians, and it should help us to realize some of the meanings of archaic astrology at the animistic stage of development.

Then it is not, as later, the motions of the celestial bodies which are the most important, but the *life-quality*, with which every single one of them is endowed. This life-quality, the characteristic particular to the star-deity, is essentially derived from the quality of the *light* of the star. Curiously enough, we are not so far from a classification of stars on the basis of *spectrum analysis*! Only instead of using a prism to determine the quality of the light, objectively and analytically, primitive man *experienced subjectively* this light, and projected back into the star the result of this psychic identification.

As for the Sun, the determination of the characteristics and power of this life-giver is made easy by witnessing the changes which take place in the vegetation. But with this idea of correspondence between earthly biological phenomena and the motion of Sun—and also of Moon—we come to a new phase of astrology which may be characterized, following M. Berthelot's example, by the term *vitalism*.

The Vitalistic Stage

According to the vitalistic conception, Life is in everything, interpenetrates every entity, every substance. It is a vast, universal ocean of energy in which all that is "moves and has its being." This world-viewpoint originates in mankind when the primordial fear of nature is somewhat overcome, when what we may call symbolically the "jungle" is left behind, and men become either cattle-breeders or agriculturists. Nature, in other words, is in the first stage of *domestication*. It becomes a "home," and within this home Life is seen to flow with the majestic sweep of its season, waxing and waning like the Moon, ebbing and flowing like the Nile or other big rivers whose waters mean fertility.

Animism reveals man as merely one among the myriads of entities struggling for subsistence; trying desperately to overcome fear by identifying himself with the feared object, or with the fire and the light that save his life, placating evil by sacrifices: a creature of chaos, with dim perceptions, yearning for a grasp of some sort of knowledge which will enable him to face the myriads of hostile entities with equal strength. He must understand these entities *singly*, know their nature, name them. Consciousness gives power. Naming the foe means already overcoming it . . . which is, in fact, the principle back of Freudian psychoanalysis, at another level. On the other hand, vitalism presupposes that at least a part of nature— within man as well as without—is conquered and utilized. Security of a sort has been attained.

However, this domesticated part of nature must be watched carefully, protected from evil, made fruitful. The land must be tilled; the cattle must be cared for. The keynote is no longer exclusively *defense*, but *production*. There are still enemies; but they do not attack man himself as much as man's *property*. The problem of property becomes then paramount. Production depends on property. Human life depends upon the safe-keeping and fructifying of property; and soon, also, upon the continual expansion of property. This applies also to the inner nature of man. A portion of man's being, or "psyche" has become "domesticated," that is, made conscious, prolific with ideas and knowledge. Consciousness must be preserved, safeguarded against the possible in-rush of evil forces from the "unconscious" (the jungle within). It must be cultured, just as the soil must be cultivated and the cattle attended to.

Cultivation, breeding, culture—all these things mean one thing: working in harmony with and, to some extent at least, controlling life-processes. Life in the jungle state was mostly a collection of evil entities. Life at the vitalistic stage is a force which can be either good or evil; a force which pervades all things, operates in all things. There is no way of opposing it, for it is all-powerful. But knowing the law of its cyclic increases and decreases, working in harmony with its tides, man may utilize Life. He may produce instrumentalities, magical formations which attract this life-power, and by means of which nature may be made fruitful. Such magical formations become "sacred." They concentrate the diffuse life-energy, either to reinforce or to destroy the individual or any product of nature.

At this stage of human development astrology becomes supremely important. It does not deal any longer *exclusively* with celestial entities as separate beings to be worshipped and placated—even though this animistic attitude remains still the main feature of the exoteric, popular astrology. The new astrology of the vitalistic period deals especially with an understanding of the periodicity of life-processes. These, experienced in the growth and decay of vegetation and of natural entities in general, are believed to be controlled by divine agencies which are identified with Sun, Moon, planets —and to some extent with stars.

Astrology becomes a study of the universal mystery of periodical dynamic transformations, which is seen to be the very essence of Life itself. The ancient Chinese symbolized this law of natural transformation in their series of hexagrams constituting the *Yi King*, the *Book of Changes*. This is, however, obviously a later and more abstract transmutation of early astrology. Vitalistic astrology may have been born in ancient Chaldea, where it studied first of all the celestial phenomena associated with the changes of the seasons. The movements of the Sun and the Moon became the basis of the astrological system. But these movements are considered not principally as celestial phenomena in themselves, but as pointers to the dynamic changes of the solar and lunar life-force as expressed on Earth. Nomadic races, depending on their cattle, seem to have emphasized the lunar periods, because these correspond more with the periods of *animal* life, and with sex and procreation through mating. Agricultural races, on the other hand, emphasized the solar cycles which correspond to the cycles of vegetation. From these basic solar-lunar correspondences came by generalization the great "Law of Analogy," which is the very foundation of all occult science.

The Law of Analogy presupposes a universal agent permeating the entire universe—a life-substance or life-force filling in all space; filling in the dome of the heavens, as well as the *domus* (domicile, home) in which the tribal group lives, procreates and dies but to renew and continue itself through blood-propagation. The tribal home becomes a small replica of the universal home bound by the spheres of the stars. The Earth is the microcosm; the universe, the macrocosm. It is only later, in Alexandria and in the Middle Ages, that man, the individual being, is considered to be the microcosm. Then astrology is individualized. In ancient Chaldea and China it refers only to the Earth and to the State or community. The State is the microcosm, and the Emperor or King its Sun and center of life.

In such agricultural states, built in vast plains, the framework of all living is produced by the four great moments of the cycle of solar changes: the equinoxes and solstices. These are indissolubly associated with the four cardinal points of space. Consider ancient China, around 2,000 B.C. The capital and the palace of the Emperor within it are oriented to these four points. The palace has four sections, each corresponding to a season. The Emperor lives in the East section during the spring, in the South section during the summer, in the West section during the fall, and in the North section during the winter.*

This four-fold division is obviously associated with the idea of duality and sex. The Chinese build their cycle of change upon the alternate waxing and waning of the two principles *Yang* and *Yin*, masculine and feminine. This dualism is transferred by correspondence to the dualism of day and night: the Sun, lighting the day; the Moon, lighting the night. The female animal has periods of heat and of indifference, just as the Moon is either bright or dark. Astrology is thus based on purely *biological* concepts. It is dynamic, vital. It explains the *causes* of all biological phenomena on Earth—later of all social phenomena, as in Chinese civilization, in which social organization, politics, music and all culture are ruled by the pattern of harmony revealed by the movements of the celestial bodies, themselves considered to be the vehicles of symbols of the Divine Powers which collectively represent universal life.

On this vitalistic foundation, however, a more mental superstructure grows progressively, as centuries roll by. Planetary cycles are added to those of the Sun and the Moon. More and more the priests who record, tabulate, compare and study the movements of the celestial bodies realize the abstract values involved in their cyclic revolutions. The idea of "precise changeless numerical ratios" takes hold of the mind of men whose profession it is to be symbols of order and law to a humanity still gripped by the fear of elemental forces. The notion of Heavenly Order becomes the one great security against the chaos of elemental nature, still so apparent in storms, inundations, droughts and cataclysms of all sorts. An archetypal, divine world of Order is shown in the Heavens where every object moves according to immutable laws.

* Henri Maspero: *Le Chine Antique II, Chap. 1.*

Man's task is then obviously so to operate upon the "earth" (the soil and cattle, but also his own earthly instinctual nature) that it becomes a perfect replica of the celestial Order.

From such premises two basic needs can be deduced: the need for a *calendar* determining at first solely the time when all agricultural operations must be performed (sowing, harvesting, etc.), and the days which are favorable and unfavorable to any such operation; then the need for an *Ethical Law* determining how man is to deal with and to cultivate his own nature, his own earthly being; how man is to behave in relation to man within the framework of the State—if this State is to conform to the celestial law. Thus, in ancient China we see the Emperor as high-priest of this celestial religion, mediator between the Heavenly Order centered around the Pole Star (where resides the great God of Order) and mankind. He is assisted by four astronomers who together with him determine the agricultural Calendar—besides establishing a moral-social law and musical scales, music being the agency whereby the earthly State may become tuned up to the "Harmony of the Spheres" (also a Pythagorean idea). Music includes tones and ritualistic dancing as well, for there again the principle of duality must reign. Bodily motions harmonized to musical tones and rhythms—such a harmony symbolizes and *magically calls for* a corresponding harmony between human emotions and celestial motions.

The Emperor is the fixed point of reference for all ethical social measurements, as the North Pole is astronomically. His voice is a paragon for all tones; his body, for all measurements. All roads are measured from the center of his palace, where he lives; or rather, because he cyclically changes his residence, where stands the tomb of the Great Ancestor, the origin of the State. The Emperor is the One Man, the One Individual, the One Mediator through whom the Order of the Heavens is infused into the State. He is thus the Supreme Astrologer. Or rather he is the very Condensation of all Heavenly Virtues, and his four astrologers through him are able to partake of the mystery of the Heavens.

This represents a perfected stage of astrological civilization; but—is it not astonishingly like the Christian religion, on a different plane? For is not Jesus the Christ the One Mediator between mankind and God, the One Spiritual Individual (being the Only Begotten Son), the paragon of all celestial virtues, the only fountain of salvation? And are not His Apostles and the popes by apostolic succession the dispensers of His wisdom, the establishers of a Church militant, which is to become a replica on earth of the Church triumphant in Heaven?

Christianity came at a time of great psychological chaos, when a new world was being born out of the ruins of the East-Mediterranean past, when Greek intellectualism and individualism had led to utter psychological confusion. The Christian Church became then the symbol of a Heavenly Order, the only security in a period of chaos, the one integrating force in a welter of passions and decadent perversions. But so was the astrological State of Chaldea and of China the only security against elemental chaos. The cyclic courses of the celestial bodies alone were tokens of a universal Order. The knowledge of the solar and lunar motions alone could save man from ruined crops—which meant starvation and chaos. What this astrological knowledge represented is shown by the fact that in China the fall of the first dynasty of Hia is said to have been caused by the failure of the imperial astrologers to announce an eclipse. Whenever, because of incomplete knowledge of celestial motions, a planet did not appear exactly where expected, this was taken to foretell chaos and ruin to the imperial house. If the rulers failed to know accurately the celestial happenings, the only bulwark against chaos was destroyed, and the rulers had to go. They were to be the Integrators, the Organizers, the Custodians of the Universal Order. If they failed to know that Order, they proved themselves unworthy. They *had* to be overthrown for the very salvation of the people.*

On the biological plane of agricultural operations, and on the plane of ethical and social organizations, astrology was, then, the Great Knowledge which alone insured security and that spiritual trust in a Cosmic Law *without which no civilization is possible*. It was vital, living knowledge, for at every step it filtered into the operations of all life-processes! It was the *Science of life*, or, as M. Berthelot says, *Astrobiology*—the science of a life conceived as archetypally ordered and cosmic, operating identically in the microcosm, Earth, as in the macrocosm, the universe.

The Change of the Sixth Century B.C.

Then man began to develop a new basis for living and to know himself as an individual, a free being; and a new jungle arose at a higher level, the psycho-mental level. This meant the start of a new cycle of human development, calling for a New Astrology, a new understanding of Order, of Cosmos, of God.

This momentous change occurred, archetypally as it were, during the sixth century B.C.; the time of Gautama the Buddha, followed by Lao-Tze and Confucius, the last Zoroaster and Gushapt, Pythagoras and, later, Plato—to mention only the most outstanding spiritual figures of this critical time which marked a potential reversal of all human values. Twenty-five hundred years later humanity is trying to bring into actual and organic manifestation what was then a mere potentiality.

The main significance of the change, as far as this present study of ours is concerned, is that the emphasis which had so far been exclusively placed on *physiological* matters began

---

* The Greek historian Megasthenes (302 B.C.), describing the duties of the Brahmin astrologer, adds, "The philosopher who errs in his predictions observes silence for the rest of his life." A list of the qualities expected of an astrologer, found in the old Sanscrit texts, is quite appalling.

to be transferred to *psychological* values. Everything before 600 B.C. was based upon the human "body." Since then, more and more, a new foundation has been raised, and almost everything is sooner or later to be focussed upon the human "psyche"—using this term to represent man's inner nature: mind, soul, and their various activities and functions, conscious and unconscious.

Everything was, of old, centered upon the body—including all spirituality. For the body was not then what it is to us Christians. It was the pure vehicle of instincts and of the spirit, but only *potentially* the vehicle of spirit. Spirit was asleep in the body and had to be aroused, made active—this being the basis of the pure archaic form of *Hatha Yoga* before the sixth century, B.C. This arousal could be induced by control of the life-force, through breathing, sounds and ritualistic postures or movements—but also in relation to cosmic processes involving Sun, Moon, planets, and stars. In the *Kundalini Yoga*, man is understood as a system of vital centers or whirls of energy which correspond to these celestial dynamos, the planets, and Sun and Moon. Finally the life-force is completely transfigured by its marriage with Spirit and the thousand-petalled lotus blooms, the *Sahasrara chakra*; that is, the solar system is transcended and the myriads of stars shine, chrysanthemum of the Heavens, the Cosmic Rose—while is heard the mystery sound, *Nada* in *Sahasrara*, the Voice of the God that dwells within the Pole Star.

In other words, what the Chinese State as a whole was to be, the *Yogi* sought to fulfill in himself, as an Individual. To the Chinese Emperor corresponded the "*Ishvara*-in-the-body," the "Jewel in the Lotus" of Thibetan lore. Astrology here meant practical spiritual development—but spiritual development through the body, through the human earth made perfect and cosmic in the likeness of the celestial harmony.

It seems to us a mistake to believe that the old *Kundalini Yoga* and similar methods of development referred to psychological facts—as C. G. Jung apparently believes. If it did, it was only after the reforms of the Buddha. For then the chaos of the world was shown not to be overcomeable through means which were almost entirely psychological and rational, or suprarational. And a new type of astrology soon began to develop: *alchemical astrology.*

Alchemy, when not perverted or materialized, is an attempt to do with the human psyche what the Chinese Emperor was supposed to do as supreme Ruler of Agriculture and Establisher of the Calendar. Its purpose is to raise psychological crops and to domesticate the wild herd of human desires. The *Yoga* of Pantanjali and the mental training of the Buddha dealt more specifically with the mental processes. "*Yoga* is the hindering of the modifications of the mind," wrote Patanjali. But Chinese alchemy, along the lines pursued by the Taoists, and European alchemy, from Geber to Boehme *via* Paracelsus, are more particularly dealing with the energy-aspect of the psyche, or we might say, with the soul-nature of man—its purification, redemption and fructifying by the "virtue" of Christ, or in another sense, of *Tao.*

In alchemy the human "earth" to be tilled and transmuted until it bears forth the immaculately-born "Son of God," the Christ-body, is symbolized by metals and by planets. The processes of transmutation are symbolized by "codes" which are either series of symbols drawn from natural agricultural processes, in China; or interpretation of incidents of the life of Jesus as recorded in the Gospels, in European alchemy (especially with Boehme). The *Book of the Golden Flower* translated from the Chinese by Richard Wilhelm, as well as the archaic *Yi King*, will show what the former are. The latter can be studied in Boehme's writings and those of older alchemists.

The use made of astrology in alchemy is largely symbolical. But in a sense astrology is always symbolical when properly understood. All depends upon what is meant by "symbol."

Algebra is also purely symbolical, and yet algebra and higher mathematics have made possible modern science and the age of machines. *Astrology is fundamentally the algebra of life.* But its applications are as numerous as the types of life it co-ordinates, integrates, and to which it gives the significance of Order.

The old Chaldean astrology was based on the principles of correspondences—purely symbolical principles. True, the Chaldeans did believe that planets were the bodies of gods according to whose dictates the universe was run. But this was merely an *interpretation* of astrological symbolism. The symbols were interpreted as gods because man's consciousness was essentially physiological and biological, because his objective and subjective worlds were still very much confused, and there was no clear-cut division between what was physiological and what was psycho-mental; because animism had still very strong roots in man's consciousness.

As mind developed independently, especially after the sixth century B.C., as abstract thinking began to separate thought from its concrete life-foundation, the biological valuation of "practical utility" receded into the background, and the interpretation of "pure knowledge," "pure science," was given to astrology. Then it became astronomy. This, as M. Berthelot points out, occurred preëminently in Chaldea; while in Egypt the transformation was more characteristically from cere-monial magic to spiritual ethics. In China, the old agrarian interpretation gave place to a social-ethical one. In India, what used to refer to the body and to the life-force within the body (escape from the jungle-world of men's senses by a process of detachment and unification of energies), came to be ap-plied to the mind. In Greece, the old Orphic religion also became transmuted into Pythagoreanism.

In every case what occurred was a change of level, a change of interpretation. The personal God became (theoretically and potentially only!) an impersonal Law or Principle of

Order; just as in original American democracy we see the idea of personal Kingship give place to that of an inviolable Constitution. "In America the Law is King," said Thomas Paine. At the same time and for the same reasons the principle of blood-relationship, which represented the only bond valid to a humanity focussed at the physiological level, began to be challenged by a new type of human relationship, the spiritual brotherhood including men (and at times women) of different bloods and races. Witness the Buddhistic *Sangha*, the Pythagorean sodalities, the Gnostic brotherhoods (whence the Catholic monastic orders), and finally such brotherhoods as those of the Druzes in Mount Lebanon (originally composed of mystics of all races).

Unfortunately, yet most naturally, such a tremendous change of level could not possibly be operative among the masses. The tragic thing was that even the élite of mankind failed to live up to the potentiality of the vision opened up to it by the Great Teachers of the sixth century B.C.; and the five or more centuries which followed are the story of the relative failure of mankind to adjust itself to a new level of being. Whether in China, or India, or Greece, or Persia, the result was the same, the depth reached varying, of course, with each civilization.

In Greece, mind turned into mere analytical intellect, wisdom into sophistry. Individualism developed in an unbalanced manner, and humanity entered a phase of large-scale psychological chaos, with the usual result of physiological disequilibrium, sensuality, perversion, etc. This led, by reaction, to popular Christianity, and in India to the *Bhakti* movement and *Mahayana* Buddhism. A wholesale psychological revulsion against mind set in, and religions of feelings and love, devotional and compassionate, swept over the world.

In the meantime astrology had experienced a deep transformation. It had ceased to be vital and necessary to the collectivities as a principle of order, because the growing domination of the intellectual rational principle enabled man to project speculatively his own order into the world. But—and this is the important point—the rational order of the intellect is of a different quality than the biological order. The intellect is but an instrumentality which helps man to raise his consciousness from the physiological to the psycho-mental level. It cannot fill a human life with vital significance. It creates a separative kind of individualism, based on analysis but not on synthesis—and all life is synthesis. As individuals became more and more the important thing, astrology began to cater to them and to their fears. Then its long cycle of outer degeneration began. It became increasingly, on the surface, mere fortune-telling—while the deeper phases of astrology found themselves reborn, as already stated, as the foundation for alchemy.

The turning-point came probably as astrological ideas swept from Chaldea westward; first "through the Babylonian sage Berosus who founded a school about 640 B.C. in the Island of Cos and perhaps counted Thales of Miletus (639-548) among his pupils." (Cf. *Encyclopedia Britannica* "History of Astronomy"); and, even more definitely, during the middle of the fourth century B.C. (according to Bouché-Leclercq and others). While in Chaldea, as in China, astrology was solely a matter concerning the community or the state, with the King as center and guiding principle of the state, in Greece, and later, in Rome, the practice of making *individual horoscopes* developed. Astrology fell soon into the hands of commercially-minded people, who came rapidly to be known as charlatans. In Rome, these were called first "Mathematici," then "Chaldeans," and, just as in modern times, so much trickery or foolishness became connected with their practice that they were at times forced by imperial edicts to discontinue their trade.

In ancient India an official astrologer was attached to every village-community, and it appears that one of his functions was to cast the horoscope of the new-born children of the high castes. But in this case the practice had a very ritualistic and *physiological* or *biological* significance; for marriages were often made by comparing birth-charts, and even the connubial life was regulated by the stars. In other words, here again we find a biological type of individualism in operation. The *bodies* of the individuals (of the high castes) had to be "cultivated," or in fact bred, so that they might become perfect instruments for the release of the spirit. Racial purity was another expression of the same ideal; and it was forced by circumstances, for Aryan blood had to be carefully preserved, or else the overwhelming mass of non-Aryan people in India would have corrupted the race type. This would have meant *physiological chaos.* Thus here again astrology served as a means to bring—or to keep—biological order; as a defense against elemental nature and as a technique of developing the "domesticated" nature, i.e., nature true to the celestial pattern represented by the *Manu*, the great divine Ancestor. Such a biological problem arises always when a more or less nomadic race living on the highlands invades the plains teeming with a decadent humanity.

There are, however, no evidences that the individualization of astrology and its use for personal purposes in Greece and Rome had a similar physiological basis. There may have been an archaic type of Greek astrology connected with the Orphic mysteries, as there was an archaic Egyptian astrology connected with ceremonial magic; but to our knowledge no traces of it have been preserved. It is evident, however, that Pythagoras used astrology in relation to music—and there perhaps we should have to look for the origin of the ethical-psychological-alchemical astrology of later times.

Such a type of astrology—which must be sharply differentiated from the type to which Ptolemy refers—is an attempt at bringing some sort of psychological order into the inner natures of men who had been unbalanced by the new emphasis which Greek civilization (and similar manifestations in the Orient) had placed upon the intellect. It is true that classical Greece had also stressed the elements of physical beauty and bodily form. But the Greek cult of the body was esthetical—not biological, or "occult" in the sense of the early Hindu *yoga*. The Greeks worshipped form and proportion, not the organic *life* that made and that sings within the body-earth. They were ideologists, and finally estheticians.

It was the impact of this previously unknown ideologism, which deals with order, form, measure as abstractions valid on their own mental plane without the necessity for a physiological foundation or even context, that shook the human world—and destroyed the vital meaning of astrology. Astrology had discovered the order that is within the sphere of biological phenomena. It was the promise inherent in nature—outer or inner—that the apparent chaos of natural energies can be resolved into a cosmos; that therefore prevision based on law is possible; that the living future can be deduced from the living past. Now men were beginning to deal with an abstract order; no longer with cosmos within nature—living cosmos—but with ideological patterns, with *logic*.

Greek logic killed the meaning of physiological astrology. If man could make his own order abstractly, and satisfy in that way his innate yearning for security, there was no longer vital value in trying to search painfully for order *within* outer nature. Man could command order. He could project it outwardly—which means estheticism—out of his own self, his own mental self. He could make the world again out of ideas. What an incredible revolution! Before that time, ideas were merely connective links between natural phenomena concretely perceived. Now they were said to live in their own world, a world where man also could dwell far away from the realm of natural chaos and of biological fear. Such a conception transformed the entire human outlook in a way which it is very difficult for us moderns to appreciate, especially as most of what we have known of the archaic ages was more or less rewritten, or for the first time recorded, *after* the sixth century B.C.

If order was existing in an archetypal world *outside* the world of biological nature, then the thing to do was, of course, to leave the latter and its fears—and to enter the blessèd realm. The Buddhists attempted to do that by meditation, by severance from physiological life, and by a thorough mentalization of the body. This was quite different from the "archaic" *yoga* which was an attempt to rouse the vital spirit in the body, to free it from sense-bondage and "jungle" fever, and integrate it to a point of perfect unity with the "God that dwells in the Pole Star"—as the Chinese had it. The Greeks looked for an escape from the tragic world of nature and its passional fate by pure thought, pure esthetical contemplation and "platonic" love.

Finally, when these types of escapes ended in ratiocination and sophistry, or in the absolute selfishness of a fallacious *nirvana*, then a strong psychological reaction set in, and religions of feelings arose: the *Boddhisattva* ideal of compassion, or in India and Persia the *bhakti* ideal of a love—so personal in its ecstasy as to be expressed in symbols taken from the most sensual passion; or the Christian ideal of charity, sacrifice and martyrdom. These religions had also a world freed from the sufferings and fears (now become "sins") of earthly nature; but this world could only be attained after death. It was the "other world;" and its entrance was guarded by the Church, without recourse to which man was confronted with a still more horrible realm of fear and chaos—hell. It is true that archaic religions did often imagine a world of gods to which mortals might be admitted after death, but the significance of this world was entirely different psychologically from that of the Christian "other world." For the latter gave a pejorative and sinful meaning to anything connected with physio-biological nature, which is the important point. Then faith, blind obedience, love, became exalted; exalted *against* natural biological living. Thus the long story of repressions began, the divorcing of the spirit from the flesh. Men lost the solid order of natural instincts and were unable as yet to reach *another solidity*, that of a higher order of life at the psycho-mental level. They therefore found themselves dwelling in an intermediate realm, a realm peopled by the results of suppressions, denials, thwarted feelings and intellectual sophism—a psychological jungle indeed.

In this jungle, as in any jungle, there was fear. Monstrous creatures, *incubi*, *succubi*, evil forces crowded it; no longer physiological creatures connected with earthy elements, but products of sins, of self-deceptions and of biological starvation. From this arose a psychological type of *animism*. It is true that the Church offered order and security to those who entered her realm. But how many monasteries did really keep the jungle out?

Yet the Church was a refuge, a token of the possibility of a supernal world to which she alone led. And therefore the Church took the place of astrology. It did so with many festivals and ceremonies arranged with great order throughout the year—in fact duplicating the old biological festivals based on the astrology of the archaic era. It did so for its consecrated children with a daily series of masses, prayers, services, extending through night and day. All these church ceremonies represented the Christian year, the Christian zodiac (now inhabited by saints and archangels), the Christian cosmic order. Observance of those ceremonies kept the jungle away from the soul.

But it was still astrology under a different garb! Astrology without the name. The wheel of the zodiac was replaced by a system of permutations of the four elements: hot, cold, dry, humid—not unlike the Chinese *Yi King*. To those permutations corresponded the many festivals of the year, some liturgy appropriate for those, and to them were attached, as symbolical illustrations, episodes of the Gospels.* Boehme was to extend the same system, using alchemy as a foundation—not unlike that of the Chinese Taoists.

Kabbalistic Astrology

There came, however, during the Middle Ages (especially after the eleventh century) a great renewal of astrological ideas proper, which, while repudiated and combated by the Church, still came more and more to control the minds of the period. This astrology was the result of the "psychological animism" already mentioned; and it can be generally characterized by the term *Kabbalistic*. It was linked very definitely to various forms of ceremonial magic, and came to Europe, mostly, it seems, through Spain and from centers of Arabic culture, especially perhaps, Fez, in Morocco.

The origin of this trend of astrology, essentially magical, appears to have been a mixture of Egyptian and Hebrew traditions. The books of Hermes Trismegistus, compendium of Egyptian gnosticism, were partly a foundation for it—and presumably a great number of oral traditions possibly descending from the old Mysteries, Babylonian and Greek. At any rate, we find there a rather curious mixture of elements, many of which are not altogether fortunate. That which once had been a *vital function* in archaic society appeared after the great psychological transformation of humanity as an *inferior function* (to use the terminology of Jung's psychology). It was the old magical idea of animism translated to the chaotic "astral" realm in which the collective psyche of the Middle Ages was so definitely centered. Thus the element of fear was strongly present. The magician uses a sword to combat the evil spirits, protects himself by magical circles. Yet fear is

---

* This can be seen especially in books written by Syrian authors; for Syrian churches had remained closer to the biological foundation of the ancient East; while the Roman Church had become more intellectualized under the influence of neo-Pythagoreans and neo-Platonists. Cf. The book of *Bar-Hebraeus* called *Ethicon*, and many others (thirteenth century).

often in his heart, and the door is thus opened to psychological disintegration. Witness the horrors of ceremonial magic in Europe, even to this day.

Such types of magic, pure or impure as might be the case, used astrology consistently. According to Kabbalistic ideas, the Universe consisted of ten concentric spheres, each sphere being under the influence of one of the ten *Sephiroth*, or Emanations from the Absolute. These spheres were in order:

> The primum mobile
> The sphere of the zodiac
> The sphere of Saturn
>   ”   ”   ” Jupiter
>   ”   ”   ” Mars
>   ”   ”   ” Sol
>   ”   ”   ” Venus
>   ”   ”   ” Mercury
>   ”   ”   ” Moon
> The mundane sphere

Each of the planetary spheres presided over a certain section of human affairs, and the man who wished to succeed in these affairs had to know the mystic symbols of the governing planet and the names and attributes of the operating genii. (Cf. E. Y. Pilcher—*Two Kabbalistic Planetary Charms*—Soc. of Biblical Archaeology—1906.) Magic squares were also used, and talismans were made to secure the offices of the spirits or the influence of the planetary spheres.

What these genii were supposed to be can be seen from the following excerpt:

"The Creation of Life by the Sun is as continuous as his light; nothing arrests or limits it. Around him, like an army of Satellites, are innumerable choirs of genii. These dwell in the neighborhood of the Immortals, and thence watch over human things. They fulfill the will of the gods by means of storms, tempests, transitions of fire and earthquakes, likewise by famine and wars for the punishment of impiety. . . . Under the Sun's orders is the choir of Genii, or rather the choirs, for there are many and diverse, and their number corresponds to that of the stars. Every star has its genii, good or evil by nature, or *rather by their operation, for operation is the essence of the genii.* . . . All these genii preside over mundane affairs, they shake and overthrow the constitution of States and of individuals; they imprint their likeness on our Souls, they are present in our nerves, our marrow, our veins, our arteries, and our very brain-substance. . . . They change perpetually, not always identically, but revolving in circles. They permeate by the body two parts of the Soul, that it may receive from each the impress of his own energy. But the reasonable part of the Soul is not subject to the genii. It is designed for the reception of God, who enlightens it with a sunny ray. Those who are thus illumined are few in number, and from them the genii abstain; for neither genii nor gods have any power in the presence of a single ray of God. But all other men, both soul and body, are directed by genii, to whom they cleave and whose operations they affect."

From *Hermes Trismegistus* (quoted in *The Secret Doctrine*, I, p. 294)

Here we have a typical attitude, probably of Brahmanical lineage, according to which nature is conceived from the animistic point of view, as something evil, something from which (because of its changeful, unsteady, monstrously prolific and unmoral quality) man must escape. There is a part of man's soul through which man can contact That Which is changeless, attributeless, limitless—the Self. As the contact is permanently established, man reaches safety. The jungle becomes harmless. The genii, good or bad, can no longer seduce, delude or attack man. He is an Illumined One.

The Kabbalist, on the other hand, ordinarily pursued another tactic. His task was to master these "astral" forces. He was the magician of the jungle. By propitiation (through physiological or psychological sacrifices) or by command (using a knowledge of the Names and Signatures of the genii) he made nature subservient to his will. This, of course, is just what the modern engineer does. The latter may have nothing but contempt for the magician—but the fact remains that the two basic attitudes are the same; for the formulas of the chemists are the signatures of the elements—except that they are arrived at by a process of intellectual analysis, while the Kabbalist's hieroglyphs are the result of a process of psychological identification. But what is still more important, the results attained by the controllers of nature's forces are in the end often similar. The magician commanded genii, but soon became their slave. He had to feed them with his own soul. His creatures devoured him. And today this society of ours, made up of actual or potential engineers, has become obviously the slave of its machines, of all the instrumentalities and agencies by means of which it commands the elements.

Such an analogy will, of course, seem beside the point and untenable to most people; but if one realizes the cleavage which has occurred for so many centuries between the physical world ruled by the intellect and the world of the psyche left in a state of chaos reminiscent of the primitive jungle, in spite or because of moral systems and codes of behavior—then one may see all things in their proper relationship. Modern science belongs to one side of the chasm; and all the so-called occult or esoteric systems, plus modern psycho-analysis and its derivatives, to the other.

Alchemical Astrology

If Kabbalism and the type of astrology used in its magical practices represent a sort of psychological animism, the true kind of alchemy stands for what we might call "psychological vitalism." Alchemy does not try to renounce nature and to center consciousness, as it were, outside of it, on the high peaks of the soul; nor does it try to command it by compulsion and the exercise of intellectual self-will. It assumes a universal life-substance which fills in the whole universe, physical and spiritual. It sees man and the universe as two examples of the same basic harmony of principles operating in and through this life-substance, and aims at establishing man at his own level of manifestation as a perfect cosmos, just as the universe at its level is a perfect cosmos. Evil is due to the fact that the respective spheres of man and of the universe become mixed, as man ceases to be a mere *part* of universal nature and becomes in his own right a cosmic *whole*.

This explains why in archaic times vitalistic philosophy considered the earth as the microcosm, and in modern times alchemy, its counterpart, considers man as the microcosm. Before the sixth century B.C. man *was not* actually a microcosm, but only, in a sense, the fruition of the earth. Even so, few men really are microcosms! But since man found in himself, independently from nature, his own principle of Order, his own Measure and Proportion, the Idea, the God within—then man can be said to be, generically at least, the microcosm.

"To understand correctly the meaning of the words alchemy and astrology, it is necessary to understand and to realize the intimate relationship and the identity of the Microcosm and Macrocosm, and their mutual interaction. All the powers of the universe are potentially contained in man and man's physical body, and all his organs are nothing else but products and representatives of the powers of Nature. . . . If I have 'manna' in my constitution, I can attract 'manna' from heaven. 'Saturn' is not only in the sky, but also deep in the earth and in the ocean. What is 'Venus' but the 'Artemisia' that grows in your garden? What is 'iron' but 'Mars'? That is to say, Venus and Artemisia are both the products of the same essence, and Mars and iron are both the manifestations of the same cause. What is the human body but a constellation of the same powers that formed the stars in the sky? He who knows what iron is, knows the attribute of Mars. He who knows Mars, knows the qualities of iron. What would become of your heart if there were no Sun in the universe? What would be the use of your 'vasa spermatica' if there were no Venus? To grasp the invisible elements, to attract them by their material correspondences, to control, purify, and transform them by the living power of the Spirit—this is true alchemy."

Franz Hartmann, *Paracelsus*, pp. 287-288

The following quotation shows, even more than the preceding one, the difference between vitalistic and animistic astrology (in the modern sense), for in it Paracelsus himself, one of the greatest figures in European history, denounces the popular attitude toward astrology, which was then very much the same as it is today, and as it had been also in the last period of the Greco-Latin world:

"No one needs to care for the course of Saturn: it neither shortens nor lengthens the life of anybody. If Mars is ferocious it does not follow that Nero was his child: and although Mars and Nero may both have had the same qualities they did not take them from each other. It is an old saying that 'a wise man may rule the stars' and I believe in that saying—not in the sense in which you take it, but in my own. The stars force nothing into us that we are not willing to take; they incline us to nothing which we do not desire. They are free for themselves and we are free for ourselves. You believe that one man is more successful in the acquirement of knowledge, another in the acquisition of power . . . and you think that this is caused by the stars; but I believe the cause to be that one man is more apt than another to acquire and to hold certain things, and that this aptitude comes from the spirit. It is absurd to believe that the stars can make a man. Whatever the stars can do we can do ourselves, because the wisdom which we obtain from God overpowers the heavens and rules over the stars. . . . Man's soul is made up of the same elements as the stars; but as the wisdom of the Supreme guides the motions of the stars, so the reason of man rules the influences which rotate and circulate in his soul.

"The planetary influences extend through all Nature, and man attracts poisonous qualities from the moon, from the stars and from other things; but the moon, and the stars, and other things also attract evil influences from man, and distribute them again by their rays, because Nature is an undivided whole whose parts are intimately connected. . . . The sun and stars attract something from us, and we attract something from them, because our astral bodies are in sympathy with the stars, and the stars are in sympathy with our astral bodies; but the same is the case with the astral bodies of all other objects."

Franz Hartmann, *Paracelsus*, p. 309, etc.

This expresses clearly the idea of the exact correspondence between the macrocosm whose principle of order is "God" and the microcosm, man, whose principle of order is "reason" —or the "God within man." The life-substance circulating and differentiated within both macrocosm and microcosm is one and the same. The Light is the same, whether it shines as Sun and stars, or as the radiant centers *within man's psychomental organism*—once the latter is built by a long process of psychological integration. This is the Great Work of the true alchemists, the process of "individuation" which is the goal of C. G. Jung's psychological work, the birth of the "Living God" as a contemporary mystic-occultist Bo Yin Ra speaks of it, following the tradition of Meister Eckhart and Boehme.

In the meantime, of course, during the centuries which led from the Middle Ages to the Renaissance and up to the present day, astrology, as the Greco-Latin world had bequeathed it to us through Ptolemy, flourished in the courts, among the merchants eager to increase their wealth, and wherever man's insatiable curiosity for the future—as an escape from fulfilling the present!—held sway. Whenever an astrologer succeeded in foretelling some striking death, birth or calamity, he became famous, a favorite of kings; but when his prophecies failed in some notable instance disgrace became his lot. Nostradamus, physician of King Henry II of France and a favorite of Catherine de' Medici, William Lilly, born in 1602, and his pupil John Gadbury who died in 1691—and many others whose names can be found in various modern works on astrology, continue the tradition of Ptolemy, adding here and there, but without bringing in any new element of importance. European "classical" astrology is a spiritually lifeless rebirth of Greco-Latin intellectualism, as is practically all European classicism. The entire progress of humanity is then concentrated upon pure intellectual analysis and physical "scientific" experimentation. The vitality that was in astrology is now centered in astronomy. Man's *reason* plays at recognizing itself in the outer world, *which it makes in its own image,* just as primitive man's *psychic sensitiveness* projected itself into a world made in its own image and peopled with "spirits" and deities with human moods. Recently electricity and radioactivity broke the spell and led man to the startling concepts of twentieth century physics, to Einstein's theory of relativity, to the quantum, and to Heisenberg's principle of indeterminacy. This means the birth of a new world of thought, widely open to the Unknown and Unknowable, which the last centuries had hoped to kill with the magic sword of Reason. It is this new world which is now demanding an account from astrology.

Astrology must be reborn and must perform again for our modern world, made chaotic by an unbridled and false individualism and by the sudden opening of psychological dams, the task of practical integration which has always been its own. Wherever the correlated motions of Sun, Moon, planets and stars are used to bring order into the confusion of our everyday world—there is astrology. The type and range of the phenomena of nature which astrology correlates, interprets and makes significant in terms of a cosmic principle of Order, change age after age. At first they were physiological and elemental. Now they are to be essentially psychological and mental. But the fundamental work of astrology remains the same. It is to reveal the "Harmony of the Spheres" at whatever level man's consciousness is centered. It is to carry the symbol of Order wherever man finds chaos. In modern terminology, it is the *algebra of life.*

FIRST SECTION

I. *Astrology Faces Modern Thought*

Can Astrology Ever Become an Empirical Science?

ASTROLOGY, the *algebra of life*. Such a statement demands explanation; and in order to provide such an explanation we shall find it convenient at first to examine briefly the views of one of the most representative of modern scientists in reference to the characteristic evolution of scientific thought throughout the ages. These views are particularly significant, inasmuch as they show a remarkable parallelism between the evolution of natural science and the evolution of astrological thought as outlined in the last chapter. On the basis of such a parallelism it will be easier to understand the new developments of astrology, developments which —because of their symbolical and relational character—led us to define astrology-in-the-making: the algebra of life.

Writes Sir James Jeans in *The New Background of Science:*

> "Reviewing the history of man's efforts to understand the workings of the external world, we may distinguish three broad epochs, the nature of which may be suggested by the words *animistic*, *mechanical* and *mathematical*. (Italics ours)
>
> "The animistic period was characterized by the error of supposing that the course of nature was governed by the whims and passions of living beings more or less like man himself. Before our infant can distinguish between animate and inanimate objects, he is destined to pass through a stage of confusing the two. . . . Because personality is the concept of which he has most immediate and direct experience, he begins by personifying everything.

37

The Astrology of Personality

"As the history of the individual is merely the history of the race writ small, our race did much the same in its infancy as its individuals still do in theirs. . . . Then in Ionian Greece, *six centuries before Christ*, the human intelligence began consciously to apply itself to the study of nature. It felt very little desire to increase its factual knowledge of nature, so that Greek science consisted in the main of mere vague questionings and speculations as to why things came to be as they were rather than otherwise.

"It was not until the time of Galileo that science turned from cosmology to mechanics, and from speculation to experiment. The simplest way of affecting inanimate matter was to push it or pull it by means of muscular effort. So long as men could only experiment with objects which were comparable in size with their own bodies, they found *inanimate nature* behaving as though its constituent pieces exerted pushes and pulls on one another, like those we exert on them by the actions of our muscles. In this way the science of mechanics came into being. Pieces of matter were supposed to exert 'forces' on one another, and these forces were the causes of the motions of the bodies in question, or rather of the changes in their motion. And it was found that the behavior of every object was determined, entirely and completely, by the pushes and pulls to which it was subjected. . . ." (pp. 33-34)

The author goes on to discuss the implications of this mechanistic view of nature, how it involves absolute determinism, how Descartes, in order to avoid some of these implications, "regarded mind and matter as entirely independent 'substances,' each existing in its own right apart from the other and of such essentially different natures that they could not possibly interact." However, in order to show the intimate correlation between our thoughts and the atoms of our world . . . Descartes insisted, as in a different way did Leibnitz at a later date, that at the first morning of creation a supremely benevolent God had miraculously arranged for a perfect and continuous synchronization between bodily and mental events.

Jeans goes on to say:

"Throughout the mechanical age of science, scientists had proceeded on the same general lines as the child and the unreflective savage. Out of the impressions registered through their senses, they had built an inferential world of objects which they believed to be real, and affected by events of much the same kind as occurred in everyday experience. They described this as the 'common-sense' view of science; and defined science as 'organized common-sense.' . . . Then new refinements of experimental technique brought new observational knowledge, which showed that the workings of nature could not be explained in terms of the familiar concepts of everyday life. . . . Mechanism, with its implications, has dropped out of the scheme of science. . . . We are beginning to see that man had freed himself from the anthropomorphic error of imagining that the workings of nature could be compared to those of his own whims and caprices (animism), only to fall headlong into the second anthropomorphic error of imagining that they could be compared to the workings of his own muscles, and sinews (mechanism).

"Whether determinism has also been banished from nature is still a question for debate. . . . But that those particular causes which seemed until recently to compel determinism have gone—this is hardly open to question." (pages 41-43)

It is easy to see how the three stages of knowledge which Jeans mentions (animistic, mechanical and mathematical) correspond to the three stages of astrological thought discussed in our preceding chapter. The "mechanism" of science is not basically different from the "vitalism" of astrology; the "push and pull" of the former corresponds in terms of material activity to the "*yang* and *yin*" principles of vital operations. In both cases a tangible dualism of forces is considered to be the substratum of reality; and if mechanism originated in a generalization of muscular action, then vitalism can indeed be traced to a similar generalization of the reproductive act—the union of male and female organs. In the new type of astrological vitalism, the stars and planets are considered as magnets or radio sets, and electrical action, being always of a polar nature, is the new name given to the "vital force" of older thought.

The third stage of thought is called by Jeans "mathematical." The main feature of it is that pure mathematical speculation is seen to fit perfectly the results of ever more complex and refined experiments; in fact it often precedes experiments. Mathematical theories are built, and as the physicist looks for a type of phenomena to which the theory might apply he often finds one, hitherto unexplained, which fits perfectly the purely abstract formulas. Moreover the striking thing is that a few symbols—as are all algebraic or mathematical letters or figures—are seen able to bring order and logical succession to the vast complexity of natural phenomena. In other words, a few symbolical relations (i.e. formulas) are seen to suffice for the ordering of the multitude of the world's events into a pattern, knowing which man will gain relative mastery over natural elements through the power of foreseeing.

Quoting again from Jeans' book:

"Einstein has written (Introduction to *Where Is Science Going?*—page 13): 'In every important advance the physicist finds that the fundamental laws are simplified more and more as experimental research advances. He is astonished to notice how sublime order emerges from what appeared to be chaos. And this cannot be traced back to the workings of his own mind but is due to a quality that is inherent in the world of perception'. (*This conclusion is disputed by many thinkers. D. R.*)

"Weyl has made a similar comment, writing (*The Open World*, p. 41): 'The astonishing thing is not that there exist natural laws, but that the further the analysis proceeds, the finer the details, the finer the elements to which the phenomena are reduced, the simpler—and not the more complicated, as one would originally expect—the fundamental relations become and the more exactly do they describe the actual occurrences.'

"We have had ample evidence of this tendency toward simplicity in the present book. We have seen Hero's simple synthesis of the two laws of Euclid gradually expanding in scope until it embraces almost all the activities of the universe, and yet maintaining its original simplicity of mathematical form throughout. This refers to Einstein's recent 'Unitary Field-Theory,' which, if it achieves complete success 'will remain valid whatever physical agencies are in action, so that we shall be able to combine all the operations of nature in one synthesis: they will have become shortest courses in a curved four-dimensional space' (page 126). Phenomenal nature is reduced to an array of events in the four-dimensional continuum, and the arrangement of these events proves to be of an exceedingly simple mathematical kind. . . . This simplicity . . . seems to admit of a very simple mathematical interpretation and of no other, as though, in Boyle's phrase, mathematics is the alphabet of the language in which nature is written. The words of this language may or may not be mental in their meanings; the immediate point is that, even in the alphabet, we can discover no reality different in kind from that we associate with a mere mental concept. These mental concepts are not of the kind we associate with the work of the engineer or the poet or the moralist, but with the thinker who works with pure thought alone as his raw material, the mathematician at work in his study. . . . For three centuries science had projected mechanical ideas on to nature, and made havoc of a large part of nature by so doing. Twentieth-century science, projecting the ideas of pure mathematics on to nature, finds that they fit as perfectly and as uniquely as Cinderella's slipper fitted her foot."

The phrase "projecting the ideas of pure mathematics on to nature" is significant. It shows that in such a science as physics or chemistry—and in general in all *empirical sciences*—three elements are to be considered: 1) natural phenomena or data; 2) ideas of pure mathematics; 3) a system of interpretations or "laws," which enable man to prophesy more or less accurately future natural phenomena. This is an important fact to consider; for thereby it is shown that a fundamental distinction exists between mathematics and the empirical sciences. Mathematics is used as the integrating factor in the building of the empirical sciences. In a sense the latter are applications of mathematical ideas. *Mathematics provides the form of knowledge, empirical sciences the organized contents of knowledge.*

This distinction is capital. For by defining astrology as the *algebra of life*, we place it in the category of mathematical thought—and not in that of empirical sciences. The results of such a conception are far-reaching.

The word "algebra" comes from an Arabian word "*al-jebr*" which means: the reduction of parts to a whole. The word "*jabara*," from which it is derived signifies: to bind together (Webster). Algebra has therefore as its basic function the binding together, or correlating, or integrating of elements into a formulated whole. The nature of these elements can be grasped when we consider the definition which Webster gives of "mathematics": "The science treating of the exact relations existing between quantities or magnitudes and operations, and of the methods by which, in accordance with these relations, quantities sought are deducible from others thought or supposed."

Two important points stand out in such a definition. First, mathematics is seen as a "science of pure correlation" (Bertrand Russell). Second, what it correlates are "quantities or magnitudes and operations." Algebra is a branch of mathematics, but besides correlating quantities it also deals with a category of conventional symbols which can be made to represent any element considered or the relations between any groups of elements. According to our conception, astrology is a kind of algebra, inasmuch as it deals with symbolic elements (planets, stars, segments of geocentric space, astrological Parts, Nodes, progressed positions, etc.) which it "binds together" into a formula describing a living whole: the native. However, these symbolic elements do not belong to the realm of quantity. They represent, on the contrary, *universal life-qualities.* Astrology is thus a kind of algebra of qualities; and

42

these qualities are not mere sensorial qualities (such as white, blue, thick, heavy, painful, etc.), but qualities which refer to *living processes*—whether on the physiological or the psychological and super-psychological planes.

We shall discuss these statements step by step; but it seems necessary at first to emphasize what astrology is not, before we can specify what it fundamentally is. In other words, we have to show briefly that astrology is *not* an empirical science, as are for instance physics, chemistry, or even biology, zoology and history. These empirical sciences deal with experimental data which they organize by using mathematical formal concepts. Such experimental data are sensorially perceived— directly or by means of instruments which extend the field of direct sensorial perception. Then by a process known as "scientific induction" correlations are established between data which form the basis of empirical *exact knowledge*.

Scientific induction is the basic postulate of exact sciences. It can be formulated in various ways but, according to Bertrand Russell (*The Analysis of Matter*, p. 167), "it must yield the result that a correlation which has been found true in a number of cases, and has never been found false, has at least a certain assignable degree of probability of being always true." This definition is of great importance to us, for who, among astrologers, will claim that *any* astrological correlation for which a definite meaning has been recognized "has never been found false"?

But this is not all. The problem of making astrology "scientific" in the sense of an empirical science—even if not an "exact" science—is involved in the proposition, or belief rather, that planets or stars actually influence individual beings by the fact of their sending to earth radio-like waves, or rays, which affect biological and psychological processes. Now, even if these "rays" were discovered, and if it became clear that they act upon the atoms and molecules of earth-substance in definite and measurable ways, this would in no way prove the usual findings of astrology. A restricted kind of natal astrology might be evolved which might claim—after centuries of research—the status of an experimental science; but this would solve only a fragment of the problems involved in the sum total of astrological ideas.

The reason for this is obvious. Let us admit that stellar or planetary rays produce physical and chemical changes in the substance of atoms and cells, and are thus able to condition psychological states. Let us suppose, moreover, that these changes are proven to be measurable in terms of the angular relationship of the planets (astrological aspects) and are affected by the section of the earth's orbit (zodiacal sign) or of the geocentric space at birth (house) in which the planets or stars are found. This in itself is an enormous order, which may never be filled. But even if all of it were scientifically proven —the following *basic* factors in astrology would remain most unscientific mysteries, as far as we can see.

Why should the first house represent matters affecting self and the structure of the body; the second house, finances; the seventh house, marriage, etc.? Why should zodiacal signs be related to certain parts of the body? Why should certain planets "rule" certain signs? Furthermore, how could "progressions" be "scientifically" explained? What could ever *prove* scientifically whether primaries are true and secondaries false, or vice versa; that the distance in degrees between two planets gives (usually) the number of years between birth and an occurrence which is characterized by the two planets' natures?

Then what of horary astrology, i.e., solving life-problems by interpreting the configurations of space and planets at the moment the problem arises in one's mind? "Scientific" astrologers may frown at horary astrology as being mere fortune-telling. Nevertheless it is easy to show that natal astrology (study of birth-charts) is a special case of horary astrology; for, as Marc Jones stated, studying a birth-chart is merely answering the question: "How is the problem of my life to be solved?" At least, this is just as logical a way of looking at the relationship between horary and natal astrology as the one formulated by saying: "An horary chart is the birth-chart of an idea." One may prefer the latter interpretation, but the former cannot be dismissed easily, and the truth of the matter must in some way include both approaches.

It is useless to add more "whys" to this already long list. We trust it will be apparent to everyone after some clear thinking on the matter that attempts at making astrology an exact empirical science by basing it on measurements of actual influences and rays are, if not doomed to failure, at least bound to explain or prove only a fragment of the entire body of ideas which constitutes and has always constituted astrology. Whatever science may discover concerning cosmic radiations, we do not believe that the *philosophy* of astrology can or should ever be the same as that of an empirical science, like physics or mechanics or biology.

There is, however, a somewhat different category of sciences which are based not on exact scientific induction and strict causality, but on statistical knowledge. Dr. A. Ritchie-Scott mentions as belonging to this type in the practical world "the whole theory of Insurance, Life-Annuities, the modern theory of heat, the construction of telephone exchanges, the Mendelian theory of inheritance, the study of Population Statistics, Blood Testing, sampling of ores, etc. . . . all based on the Theory of Probability and none the less valid for that." (*American Astrology*, July 1934)

Besides these examples, it is now well known that atomic physics is becoming more and more a statistical science, especially if Heisenberg's theories are proven to be correct; for they "give us a picture of a *statistical atom* whose properties and qualities are the average of the properties and qualities of all the actual atoms concerned in the emission of light." (Sir James Jeans, op. cit., p. 183). The new wave-mechanics "deals

45

only with probabilities and statistical assemblies, and its apparent determinism may be only another way of expressing the law of averages. The determinism may be of a purely statistical kind, like that relied on by an Insurance Company, or the Bank at Monte Carlo." Jeans further asserts:

"This being so, there is no assignable reason why the apparent determinism of the wave-equation should not conceal a complete objective indeterminism. In the mathematical problem known as the 'random walk,' we imagine that a traveller walks 20 miles a day, but with no causal relation between the directions of his walks on successive days—we can, for instance, imagine his throwing a stick up in the air at random every morning, and letting the direction of its fall determine the direction of his walk for the day. A mathematical formula can of course be obtained to exhibit the chances of his being at various points at successive nightfalls. If we now reduce the unit of time from a day to a second, so that his every step is indeterminate, we find that the probabilities spread out in waves, much as in Schrödinger's equation; the spread of the waves corresponds to a strict determinism, although the underlying physical cause is a complete indeterminism." (op. cit. p. 255)

"The only determinism of which modern physics is at all sure is of a merely statistical kind. We still see the actions of vast crowds of molecules or particles conforming to determinism—this is of course the determinism we observe in our everyday life, the basis of the so-called law of the uniformity of nature. But no determinism has so far been discovered in the motions of the separate individuals; on the contrary, the phenomena of radioactivity and radiation rather suggest that these do not move as they are pushed and pulled by inexorable forces . . . they are not controlled by predetermined forces, but only by the statistical laws of probability." (pp. 275-276)

These statements have a very direct bearing on the subject of astrology, and besides will bring joy to the heart of the convinced believer in the principle of free-will. While the subject is too vast to be discussed here, two basic points must be mentioned, for they have a capital importance in any solid philosophy of astrology. The first is that we shall always find in any type of thought dealing with life a fundamental inter-penetration between individual values and collective values. The individual may be free, but that freedom is certainly bound by the magnetic field, or *aura*, of the collectivity to which he belongs—the "Ring-Pass-Not" of Oriental occultism. On the other hand, the collectivity is also influenced and fecundated by the creative activity of those of its members who act as individuals and not merely as photostat copies of the collective pattern, or soul.

These two elements, individual and group, must figure pre-eminently in any astrological judgment; and this in various ways with which we shall deal succinctly as we go on in our study. It may be well, however, to state now that no astro-logical birth-chart can be judged *with accuracy*, if the general conditions of the group to which the native belongs as an individual, are unknown. This refers both to the social group (family, race, religion) and to that other grouping in con-sciousness which creates *levels of being*. The birth-chart will reveal individual tendencies, but these will manifest actually in terms of the condition of the family, city, nation, race in which the individual is born. A Chinese coolie may have exactly the same birth-chart as a European nobleman of a highly cultured family, born at the same latitude. And it is obvious that no one could infer accurately from the birth-chart alone what the Chinaman's life would be, especially if he were believed to be a European nobleman. For a life, and even an individual's character, are determined not only by the individual equation (birth-chart), but by the group in which these manifest. Group-values may be vaguely suggested in a chart, but only insofar as they affected the pre-natal forma-tion of the individual.

Does the above invalidate astrology? We do not believe so; but it serves to define its sphere. A birth-chart *as a whole* re-fers to an individual as such (potentially or actually) and deals with individual values. But any separate astrological factor—as for instance the position of a certain planet or an aspect between two particular planets—has only a *statistical value*. And this is why no particular astrological factor does necessarily operate in the same very definite way in all individual birth-charts. It is only statistically accurate—or, as we shall see presently, symbolically significant.

Bertrand Russell's words concerning the statistical principle will add more clarity to the above statements:

> "It might be thought that a statistical average is not very different from a rule with exceptions, but this would be a mistake. Statistics, ideally, are accurate laws about large groups; they differ from other laws only in being about groups, not about individuals. Statistical laws are inferred by induction from particular statistics, just as other laws are inferred from particular single occurrences." (op. cit. p. 191)

In other words, a science is no less "scientific" because it deals with statistical averages rather than with single occurrences; only it is to be clearly regarded as a science dealing with large groups and not with individuals.

From this it might seem that astrology could be considered as an empirical science of a statistical type. But such a conclusion does not seem to be fully warranted. Astrology may utilize the statistical method to check up its statements, and will do well to adopt such a technique—which has never been used with any great degree of scientific accuracy and on a large enough scale. But to say that, is quite different from claiming astrology as a true statistical science. Statistics may show that among famous people the sextile Sun-Moon occurs in a 12 per cent ratio; while in ordinary human beings it occurs only in about 5 in 100 cases (the example is given by the French mathematician-astrologer Paul Choisnard). This might indicate a certain correlation between that aspect and "celebrity" (whatever is meant by that!). But the inference is rather inconclusive. And even if it could be proven that

90 per cent of especially gifted musicians have a dominant Neptunian influence, and that as many prominent soldiers have the Sun in Aries, etc., it would merely mean that certain astrological statements are corroborated by statistical research. It would neither indicate *how* these astrological facts had originally been discovered, nor, I believe, the correct method of discovering new astrological truths; and still less *why* the statements are correct. Moreover, it would apply only to single separate factors in astrology and not to the quite different problem of interpreting an entire birth-chart as the symbol of an individual.

How are discoveries made in modern physics? The classical explanation is that a physicist observes a fact which is new, or ponders upon some flaw in an old theory, and formulates a new hypothesis which explains the new fact or solves the old unsolved enigma. The hypothesis is then checked by testing all the possible consequences thereof; and it becomes an accepted theory if it fits in with every known fact and is invalidated by none. We might assume that astrology originated in a similar manner. Some striking event coincided with an equally striking planetary conjunction. The hypothesis that both were related arose in the mind of an observer, who checked it up with similar occurrences—and after a few generations of checking up, this conjunction was definitely considered to bring about a certain event, or at least a certain type of event.

Whether astrology originated in such a manner or not can hardly be proved or disproved. If it did so originate, then we claim that astrology has reached a time when its value is to be keyed up to an entirely different plane of consciousness, to another mental level. In this, it would follow the course of development which mathematics and geometry have presumably taken. We may believe that men began to think of numerals purely in relation to concrete objects—two apples, three stones, etc.; or thought of a triangle as a class of objects

49

having a certain apparent shape. Then the abstract idea of number, or triangle, developed in man's mind—yet always with some sort of concrete background not entirely separated from sensorial experience. Finally the modern stage was reached in which non-Euclidian geometries and the higher forms of algebra completely robbed number and geometrical form of any representative elements, and reduced them to strictly logical symbols.

Says Bertrand Russell (op. cit., p. 171):

> "Propositions which form part of logic, or can be proved by logic, are all *tautologies*.—i.e., they show that certain different sets of symbols are different ways of saying the same thing, or that one set says part of what the other says. . . . Such propositions, therefore, are really concerned with symbols. We can know their truth or falsehood without studying the outside world, because they are only concerned with symbolic manipulations. . . . All pure mathematics consists of tautologies in the above sense. . . . Our certainty concerning simple mathematical propositions does not seem analogous to our certainty that the sun will rise tomorrow. I do not mean that we feel more sure of the one than the other, though perhaps we ought to do so; I mean that our assurance seems to have a different source. . . . It is obvious that, whenever it is actually useful to know that two sets of symbols say the same thing, or that one says part of what the other says, that must be because we have some knowledge as to the truth or falsehood of what is expressed by one of the sets. Consequently logical knowledge would be very unimportant if it stood alone; its importance arises through its combination with knowledge of propositions which are not purely logical.
>
> ". . . In an advanced science such as physics, the part played by pure mathematics consists in connecting various empirical generalizations with each other, so that the more general laws which replace them are based upon a larger number of matters of fact."

Astrology Compared to Logic and Mathematics

This quotation contains several statements which are very important at this stage of our inquiry into the essential nature of astrology. Mathematics, it is said, is concerned with symbols, the truth or falsehood of which can be known without studying the outside world. Mathematical propositions, Bertrand Russell adds in another paragraph, are thus purely formal. He further makes clear that mathematics and logic are sciences in an entirely different sense from the sense in which, for instance, physics is a science. The former are analytical and formal; the latter is empirical. Yet physics without mathematics would lack the very power of correlating logically its generalizations.

If, now, we come back to our definition of astrology as the *algebra of life*, we shall make our meaning plainer by stating that astrology is to all the empirical sciences dealing with the formation, growth, behavior and disintegration of organic wholes what mathematics is to physics and in general to sciences of inanimate objects. We do not say that it is recognized as such, but that such is its true function. And this is to some extent a verifiable statement.

Astrology of itself has no more meaning than algebra. It measures relationships between symbols whose concreteness is entirely a matter of convention, and does not really enter into the problems involved—just as the symbols of algebra, x, y, n, are mere conventions. The astrologers use terms like opposition, conjunction, squares, exactly as the mathematician uses signs of addition and multiplication. Their "progressions" are also very much in the same category as the more complicated symbols of calculus—the function sign, etc. The revolutions of celestial bodies constitute in their totality a vast and complex symbol which, of itself, is made up solely of *cyclically changing patterns of relationship*. It does not matter in the least whether it is planets, or abstract points derived from planetary motions, or segments of orbits, or symbolical points of reference like meridian, horizon and the like, which are considered. Planets are significant and convenient vehicles for symbolical meaning because they bear relatively simple relations of distance, velocity, mass, period, to a central point of reference, the Sun—or rather to the Earth's orbit around the Sun.

In other words, the astrological realm of moving celestial bodies is like the realm of logical propositions. Neither one nor the other has any real content. Both are purely formal, symbolical, and conventional. They acquire real value only in function of the actual living experiences which they serve to correlate. Alone, astrology and mathematics are without substance. But they invest with coherence, pattern, logic and order whatever substantial reality is associated with them. Thus mathematics associated with physical experimentation produces modern physics. In a similar manner (yet obviously not identical) astrology can and probably should be associated with physiology, geology, medicine, history, sociology; and above all, with psychology.

The fact is that when astrology played a really vital part in ancient civilizations it was so considered—if not by the rabble, at least undoubtedly by the initiated astrologers. We saw in our first chapter that the function of astrology was to bring into the chaos of the natural world on Earth the supreme order of which celestial revolutions are so conspicuous and psychologically exalting a manifestation. Chaos and imprevisibility and blind chance on Earth; but above in the heavens, perfect order, previsibility, law. Astrology took its significance from such a contrast. The skies were regarded as a *cosmic measuring device*, an archetypal paragon of order, which could be juxtaposed with any system of natural phenomena. From this juxtaposition would result a new view of the system of natural phenomena: an ordered, coherent view, which would lead to the possibility of making prognostications as to the future behavior of the system.

This is not very different from what science does when measuring with a yard-stick or timing with a clock a natural phenomenon. The complete set of planetary, solar, lunar and stellar revolutions, *as seen from the Earth*, has ever served in astrology as a complex many-dimensional yard-stick and as a clock, in order to determine the periodical behavior of natural organisms—in fact, as we shall see presently, of any *whole* (the Earth as a whole, a living body, a human psyche, a nation, etc.).

Modern physics has rightly stressed the fact that such measurements involve certain difficulties and are relative to the position and motion of the observer. In order to measure a distance, one must put the beginning of the yard-stick first at a definite point. In astrology, all measurements begin with the *first point of independent existence*; in the case of a human destiny, the first breath. The zodiac—(which, let us not forget, is *only* the orbit of the earth divided into twelve thirty-degree sections, and has little or nothing to do with constellations)—is measured as if beginning at the spring equinox, because at such a time a new cycle of vegetation begins in the Northern latitudes, where apparently astrology originated.

In other words, if we wish to investigate the *laws of periodicity and of structural relationship* which will apply to a human life starting on a certain day, we project on paper the state of our cosmic measuring rod (the solar system viewed from the place of birth) at that time, and measure with it the organism of natural elements which has just reached the condition of independent existence. Does the cosmic measuring rod and time-piece combined—the birth-chart—mean in itself anything substantial? Not in the least—no more than any yard-stick or clock. It is merely a symbol of measurement. Unless we know first of all what it is we want to measure, we shall know nothing practical after having measured—only a set of algebraic symbols on a wheel. If we do not know human nature, a birth-chart will give us no indication whatsoever on the nature of a particular human being. Unless we know about air-currents, atmospheric pressure, etc., an astrological chart will tell us nothing of the weather. Jupiter and Mars do not mean anything concrete whatsoever. They mean no more, no less, than 3 and 4, or a spiral and a straight line, or *m* and *p*. But if we say: Here is a newborn human body. It contains in itself the power to grow to full stature, the powers of blood-circulation, of food-metabolization, of self-reproduction through sex, and many other life-properties which characterize this body as belonging to the human species—then we can attempt to bring order out of this apparent chaos of powers, functions and life-properties by juxtaposing our celestial symbols to them.

Jupiter will symbolize the power of expansion; Mars the power of out-going impulses; Venus the power of combining reactions to stimuli as conscious judgment and emotion, etc. But, if we dealt with atmospheric conditions instead of with a human being, Jupiter, Mars, Venus would of course interpret altogether different things—like atmospheric pressure and other telluric factors. Because the latter are as yet very little known and the planet Earth has not yet been understood and studied *as an organic whole*—astrological symbolism is not very useful to meteorology and related sciences. At best, the astrologer will say that a strong Jupiter may indicate an intense state of expansion. But expansion applied to what? The "what" can be known accurately only when the organic behavior of the Earth as a whole is well understood; that is to say, when all the functions of this planetary organism are isolated. Then astrology can correlate and interpret these functions—just as mathematics correlates and interprets observations furnished by the microscope and electrical devices, bearing upon the inside structure of the atom.

To the above, objections undoubtedly will be raised. Textbooks on astrology will be shown, in which the planets, their positions and aspects, are given most definite and concrete meanings. Indeed, it is so; but these text-books are merely popular presentations of traditional data concerning the correlations of astrological symbols to certain realms of experience which happened to interest men most particularly. They do not deal essentially with pure astrology, but with certain particular applications of astrological symbolism. These applications are based on traditional knowledge concerning such things as psychology and old-time government; and are valuable only insofar as this traditional knowledge is valuable.

The interpretations of astrological elements given by most of our contemporary text-books on astrology are just as valuable as the traditional knowledge of human psychology and government was at the time of Ptolemy, in Alexandria. Insofar as human psychology and sociology have changed since that time, they are *valueless*. But as human nature is after all quite constant on the whole, the *applications* of astrological symbolism made by Ptolemy and his predecessors are still largely true today—but obviously quite false, or beside the point, or incomplete, in innumerable cases.

The fundamental point to grasp however—and it seems a difficult one for so many people!—is that ordinary books on astrology today give merely the application of astrological symbolism to a few traditional subjects: character, health, happiness, and matters affecting the State, etc. These applications are based on a traditional common-sense view of the subjects involved, and stand or fall with this traditional view. If they fall it does not in the least imply that the principles on which astrology is based, as a science of symbolism, are wrong. No more than mathematics proved to be a failure when the discovery of the quantum upset the whole fabric of modern physics. Similarly, the discoveries of psychoanalysis, as well as the new social conditions prevailing today, have invalidated many of the traditional statements reproduced in modern astrological text-books with regard to psychology and social behavior and professional abilities. But astrology proper remains untouched by such changes: for, just as Bertrand Russell says of logic: "We can know (its) truth or falsehood without studying the outside world, because (it is) only concerned with symbolic manipulations." Paraphrasing him further, we would add: Our certainty concerning simple astrological propositions does not seem analogous to our certainty concerning simple psychological facts, like the fact that a girl will fall in love some time in her life, or pass through an emotional crisis in her forties. Our assurance comes from a different source.

To try to define or at least suggest what this source is— such is our next task; a difficult one, because it involves a type of attitude to life and to consciousness which is quite removed from the official and normal one prevalent in our academic and intellectual civilization. We shall approach the subject first of all by studying briefly a type of development in modern thought which is at the same time new in its formulation, yet very ancient in its ancestry: we refer to the philosophy called "*Holism.*"

The Philosophy of Holism

This philosophy is expounded fully in a remarkable book, "Holism and Evolution," written in 1926 by a still more remarkable man, General Jan C. Smuts, statesman, philosopher and scientist. An article in the latest edition of the *Encyclopedia Britannica* under the name "Holism," also written by General Smuts, gives a general summary of the ideas developed in the book. We shall quote somewhat extensively from this article:

"Holism is the theory which makes the existence of 'wholes' a fundamental feature of the world. It regards natural objects, both animate and inanimate, as wholes and not merely as assemblages of elements or parts. It looks upon nature as consisting of discrete, concrete bodies and things, and not as a diffuse homogeneous continuum. And these bodies or things are not entirely resolvable into parts; in one degree or another they are wholes which are more than the sum of their parts, and the mechanical putting together of their parts will not produce them or account for their character and behavior. The so-called parts are in fact not real but largely abstract analytical distinctions, and do not properly or adequately express what has gone to the making of the thing as a whole.

"Holism is therefore a viewpoint additional and complementary to that of science, whose keywords are continuity and mechanism . . . (Science's) mechanistic scheme applies even to living bodies, as their material structures determine the functions which constitute life characters. . . . Life and mind are considered as derivative and epiphenomenal to matter. . . . The scientific scheme has been seriously undermined by the most recent discoveries in physical and mathematical science.*
. . . The value of the mechanistic concept for research is not questioned, but it can no longer be considered as a true index of the concrete character of the universe and its contents. Holism is an attempt to explore an alternative scheme which will yet avoid the pitfalls of vitalism.

"What is involved in the concept of a whole? In the first place, insofar as a whole is consisting of parts or elements, they cannot be fixed, constant, or unalterable. . . . Whole and parts mutually and reciprocally influence and modify each other. . . . The parts are moulded and adjusted by the whole, just as the whole in turn depends on the co-operation of its parts. . . . The concept of the whole as applied to natural objects thus implies two great departures from the orthodox scientific scheme. In the first place, matter, life and mind do not consist of fixed, constant and unalterable elements. And in the second place, besides the parts or the elements in things, there is another active factor (the whole) which science does not recognize at all.

"Evolution is the progressive complexifying of parts or co-operating elements, with a simultaneous increase in unity of pattern with which they are blended. It is thus a rising series of wholes, from the simplest material patterns to the most advanced. . . . Wholeness, or holism, characterizes the entire process of evolution in an ever increasing measure. And the process is continuous in the sense that the older types of

* This is especially true of the quantum theory which is perhaps the deepest basis of scientific Holism, insofar as it pictures the universe as functioning by means of wholes of "action":—quanta. The theory opposes the view of continuous movement, giving thus a discrete appearance to the universe. The philosophy of the quantum theory is yet to be formulated. (D. R.)

wholes or patterns are not discarded, but become the starting point and the elements of the newer, more advanced patterns. Thus the material chemical patterns are incorporated into the biological patterns, and both of them into the subsequent psychical patterns or wholes. . . . Electrons and protons, atoms and molecules, inorganic and organic compounds, colloids, protoplasm, plants and animals, minds and personalities are but some steps in this movement of holism. . . .

"The whole is creative; wherever parts conspire to form a whole, there something arises which is more than the parts. . . . The origin of a whole from its parts is an instance of the more arising from the less, the higher from the lower, in a way which does no violence to reason . . . because the concept of a whole in relation to its parts is a product of reason. . . ."

(Encyclopedia Britannica: "Holism")

General Smuts explains further how the concept of purely mechanical causation is unsatisfactory and possibly a fiction, for if the effect is never more than the cause, if cause is and must always necessarily be an exact measure of effect, this cannot be a creative progressive universe. Holistic causation (where several factors contribute to the making of new wholes) is the real process, and makes possible the increase and advance which is actually the fact in nature. Also if the cause determines the effect completely, determinism is absolute. In the holistic universe freedom is recognized as inherent in nature.

The organic unity which constitutes a whole is the ultimate basis of individuality. Hardly noticeable in the inorganic realm, individuality increases throughout the organic world until it becomes the basis for the latest and greatest whole of evolution, the human personality. Out of the progressive evolutionary combination or integration of material, chemical, biological, and mental patterns, the complete personality is born, which constitutes and explains the unity and interrelations existing between these three sets of patterns.

The whole, looked at from an external mechanical standpoint, is what we call parts. But from an inner integral standpoint, the whole is the self. The relation of whole and parts is thus transformed into the relation of self to not-self, with which we are acquainted as the subject-object relation in psychology. Wholeness is selfness. The world-process tends from matter, through life, to mind and spirit; from necessity to freedom; from the externality of the elements to the inwardness and selfhood of wholes. Whole-making characterizes this process at every stage. This applies to psychological processes, in which there is an increasing building-up of higher patterns out of lower ones. *Gestalt* psychology has shown, for instance, that mental activity produces patterns or structures of experience which behave as wholes and enter into other experiences as undivided and indivisible wholes.

While the same is true with regard to social, religious and political structures, these are holoids rather than wholes; and the real wholes are always the personalities who have built these structures for the purpose of the growth and spiritual advancement of all human individuals. General Smuts does not believe that the individual is for the sake of State or Church, but *vice versa*. As to the possibility that the universe might be also a whole, he refuses to take a positive stand, saying only that "this is not a completed universe, but a universe in the making; and there may be wholes great and small in the making beyond the comprehension of our limited faculties." And he concludes with these beautiful words:

"Although the theory of holism frankly accepts the material basis of the world and recognizes the natural order as idealism cannot, yet it fully justifies the claims of the spirits in the interpretation of the world. . . . We are constantly confronted with the opposition between matter and spirit, between the temporal and the eternal, between the phenomenal and the real. Holism shows these opposites as reconciled and harmonized in the whole. It shows whole and parts as aspects of each other; the finite is identified with the infinite, the particular with the universal. Eternity is contained in time, matter is the vesture and vehicle of spirit, reality is not a transcendent other-worldly

59

order, but is immanent in the phenomenal. To attain to reality, we need not fly from appearance; each little centre and whole in the world, however lowly, is a laboratory in which time is transmuted into eternity, the phenomenal into the real. The wondrous truth is everywhere; the plummet let down anywhere will reach to unknown depths; any cross-section in the world of appearance will reveal the very texture of reality. Everywhere the whole, even the least and most insignificant apparently, is the real wonder, the miracle which holds the secrets for which we are groping in thought and conduct. There is the within which is the beyond. To be a whole and to live in the whole becomes the supreme principle, from which all the highest ethical and spiritual rules (such as the Golden Rule) follow. And it links these rules with the nature of things, for not only do goodness, love and justice derive from it, but also beauty and truth, which are rooted in the whole and have no meaning apart from it. The whole is in fact both the source and the principle of explanation of all our highest ideals no less than of the earlier evolutionary structures."

Astrology and Holistic Logic

The whole is also "the source and the principle of explanation" of true astrology. As we understand it, and as it has perhaps always been understood by those who probed its most essential significance, true astrology is the *mathematics of wholeness*. It is "holistic logic" in opposition to the "intellectual logic" of this present Western civilization. It deals with wholes. It studies the structural harmony, the growth, development and the disintegration or transfiguration of wholes—whether these be the usual biological organisms or more transcendant mental and spiritual wholes.

Intellectual logic deals with "parts;" holistic logic with "wholes." All intellectually logical propositions, as Bertrand Russell says, are essentially tautologies. They equate judgments concerning the realm of "parts." They see that parts fit well causally, one with the others. They are strictly analytical propositions and are perfectly adapted to the mechanistic conception of the world—which will always remain an essential factor in human knowledge. This concept, so strongly (almost exclusively) developed in the European civilization (and its Greek prototypes), is a marvelous instrument of knowledge. But only an instrument. It does not make us understand reality. It only establishes a basis of "intellectual honesty" for our approach to reality. It helps remove the parasitic growths of subjective emotionalism, which so easily corrupt any type of vital knowledge. It filters the waters of knowledge, so to speak; or in another sense, it is a scaffold which lifts up knowledge to a really human plane. Intellectual logic and the idea of strict causation (its result) are marvelous tools for the training of a crystal-clear, honest and un-emotional or un-devotional mind. They serve to root out the delusion of the miraculous, the fallacies of the religious, tribal mind. They are great cathartics. But while one may guess at the shape of a building by studying the scaffold used to build it—the scaffold is not the building.

The scaffold represents the outside view of the world, a view which deals with parts as if they were not integral components and, in a sense at least, products of the whole. But the moment the whole becomes an *operating unit*, parts cease to be merely parts; they become *functional organs* of the organic whole. We usually restrict the use of such terms as organism, organs, functions to what is now known in science as biological wholes. But in the holistic conception of the universe we extend the use of the terms, potentially at least, to all kinds of wholes. The fact that there is a whole implies the existence of parts which are more than what is known, from the mechanistic viewpoint, as mere parts. Again we may make a distinction between mechanistic and intellectually analyzed parts, and holistic parts; the latter being in all respects organs, cells or groups of cells, and agents of the whole.

Elsewhere we spoke at great length of the philosophy of Operative Wholeness (*The Glass Hive, Hamsa* series of articles bearing this title; 1929 to 1934). We feel that these two words "Operative Wholeness," which we used years before being acquainted with General Smuts' work or those of other English philosophers, are very significant. They at any rate give the keynote of a philosophy of astrology. For true astrology deals, exclusively and integrally, with operative wholes. It deals with them just at the precise moment when they emerge into the condition of wholes; when they become able to maintain independent operation as wholes at their own level of being; able also, at least potentially, to reproduce themselves through some sort of emanative or multiplicative process.

Here we are confronted with two definite factors: a space factor—the structure of the whole, its morphology and the sum total of its specific characters; and a time factor—the moment of integration, of "holization," when what was only a group of elements begins to operate as an independent whole. The space factor has to be known independently of astrology. It belongs to those sciences which deal with spatial arrangement or structure,—as physics, physiology and psychology. An astrological chart will never tell, of itself, whether the whole it characterizes is a man, a dog, a seed of wheat, or an idea. If one knows that the chart is to be referred to an entity of the species *homo sapiens*, and moreover to a particular race within that species (white, yellow, black, red), then a good deal of *inferential knowledge* may be had as to the individual variation of the type which the chart represents; nothing more.

This is one of the reasons why we compared astrology to pure mathematics; for mathematics does not give any information as to what its equations refer to. First, you have to have perceptual knowledge; then only can you use mathematics to give a new quality to that knowledge. Likewise in order intelligently to use astrology, you have first to know what kind of whole the chart symbolizes. Is it a human being? Is it a man or a woman? And, to some extent at least, what racial and cultural type of man or woman is it? Knowing these things, astrology can then be used to add a new quality to that knowledge. This quality is almost solely dependent upon values which refer to the *essence of time*—an almost entirely unknown factor in science. Astrology is rooted in the mystery of time.

Again let us restate our parallelism between logic and astrology. Logic is a method of testing the purity of the causal principle in any concept. The causal principle in turn is the foundation of the mechanistic theory, which refers, as seen above, to an external viewpoint from which the universe appears as a grouping of causally related elements in an abstract matrix which now is called space-time, or the continuum. In such a theory the essence of space completely absorbs the reality of time, which becomes merely a fourth-dimension of space. As Bergson pointed out in his great work *Creative Evolution*, the time of science is purely mathematical and has no intrinsic vital value. He then tried to approach the reality of time, which he expressed by the term "duration."

Time and Cycles

In the holistic universe (generally speaking, and not necessarily as General Smuts sees it) time is very real indeed. And its reality is very much to be identified with the reality of the wholeness of the wholes. Not only does real time, or Bergsonian duration, become a function of the wholeness of wholes, but it enters, in a sort of meta-causal way, into the "holization" of any group of elements. Two factors are thus involved: First, the span of independent existence of any whole is intimately united to the character of the wholeness of that whole. Second, the quality of the moment when the group became an operative whole determines the quality of the wholeness of the whole.

In other words, whether a whole continues to exist as such

a minute, a year or a billion years, is not merely a secondary matter. The span of wholeness cannot be isolated from the essence of the whole. The relation between both is not one of causation, but one of identity. Considered as a particular, living entity, a man is the length of his life: first proposition. A man is the moment of his assumption of the power of independent existence (first breath): second proposition. Such are postulates of a "time-philosophy."

Nevertheless these do not contradict the facts that a man is first of all an entity belonging to the human species, then to a particular race and physiological grouping. These facts determine a man's space-characteristics: his biological structure. But a man is not only a part of a collectivity (mechanistic view). He is an individual whole (holistic view). What is it that characterizes this individual wholeness? The moment of his first breath, and the span of his life—both being related values in *real time*.

Modern science has nothing whatsoever to say as to the quality of the wholeness of any whole; nor has it anything vital and real to say concerning the essence of time. Wholes are creatures of time. Parts, as causally related elements, are creatures of space. The term "creatures" may be somewhat allegorical; but the general idea is correct, for the relationship of time to wholes is of a genetic type. It is not exactly that time *makes* wholes; but time conditions the making of wholes. To return to our previous illustration, mathematics does not make physics, but mathematics conditions the making of physics. Mathematics makes physics a whole, through the process of logical correlation of data. Likewise time makes of groupings of elements operative wholes, through a process of correlation and "holization" of these elements. This latter process is not logical. In some cases we may call it biological; but in a more general sense it transcends what is ordinarily called "life." It might be named *cyclological*, because time is essentially cyclic in its manifestations.

Thus the science of cycles (or, more accurately, the science of "cyclicity"). *Cyclology* is to the science of wholes what mathematics is to modern physical science. Mathematics analyzes space; cyclology analyzes time—real time, the time of the living and the whole. The former starts from a strictly causal, intellectual, external (in General Smuts' sense of the term) viewpoint of the universe, conceived as *extended* in an abstract space-time continuum, in which time is interpreted as an extra spatial co-ordinate. The latter starts from a synchronistic, holistic, internal view of the universe conceived as *in-tensed* in a cyclic psycho-biological time, the unit of which might be called the "quantum of duration," viz., the creative moment. The moment is creative inasmuch as it releases the power needed to make wholes. It is a sort of "photon," as it represents a unit of release of that whole-making energy which is the innermost reality of time.

If we refer again to General Smuts' ideas and see with him the wholeness of the whole as identical with self or soul (depending on these words' definitions), then we can realize that the moment is creative of selfhood or soul; that a soul can be determined in function of the moment at which the whole, of which it is the very wholeness, arises as an independently operating individuality. Time becomes thus the universal matrix of "individual souls." Each soul (or whole) has its birth-moment and its cycle of manifestation, both of which fully determine it as a soul,—i.e., as a wholeness of parts, which, in their ancestry as parts, refer to space.

This fits in well with the old mythological symbolism. For Chronos-Saturn is the maker of individual souls, or individual selves, or personalities, or egos—according to the way these terms are defined. It is the god of cycles, the ruler of the Golden Age (i.e., of the beginning of any cycle). It is the principle of limitation, of boundaries, of finiteness, of crystallization and form. This, because *every whole must needs be finite*; because wholeness implies finiteness, selfhood implies

limitations and form. Yet the Golden Age is the age of innocence and bliss; for to live wholly within the limits and cyclic
boundaries of one's own wholeness is true innocence and
bliss; sin and tragedy coming only as one attempts to go
beyond these boundaries in search of the "infinite."

In one of his letters to students, Marc Jones writes:

> "There is no delusion so damaging to the spiritual growth
> of the seeker as the idea that infinity is something to be sought,
> and somehow to be gained. . . . Infinity is a concept of finite
> mind, to get at something which it is not, and finiteness is a
> necessity for realization of infinity, paradoxical as this may
> seem to be. . . . Fear is infinite, just as love is finite. Hate is
> infinite, as is a lie or a surrender of a soul to the immoral or
> the base; but divinity is finite, definite, that is. Finite means
> limited, infinite indicates a lack of delimitation. The utterly
> unlimited is wholly unknown, the wholly defined is the abso-
> lutely known. God was finite to Jesus: his 'father.' Divinity
> is finite to the student who knows through the spiritual bound-
> ing, the initiatory limiting of his being. Paul calls himself a
> 'slave' of an immortal master, and in this 'bondservantship'
> becomes likewise a real or immortal personality. Reality is
> finite, never infinitely gained. The quest for the real is really
> the quest for the finite absolute."

This easily brings us back to the revolution which Einstein
accomplished in the realm of world physics by declaring the
universe boundless but limited. Since this mathematical statement modern science has begun to deal with the universe as a
whole—and also with the atom as a whole composed of very
peculiar parts. All of which leads in the direction of Holism.
But we would seriously question some of the philosophical
ideas involved in Einstein's generalized theory. We would, for
instance, say that space as such is unlimited; because space
deals with the causal extension of elements, of parts-to-be. And
there is no limit to the possible number of and relations between elements. But time is limited; because it is the realm of
whole-making; and wholeness or selfhood is, by definition,

limited. Time, abstractly speaking, is *the* Cycle—whatever the apparent size of it may be. It is the "circle of wholeness"; the mythological-astronomical Ring of Saturn. That, therefore, which makes space-time limited is the factor of time. Infinite time is an absurdity. Eternity is not infinite time, but an immense cycle of time, or eon. Mystically speaking, it is the wholeness of any cycle.

In Gnostic philosophy an Eon is not only a cycle of time, but a divine Consciousness or cosmic Being—a cosmic Whole. This applies to every cycle, however small it may appear to be. A moment is an eon, in the sense that it is both a unit of time and a soul—or the formative matrix of a number of wholes that achieve then their wholeness. As to what is called the "universal Self," such does not mean an infinite Self, but on the contrary that which reaches perfect selfhood during every "quantum of duration," during every moment: viz., the whole that is whole in and through every one of the shortest moments, without any conceivable break in selfhood. It may be the smallest of the small, or the vastest of the vast. Dimensions do not count, because they belong to the realm of space. Nor does it matter whether a whole has this or that number of parts, small or tremendously large. The number of parts and the degree of extension in dimensions do not belong to the realm of wholeness—or time, but to the illusion of spatiality, the illusion of *plus* and *minus*, of intellectual logic and causation. Being is potentially whole at every moment. The supreme Being is He Who is actually whole at every moment, knowing not the disintegration that is death; Whose span of time is so full with uninterrupted wholeness that it is both the smallest of the small and the vastest of the vast.

Positive and Negative Time

All of which is undoubtedly very metaphysical; yet so intensely practical! It refers to one of the basic changes which characterize this period of transition of ours; a change very complex inasmuch as it at times appears to be directed one way, at others just in the opposite direction. Since the sixth century B.C. mankind has tried to repolarize itself in accordance with a new mental and abstract viewpoint. Its best philosophers and scientists have stressed the factor of "form." Form, which must not be confused with "body," is merely the synthetic result of purely abstract relationship. Form, however, when it becomes manifest in the ordering of material elements into a "body" (or object), implies extension in space. Thus space, as a cosmic principle, has been fundamentally emphasized during these last twenty-five centuries.

On the other hand, real time has been left in the background. Time, for archaic mankind, meant a line of successive modifications undergone by material bodies. Time was significant insofar as it seemed to cause the fateful disintegration of bodies and energies. Time was thus analogical with fate. Saturn was the god of fate and *karma*—the implacable ruler whose decrees meant cessation and death. Cessation means emotion; and so does birth. All great changes, all moments when time seems to act with particular power and significance, are causes for intense emotions. Thus time-values appear, to the "natural" man, as emotional values. Time (Saturn) operates—as we shall see later on—through changes in feelings (Moon). The changes of the Moon mould the life of feelings of man, as the solar changes affect the operation of the basic life-force in all living bodies.

Time, thus connected with change, carries always with it the significance of cessation (cf. the Saturn symbolism); and thus that of the tragic inability to perpetuate consciousness, love, youth and all such symbols of perfectly functioning organic form. In other words, time, which at first was associated with the birth of things (Golden Age) and bliss, for many centuries seems to have been essentially linked with the idea of death and the fatality of not being able to maintain one's own identity (which means, to retain a definite form). Saturn-time has been regarded thus more and more (especially throughout the Christian era) as the power that opposes life; an anti-holistic power.

This in itself is highly significant. That which actually generates wholes and gives birth to souls has been almost exclusively considered as the cause of all destruction! It is, of course, both the cause of birth and the cause of death. But because "this world" was considered evil and illusory, birth did not seem a particularly joyful event—and, curiously enough, death was even more feared; which would be indeed quite illogical, were it not for the fact that death was taught to mean in so many cases the birth of hell! Occult philosophy and the deeper types of mysticism emphasized the teaching that while the ordinary man, identifying his selfhood with his body of earth-matter, was facing extinction of personal consciousness at death, the adept, having succeeded in transferring his selfhood from the body to the abstract form (or astral prototype), knew no cessation of personality at death. His material body would disintegrate under the sway of Saturn, but having established his selfhood in an abstract form, he was able to cheat Saturn. He remained the same self minus a material vehicle for expression. The wholeness of the whole remained, even though the operative power of the whole (in terms of *earthly activity*) was gone.

Thus the fatality of cessation was overcome, through the mastery of form. Man building his "form of immortality," or extricating it from the substantial elements which gave it body, was able to retain his selfhood in spite of all changes, in spite of time. Having built his own space-structure as an impregnable fortress, he could defy time. This could be done only by the use of mind. Various levels of mind would confer upon one various types of immortality. A great book remembered throughout the ages is a sort of personal immortality for its author. The adept, however, was able to gain an even more integral type of immortality by functioning beyond

69

death in his "Christ-body" or "body of resurrection" or *nirmanakaya* body, etc.

Unfortunately, the *creative* type of mind (i.e., mind considered in relation to the process of whole-making) was soon obscured by the tremendous development of the *logical* type of mind, or analytical intellect. Through analysis, space lost its wholeness (i.e., its connection with the holistic power of time) and became mechanistic and strictly causal. It became infinite, thus meaningless. It was conceived as extending in all directions infinitely. Causality and mechanism led to the formulation of the laws of thermo-dynamics and to the idea of entropy. The universe was seen as "running down." Here also time was becoming the fatality of cessation—instead of the power of giving birth to wholes.

Of late, however, a tendency toward restating cosmology in terms not unlike the ancient Days and Nights of Brahma has come to the fore. Not only is the universe being conceived as a whole, but instead of being pictured as an exploding whole it is acquiring the power to regenerate itself, periods of contractions alternating with periods of expansion (Sir James Jeans; op. cit., p. 138). It seems probable that a new understanding of the essence of time may lead scientists to further and more satisfactory theories.

The main point for us to grasp, however, is that there are two fundamental conceptions of time possible: *Negative time* is time conceived as the fatality of cessation. *Positive time*, or holistic time, is the power of whole-making. The first view is subjective and emotional. It says: "Here I am, whole, alive, conscious; and it is all going to end. Each change is a step toward death, and thus all is suffering and all in vain." Thus speaks the individual, who has seen that individual selfhood is a mirage. "All compound entities decay," said the Buddha. From which follows logically that the only wise attitude to take is to withdraw one's consciousness from all changing compounds and to dwell in pure "abstract form," in pure

70

wholeness beyond (or within) all wholes. This is the *Nirvana* state.

The positive conception of time sees time as the eternal birthing of wholes which do not necessarily die as such but may keep combining with each other, forming in the process ever greater wholes. Through *participation in consciousness* the individual may become an organic part of a greater whole, and thus achieve immortality within that whole, as a functional agent of the wholeness of the greater whole. This kind of immortality differs in meaning from strictly personal immortality, because it is not based on the overcoming of time, but on identification with the creative power of every moment.

Man should live fully every moment, and first of all his fundamental birth-moment and his entire Destiny. As he ceases resisting time, but on the contrary accepts the creative message of every moment, every moment is seen as a birth. Man, as he lives creatively, lives in a constant process of whole-making. He is not trying to escape the limitations of any one moment by rushing off into space, but he fulfills the space and the form determined by the potency of every moment; and by so doing he constantly renews his wholeness. He creates, with the same ease and joy, in the moments which define his wholeness as that of youth as in those other moments which define his wholeness as that of maturity, old age, or death. All these time-definings are equally creative opportunities for whole-making. At every moment he is a whole combining with all other wholes within the universal Whole. When the space-structure known as his body is no longer able to define new series of whole-making, the structure is resolved into its elements, which recombine within the Whole to carry on the joy of birthing in other modes. But at the very moment the body structure loses its holistic power and breaks down, in that same moment myriads of structures are born in the universe. A star may be born, and he who has fulfilled time and identified himself with its cyclic tides is carried thereon to immediate birthing according to the fulness of the whole-making power he had developed within his then ending space-structure (i.e., species, race, family and groupings of all sorts).

Intuitions and Symbols

The new type of Astrology, which we discuss in this book, is founded upon this positive conception of time. And it involves therefore the use of a faculty which had no place in minds weighed down by the negative concept of time, its determinism and its fears. According to the negative concept of time, every whole is dying at every moment in its parts. Thus the only thing the whole can do is try frantically to get new parts, and so master the causal laws of relationship between parts that, *by engineering skill*, the fateful disintegration may be made as slow as possible, and the space-structure may be preserved. As in war offensive is the best means of defense, so self-preservation is best accomplished by means of self-aggrandizement. Which leads to imperialism and greed, on a constant background of fear. At the limit we have the symbol of the "black magician," who feeds on the death of all things, who in absolute fear preserves his formal perfection by destroying all things and sucking their life-power. Such is the supreme manifestation of negative time. It involves the use of a powerful intellect, which reduces all things to elements in order to assimilate them, which is absolutely un-creative because absolutely divorced from the holistic power of true time.

This is perhaps only a symbol, but it indicates the consummation of the process which extols exclusively intellectual logic, and the analytical, causalistic attitude of the mind. In opposition to this we see the development of the faculty of intuition, which is the power to identify oneself with the whole-making power of time. Intuition begins with biological instinct.* The latter apprehends every new situation and confrontation as a whole, and reacts to it instantaneously also as a whole. Thus there is perfect adjustment of whole to whole, and perfect fulfillment both of all relationships involved in the confrontation and of the moment itself.

Intuition is the same power at the psycho-mental level. C. G. Jung speaks of intuition as follows:

> "Intuition is a kind of instinctive apprehension, irrespective of the nature of its contents. . . . Through intuition any one content is presented as a complete whole. . . . Intuitive cognition possesses an intrinsic nature of certainty and conviction which enabled Spinoza to uphold the 'scientia intuitiva' as the highest form of cognition."

The best definition would seem to us to be that *intuition is holistic perception*. It can also be defined as *awareness of self*. It is the faculty which enables us to be aware of the self (the wholeness) of any whole. It is thus opposed to sensations, which are always fragmentary and therefore need the causal logic of the intellect (or the equivalent biological power of association of sensations) to co-ordinate them. Intuition is not based on causal logic, yet has a definite type of logicalness, to which we referred as "holistic logic." The certainty derived from intuitive realizations is not of the same type as that derived from simple mathematical propositions; and yet the intuitive realization is, in its own way, a kind of tautology.

A tautology was defined by Bertrand Russell as a proposi-

---

* Bergson defines intuition as instinct become conscious of itself, set free from slavery to the exigencies of action and able to reflect upon what it sees. The essential nature of both instinct and intuition is defined by him as "sympathy." Intellect at its highest puts into our hands the key to the comprehension of matter; intuition may lead us to the very depths of life itself. Intuitive philosophy is a type of knowledge akin to art but having for object life itself. It operates by establishing a sympathetic relation between us and other living beings. Intuition transcends intellect, but it is by means of intellect that it has grown beyond the limitations of mere instinct. Without the co-operation of intellect it must—as instinct—have remained attached to some special object of a practical utility, and have spent itself in outward act. (Cf. *Creative Evolution*, Ch. II.)

tion showing "that certain different sets of symbols are different ways of saying the same thing." In other words, the process is that of identifying two symbolical representations. The intuitive realization is similar to this because through it a whole (be it an individual or a situation) is identified with a quality. One knows intuitively that a man is honest, let us say. This means that in a peculiar way the man and honesty have been realized as identical. The quality, honesty, has superimposed itself to the concept of the man, and become one with it. We believe that all intuitions can be explained as sudden identifications of particular wholes with basic qualities held, as it were, in the unconscious. When a person (or a whole situation) becomes the subject of an intuitive realization, one or several of these basic qualities are suddenly pulled out of the unconscious and so at-one with the mental image of the person (or the situation) that the latter becomes completely significant in terms of these qualities.*

Astrology is based upon one of these intuitive realizations identifying "order" and "the celestial motions of the stars." The conceptual quality of "order" was latent in the unconscious. It was the psychological result of a yearning to find a compensation for the apparent chaos of every-day existence. Moreover, man observed that there was a striking regularity in the movements of Sun, Moon, stars. Then the inner psychological factor and the outer perception somehow appeared as identical. One became the symbol of the other. All intuitions are based on symbols.

What are symbols? They are *representations of qualities which pertain to wholes*. In contradistinction to symbols, enumerations and categories pertain to parts. Parts exist in a condition of co-extensive simultaneity—that is, in space. They are seen in juxtaposition, and they strike us basically by virtue of their differences: they occupy different places, are orien-

---

* Cf. next two chapters for a further discussion of these "qualities" and "primordial images" of the unconscious.

74

tated differently, behave differently. They have distinguishing characteristics thanks to which the mind is able to define them analytically against the background of a homogeneous space, or against each other, by contrast. Parts therefore can be enumerated; they can be given quantitative values and causal connections; they can be classified into categories, compartments, etc. But when we come to wholes (whether as whole entities, or as whole situations) we are facing truly indivisible individualities which must be understood and *lived* as wholes. In order to do so we have to establish a current of "sympathy" between ourselves (as a whole) and them. Our wholeness meets and at-ones with their wholeness. A psychic state is the result, in us. This state is purely qualitative; for, as Bergson shows in his book, *Les Données Immédiates de la Conscience,** psychological states are in themselves purely qualitative, and pure duration is a "succession of qualitative changes."

Thus, briefly speaking and avoiding lengthy metaphysical arguments, we may say that every whole as it is experienced by us at any particular moment is pervaded by a quality which represents the "genius" of this whole, the genius of the situation as a whole: its significance, its "soul." How can this soul or significance be conveyed? Not merely by an enumeration of the parts constituting the whole, but by a "symbol" which, as a "sign," reveals the significance of the whole.

Time-values, soul-values, whole-values—all similar terms—cannot be communicated directly. Intellectual analysis and its related mental operations are of no use whatsoever to convey the wholeness of a whole, the genius of a whole situation, of a whole moment. Intuition, based on identification and perfect sympathy (or perfect atunement), can alone bring us to the realization of that wholeness or genius.

But how can we arouse this state of identification? Only by

---

* Translated into English as *Time and Free Will*. Cf. Chapters I and II.

formulating a situation or image which, in an actional dramatic manner, will exteriorize the quality of the whole,—and moreover will tend to arouse the experience of that quality in others. Let us suppose that a man is living in a thick jungle, so thick that he has never seen a night-sky filled with stars. In the jungle, he constantly experiences fear and attacks from hostile living things. Jungle-life seems to him an awesome chaos of brutal instincts. Then a superior being comes to him who takes him to a mountain peak from which he can watch the orderly pageant of stars. He is taught the rudiments of astronomy and the ordered laws of celestial motions. For the first time the wholeness of him faces the wholeness of the universe, and he experiences the reality of order and harmony. Even jungle-life, he now realizes, is ruled by some vast mysterious harmony.

Then he returns to his jungle, his whole being filled with the experience. He tries to communicate the meaning of order to his jungle-fellows—without success, of course, as there is no sensorial experience of theirs which can give to them the "symbol" of order. Finally, he leads them to the top of high trees and they contemplate the clear night-sky. They see, night after night, the pageant of stars. They can sense the reality of universal order, for now they have seen a "sign" thereof. And whenever, later on, if unable to climb the high trees and oppressed by the dark chaos of the jungle, they feel lost in this chaos, another man can tell them: "Remember the stars. There *is* order in the world." And the despairing men may again experience the reality of order through the power of the symbolism of the stars.

Likewise a tiger becomes a symbol of fear; a strongly built house a symbol of protection. In other words, a life-situation which, in the more or less universal experience of mankind, is spontaneously identifiable with the quality of a particular psychological state, becomes the symbol of that state. It is that state exteriorized as a symbolic image, the image being further abstracted at a later stage of evolution into a word or a sentence or a work of art.

What makes of the image or dramatic action a fit symbol is, first of all, the fact that it constitutes *a whole situation*. It must be experienced as a "whole of action"; otherwise it would not release in another person a wholly determined psychological state. Then, it must be related to the past experience of that person, either directly or at least indirectly. No symbol is really significant to any one who has not experienced the "whole of action" it pictures. A tiger is not a symbol of fear to anyone who has never experienced a tiger, either directly or vicariously by partaking of the experience of other persons. The more vicarious and remote the experience, the less significant the symbol—because the less power it has to rouse the psychological state with which it is meant to be identical.

We said that all intuitions are based on symbols. But so, in a different way, are instincts. An animal faces a situation and reacts instinctively to it. If, in the past, no identical situations had been experienced by his species as a whole, there would be no such reaction—certainly not as perfect a behavior. The fact that the situation had been experienced many times before made of the configuration of elements constituting it, a symbol. It became a sign for a psychological-biological state which compelled immediate adaptation. The instinctive reaction is not only immediate but a perfect adaptation of experiencer to situation. This is so because the symbol has *absolute significance* and therefore absolutely compels, without any reservation or perversion, the proper vital or biological behavior.

In a modern human being, on the contrary, hardly any life-situation is ever endowed with absolute significance as a symbol, because modern man uses his analytical mind to such an extent that he can no longer realize a situation (or himself) as a whole. He is not whole in his reactions—unless under the stress of a few all-compelling biological feelings. He does not see people or situations as wholes. Therefore they do not become immediately identified by him with "qualities," of which they become symbols. Because they are not realized as symbols of qualities, fully and wholly experienced in the past, they must be analyzed, bit by bit. The result is at best a delayed reaction; or a wrong reaction. Neither instinct nor intuition analyzes a man or a situation bit by bit; but they apprehend them whole and at once. They see them whole and as identified with one or several qualities, which determines a correct reaction.

The American Indian, even today, usually reacts at once to a person never met before. This person's voice or the quality of his silence, or an indescribable something becomes for the Indian a clear symbol of the person's real selfhood (i.e., wholeness). And he acts accordingly with true judgment—on his intuition. The white man, on the contrary, usually does not meet a stranger as whole meeting whole, intuitively; but begins to analyze this and that feature or characteristic. And seeing more or less unrelated parts, instead of a significant whole symbol of qualities, he frequently reacts to the stranger in a way which proves wrong.

Intuition is thus the power to read every whole as a symbol of a basic quality of life. This actually means to see the soul in every thing, the wholeness (quality) in every whole. Through his instincts the animal lives in a world of unconsciously apprehended symbols which compels his biological functions to react in perfect patterns of behavior. The wholly intuitive man lives in a world of consciously perceived symbols, in a world of souls, full of significance. The combination of all these symbols at every moment constitutes another symbol, the seed-symbol of the moment. This seed-symbol reveals the significant quality of that man's soul as it sees itself revealed in the fulfillment of the moment.

Cosmically speaking, every moment of the universe can thus be realized as a cosmic symbol revealing the quality of the moment, and the soul of the Cosmos—call it *God* if you wish. Every moment thus realized, however, is that moment in relation to the perceiver on earth; and, at the limit, to the whole of mankind.

As we saw that each moment is a birthing of numberless wholes, it follows that, by law of cosmic inheritance, the quality of that moment determines the basic quality of the wholes issued therefrom. And as the ordered revolution of the celestial bodies is the great symbol of natural and cosmic order, it follows that the pattern made by these celestial bodies at any moment can be taken as the root-symbol of the wholeness (selfhood and destiny) of every whole born at that moment. The quality revealed by that root-symbol is the quality of these wholes. But the root-symbol (the astrological birth-chart) *must* be considered as a whole and through the faculty of intuition. For analytical intellect is of no avail in realizing holistic symbols; and if the birth-chart means anything *vital and real*, it can only be as a symbol—therefore *as a total configuration*, as a whole. The wholeness of the celestial pattern at birth and the wholeness of the selfhood and destiny of the native are identical; and both are expressions of the wholeness of the moment. In intellectual logic we have the formula: If $A = B$, and $B = C$, then $A = C$. Holistic logic gives, however, a different meaning to the symbol $=$ than intellectual logic; a genetic meaning, as it were.

We must now add that the revolutions of Sun, planets and stars are not the only material which may be used as symbols for an intuitive revelation of the soul of the moment. Theoretically everything can serve as a basis for symbolism, provided: 1) that the interpreter is able to meet every symbolic situation as a whole with the wholeness of his own selfhood, thus with fully developed intuition; 2) that this intuition, if it is to be communicated, operates according to the principles of "holistic logic"; principles which may be briefly described as of *functional coherency*.

This is where the intellect finds its proper place. In instinctive behavior the "functional coherency" is unconscious and biological. For instance, certain motions and attitudes in animal courtship are symbols of the biological urge that leads to mating. But the animal cannot fail to interpret correctly, i.e., with holistic logic, the meaning of these motions and attitudes. His instinct knows with certainty what the dance of the male or the flight of the female means in terms of the biological function of propagation. His unconscious, unerring interpretation is "functionally coherent" because the "mind" which does the interpreting is absolutely one with the vital principle, with the wholeness of the moment. Spring, as the mating moment, compels absolutely the animal's interpretation of the symbols of the dance of mating. The animal perfectly fulfills the moment. The soul of the moment and the self of the animal are identical in significance. Therefore the interpretation, unconscious and instinctive, cannot be false.

But with man's attempts to get an intuitive realization of his individual selfhood and destiny at every moment, the problem is more complex; because such realization *has to* find its foundation in the conscious mind. And the conscious mind (or the thinking function) does not at first operate upon wholes but upon parts. Thinking develops from sensations, which are discrete and separative. It rationalizes sensations or associations of sensations; and unless a new faculty re-energizes the mind, it deals first of all with space-values or form-values, rather than with positive time-values and holistic principles. To deal with the latter requires the collaboration of the feelings which, as we shall see in a later chapter, react naturally to whole situations.

The union of the feelings' whole-reactions and of thought-logic leads the mind to a new attitude or polarization. It begins then to function in terms of wholes rather than in terms of parts; in terms of psychological evaluations rather than in terms of physical intellectual concepts. It becomes holistic rather than mechanistic. It ceases to be bound to material objects and to the task of enumerating and classifying them by their space-characteristics. It turns inward, after having achieved this liberation, and begins to "feel" the living power of the moment. Then the wholeness of the moment begins to speak; and such utterances are symbols.

It matters not whether such symbols are dreams or mystical visions or omens or occult "signatures," or any one of the forms of life-interpretation and even divination that have been used for millenia. The point is that all life-encounters become endowed with significance. Man becomes thus Interpreter and Seer. He lives in a world of souls, in a world of significant wholes, because wholeness, or holism, operates through his consciousness. In the animal, wholeness operates through the physiological organism. In the man with a re-polarized mind, wholeness operates at the psycho-mental level —thus consciously. When the operation becomes perfect, there is in the intuitive interpretations of the symbols of the moment the same certainty that exists in the biological instincts; a certainty which the intellect can know only in logic and pure mathematics—the certainty of a tautology; a certainty that comes from *evident identity*. The animal interprets the mating dance with certainty because he has become identified with the mating urge within the moment. Only he does not know it. The perfect intuition is also the result of an identification (of absolute "sympathy," as Bergson wrote) between the perceiving individual whole and the perceived whole situation. This identification occurs within the moment, to the whole-making energy of which the individual is now fully open.

To such a perfected intuitive man no particular system of symbolism is necessary; and astrology is of no special value. But he cannot communicate his intuitions to others. Communication necessitates a system of interpretation; a set of symbols which can serve as spatial-mental "bridges" between the wholeness of the moment and all perceivers. It thus needs a language. Astrology is such a language, just as the series of hexagrams of the Chinese *Yi King* is such a language. And it is in the formation and use of such a language that what we called holistic logic and the principle of functional coherency come into operation.

The true foundation of astrology is such a holistic logic; and as already said, not a compilation of data or statistics, even though the latter may have great value in helping to make abstract interpretations more concrete and precise. This holistic logic, based on the perception of the wholeness of the material used as symbolical elements and of its functional coherency, is for the truly intuitive man as logical as intellectual logic. But it is not as rigid and set, at least in appearance, because it is creative. It is a function of evolving life. Like the logic of instincts, it adapts itself to new situations and to new levels of being. It is protean—and yet in a mysterious way it inheres, unchanging in its essence, in all varieties of formulations.

The Foundation of Astrological Symbolism

These unfamiliar thoughts may become clearer as we indicate briefly the manner in which astrological symbolism can be arrived at.

The problem of astrological symbolism is that of correctly (i.e., significantly) identifying the order manifest in the cycles of celestial bodies in relation to the earth-observer, and the order which is usually *not* manifest in human nature and human life, but for which man psychologically yearns; and which becomes an actual inner reality to the spiritually awakened individual. The man who is enmeshed in the continual warfare of primordial and natural elements finds in life nothing but chaos and chance; from which results fear. The man who sees these elements as functional parts of a cosmic whole, harmonized by outwardly complex, yet inherently simple laws of "functional coherency," overcomes fear. Having conceived and realized the universe as a whole, his life as a whole, his psyche and his body as a whole, he is able ultimately to identify himself with the wholeness of these wholes; and to stand in the abstract and "mystical" relation of wholeness to whole. This does not mean standing *outside* of the whole-nature, or *above* it. It does not mean exactly what is called ordinarily: considering one's nature and destiny *objectively*. It means retaining a constant position or state of equilibrium at the "center of gravity" of this whole-nature and destiny. It means not being thrown out of equilibrium by (i.e., involved into) the intensification of any one functional part of this whole. It does not mean withdrawing oneself from such an intensified function.

Here it may be well to refer to the scientific concept of "energy" which is determined in terms of acceleration of momentum, rather than in terms of a mysterious "force" residing in the object. Psychic energy, likewise, is produced by the intensification of a psychic-organic function; by the fact that the "quality" it represents so increases its significance in relation to the entire organic equilibrium that it becomes a dominant factor in the consciousness. For instance, the function of feeling may take such an overwhelming value that the consciousness is almost entirely filled with a feeling of hatred. In such a case the self, the "I AM," becomes usually involved in, thrown out of the psychic center of gravity by this hatred. And the whole being cries out: "I hate," which means: "I am hatred."

The man who remains equilibrated may feel hatred arise, but he will not say: "I am hatred," but: "There is an intensification of hatred in the whole of me." He will not cut himself off from the function of feeling, because of that; for this would be self-mutilation. But he will marshal, as it were, all his other functions and balance with them the intensified feeling-function. If he succeeds in doing this, he, the self and wholeness of the whole, will retain his position of equilibrium at the center of gravity of his whole-nature. He will have thus managed not to be swept away from this center of gravity by the energy generated by the intensification ("acceleration") of one of his part-functions, yet without withdrawing from this function and thus accepting a mutilation.

It is very likely that one cannot speak of "psychic energy" unless one or more functions become thus intensified. The powerful self depends for its power upon such intensification; and thus his equilibrium is always unstable and dynamic. There is a constant and alternating increase and decrease of the intensity of *all* functions. Yet the self remains always at the center of gravity of the whole, acting upon the parts whose relationships are constantly altered—but whose total equilibrium is never lost.

The harmony of the whole-nature can thus be pictured in terms of dynamic relationship between parts. Man as a whole is a complex of dynamic relationships between functional parts. So, in fact, is every organic whole. There is, therefore, in every organic whole a dynamic order which can be established in terms of cycles of alternate intensification and inhibition of functions. But such a picture can easily be related to that of the solar system as a whole, if intensification of function is connected with various sets of characteristics derived from the various types of planetary relationships (relationships of position in space, of distance to the Sun, of mass, velocity, stage of cosmic evolution, etc.).

The important point to realize is that these symbolical connections *must always be based upon an interpretation of the two related wholes which is functionally coherent, and grounded on concrete and incontrovertible facts of experience.* In other words, any correlation established between, say, Saturn and a particular psychological function must derive from a consistent interpretation of: 1) the solar system as a whole; 2) the human psyche as a whole. If a principle of correlation is established giving to one planet a symbolical significance in terms of its distance to the Sun, then all planets must be given their respective symbolical significance in the same way. If a strictly geocentric attitude is taken, then all symbolic interpretations must be derived from it. There should never be any *mixing up* of planes of interpretation. Many such planes of interpretation may be used successively, each in relation to a corresponding level of being. But there must not be any confusion between the types of concrete data used as bases for the various sets of interpretation. *Each set of interpretation must use its own type of concrete data,* and this one exclusively.

The following may be taken as a most significant example: In archaic times men's concrete and significant experience of celestial bodies was solely in terms of the light they gave. The concrete data at the disposition of astrologers were that the Sun was in all appearance the source of life as well as of light and heat. Man's life was divided into periods with sun-experience (days) and periods without sun-experience (nights). Jungle nights are full of fears and tragedies and deaths. At once life became subject to two interpretations, depending on the presence or absence of the Sun and of its light. Then, in temperate climates, it must have soon been remarked that the seasons and the corresponding changes in vegetation and in the biological characteristics of animals and men were all correlated to and functions of the various angles at which the Sun-rays struck the earth, whch angles seemed to regulate the intensity of light and heat as well as the even more obvious relation between the lengths of days and nights; thus the four basic points of solar change, equinoxes and solstices.

The Moon was experienced as a mysterious helpmate of the Sun in giving light. It was also presumably noticed very soon that its cycles corresponded to that of physiological change in women, etc. From these and related concrete and significant data of experience, the Moon took on a very definite symbolical meaning. All the celestial bodies were seen as pin-points of light and called "stars"; but some retain a constant relationship to each other and were called "fixed stars." Their constant relationships, i.e., the patterns they made on the darkness of space, became endowed with significance just because, almost alone of all things in nature, they remained constant. They therefore became symbols of *constant life-qualities*, of Ideas of organization or Archetypes—as constellations.

The stars which, like Sun and Moon, changed their positions periodically with reference to the constellations, were called "planets." They acted like the Sun, with respect to their periodic motion; yet they emitted only a tiny amount of light. So they became, naturally and logically, significant as "attendants of the Sun." As such they were given attributes symbolized by the intensity of their light, by the average distance they kept from the Sun and the manner of their appearance. Venus, for instance, being the star of the evening and the star of dawn in turn, was given a dual significance. From another standpoint the color of fixed stars and planets served to make of them symbols of qualities—as the redness of Mars and Antares, etc.

All these facts were concrete and significant data of experience. The intuitive man envisioning the skies as a cosmic whole distributed significances to·their component parts in terms of experienced facts. Each part became the vehicle of an organic function within the cosmic whole of the heavens above and below. All these experienced facts were of course based on a geocentric interpretation of the cosmos. The Sun symbolized the most important function, that of being the very source of the life-force, not because it was the center of the solar system (a notion incongruous to the geocentric viewpoint), but because it was the source of light and heat, and the cycle of life on earth seemed to follow exactly its cycle of change. The Moon had then no significance as the satellite of the Earth—because that also was entirely irrelevant in a geocentric system. Moreover, planets like Uranus and Neptune, not being visible to the eye, can hardly enter into such a system based on actual experience.

Nevertheless in modern astrology the geocentric and the heliocentric viewpoints are hopelessly mixed, and the basis of symbolism is lost sight of. The result is utter philosophical confusion. Most of the concepts of geocentric astrology are retained; Sun and Moon are called the "lights"; the term "fixed stars" is used for no valid reason, and these fixed stars are given archaic meaning in terms of the old geocentric concept of "constellation."

If we wish to use a heliocentric basis for our astrological symbolism, then many of the traditional concepts, phrases and denominations of ancient geocentric astrology must go overboard. For they are *illogical* in terms of our heliocentric knowledge. What, however, complicates matters is of course that we do not *experience*, actually and sensorially, the fact that the Sun is the center of a system of which the Earth is but one planet. At least most of us do not. Scientists who make experiments to prove the heliocentric system may come close to experiencing it; but ordinary mortals take it for granted on mere intellectual grounds. Only a small minority among men are far enough developed mentally to be said to experience mentally the facts of the heliocentric system.

Thus we find ourselves confronted with two definite types of interpretation of the cosmos, each of which may be taken as a basis for symbolism. If we wish to use both, we must be careful to use them separately, each one being made to correspond to a distinct level of human consciousness—let us say, the vitalistic and the mental (or ideistic, or abstract) levels. How different will be the results obtained by changing our basis of symbolism will readily be seen as we draw logical conclusions (holistically logical, that is) from the data deriving from the heliocentric point of view. Such data, let us say at once, have very little to do with what some people call today "heliocentric astrology." By geocentric viewpoint we do not mean that which relates all celestial motions to an observer on Earth—for in every case we must obviously do that very thing. We mean the attitude which interprets celestial phenomena *in terms of their actual sensorial appearances.* The heliocentric viewpoint is that of modern scientific astronomy, which interprets the apparent motions of celestial bodies according to a *theory* proved by scientific experimentation—that is, according to an intellectual type of knowledge.

From the heliocentric standpoint, the solar system is obviously to be considered as a whole, the nearest star being remote beyond the possibility of belonging to the systemic whole. In other words, the solar system appears as a closed unit, the only known links between it and the outside world being comets. This cosmic whole, the solar system, is also apparently a part of some greater cosmic whole, which is either our galaxy the Milky Way, or a fragment of this galaxy, or a group of such galaxies—the point being still more or less in doubt, on strict scientific grounds (as far as we know). However that may be, we have a somewhat accurate knowledge of the solar system as a physical unit (with the possibility of yet unknown planets, probably very remote); and that knowledge *must* be the basis of our symbolism. No extraneous elements should be retained, such as would follow from a purely geocentric viewpoint.

The Sun, as the center of the system and the source of all the planets, is obviously to be considered as the origin of life, the fountain-head of the life-force. We "know" scientifically that we, the Earth and its inhabitants, revolve around it. We are subservient to it, and its power (gravitational or otherwise) is the cause of our cyclic motion, following which we are compelled to see the universe from a series of successive viewpoints. This series of viewpoints constitutes the psychological (or consciousness) reality of what physical science calls the orbit of the earth. *This orbit as a constant series of viewpoints is what we,* in heliocentric symbolism, *call the zodiac.* Constellations are quite meaningless in themselves in such a symbolism. They have value merely as convenient points of reference. We "know" scientifically that they correspond to nothing real. The distance of the stars is such that they can hardly have any significance for us, except insofar as the galaxy to which our solar system belongs is concerned. But ancient constellations have nothing to do with our galaxy. At best they can symbolize the various viewpoints which we get from our successive orbital stations in our annual revolution around the Sun. They symbolize, to be more accurate, vistas of universal space which the Earth and man experience as a result of their ever-changing relationship to the Sun. They are symbols of the space created by the revolution of the Earth around the Sun.

The planets of the solar system have significance, in the heliocentric symbology, in terms of their relation of position, distance, mass, velocity, density, etc., to the Earth and the Sun. They are, first of all, to be divided into planets inside and planets outside of the Earth-orbit. As this orbit introduces, as far as we are concerned of course, a line of cleavage between inner and outer, we may expect a sort of balance or symmetry between inner and outer planets. Thus we pair Venus and Mars, Mercury and Jupiter—and, in a somewhat different way, Sun and Saturn. It may be that there is actually an intra-Mercurial planet Vulcan, which should be paired with Saturn; in which case, it would necessarily carry a part of the significance now given to the Sun. Vulcan may be understood also as the Sun's photosphere. For the photosphere would, in symbolical logic, balance very accurately Saturn. The interior of the Sun would balance symbolically all planets which could be found outside of Saturn's orbit.

The Moon, as the only satellite of the Earth, would be put in an interesting position. Perhaps the Biblical symbolism of the creation of Eve out of Adam's rib might help us to understand her significance! Besides the planets, all other symbols used in astrology, from this true heliocentric viewpoint, have to be also interpreted in accordance with the facts of the heliocentric theory. The Earth's revolution upon her axis creates the ever-changing horizon; this axis creates a North Pole, a Pole Star, and other points of interest. Symbols combine with symbols to give symbols of "second degree" as it were—and so on, theoretically *ad infinitum*. But any symbol, the significance of which is not justified, on the grounds of holistic logic, by the concrete data it synthetizes, must be discarded as irrelevant.

This irrelevant quality has nothing to do with statistics and tabulations of cases which "prove or disprove" the significance of the symbol. It stands on a logical basis—even if it is not the logic of intellectual and mathematical analysis. The truly intuitive person will recognize the absoluteness of this logic on *internal evidence*. But few are the men who, at present, possess such a perfectly developed faculty: the faculty of holistic perception, the power to identify themselves with the wholeness of the wholes, and to release the significance of these wholes in terms of true and compelling symbols. Great creative artists, of course, have such a faculty, but developed only in a certain direction. When the creative artist begins to *create with life*, then he begins to live in a world of never-ceasing and ubiquitous significance, for he becomes, as it were, "geared to the moment." Then his utterances become rooted in universal significance, the very images of the moment. They become pregnant with the power of life itself. Such Creative Artists were Buddha, Lao-Tze, Jesus.

11. *Astrology and Analytical Psychology*

The Synchronistic Principle

IN an address delivered in Munich, May 10*th*, 1930, in memory of the great exponent of Chinese wisdom and initiate in the psychology of Chinese *Yoga*, Richard Wilhelm, C. G. Jung made these significant statements: *

> "To me, the greatest of Wilhelm's achievements is the translation of, and commentary on, the *Yi King*. . . . This work embodies, as perhaps no other, the spirit of Chinese culture. The best minds of China have collaborated upon it and contributed to it for thousands of years. Despite its fabulous age, it has never grown old, but lives and operates still, at least for those who understand its meaning. . . . Anyone like myself who has had the rare good fortune to experience in a spiritual exchange with Wilhelm the divinatory power of the *Yi King*, cannot for long remain ignorant of the fact that we have touched here an Archimedean point from which our Western attitude of mind can be shaken to its foundations.
>
> ". . . The function on which the use of the *Yi King* is based, if I may so express myself, is apparently in sharp contradiction to our Western, scientifically-causal, *Weltanschauung*. In other words, it is extremely unscientific, taboo in fact, and therefore out of reach of our scientific judgment, and incomprehensible to it.
>
> "Some years ago, the then president of the British Anthropological Society asked me how I could explain the fact that so highly intellectual a people as the Chinese had produced no

* Printed in the book *The Secret of the Golden Flower*, a translation from the Chinese by Richard Wilhelm, with a commentary by C. G. Jung. We have used in this quotation the spelling "*Yi King*" instead of "*I Ching*" to fit in with our previous use of the term.

science. I replied that this must really be an 'optical illusion,' because the Chinese did have a science whose 'standard work' was the *Yi King*, but that the principle of this science, like so much else in China, was altogether different from our scientific principle.

"The science of the *Yi King* is not based on the causality principle, but on a principle (hitherto unnamed because not met with among us) which I have tentatively called the *synchronistic* principle. My occupation with the psychology of unconscious processes long ago necessitated my looking about for another principle of explanation, because the causality principle seemed to me inadequate to explain certain remarkable phenomena of the psychology of the unconscious. Thus I found that there are psychic parallelisms which cannot be related to each other causally, but which must be connected through another sequence of events. This connection seemed to me to be essentially provided in the fact of the relative simultaneity, therefore the expression 'synchronistic.' It seems indeed, as though time, far from being an abstraction, is a concrete continuum which contains qualities or basic conditions manifesting simultaneously in various places in a way not to be explained by causal parallelisms, as for example, in cases of the coincident appearance of identical thoughts, symbols or psychic conditions. Another example would be the simultaneity of Chinese and European periods of style, a fact pointed out by Wilhelm."

This is the very expression of the basic ideas which we formulated in our preceding chapter. Time as a "concrete continuum" is what Bergson calls "real duration." The fact that it contains "qualities or basic conditions" which exteriorize themselves in ideas, cultures and psychic conditions (individual or collective) is proof of the generative power of the moment. Each moment is a whole which begets concrete wholes. Each moment is to be considered, moreover, as the unit-cycle, or time-unit—just as the quantum or photon is the unit of release of energy. Energy is released by photons. Significance, or selfhood, is released by moments. Time is the womb of souls; just as "Light" (in the most general sense of the word) is the womb of all physical energies. As the Hindu occultist would say, *Daivi prakriti* (i.e., the Light of the Logos) is the source of all energies (or *shakti*). All Earth-energies can be traced to their parent-source, the Sun, whose total radiations are described generically by the term Light.

We have thus, in a sense, a dualism of Light and Time, of photons and moments. These two elements, to which we should add Space, are the foundation of astrology, which can be based on the emphasis of either one of them. Light and Time are symbolized by the photosphere of the Sun (Vulcan?) and Saturn, which, as we have already seen, balance each other on either side of the Earth in the solar system. Without going into lengthy metaphysical discussions we may, however, state here that Light is the *emanation* of the wholeness of the whole (theoretically, of any perfectly integrated whole—thus the "light" emanated, if tradition is correct, by the very being of great saints and mystics). On the other hand, Time is the significant quality of every whole; that is, the defining characteristic of the whole.

Every whole as a whole theoretically radiates Light (some degree or type of it, not necessarily, of course, what we usually call "light," and which is the radiation of that cosmic whole: the Sun). Every whole as a whole represents or symbolizes a quality which is the manifestation of a particular moment of Time. Time generates particulars; and every whole, as we have already seen, must needs be defined, limited. It is thus a particular. Light is the manifestation of the wholeness of these particulars. The photon is described by the formula hv, in which the letter v represents particularness (the particular velocity or frequency or "key-note" of the whole), and h symbolizes universality (the universal fact of wholeness exteriorized as Light; "operative wholeness").*

---

* Space is the abstract mathematical basis of reference for measuring the relationship of whole to whole within the universal Whole. This relationship operates through the interchange of "Light," or energies, and is thus

We might say that any cycle, as a quantum of duration, is also definable by the formula *hv*, in which *h* represents the universal potency of Time (i.e., the universal Creative Power, or God), and *v* the particlar value of the cycle's duration. Just as there is no release of energy except by whole quanta, so there is no progress in selfhood or wholeness save through whole cycles. Selfhood progresses from cycle to cycle, and only through the perfect fulfillment of these cycles (whether they last a minute or an eon). He who does not fulfill the smallest moment can never fulfill the larger cycle—a doctrine implied in the last section of Patanjali's aphorisms on *Yoga*.

This is both holistic and astrological philosophy; for astrology has *no real value* unless it enables us more fully and significantly to live the moment, or any cycle during which we are progressing. To live fully every moment is to find in every moment Light, and to become illumined by this Light. Darkness is ever the result of unfulfillment. The unfulfilled moments or cycles cast their shadow over the future moments: this is *karma*—or what we called previously "negative time," un-illumined time.

Selfhood progresses by fulfillment of the moments; and each moment or cycle presents us with a new quality which is to be fulfilled. Each birth is thus for the universal whole a problem of fulfillment. The whole finds in every nativity a quality, a new *dharma* (in Hindu terminology) to be fulfilled. It is not only that "*whatever is born or done this moment of time, has the qualities of this moment of time,*" (Jung, op. cit. p. 143), but that every moment creates for every whole the duty to

---

measurable in terms of the velocity of light—as in modern science. Space is thus, in a sense, "created" by Light. We shall see later on that it corresponds to the collective; Time, to the individual. Space is a framework for the operation of wholeness, the field created by the exteriorization, as Light, of wholeness. In other words, Wholeness exteriorizes itself as Light. Time exteriorizes itself as Space. Thus the spatial relationships of celestial bodies are exteriorizations or symbols of the qualities of moments and cycles.

fulfill the quality of that moment. This principle has a purposive as well as an explanatory meaning. And this brings to it an ever greater psychological value. As we shall see later on, the function of astrology is not to tell us what will, or rather what *may*, happen in the future, but what significance there is in every moment or cycle lived or about to be lived. It reveals the quality of particular moments and of the larger cycles rooted in those moments.

This is apparently well understood by C. G. Jung who said, in the same memorial address:

"Astrology would be a large scale example of synchronism, if it had at its disposal thoroughly tested findings. . . . In so far as there are any really correct astrological deductions, they are not due to the effects of the constellations, but to our hypothetical time-characters. In other words, whatever is born or done this moment, has the qualities of this moment of time.

"This is also the fundamental formula for the use of the *Yi King*. As is known, one gains knowledge of the hexagram characterizing the moment by a method of manipulating sticks of yarrow, or coins, a method depending on purest chance. As the moment is, so do the runic sticks fall. . . .

"The type of thought built on the synchronistic principle, which reaches its high point in the *Yi King*, is the purest expression of Chinese thinking in general. With us this thinking has been absent from philosophy since the time of Heraclitus, and only reappears as a faint echo in Leibnitz. However, in the time between, it was not extinguished, but continued to live in the twilight of astrological speculation, and remains today at this level."*

* In this and other unquoted paragraphs Jung does not give an altogether correct picture of the basis of the symbolism of the *Yi King*. The Chinese hexagrams are based on a cosmic formula of change. Out of the Unknown Principle arise two principles *Yang* and *Yin*, positive and negative, expansive and contractive; and all cycles are considered as the time-symbols of the interaction of these two principles. They are particularly related to the cycles of the year, *Yang* dominating at the summer solstice, *Yin*, at the winter solstice. *Yang* is represented by a straight line, *Yin*, by a line broken in two. The hexagrams constitute the 64 possible combinations made by the six-fold superposition of these lines. Each is referred thus to a section of the yearly cycle, and carries a symbol which has significance

Astrology and Its Application to Psychology

The great value, for us, in the above quotations is the fact that they come from probably the greatest psychologist of our time. If Dr. Jung, first scientist and practicing psychiatrist, then pupil of Freud, finally exponent of his own findings and interpretations as founder of the Zurich school of analytical psychology, discovered this "synchronistic" principle as a result of his psychological practice, the fact is indeed significant. For it shows that while causalism and mechanism have proven invaluable in the study of physical phenomena, they have failed to explain many of the most characteristic among psychological phenomena. Thus, in a way, the thesis of Bergson is justified. Spatial values refer to matter; but everything psychological needs for its explanation values based on time, —real time that endures. Thus the synchronistic principle fits in the psychological picture, for it represents a time-evaluation. It is based on the *formative potency* of the moment. Thus astrology and psychology become intimately linked. In fact, Dr. Jung says:

> "Astrology is assured of recognition from psychology, without further restrictions, because astrology represents the summation of all the psychological knowledge of antiquity." (op. cit. p. 143)

Important and valuable as this statement undoubtedly is, we must say, however, that it implies a conception of the nature of astrology which we have shown to be, strictly speaking, incorrect. Astrology, even as traditionally handed down by Ptolemy, is not the summation of ancient psychology. First, because it refers to many things besides psychology—from

---

in terms of that section. Each hexagram is thus a sort of zodiacal sign, or cosmic viewpoint measured on the circumference of the orbit of the Earth. The symbols themselves were apparently written down by King Wen around the year 1100 or 1000 B.C.; but it could undoubtedly be shown that their symbolism is based on "holistic logic," just as astrological symbolism. Jung is too much of an experimentalist, it seems, to realize this fact.

governmental matters to weather and the condition of crops. Secondly, because—as we saw in the first part of the preceding chapter—astrology is not to be identified, in its essence, with any experimental or empirical science, but rather is the *organizing principle* of such sciences as deal with life and significance in relation to "organic wholes," much as mathematics is the organizing principle of sciences dealing with inanimate matter and the realm of "parts."

It is true that the body of concepts, judgments and opinions handed down to us by Ptolemy and the Arabian astrologers can give us an excellent idea of what the psychology of antiquity was. But this is because the books which we have on astrology are *collections of particular applications of the principles of astrological symbolism.* They are text-books telling how to apply astrology to various matters—psychology and human nature being the foremost of those. They are not, directly and consistently, text-books of strict astrology. We must insist upon this point, because it is a basic one. Lacking an understanding of this, the ideas of the huge majority of people concerning the value of astrology have been consistently biased.

A text-book of strict astrology should deal with:

1) A study of the principles of what we called "holistic logic."

2) A study of the concrete data and symbolical implications of both geocentric and heliocentric astronomy.

3) A study of all elements used by astrology, not in terms of any particular application thereof, but in terms of the logic inherent in their definitions and mutual correlations.

4) A general survey of the concrete fields (or empirical sciences) to which these symbolical elements can be applied, and of the particular technique of application, which must somewhat vary in each of these fields. This would, of course, include characteristic examples of application.

Instead of embodying such a program of studies, traditional

astrology is satisfied with stating the way in which a birth-chart (or horary, or progressed chart) is to be erected, and to tabulate the traditional meanings attached to every aspect and position, mixing up rather hopelessly psychological, physio-logical and purely divinatory concepts. Of the *rationale* of the elements used in passing judgment (positions, aspects, etc.) very little is usually said. It is only within the last twenty years or so that books on astrology have attempted to study the "why" of astrological symbols; and it is only in the case of the courses recently delivered by Marc Edmund Jones that astrology has been taught as a vast system of symbolization of all realms of being in their triple correlations as form, sub-stance and activity.

This book is no attempt to cover adequately the types of studies enumerated above. Its purpose is to pave the way to a new type of astrology which would be philosophically sound and whose application to modern psychology would help men to live more significant, therefore more spiritual, lives.

Philosophical "soundness" rests upon absolute coherency of ideas and consistency in the development and application of the basic principles and symbols used. As for psychological "helpfulness," this would obviously depend largely on the type of psychological materials being correlated with the astrological symbols. As already said, most astrological text-books deal only with a sort of "common sense" psychology, rather superficial in character; others, with a psychology in-fluenced by more or less valid theosophical ideas, not always philosophically coherent nor rooted in the experience of mod-ern Western man. Our aim has been to interpret astrological symbols in terms of an "up-to-date" Western psychology, consistently backed up, as it were, by a philosophy which brings into clear relief some of the most recent and the most vital concepts of this century.

We are above all stressing values and using a terminology which are found in C. G. Jung's works, because we are deeply convinced of their inherent validity, and also because they dovetail so remarkably with the general set-up of astrological symbolism. Our first task therefore is to acquaint the reader with the general principles of Jung's "analytical psychology," a psychology whose roots may be grounded in Freudian psychoanalysis, yet whose stem and flowering live in strata of being almost as far removed from Freudian thought as the vision of a Lao-Tze or a Plato is removed from that of a laboratory vivisectionist.

Three Basic Types of Psychology

In order to clarify some matters which are a source of constant confusion it is necessary to recognize that the term "psychology" is used to mean several different branches and types of knowledge. It will probably be of great help to take for granted, for the time being, the ancient division of man's being into spirit, soul and body, and to say that psychology can be and has been considered from three basic points of view. Thus there is:

1) a *spiritual* psychology, which is a branch of philosophy or religion, and contemplates all human values, introspectively and intuitionally, in terms of beliefs, or intuitions, or transcendental perceptions.

2) a *physiological* psychology, which considers all the processes usually classified as "psychological" (sensation, attention, feelings, thoughts, etc.) from the standpoint of physiological functions.

3) an *analytical* psychology, which deals primarily and directly with the facts of consciousness and the structural relationship existing between the various functions of the psyche *per se*.

The spiritual type of psychology considers man to be essentially and in reality a spiritual being using a body for the purpose of acquiring concrete experiences and certain faculties which can be generated only in contact with matter. Corporate existence is, however, taken to be the result of a "fall" and as such has a pejorative connotation. The soul is immortal insofar as it has assimilated to itself the spiritual essence, and liberation from the thralldom of natural energies is the goal. Such a psychology, which is particularly exemplified in the Christian Fathers' ideas and, to a very large extent, in Platonic psycho-philosophy, is bound up with ethics. The physical world is the world of shadows, if not of sin; and truth, goodness and reality abide in an archetypal world, which is, in a sense, a concrete (or at least substantial) spiritual realm. Psychology is largely a matter of understanding how these archetypal realities and the human soul (which belongs to their realm essentially) react to the illusions and shams of the natural world; and by what process the soul, lost in the mesh of the body, can disentangle itself and regain its primordial status—plus a "consciousness of relation" which is the fruition of the embodied state.

This type of psychology is found predominant in the Orient (but by no means exclusively held there as true), and wherever religious, ethico-spiritual, alchemical valuations are emphasized at the expense of physical or materialistic ones. It is found in a great variety of manifestations, each philosophical or religious system giving it a particular formulation. It is the usual foundation of traditional occultism, but there we find it sometimes strongly associated with a type of structural psychology which differentiates occult psychology from the purely religious type. Yet the differentiation is not sharp, and is, in appearance at least, a mere matter of relative emphasis.

The physiological type of psychology is one in which psychic reactions—as sensations, feelings, ideations and volitions—are considered as emerging from and strictly conditioned by physiological processes. The method of such a type of rigorously empirical and experimental psychology is the purely scientific method, and it is to such a psychology only that scientists usually refer as "psychology." Barring whatever there may have been in India which could be referred to that class of psychological study, we can date the beginning of such a type of psychology from Aristotle. Before him there was of course a long period of archaic psychology, which could be called "physiological" in the sense that in archaic thought the soul was not differentiated from the body in the way in which it became so distinguished after Pythagoras. As we saw in a previous chapter, the unity of living nature and of living man became definitely broken into a physical and a psycho-mental realm only around the sixth century B.C. And therefore the care of the body (medicine) included to some extent matters pertaining to the psyche.

In fact, however, considerations pertaining to the united body-psyche belonged to the nascent province of alchemy. Alchemy is the science of the human being considered as a compound of physio-psychological processes. The doctrine of the four humors of the body (blood, phlegm, black bile and yellow bile) corresponding to the four elements of astrology (fire, earth, air and water), and leading to the Arabian enumeration of four temperaments (sanguine, phlegmatic, melancholic and choleric), is an alchemical doctrine. In archaic alchemy (which is closely related to the original forms of the Hindu *Hatha Yoga*, and still more to *later Taoism*) the conception of the soul is not very well defined, because spirit and matter are seen in adunation. The vital body (or pneumatic body) is within the physiological organism, as the fibres of the mango fruit are within the fruit itself—and the aim of the ancient practical applications of alchemy is to disentangle the former from the latter—thus releasing for use a spiritual body, free from the earthly quality of the physical body, and the seat of a new consciousness, which can then be called the Soul.

In other words, archaic psychology is only most superficially to be related to the scientific type of physiological psychology, just as chemistry is to alchemy. From Aristotle the lineage of modern scientific psychology passes through

Galen and the medieval physiologists, through Francis Bacon, Thomas Hobbes, Malebranche, James Mill, Johannes Müller, Lotze, Wundt, William James, reaching finally to the Behaviorists, the "Gestalt" group, and an endocrino-psychologist like Dr. Berman (*Glands Regulating Personality*). The latter emphasizes what he calls the "body-mind"—i.e., the unity of physiological and psychological processes—in a way which is similar, though diametrically opposite in its practical methods, to archaic alchemy. Dr. Berman aims at the production of the perfect human being through generalized gland-treatment and the establishment of perfect functional harmony. The true alchemists had the same purpose, but they had it on different grounds, and tried to reach it by different methods.

The third basic type of approach to psychology, what we called the analytical type,* deals directly and immediately with facts of the mental life, or rather with what it calls "psychic contents."

It does not lay any emphasis on the problem of the exact origin of these contents; that is to say, it does not particularly study the process by which a nerve-impression or series of impressions becomes a truly psychic sensation which in turn transforms itself into habit, thought, instinct, etc. It considers the psychic life of man as a domain in itself, and is mainly preoccupied with the study of what happens in this realm considered as a more or less self-sufficient and autonomous one.

This, however, must not be construed as meaning that the analytical psychologist considers the psyche as essentially different from the body. On the contrary, Freud and Jung began their psychological work as physicians; and even in the latest formulations which have been presented by Jung, the thera-

---

* The term "Analytic Psychology" was used as the title of a book by G. F. Stout (1896). C. G. Jung calls his type of psychology "Analytical Psychology." We use the term here in its broadest sense, but specifically in the direction of Jung's interpretation—although Dr. Jung would presumably disagree with much that we say in this chapter.

peutic element is very strong. But *psychic* health is emphasized. The point of approach of analytic psychology is actually from the body to what it calls the *psyche*. But while the Behaviorist and the strictly "scientific" psychologist are to be compared to laboratory investigators in their study of the chemistry and physics of separate psychic elements, the "analyst"—especially Jung—is essentially the physician or healer, who deals with the functional balance of the psychic organism as a whole.

In other words, the analyst studies the facts of psychic functioning, the structural pattern made by the inter-relationship of all these facts, the behavior of the whole psyche. What also differentiates analytical psychology from the "physiological" type above mentioned is the fact that it is purposeful. It does not analyze for the sake of mere investigation, but with the definite aim to heal, to cure, to make whole. What it attempts to make whole is first of all the psyche. But not only does it recognize the interdependence of body and psyche. It almost postulates their identity. Jung writes in *Modern Man in Search of a Soul* (p. 85):

> "The distinction between mind and body is an artificial dichotomy, a discrimination which is unquestionably based far more on the peculiarity of intellectual understanding than on the nature of things. In fact, so intimate is the intermingling of bodily and psychic traits that not only can we draw far-reaching inferences as to the constitution of the psyche from the constitution of the body, but we can also infer from psychic peculiarities the corresponding bodily characteristics."

The same thought is even more strongly formulated in his Commentary on *The Secret of the Golden Flower* (p. 131):

> "It is characteristic of the Westerner that, for purpose of knowledge, he has split apart the physical and the spiritual sides of life; but these opposites lie together in the psyche, and psychology must recognize the fact. The 'psychic' is both physical and mental."

In another place he writes:

> "The psyche is a self-regulating system that maintains itself in equilibrium as the body does. Every body that goes too far, immediately and inevitably calls forth a compensatory activity. Without such adjustments a normal metabolism would not exist, nor would the normal psyche. We can take the idea of compensation, so understood, as a law of psychic happening. Too little on one side results in too much on the other. The relation between conscious and unconscious is compensatory."
>
> (*Modern Man in Search of a Soul*, p. 20)

A brief study of the meaning which Jung attributes to the terms *conscious* and *unconscious* may help the reader to get a clearer picture of what Jung intends to convey by the word *psyche*.

Conscious and Unconscious

According to Freud, all mental processes (apart from the reception of external stimuli) are derived from the interplay of forces which are originally of the nature of instincts; that is to say, which have an organic origin. There is, however, a force in the mind which can exclude from consciousness and from any influence upon action all tendencies which, for some reason, are not acceptable to it. Such tendencies are "repressed." They fall below the threshold of consciousness and become unconscious contents. These repressed instinctual impulses, however, are not made powerless; they act indirectly, causing psychological and physiological disturbances.

Jung admits the existence of these repressed contents which in their sum total constitute what he calls the "personal unconscious"; but he also speaks of a "collective unconscious" which has an entirely different origin and significance:

> "Just as the human body shows a common anatomy over and above all racial differences, so too, does the psyche possess a common substratum. I have called the latter the collective

unconscious. As a common human heritage it transcends all differences of culture and consciousness and does not consist merely of contents capable of becoming conscious, but of latent dispositions toward identical reactions. Thus the fact of the collective unconscious is simply the psychic expression of identity of brain-structure irrespective of all racial differences. By its means can be explained the analogy, going even as far as identity between various myth-themes and symbols, and the possibility of human understanding in general. The various lines of psychic development start from one common stock whose roots reach back into the past.

"Taken purely psychologically, it means that we have common instincts of ideation (imagination), and of action. All conscious imagination and action have grown out of these unconscious prototypes and remain bound up with them."

(Commentary on The Secret of the Golden Flower, p. 83)

The relation of conscious to unconscious is further described in the following statements:

"Without a doubt, consciousness is derived from the unconscious. This is something we remember too little, and therefore we are always attempting to identify the psyche with consciousness; or at least attempting to represent the unconscious as a derivative, or an effect of the conscious (as for instance in the Freudian repression theory)."

(Commentary on The Secret of the Golden Flower, p. 119)

"The unconscious has contents peculiar to itself, which, slowly growing upward from the depths, at last come into consciousness."

(Modern Man in Search of a Soul, p. 37)

Such contents, which arise from the depths of the collective unconscious are usually given the name of "archetypes" or "primordial images." It is also said that "instincts are archetypes," and that "the contents of the collective unconscious are not merely the archaic residua of specifically human ways of functioning, but also the *residua* of functions of the animal ancestry of mankind." They . . .

"can be found in all minds. The primordial images are the deepest, the most ancient and the most universal thoughts of humanity. They are as much feelings as thoughts, and have indeed an individual, independent existence, somewhat like that of the 'partial souls' which we can easily discern in all those philosophical or gnostic systems which base themselves upon the apperception of the unconscious as the source of knowledge, as for example, Steiner's anthroposophical *Geisteswissenschaft*. The conception of angels, archangels, 'principalities and powers' in St. Paul, of the *archontes* and kingdoms of light in the Gnostics, of the heavenly hierarchies in Dyonisius the Areopagite, all come from the perception of the relative independence of the archetypes of the collective unconscious."

(Two Essays on Analytical Psychology, p. 68)

We shall not attempt to discuss here the most debatable statements contained in the last part of this quotation, as our present purpose is merely to present some of the basic concepts of analytical psychology, to which we shall make frequent references in the rest of this book. As, however, the problem of the "real" existence of "gods" and "occult beings" is of great interest to most students of astrology, we shall mention it again in the chapter "Individual, Collective, Creative and the Cyclic Process," and we shall try to show what relation exists between Jung's "primordial images" and at least certain of the classes of cosmic beings mentioned by religions and occultism.

The main point to consider is that, while Freud gives to the unconscious a purely secondary and negative character, Jung sees it as a positive and primordial factor, in fact as the very matrix out of which the conscious grows by differentiation. He recognizes, however, the existence of a "personal unconscious" which is the result of inhibitions and perversions occurring during the process of differentiation of the conscious. This "personal unconscious" is almost identical with Freud's unconscious. But, though a basic factor in Jung's psychotherapy, it leaves to the "collective unconscious" the place of main importance in his general philosophy and attitude to life.

With Freud and Adler, psychology is almost entirely a matter of psychological healing. The former emphasizes the cure of psychic disturbances which are almost strictly considered as illnesses, and, after having tentatively removed the causes of the condition, "nature" is more or less left to handle the situation. On the other hand, Adler deals more particularly with the problem of readjusting to social conditions and collective values the individual who, for some reason, was unable to make a correct social adjustment in youth or thereafter. He starts from the individual and his inability as an individual to function in the collectivity; whereas Freud attempts rather to remove from the submerged parts of the individual psyche the results of the lies and the perversions imposed upon the individual by the collective (family and race habits, inherited tendencies, environmental influences, etc.).

Jung attempts not only to synthetize the two approaches in his therapeutic practice, but he reaches much further. He tends to become a "healer of souls" in a manner reminiscent of spiritual teachers and of Oriental *gurus*—especially perhaps the teachers of the Zen school in Japan. We said only "reminiscent;" for obviously Jung's technique is quite different from those of ancient "spiritual teachers." The point is, nevertheless, that he holds definitely an ideal of human consummation before his clients and before humanity in general. His work is purposive and integrative. He yearns for the complete human being. He envisions, not exactly a "superman," but a "whole-man." And he attempts to lead man toward the fulfillment of this vision—toward the goal of what he calls *individuation*.

Individuation

To understand the full meaning of this term it is necessary to grasp first the situation created, philosophically and practically, by Jung's division of the psyche into two positive realms—conscious and unconscious. Freud's unconscious offered no special problem, save that of getting rid of it. It was a negative quasi-pathological shadow which the light of increased and normalized consciousness at least theoretically dissipated. But Jung's collective unconscious is not to be dissipated, but to be assimilated. It is the sea from which the conscious ego emerges; a sea which may drown this ego, but which on the other hand, once functioning within the structure of an organic and complete conscious being, a Self, becomes as the blood thereof—the blood which is individualized sea-water.

This is of course a symbol. But it holds some truth as to the nature of the relationship of the conscious to the great unconscious. The latter is to be integrated to the former, and this process of integration which reunites the two polarities of the psyche is a process of constant assimilation of unconscious contents by the conscious. Through this process, which is also one of psychological "marriage" within the individual man, the ego—the center of the conscious—grows as it were beyond itself and becomes the fully integrated Self—the center of the totality of man's fully developed being. This consummation (which, in a sense, is never final, for the existence of spheres within spheres of collective unconscious can be conceived or postulated) is *individuation*: the "making whole," or "making perfect" of older systems of spiritual development—yet with a difference due to the new mental level reached by mankind.

Jung is careful to distinguish between the ideal of individualism (especially "rugged individualism"!) and that of individuation. He writes:

"Individuation means to become a single, discrete being, and, inasmuch as the concept individuality embraces that innermost, last and incomparable uniqueness of our being, it also includes the idea of becoming one's own real self. Hence individuation could also be translated as 'coming to selfhood' or 'self-realization.' . . . Individualism is a purposeful attempt to stress and make conspicuous some ostensible peculiarity, in opposition to collective considerations and obligations. But individuation means precisely a better and more complete fulfillment of the collective dispositions of mankind, since an adequate consideration of the peculiarity of the individual is more conducive to a better social achievement, than when the peculiarity is neglected or repressed. For the uniqueness of an individual must not be understood as mere strangeness, or singularity of his substance or components, but rather as a peculiar combination of elements, or as a gradual differentiation of functions and capacities which, in themselves, are universal. . . . Individuation can only mean a psychological evolutionary process that fulfills the given individual disposition. In other words it is a process by which a man can create of himself that definite, unique being that he feels himself, at bottom, to be. In so doing he does not become 'self-centered' in the ordinary sense of the word; he is merely fulfilling the particularity of his nature, something vastly different from egoism or individualism.

"Inasmuch as the human individual, as a living unity, is made up of universal factors, this unity is wholly collective, and therefore in no sense opposed to collectivity. . . . Individuation aims at an essential cooperation of all factors."

(*Two Essays on Analytical Psychology*)

Esthetics vs. Ethics

Before we point out briefly the main features of the technique which Jung uses to bring about the goal of individuation, it seems important that we should establish at once how the ideal of individuation, of "an essential cooperation of all factors" within the total human being, leads to a revision of our traditional concept of ethics and morals. This is of course a very delicate subject which allows of grave misunderstandings, and so we beg our readers not to infer, from what we shall say, conclusions which would in no way be warranted.

As we shall see in the beginning of our second part, the very act of living implies two basic directions of functional operation which can be characterized by the terms *awareness* and *experience*. In a sense, the division is not unlike that of stimulus and response, but with a much more general significance attached to it. We become "aware" of internal as well as external facts, of the subject, or self within, as well as of the object, or outer world. Awareness, following a well-defined process, leads to a more or less concrete, or at least a formed reaction, in which the ego and what he has become aware of interpenetrate. The result of this interpenetration is what we call, in the philosophical sense of the term, an experience, that is "a moment lived through."

Every kind of "living through" implies a sort of judgment passed upon: 1) whatever one has been aware of; 2) the relation of oneself to that thing or quality. But the judgment can be fundamentally of two kinds. In one case it manifests as a *feeling*, in the other as a *thought*. Jung describes feeling as follows:

> "Feeling is primarily a process that takes place between the ego and a given content, a process, moreover, that imparts to the content a definite *value* in the sense of acceptance or rejection ('like' or 'dislike'); but it can also appear, as it were, isolated in the form of 'mood' quite apart from the momentary contents of consciousness or momentary sensations. . . . But even the mood . . . signifies a valuation; not, however, a valuation of one definite, individual conscious content, but of the whole conscious situation at the moment. . . . Feeling is also a kind of *judging*, differing, however, from an intellectual judgment, in that it does not aim at establishing an intellectual connection but is solely concerned with the setting up of a subjective criterion of acceptance or rejection."
>
> (*Psychological Types*, p. 544)

Without going further into the matter it will be clear that all purely moral or ethical valuations are related to feelings; that is to say, they are immediate judgments passed on the value of a content of the psyche or of a whole situation. The image that came into the consciousness or the situation in which one finds oneself in relation to other objects or persons is "good" or "bad." The ego accepts it or rejects it in an immediate direct manner and on the basis of either a deep-rooted instinct or an equally deep-rooted traditional collective attitude. Morals are constituted by a set of traditional judgments concerning more or less clearly defined situations or relationships, some of which are based on what appears as biological instinct, others of which are the results of an attitude to life consciously and deliberately stressed by a religious, social or philosophical code of values.

Feeling-judgments, and more specifically ethical judgments as to what is "good" or "bad," are valuable in that they consider the whole of a situation and its bearing upon the whole organism of the experiencer. No time is wasted in intellectual analysis and "maybe." On the other hand, barring those feeling-judgments which are really instinctual reactions and deal with biological necessities, ethical valuations are determined by a "pre-judgment" and often a prejudice, and by the quality and limitations of either the conscious ego or of some powerful racial image in the unconscious. In other words, they take things for granted.

While the real intuition springs from an immediate adaptation of the whole of the experiencer to a whole situation—including all its new and never-before-realized implications—an ethical feeling-judgment values every new situation in terms of set traditional estimations. Thus morals are periodically changing their dictates, and while they may be the expression of real collective intuitions when they are "fresh," they soon lose their real significance, as soon and insofar as a new lay-out of basic factors in human nature manifests.

The main point, however, which we have to make is that all ethical judgments divide the sum total of experiences into two categories; one which is acceptable, the other which must be rejected. While this may be a necessity of living in a world where the law of opposites rules and all "living whole" faces destruction, from without and even from within—the fact remains that by living almost exclusively by ethical standards or feeling-judgments, man cuts himself off from experiencing half of his life-contents.

Ethical living is "safety first" living. It is living based upon fear. In the jungle, fear is a real thing and is really the working out of the instinct of preservation. Run or die is the basic law, in most cases. The other solution is to shut yourself within walls which define a zone of safety (the home) and a zone of danger (the outdoors).

Now, if we recall what was said in a previous chapter, mankind is now, and has been for many centuries, in a sort of psychomental jungle, which the relative safety of our civilized *physical* world does not make any more safe; just the contrary. Mentally speaking, we may say that the European emphasis on intellectual logic and scholasticism had for its aim the building of a zone of mental safety in the jungle of the newly-entered realm of ideation. Logic and mathematical discipline teach us how to build an intellectual home within the confines of which the power of ideation can function safely. Mathematical formulas constitute a framework of operative safety. As long as you keep within it you can trust the results of your ideas; but if you go off, then your chaotic imagination may lead you astray.

Psychologically speaking, the same has been true. European ethics and philosophy taught us to build a strong and well-guarded home (or rather, fortified castle): the conscious, over which ruled in omnipotence the feudal lord: the ego. The woman was enslaved by the lord, and the children were cowed into submission. The peasants who toiled around the castle (the instinctual contents of the psyche) were admitted to the castle under strict supervision of an armed guard, when the enemy menaced the gates, safely locked. Of course, a lovely chapel was built within the fortress in which an autocratic God, camouflaged into a compassionate Savior, was worshipped. The whole picture of the feudal civilization is an exact symbol (as is always the case) of what was happening then *within man's psyche*.

Music also, the direct expression of the psyche, gave, as is always the case, a symbolical picture of this feudal world; formalism and tonality, being splendid illustrations of this domination of the ethical *principle of exclusion*. The whole of the Christian European civilization is based on that principle. It is based on psychic and mental fear; and on the sometimes necessary yet always thwarting ideal of "safety first." It did achieve greatness within the strict boundaries of what it had enclosed within its fortress; and in that sense, European civilization means an over-focalization which threw great and penetrating light upon what it had admitted as valuable and safe. Its fruits constitute therefore a treasure of great price.

But . . . oh! what a terrible mess was made of what it left outside of the walls! How dearly is mankind paying for a Descartes and a Bach! How festering and decaying the contents of the subconscious—the sum total of our inherited repressions, moral condemnations and fears! Every focalization means limitation, and thus exclusion of experiences and psychic contents. It must therefore be paid for. The more one excludes—the more ethical judgments control the outer and inner behavior—the more future generations (or in an individual life, the years after 40) will have to suffer the consequences. On the other hand, not to focalize, not to build a fortified home (or conscious) may mean a life of dispersion and constant dodging of enemies (within and without); a life in which no solid and lasting achievement is performed—save perhaps that of one's own free selfhood . . . which may be the greatest of all achievements, after all!

But we do not wish to pass here any feeling-judgment against feeling-judgments or ethical valuations! On the contrary, we intend to show that there is another attitude which, while it does not deny the validity of organically rooted and instinctive-intuitional feeling-judgments, emphasizes a different principle of conduct: the principle of *esthetics*.

Esthetics (in the strict philosophical sense of the term) is opposed to ethics (also in the strict sense of this word) very much as thinking is opposed to feeling. Thinking is defined by Jung as:

> "that psychological function which, in accordance with its own laws, brings given presentations into conceptual connection. . . . The term 'thinking' should be confined to the linking up of representations by means of a concept, where, in other words, an act of judgment prevails, whether such act be the product of one's intention or not."

What characterizes thinking is the fact that it is a *linking up* of factors. In other words, it establishes "conceptual connections," or in general well-defined relationships. It is the climax of the process of awareness of relationship. It brings to light the inherent form (structure or configuration) of things and situations. The thinking judgment is not as to whether a thing is in itself "good" or "bad," but as to whether the form of a presentation establishes a valid set of relationships or not. It does not say: "This thing is bad"—meaning always "for *me*." It tells whether the disposition of factors in the situation established by the relationship is, first, coherent, then, significant. Having analyzed this disposition of factors, it is moreover able to pass judgment as to whether, by emphasizing or restricting some of these factors, a new configuration can be established which would be more coherent and more significant.

Thinking establishes or analyzes connections which, in their total configuration, constitute a form. The form is coherent and significant, or it is not. In this process we find the foundation of esthetics. The esthetical judgment is opposed to the ethical judgment in that it does not exclude any group of elements; but, at most, subordinates some to others of greater significance. It is said that the esthetical process is one of selection. But selection does not mean condemnation of what is not selected. If a painter paints only the outlines of a body with his ink-brush, this does not mean that he condemns the elements of flesh, etc., within this outline. It does not pass an ethical judgment against them. He transforms them into *implied values.* He selects certain factors and stresses certain elements or phases of the total configuration presented by the life-experience (for instance, by the scene his eyes behold). But this stressing must be so produced as to give the *suggestion* of all the elements which have been left obviously unrepresented. In a really great work of art *all* elements of a life-situation are contained; but some are represented by actual presence, others are implied in the total configuration.

This, translated in terms of everyday living, may be illustrated by the following example. A man determines by ethical-judgment or feeling-judgment that sexual experiences are "bad," and acting upon the judgment, castrates himself (like, for instance, Origen). This is an extreme case insofar as it involves violent physical action; but in a less accentuated form, all self-compulsive asceticism is of the same type. On the other hand, we may think of a spiritual person who has reached normally beyond the desire for sex-experience. The sex-force is active in him, but transformed. It is "implied" but not actually represented. There is no ethical judgment passed against it; but, in the esthetical configuration of the whole of his being, sex is suggested, but not stressed or even concretely represented; while in the self-mutilated man, sex is always present *but in a negative form,* that is, as a positive shadow—therefore as "evil."

Ethical judgments *create* evil. Esthetical judgments produce stresses, emphases, *relief,* contrasts, light and shade, actual and implied representation, climaxes and suggestions. They balance opposites, and never condemn absolutely. They harmonize; never discard. They deal with whole relations, which they estimate in the totality of their elements. No element can be cancelled without impairing the relation. In fact, *no element in any relation can ever be cancelled. One can only transform it, by apparent cancellation, into an evil force.* But for him who acts according to the true principle of esthetics, there is no "evil"; neither is there any "good." There is only form or relationship, linking all elements into a wholeness which includes light and shadow, crest and trough, emphasis and mere implication—*all equally significant*; but each with a particular significance of its own, a significance which may be marked either with a *minus* or a *plus* sign. In esthetics the only evil is—lack of significance; but it does not reside in the thing or the situation. For all things and all situations, being expressions of the moment of their manifestation, are inherently significant. Lack of significance is due only to man's inability to perceive significance. Thus there is no evil, except ignorance.

The result is that man can be educated into perceiving significances. Ethical compulsion, based on fear, leads to evil. Esthetical education, based on the perception of coherent and significant relationship, destroys the dark fantasy which evil is. It makes of all living an esthetic activity—a creative activity. It destroys—or should destroy—all valuations based on past judgments and the compulsion of tradition, as these are hindrances to the full living of the wholeness of the moment. The wholeness of the moment is the Soul of the moment. And the Soul of the moment is your Soul and mine, ever new, ever young, ever rooted in significance, ever rooted in the "quality" which is our own, the great theme which "life" develops by making it integrate and transfigure into individual significance the completeness of our own ever-receding horizon.

So to educate man is the task of the new Psychology and of the new Astrology outlined in this book.

Astrology and Analytical Psychology

Dream-analysis and the Assimilation of Unconscious Contents

We shall refer later on to the relationship which Astrology, as re-formulated in this book, bears to the esthetical attitude to life. We shall particularly see how this attitude invalidates all notions of "bad" aspects and "evil" planets, at least in *natal* astrology. But we wish first of all to conclude our brief survey of Jung's analytical psychology by outlining the method he advocates for furthering the process of individuation. It will be indeed a most sketchy outline and we must refer the reader to Jung's books, especially *Two Essays on Analytical Psychology, Modern Man in Search of a Soul,* and the Commentary on *The Secret of the Golden Flower.*

We might say that the first step on the way to individuation is to remove the impediments obstructing it. The process of individuation is no mysterious or hallowed performance. It is the full living of an ethically and socially uncastrated life. As Jung says: "Life, . . . if lived with complete devotion, brings an intuition of the self, the individual being." Unfortunately, to live with complete devotion is made difficult by the inheritance of mankind which makes itself felt in the influence of environment, tradition and education. Collective elements press upon the tender sproutings of the plant of personality; and so the natural flow of life is disturbed, hindered, and the very waters of the soul are poisoned. The tendencies and energies repressed accumulate in the personal unconscious, whence they affect in subterranean ways the outer behavior and physiological health. Psychological analysis, in its first stage, must therefore release these repressions; the repressed wishes must be made conscious.

Dream-analysis helps us to get at these repressions and to bring them into the light of consciousness, thus robbing them of their power.

"Dreams give information about the secrets of the inner life and reveal to the dreamer hidden factors of his personality. As

117

long as these are undiscovered, they disturb his waking life and betray themselves only in the form of symptoms. This means that we cannot effectively treat the patient from the side of consciousness alone, but must bring about a change in and through the unconscious. As far as present knowledge goes, there is only one way of doing this: there must be a thorough-going, conscious assimilation of unconscious contents. By 'assimilation,' I mean a mutual interpenetration of conscious and unconscious contents, and not—as is too commonly thought—a one-sided valuation, interpretation and deformation of unconscious contents by the conscious mind. . . . The relation between conscious and unconscious is compensatory. This fact, which is easily verifiable, affords a rule for dream interpretation. It is always helpful, when we set out to interpret a dream, to ask: What conscious attitude does it compensate? . . . Every dream is a source of information and a means of self-regulation. . . . (Dreams) are our most effective aids in the task of building up the personality."

(*Modern Man in Search of a Soul*, pp. 18-20)

"The dream speaks in images, and gives expression to instincts that are derived from the most primitive levels of nature. Consciousness all too easily departs from the law of nature; but it can be brought again into harmony with the latter by assimilation of unconscious contents. By fostering this process we lead the patient to the rediscovery of the law of his own being. . . . I could not put together (in so short a space) before your eyes, stone by stone, the edifice that is reared in every analysis from the materials of the unconscious and finds its completion in the restoration of the total personality. The way of successive assimilations reaches far beyond the curative results that specifically concern the doctor. It leads in the end to that distant goal (which may perhaps have been the first urge to life) the bringing into reality of the whole human being—that is, individuation."

(*Modern Man in Search of a Soul*, p. 30)

Dreams, however, are not the only projections of the unconscious which can be assimilated. There is another field of psychological activity, which Jung names "phantasy," and which is rooted much more in the unconscious than in the conscious. From the most inconspicuous day-dreaming to the most significant sudden "inspiration" of the creative artist, the scientist, or the philosopher, the realm of creative phantasy extends. Creative phantasy is the bridge between feeling and thought. "It is not born of either, for it is the mother of both—nay, further, it is pregnant with the child, that final aim which reconciles the opposites. . . . What great thing ever came into existence that was not first phantasy?" (*Psychological Types.*)

Phantasy operates, like dreams, through the projection of symbols. By an understanding of these symbols we can tap the deepest levels of the unconscious, and assimilate the profound wisdom of the ages which is deposited at those levels.

"The unconscious can give us all the furtherance and help that bountiful nature holds in store for man in ever-flowing abundance. The unconscious . . . commands not only all the subliminal psychic contents, all that has been forgotten and overlooked, but also the wisdom and experience of uncounted centuries, a wisdom that is deposited and lying potential in the human brain. The unconscious is continually active, creating from its material combinations that serve the needs of the future. It creates subliminal prospective combinations just as does the conscious, only they are markedly superior to the conscious combinations both in refinement and extent. The unconscious, therefore, can also be an unequalled guide for man."

(*Two Essays on Analytical Psychology*, pp. 118-119)

The use of what is called "phantasy-material" is one of the most significant features of Jung's technique. He writes: "We must be able to let things happen in the psyche. . . . Consciousness is forever interfering, helping, correcting and negating, and never leaving the simple growth of the psychic process in peace." We must "release the cramp in the conscious." A new attitude is to be created, "an attitude which accepts the irrational and the unbelievable, simply because it is what is happening. This attitude would be a poison for a person who has already been overwhelmed by things that just happen, but it is of the highest value for one who, with an exclusively conscious *critique*, chooses from the things that happen only those appropriate to his consciousness, and thus gets gradually drawn away from the stream of life into a stagnant backwater."

(Commentary on the Secret of the Golden Flower, p. 91)

The "Commentary" on the *Secret of the Golden Flower* gives a great deal of information as to the meaning of this creative phantasy and the manner in which the way can be cleared that leads to the condition of integration and individuation. It shows, besides, how the modern method fits in with some of the oldest conceptions of Chinese wisdom, when these are seen as referring to psychological processes—to the integration and birth of a superior personality, the consciousness of which, detached from the world, which it contains without being in bondage to it, has become pure vision.

The philosophical motive underlying all of Jung's conceptions is that of the reconciliation of the opposites—an old and universal motive which Chinese and Aryan-Hindu civilizations featured, each in a somewhat different way, each emphasizing one of the opposites. The Chinese set-up is particularly clear, and there is little doubt that, in a renewed formulation, it will gain an ever greater ascendancy in the new era. Through Richard Wilhelm, Jung became intimately acquainted with it and with the *Yi King*, the great book in which ancient China pictured symbolically a wonderful synthesis of all life-activities, embracing all knowledge and all performances of action in a vast formula, the *Formula of Change*.

The application of the principle back of the formula in reference to psychology and to the process of individuation is striking, and, in a deep sense, constitutes the background of Jung's conceptions and technique—consciously or uncon-

120

sciously to him. As presented in *The Secret of the Golden Flower*, we find the following metaphysical picture:

> "*Tao* the undivided, Great *One*, gives rise to two opposite reality principles, Darkness and Light, *yin* and *yang*. These are at first thought of only as forces of nature, apart from man. Later the sexual polarities and others as well, are derived from them. From *yin* comes *ming*, life; from *yang*, *hsing* or essence."

Tao is "that which exists through itself," paralleling thus the "Self-Existent" (*Svayambhuva*) of Hindu Buddhism. But it is also the Great Integer and the Process of Integration. The Chinese sign for *Tao* is made up of two signs, one meaning "head," the other, "going." Wilhelm translates *Tao* by "Meaning"; but it has been translated usually as "the Way." It is, in one sense at least, the Way, or rather the Process, in the head. Jung, referring "Head" to consciousness, comes to the meaning: conscious way. *Tao* is the synthesis of *ming*, life; and *hsing*, essence. Essence and life, originally one in *Tao*, become separated at the conception of the child. To reunite them is the goal of psychological development. *Tao* becomes thus "the method or conscious way by which to unite what is separated," that is essence (which is interchangeable with consciousness) and life. Consciousness separated from life refers to the condition Jung describes as "the deflection, or deracination of consciousness." Also "the question of making the opposites conscious means reunion with the laws of life represented in the unconscious." To live consciously is to bring about *Tao*. To do this fully is to integrate consciousness (essence) and the energies of the collective unconscious (life). This comes as a result of a "psychic process of development which expresses itself in symbols." The great symbol of individuation is the *mandala*: that is, a magic circle containing a cross or some other basically four-fold formation.

Such a symbol is the zodiac—and the typical quadrature of

an astrological chart (the 4 angles). All natal astrology is the practical application of this "squaring of the circle"—the conscious Way: *Tao*. Fourfold T-A-O gives the 12 signs or houses of astrology (3 x 4 = 12). Every birth-chart is the *mandala* of an individual life. It is the blue-print of the process of individuation for this particular individual. To follow it *understandingly* is to follow the "conscious way;" the way of "operative wholeness;" that is, the way of the active fulfillment of the wholeness of being that is Self.

III. *Individual, Collective, Creative and the Cyclic Process*

AT THE close of the last chapter we referred to the *Yi King* of ancient China and to its "Formula of Change" based on the interplay of the two cosmic polarities *Yang* and *Yin*. As already mentioned, such a formula is of special interest to us because it had obvious astrological origins. Moreover it is a characteristic expression of a philosophy of time, such as we postulated in a previous chapter as the necessary background for any consistent and valid astrological thought. Astrology is philosophically meaningless unless it rests on a thorough understanding of cycles and of the creative potency of every moment—especially those "seed-moments" which become such by reason of their being the points of departure of cycles. The "Formula of Change" of the *Yi King* is a cyclic formula, which purports to determine symbolically the universal and essential structure of all cycles; better still, of *the* Cycle or of *cyclicity*. As all life-processes are cyclic—in essence, if not in outer appearance—such a formula becomes the basic law of all life-processes. Thus a truly universal synthesis of being and becoming is reached—a synthesis probably grander and more absolute, in its symbolical applicability, than that contemplated by Einstein through his "unified field theory" reducing all natural phenomena to a simple law.

The Chinese formula is not unique in the history of human thought. We shall see presently that the old Hindu civilization also had conceived a universal synthesis of knowledge which could be expressed in terms of a cyclic formula defining the universal life-process whose poles are being and becoming. And we claim that the new civilization, now slowly in the making, will also evolve such a formula on a new basis of life-analysis and at a new level of mental functioning.

The discussion of such matters obviously goes far beyond the scope of this book; and yet we find ourselves obliged to outline them briefly, because the values on which the new formula of the cycle is based are—in our estimation—the very factors upon which our classification and interpretation of astrological elements will depend. The old Chinese dualism of cosmic polarities does not suffice to interpret our modern approach to being and becoming. As already said, humanity is establishing its consciousness, slowly but steadily, at a new mental level; and therefore it contemplates the universal life-process from another point of vantage. New values must therefore be determined: values which do not, however, negate either the old Chinese or Hindu ones, but which complement and supplement them—Western values, which presumably will flower upon the American continent, the seat of an emerging civilization.

In outlining the new cyclic formula we shall have merely to state ideas, rather than discuss them in relation to other more traditional points of view. Our aim is not to write a philosophical treatise, but merely to establish a philosophical background to astrology. The new philosophy of Time, or of the Cycle, is yet to be written. The following will be a mere suggestion of its existence and a mere sketch of those of its aspects which refer more especially to psychology and astrology.

The Cycle: from Seed to Seed

Every cycle can be interpreted structurally as being composed of beginning, middle and end. These three terms, however, are to be understood in a metaphysical sense rather than in the sense of values of time. They represent three essential factors or principles which constitute in their trinity the wholeness of the cycle. The simplest way of approaching a complex subject will be to examine successively each of these three terms and to determine what it refers to, in a general sense.

BEGINNING. The beginning of every cycle is a One: a monad. By definition we shall say that a monad is the initial point of emanation of any life-cycle. It is the germinating seed, or that point within the seed whence arise root and stem. The beginning of the cycle is the moment of unity, the moment which reveals the actual presence of the One. Absolute unity is a postulate, a desideratum, an abstract goal, a metaphysical concept. It is incompatible with life or manifestation. But the One-that-is-in-the-beginning is a representation of this abstract and metaphysical unity—an *avatar* thereof. Unity can be reached in consciousness by devotion to this One—the Father-Mother of the whole cycle. Devotion is concentration upon the One—as if this One existed.

Actually the One does no longer "ex-ist" as a manifested Father; but the One *is* as a psychological reality in the memory of those of His sons who become the bearers of His integrative power—the hypostases, or avatars, of this power. This power is *Tao*, and, in another sense, it is the AUM of the Hindus. It is the integrative power *which is Life itself*; and which alone makes possible the process of integration or individuation spoken of in our last chapter. In the human physiological organism this power is that of blood-circulation rooted in the heart; in the human psyche this power is less well defined, for the psyche is in most persons far from being as yet an "organism." But it is the power which may be called the will to wholeness or the will to sanity and health, with which the psychologist must deal if his analysis is to lead the patient to psychological health and eventually to individuation.

He, therefore, who worships the One as a form or entity, as the All-Father, worships actually a memory, the most primordial of all "primordial images." This worship keeps the memory alive and offers channels through which the energy of this One can flow. The One is no longer there, just as the seed is no longer existent in the growing tree. But the power of growth that was in the seed is active throughout the cycle of the plant's manifestation. This power is an integrative force which constantly "bears witness" to the one Seed.

In other words, once the period of germination is ended, the seed disappears, having sacrificed itself so that the plant might be. But the energy that was in the seed keeps operating. It is the power of operative wholeness. The One, having ceased to be a manifested entity, has now become a *process*.

MIDDLE. This "process" is the fundamental reality of the "middle" of the cycle. By the term "middle," however, must be understood *the whole of the becoming*: The entire series of moments that occur between the initial moment of emanation and the final moment of consummation. These two moments (of emanation and consummation) are in a sense unique; they constitute the *alpha* and the *omega* of manifestation—or rather they represent the two aspects of being, the two aspects of the One. As D. H. Lawrence once wrote in an inspired article, they are the God-of-the-beginning and the God-of-the-end. In *The Secret Doctrine*, H. P. Blavatsky refers to these two "Gods"—that are one in essence—respectively as the Root-Manu and the Seed-Manu. Outside of them, all else belongs to the process of change, to the flux of becoming; that is, to that which men today call "life"—the series of activities which constitute living.

However, throughout this process of change a power of integration is more or less evident: a power that gives cohesion and direction to the multitudinous transformations of the becoming. This power is the energy of the Father, the Holy

Ghost, the Comforter. It is the Life-force that integrates all the multiplicity of parts into organic wholes. It is the power of "holism."

END. The moment of consummation of the cycle is a moment of concentration, conclusion and in-gathering of the fruits of the process of manifestation. It is the "Day-Be-with-Us" of the occultists, the Seventh-Day. As this moment of consummation is reached, all the forces which were the differentiated streams which issued from the Original Source (or Monad) and which animated the many Sons of the one Father, become gathered in a vortex of power and light which constitutes the creative reality of the God-of-the-end—creative, because this God will become in turn, by imaging Himself forth, the Creator of the new Cycle's "archetypes" or generic Forms.

Though such a characterization of the three basic terms of the Cycle is most incomplete, it will at any rate help us to define the three fundamental world-viewpoints which gave and are to give rise to three equally fundamental formulas of being and becoming. Each world-viewpoint and its formula emphasizes one of the three terms of the Cycle—an emphasis which of course does not negate the other two terms but which either leaves them in the background or gives to them a more or less subaltern, or negative, or illusory valuation. The two first types of emphasis, stressing the "beginning" and the "middle" of the Cycle—the original One and the process of becoming—are well known to mankind. The former is typical of the old Hindu civilization, and of all religious and spiritual movements which are more or less dependent upon the old Aryan tradition. The latter received a characteristic formulation in the old Chinese civilization, and is also exemplified by the largest part of the philosophical-psychological and scientific thought of the twentieth century. A third type of emphasis—stressing the value of consummation and the end-term of the Cycle—is slowly emerging from the general body of modern thought. It is such a type of emphasis that we shall attempt to characterize in a new cyclic formula.

The Aryan-Hindu Formula

India represents typically (but of course not exclusively) the attitude of devotion; that is, the dependence upon the One-that-is-in-the-beginning. It stresses—in many ways—the First Principle, the *alpha* of evolution and the yearning toward absolute Unity. The fact that there existed in India a universal synthesis of knowledge is not always recognized; but it can be discovered in the great days of the old *Aryavarta*, of Aryan civilization, underneath the many accretions and perversions which have marred the pure beauty and simplicity of the ancient system, long antedating Buddhism—just as the *Yi King* long antedated Confucianism. This system seems to have been recovered, in part at least, in a somewhat mysterious way, by Bhagavan Das, and we refer the student to his great work, the *Pranava Veda*.

India's integration, being based on the original One, is essentially *hierarchical*—much more so than China's, which is *equilibrative*. All activity and knowledge are seen in their root-relationship to the triune One, which is the AUM, the world-process derived from the absolute unknowable and incomprehensible Unity. In AUM, *A* stands for the universal monad, *U* for the world of illusion, *M* for the relation between both. This relation is a relation of negation. For the old Hindu wisdom, based on the One, denies the Many except as a shadowy objectivication of this One.

Thus the formula of the world-process is given as: "The Self—is not—the Not-Self." The formula of knowledge is that the object (Not-Self) must be known so that the subject (Self) realizes by seeing the illusory character thereof that there is nothing but the subject. The integration is reached by denial and renunciation. The world-process is seen as an illu-

sion (*maya*). The personality and change are illusions; and at
the end of the cycle, the original One finds himself again what
he originally was—uncorrupted by change. What has he
gained through the process of change? This, that he now
knows consciously that "I am that I am." Thus consciousness
is the end of the process, but a consciousness which identifies
itself completely with the subject and withdraws from the
object all reality. However, all fire leaves ashes; and so a new
cycle is necessary to reincorporate these ashes into a new
living and growing tree. Thus the world-process goes on end-
lessly through incarnation after incarnation of the same Self.
Time becomes thus the fatality of being—the warp and woof
of *karma* and of misery.

This basic attitude to life follows necessarily a strong emphasis upon the One-that-is-in-the-beginning. For this One,
the "process" of the middle cycle means dismemberment,
tragedy—or sacrifice. The end means return to the integrity of
the beginning. Thus the AUM: which is to be repeated in
succession; for the *M* is cessation, deliverance. But it brings
again re-birth. And the true AUM is the inaudible one; truth
residing in withdrawal and abstraction. *A* and *U* are also
sounded as *O* to show that the distinction between self and
not-self is a mere concept, an illusion. Thus OM is the integrated tone—the simplest vocal sound: exhaling of air and
closing of lips. A true symbol of the One without a second.

The synthesis of universal knowledge and activity followed
upon such concepts. Out of the OM emanated the *Gayatri*,
the sacred invocation to the Sun and the unity of all life.
From the *Gayatri*, and some other basic mantrams, issued
forth the four Vedas; from the Vedas came the Vedantas;
from those, representing the basic sciences of the self, originated the six schools of Hindu philosophy, synthetized at last
in the secret seventh—*Atma-Vidya*—the consciousness of the
"end," leading to the re-utterance of the AUM in a universal
way. All of this is but a most sketchy outline of one of the

basic systems of consciousness of mankind, a system which is still the foundation of most religions and of most types of occult philosophies.

The Chinese Formula

This system is of course fundamentally different from the Chinese system, which emphasizes the reality of the "process" and the dualism involved therein. *Yang* and *Yin*, the two cosmic polarities, are seen in their cyclic interplay. Time is no longer the fatality that forces the spirit into reincarnation, but is the basic reality of the process of change. All life is a ritual of change, a drama picturing the related activities of *Yang* and *Yin*, and featuring their successive permutations. These permutations are symbolized geometrically, first in a threefold scheme of archetypal manifestation (for every relation between two elements involves action, reaction and interaction); then in a sixfold realm of activity, which is the realm of actual drama or outer performance. Thus 64 hexagrams are formed, representing all the possible phases of interaction between the two principles in the sixfold realm of activity. These hexagrams are then distributed in a circle, very much as the signs of the zodiac in modern astrology.

What this cyclic series of hexagrams represents is the universal drama of life, the cosmic pattern of all activity and of all reaction to activity (which is what we call knowledge). More specifically, it stands as the graph of the changing relationship of Sun to Earth during the cycle of the year. But this relationship, which curves along the path of the Earth's orbit, is in fact the very origin of the vital principle in everything. Life does not come from the Sun. Life is the result of the enacted relationship between Sun and Earth, between energy and substance, between Light and Darkness.

At the summer solstice, *Yang* dominates; at the winter solstice, *Yin*; at the equinoxes, they are in a state of dynamic equilibrium. But in the Fall, *Yin* increases; while in the Spring,

Yang increases and *Yin* decreases in intensity. Thus four crucial points, the Cross of activity, the Four Acts of the drama —which a Fifth Act may, or may not, synthetize. This Fifth Act is the "Quintessence," of alchemical lore. It is the Fifth Limb—the house of the Creative, whether above or below. It is the sacred place where dwells *Tao*, the Great Meaning, the apex of the pyramid based on the four crucial points of the year, the Symbol of all symbols. *Tao* is the solution of all conflicts; and therefore it is not a thing or even an essence, but a process. It is the Process in the Head; the going of the Initiate up the steps that lead to the top of the pyramid—a flat top, originally, for the apex itself could only be the mystic Fire rising from the exalted altar; the altar where the Four Errors (which are really limited viewpoints) are burnt and are solved, resolved, integrated into the One Meaning.

This One Meaning, resolving all conflicts by equilibrating and transcending them, is embodied in the Chinese Emperor. He is the neutral point where all cosmic energies are balanced, the Great Empty, the hub of the wheel. This, within the State. But, for the mystic, there was potentially in every man an "imperial palace." There, within the head, *Tao* reached completion as a process, the process of "circulation of the Light," and the "Diamond Body" was born—the Emperor: the God-of-the-end, the Light-Seed.

The word *Tao* can be symbolically analyzed so that each of its three letters refers to one term of the Cycle. *A* refers to the One-that-is-in-the-beginning, the monad; *O* connotes the ultimate consummation which in man means integrated Personality centered around the Self (and not only the merely conscious ego)—and, at a later stage of abstraction, the quintessence of Selfhood; and *T* stands for the world-process of change—in man, for that state of being which is a continual flux of thoughts, feelings, intuitions and sensations; the state of the evolving ever-changing personality. The letter *T* came first, in this sacred word of China, because Chinese civilization emphasized the element of "process"; and the letter T, in universal symbology, signifies the life-power that flows through the process of becoming, the power born of the "crucifixion" of the One into the realm of duality. However, this life-power, when controlled by man in equilibrium of action, becomes the energy that leads inward along the "Conscious way" which is *Tao*.

Thus the goal of the Sage was to equilibrate within himself the opposite polarities, to reach a point of balance from which all conflicts could be symbolically resolved through objectivizing and transcending them, and to draw within the creative center of his ultimate selfhood the quintessence of the entire process of change so as to build therewith the spiritual vehicle for a relative type of individual immortality as one of the true "Celestials"—i.e., as the spiritual manifestation of one of the archetypal Principles within the realm of Universals.

The "New World" Formula

Thus the Chinese and the Hindu *Weltanschauungen*, or world-viewpoints. We claim that a third type of universal integration is possible, which would emphasize neither the One-in-the-beginning, nor the "process" which we call "life" —but the ultimate sum total, the con-summation, the in-gathering of all elements within the "circle of wholeness." Such a system would obviously integrate some of the features of the Chinese and the Hindu typical philosophies. It would, moreover, incorporate the particular stress laid by Christianity upon "personality" and the process of crucifixion—a stress seemingly absent from the Chinese system. Finally, it would have to give hospitality to the new scientific mentality, insofar as it involves a critical and analytical approach to the world of natural phenomena, and an attempt at thus deepening the understanding of the process of change.

Such a system, such an attitude to life, is slowly in the making under our very eyes. It lacks only some basic coordinating factors, a larger vision free from European bias, a truly esthetical and creative temperament—and a collective spiritual impulsion which even now may be gathering its momentum out of the collapse of the old European civilization. To the building of such a new world-viewpoint pioneers in practically all spheres of human activity are contributing. Perhaps the term "Holism" is as good as any to characterize this new attitude to life, if the meaning of the term is broadened beyond General Smuts' definition. We have used the phrase "philosophy of operative wholeness." We defined in our last chapter the truly "esthetical" approach to life and its relation to the new psychology, especially as formulated by Jung. We touched in an earlier chapter upon the new attitude of science, whose findings will do perhaps more than any other factor toward establishing the new philosophy of living and being. We must mention not only those movements in the field of social organization, politics and jurisprudence which stammer the first sentences of the new human language, but above all, the momentous pressure of economic factors, the influence of our machines and our technology, which will be the practical determining factor of material changes.

Then, there is the new religious consciousness and the power of movements which deal with occultism and mysticism—even spiritualism. In Alice A. Bailey's books the characteristics of the new type of consciousness, emerging here and there everywhere, and the broadest implications of the idea of group-work on a world-wide basis, are stated with unimpeachable clarity. Her study of the activities of what she calls the New Group of World-Servers, even though made on the basis of occult ideas which may disconcert not a few, is a masterly expression of a vision which encompasses the whole of mankind.

What is needed, however, is a simple symbolic presentation of life-principles such as we find in the old *Yi King*: a general formula which relates, centers and crystallizes all the new ideas and ideals; which brings to formulation in a new and significant manner the basic forces which in every field seek a new type of adjustment. Realizing the apparent magnitude of the task, it would seem presumptuous even to attempt it. Yet what is more simple than the basic principles of the *Yi King*? Our civilization is overburdened with complexities. What it needs is a few simple and synthetizing ideas, which at last can structurally co-ordinate the bewildering maze of our intellectual knowledge. It needs one, or a few, *significant symbols* to integrate the whole mass of materials, data and sciences which are crowding our encyclopedias. Can such be found, at this present moment? It is hard to say. But we may at any rate contribute a suggestion toward the eventual solution. On the other hand, the following concepts will be of essential value to us in determining the bases of astrological symbolism. And let us not forget, astrological symbolism, *as symbolism*, may yet play a most important part in making concrete and intelligible some of the deepest ideas involved in the philosophy of the new civilization.

Individual and Collective

All manifestations of life can be seen to involve a dualism of elements or tendencies. Where the Chinese spoke of *Yang* and *Yin* we shall use the terms: "individual" and "collective"; and we shall presently see that this dualism is resolved through the operation of a third principle: the "creative." The words themselves, of course, are not new. They have been used especially in psychology and in relation to social organization, politics—and even, of late, have been implied in the recent theories of modern physics (especially in the dualism of "particle" and "wave"). What, however, has not yet been done—as far as we know—is to use these basic concepts in an attempt at integrating the whole of human knowledge and at offering a consistent interpretation of being and becoming. Again, we must repeat that we are here barely suggesting how such an attempt could be made, and this in order to establish our re-interpretation of astrological symbols on a foundation truly all-inclusive in its scope.

The philosophy of Holism, to which General Smuts gave a most interesting though not by any means complete formulation, will help us greatly in showing how the evolutionary life-process and its contributive factors can be re-interpreted in a way that is true to the spirit of the future civilization. Whole and parts are presented as the two terms of the life-process. And the introduction of these two terms as cosmic ultimates is a tremendous step—even though General Smuts appears somewhat shy of truly metaphysical and cosmic generalizations. However, he characterizes the nature of the World-process thus:

> "This is a universe of whole-making. . . . The ultimate reality of the universe is neither matter nor spirit but wholes. . . . Holism as an active creative process means the movement of the universe towards ever more and deeper wholeness. This is the essential process, and all organic and psychic activities and relations have to be understood as elements and forms of this process. . . . The rise and self-protection of wholes in the Whole is the slow but unerring process and goal of this Holistic universe."
>
> (*Holism and Evolution*, 1926)

Such a picture, when completed by the idea that soul or self must be understood as the wholeness of the wholes (cf. Chapter II), constitutes a revolutionary revaluation of man's attitude to life. The dualism of spirit and matter, which was another form of physiological dualism, as it meant originally that of motion and inertia, is replaced by that of wholeness and parts. And the unity of the process is stressed in that "Holism is a process of creative synthesis . . . the movement of the universe towards ever more and deeper wholeness."

We cannot here thoroughly discuss the metaphysical implications and some of the metaphysical weaknesses of the picture General Smuts presents. All that we may say is that in such an idea of infinite progression, apparently from chaos to perfect wholeness, as well as in the opposite idea, held by many contemporary scientists, of a universe running down to a neutral level, we find lacking a conception of the cyclic nature of time, and of the relation of time to wholeness. We do not see how a formula of universal integration can have real validity unless it is cyclic—unless the beginning and the end, as it were, meet; and that point of meeting can be considered as absolute and timeless—the Eternal Now.

In other words: 1) the life-process is not a mere progression upward; 2) it involves two complementary motions which, seen separately, operate in opposite directions; yet which can be integrated into a third term. This term is not a motion. There is no progress involved in it.

The first motion can be termed "individuation"—provided the word is taken in a much more general sense than the one given to it by Jung.

The second motion can be termed "collectivation."

The third term is "the creative." The crux of the whole matter lies in the correct understanding of this third term. To grasp the somewhat difficult significance of it, we shall have to see how the two motions which it synthetizes and equilibrates operate.

Individuation. This is the process through which elements, which are relatively unrelated (absolute unrelatedness being inconceivable), gather or are gathered together and constitute a whole. So defined, the term is synonymous with "integration."

Collectivation. This is the process through which characteristic features, faculties or energies which had been acquired by individuals as individuals become by direct or indirect transmission the property of groups.

In order to grasp these definitions clearly it will be necessary to analyze the two concepts philosophically—*individual* and *collective*—and thus to get a well-defined picture of what these terms, often loosely used, signify.

An *individual* is an entity in which are integrated in a unique manner a number of elements. These elements are inherited from the linear ancestors of that individual, or assimilated by him in one way or another since he began to exist in a state of relative independence. What constitutes individualhood is the fact that the manner in which those inherited and assimilated elements are combined is *unique*.

This uniqueness, however, may not be absolute. It may be relative to a certain fortuitous grouping of entities, or to the possession of characteristics fortuitously singled out. For instance, if in the midst of a group of fish going in one direction in the stream, you see one fish swimming in the opposite direction, this fish acts as an individual. His behavior has a characteristic which is unique. If three fishes behave in one way and thousands of fishes behave in another, the three fishes still can be said to have relatively individual behavior. Yet considered as entities in themselves, they are probably fish just in the same way as the other fishes; and thus cannot be said to be "individuals."

Then, if you look at a brick wall, you may say that all the bricks are alike. Yet you may say that they hold individual places, for each brick, in terms of the fact that it occupies one definite place, is unique. No two bricks occupy the same place.

On the other hand, the word "collective" refers to aggregates which, at least relatively speaking, have no uniquely defined characteristics or basis in time and space; or to attributes which are found to be possessed in common by many entities. Blue eyes are collective factors; but the eyes of my friend Mr. X. are individual—for they are unique and one of the characteristics of the unique constellation of human factors which is known as Mr. X. In other words, the relation between individual and collective is somewhat analogous to that between particular and universal; only the word "universal" has various connotations and an etymological sense which are beside the point which we are making now. It must be added also that the strict meaning of individual and collective varies according to the type of entities to which they are applied. The general meaning, however, remains the same.

Every living entity can be said to possess both individual and collective elements. As with any basic dualism of principles, the two are never separated. What counts and what can be measured is the relative proportion in which the two coexist. In the Chinese yearly cycle of transformation no day was found in which either *Yang* or *Yin* was not operating. But as *Yang* increased in potency, *Yin* decreased; and *vice versa*. Likewise from the standpoint of Holism there is no whole that cannot be considered as part of a greater whole (at least potentially), and no part which is not the whole for lesser parts of which it is the sum total and synthesis.

As we deal with complex beings, with organisms which hold together myriads of cells and lives by means of a more or less well-defined structural arrangement, we find ourselves confronted with the necessity of using the terms individual and collective as adjectives qualifying the constituent elements of these complex wholes. Individual and collective are forever qualifying everything that is. Everything that is is forever pulled by the two mighty powers toward the individual qualification or toward the collective qualification. This is the great universal drama of being.

It is naturally in man that the drama is the most significant and the most complete—to men at least! Thus, by watching it operate within our total being, we shall be better able to see it operate in simpler or in more grandiose ways, in atoms or galaxies.

The Formula of Cyclic Transformation

The following cyclic formula is evidently but the simplest kind of framework, which has to be supplemented in every particular case by a much more complete one; but it parallels the equally simple *Yang-Yin* formula of China, and we claim that it has the same universal validity. Its value lies in that it gives us a new perspective on psychological factors (conscious and unconscious) and enables us to interpret all life-processes at the psycho-mental level.

We begin the cycle with the individual, that is, with a unique entity wherein are integrated a number of collective elements. From this individual emanate, through an operation which we shall study presently, new elements which are the exteriorization of his individual selfhood.

These elements, once released by the individual, become collective elements. They register upon the minds of other individuals who may or may not assimilate them; they become the common property of all men. Such collective elements, emanated by individuals, are all added to the store of collective experience and collective knowledge. They accumulate and constitute the racial-memory, out of which emerges a culture, or in general, civilization.

Civilization, in its highest sense (and *not* as pictured by Spengler who sees only its shadow), is really a process. It is the process of integration of collective elements. Each generation of men pushes the process a step further, insofar as individuals within this generation emanate out of their own individual selfhood new elements. Civilization, as a process, culminates in the formation of what mystics have called the "Holy City," the "New Jerusalem"—and in one sense, at least, the "White Lodge." That is to say, it ends in the building of an individual formation or entity—*at the psycho-mental level* —which we can call, with H. P. Blavatsky, the "Seed-Manu." It is the seed of the psycho-mental plant of civilization.

This seed, as a psycho-mental and, in a sense, *cosmic* Individual, emanates at the beginning of a new cycle collective elements. These collective elements constitute the "primordial images of the unconscious" of which Jung speaks. Also they are the "primeval revelation" of theosophy, the "sum total of innate ideas" of other philosophical systems. These, combining with a new earth, or generally speaking new substantial materials, constitute in turn the *archetypal structures* ("the astral selves") of a new race-type. Out of the matrix, which this new race-type constitutes, will emerge, by the process of evolution or individuation, individuals. And the cycle begins again.

The phase of the cyclic process during which the individual emanates elements which become the collective psycho-mental "stuff" of civilization is the phase of collectivation. The phase during which this "stuff" becomes integrated into the "Seed-Manu" or "Holy City" is the phase of individuation. It reproduces on a larger scale the process following which a particular man integrates all the psycho-mental energies of his being and becomes "individuated," in Jung's sense of the term. A similar process is that which modern science calls "evolution"—from the amoeba to man; but instead of this process being a straight progressing line, it is cyclic.

What is liable to confuse the reader is the simultaneous development of man as a species and of a multitude of men as relatively individuated personalities. We must therefore distinguish between *generic man* and *personal man*, between the "lesser individual" and the "Greater Individual." Generic man is the emanated image (or "shadow") of the "Seed-Manu" of the preceding cosmic cycle; and this Seed-Manu represents the "Greater Individual" who is an "emergent Whole" made up of the quintessence of "lesser individuals"—viz., human personalities. This "Greater Individual" of the end of the cycle manifests as the "Creator" of the beginning of the cycle. He "creates" a new species: his own image. Thus "God" created man in his own image; but "God" is the individuated sum total of all collective psycho-mental elements emanated by the individuals of the preceding cycle. Individuals among men today are emanating "ideas" and "energies" which, once individuated at some distant time into the end-synthesis of all human civilizations, will *be* the "God" that will "create" some new species of "men" at the beginning of the future cosmic cycle on Earth (or perhaps elsewhere).

We must not forget, however, that generic man, being thus the creation or emanation of the "Greater Individual," is originally a mass of collective elements. Generic man is not an individual, but the matrix out of which the individual will arise after a long process of individuation. Still more important perhaps, we must realize that this process takes place, *first at the physiological, and then at the psycho-mental level.* Thus ancient mythologies speak of several "Creations"; thus *The Secret Doctrine* mentions first the projection of the "astral shadows" (i.e., the archetypal forms) of men, then that of the "sparks of Mind"—the nuclei whence germinates and develops man's psycho-mental being. The two are one, in a sense, but they operate at different levels of being and by organizing a different kind of "substance."

Without entering into the discussion of difficult points of "occult" cosmogony, we can say, however, that *no* creation is born out of, or emanated by, its creator, *as an individual*—it is born only with a potentiality (more or less compelling) of individual selfhood. Thus we have to differentiate in every man between race-self and (potential or fulfilled) individual-self. The former is collective in nature; the latter, individual. In other words the generic type of man (*homo sapiens*) reaches first a certain point of crystallization, which is generic individuation; then the process of personal integration begins from such a generic foundation.

Generic individuation is a process affecting the sum total of human beings which belong to a more or less clearly determined group. It operates by gathering together in a definite geographical environment human beings which have been projected (as "emigrants") out of several relatively individuated groups and thus have become, from the race's standpoint, "collective elements." These collective elements of various descriptions become slowly homogenized. That which homogenizes them into a generic type (or later "culture") is a series of common experiences and the common assimilation of certain ideas and "creations" emanated by the creative individuals of the group. And by the terms "creative individuals" we do not mean only "creative artists." Any one who has a new idea and discovers a new significance in any experience, or relates together certain facts of experience in a new, and especially in a symbolic way—is a creator. As what he has thus created is assimilated by several men of his group, a new step is taken toward group-integration or generic individuation.

Our bodies have been built, and their type and functions set, just in this way—but through millions of years of generic individuation. The common inheritance of mankind has accumulated for thousands of millennia. This common inheritance is the "collective unconscious" formulated by Jung. It has tremendous formative power. And its formations set the generic type—both of our bodies and our psyches. But, let us not forget, these energies-formations of the collective unconscious are not only the result of the assimilation of the "lesser individuals'" creations (as above defined); they are also connected causally with those "primordial images" or "innate ideas" which emanated at the beginning of the cycle of our present humanity from the "Greater Individual," the "Seed-Manu" of the preceding cycle.

Again, what makes matters rather complex is that individuation and collectivation operate at various levels and dovetail into each other. But if we grasp the following formula, an Ariadne thread may lead us safely through the labyrinth of the cyclic life-process: this life process is *from collective to collective through the individual*. But we might also say: *from any level of individuation to the next higher level through the*

creative. The first formulation is from the standpoint of substance; the second, from that of spirit, or unity.

If we take the formulation according to spirit, we have the
cyclic formula mentioned at the beginning of this chapter;
beginning-middle-end; or God-of-the-beginning—the dualistic
life-process—God-of-the-end; or Seed-plant-seed; or monad-
personality-Self, psychologically speaking. Using the *alpha*
and *omega* symbolism, we could symbolize the formula by
the word *amo*, which means in Latin "I love." Comparing it
to the Latin *Amen*, the Sanskrit *Aum* and the Chinese *Omi*,
may prove interesting to the student of symbolism. According
to our present alphabet, the symbolic formation ought to be
Amz; *M* stands for the collective—which is of course analogical to the mother-element *ma*, and the sea (*mar* in Latin); *A*
and *Z* represent the two stages of the Seed or the Individual,
the initial and the culminal or synthetic. *A* stands psychologically for the monad; *M* for the personality (in our sense of
the term, the equivalent of the Sanskrit *manas*); *Z* for what
we call, with Jung, the Self (in Sanskrit *Sva*; *S* being the
Sanskrit equivalent for *Z*; a root found with slight difference
in practically all Indo-European languages).

If we accept, however, the formula: from collective to collective through the individual, we posit as primordial the
world-process of change, the vast sea of cosmic elements,
forming into more or less individual wholes which break
again into parts. The individual is then merely the momentary
flowering of a process, the crest of the waves of an ever restless ocean.

Quality, Structure and Substance

Collective elements (whether cosmic or human) represent
always the pole of substance, as opposed to the individual
which stands for spirit. As there are elements of all kinds and
at all levels of being, substance may be of many types. Thus
we speak of physical and of psycho-mental substance. Sub-

stance is the result of the process of collectivation (whether as disintegration or as creation). The substance which results from disintegration is the humus made of decaying leaves which will provide the new Spring vegetation with chemicals. The substance which results from creation is symbolically of the nature of the seed-substance.

In her exceedingly valuable book, attempting to effect a reconciliation between Oriental and Occidental psychologies, Alice Bailey writes: "The key-word 'substance' with its suggestion of materiality is a misnomer. It is helpful, however, to reduce this word to its Latin roots: 'sub' *under*, and 'stare' *to stand*. So substance is that which *stands underneath*, or underlies." Substance, in its philosophical sense, means *substratum*. It is defined in Webster's dictionary as "That which underlies all outward manifestations; that in which properties inhere." On philosophical grounds of logical consistency we have to postulate a "psycho-mental substance" as a substratum to the psycho-mental activities of spirit (or in man, the individual "quality" which is his spiritual reality). Every realm of manifestation of spirit must have a corresponding type of substance, spirit and matter being absolutely correlated. Psycho-mental substance may be considered an emanation, and a refined product of physical substance. Or it may be that physical substance is the condensation of a universal "mind-stuff."

If such an argument is to be dismissed because of its being "metaphysical" and not based on experience, then let us dismiss all the new atomic physics. The ether, or the curvature of space, or electrons and photons, are all postulated as the substrata of recorded activities. The activities are recorded, but no eye may ever see the ether, or the electron, and still less "curved space." There is as much evidence, in fact much more, for the existence of a "psycho-mental" substance as there is for the existence of electrons, which are *only logical necessities*. Besides, any concept of survival of consciousness, or immortality—a concept which Jung considers a normal requirement for psychological health—requires of course a psycho-mental substance. For once physical substance is gone, there must obviously be some other kind to serve as a substratum for the consciousness. If this is denied, then the denial is merely a quibbling over words, and an archaic attachment of the consciousness to the "primordial image" of a *tangible* substance.

It must be added, however, that the question whether or not such a postulated psycho-mental substance can be *actually experienced* by man depends on whether or not man is susceptible of developing superphysical senses, or organs of direct perception. Even if he cannot, there is such a thing as "inferential evidence."

In opposition to substance, what we call "quality" represents the spiritual identity of the living whole. In our discussion of the philosophy of time in Chapter II and at the beginning of Chapter III we saw that every moment of time is creative of a particular quality which is, figuratively, stamped upon any whole reaching the condition of independent existence at that moment. The quality of the moment and the quality of the wholeness of the whole are identical. This quality as it is projected out of time, so to speak, is the monad of the particular whole considered. It is the One-in-the-beginning. It represents the individual pole.

Quality, or monad, may refer to a species, or to a single human person. It should be evident from what was said previously that *at the physiological level quality is generic, not personal.* In other words, physiologically speaking, there is but one monad for the whole of mankind, just as there is only one monad for the cat or the dog species or genus. Individualhood resides in the species or sub-species, not in the particular specimen thereof, a particular cat or a particular dog. There are, however, an infinite number of gradations. Individualization, the becoming different from the norm, has some place at the physiological level. But, and this is the important point, only insofar as it provides a basis for (substantial viewpoint), or is the expression of (spiritual viewpoint), psycho-mental factors.

What might be better to say is that physiological individuation is of a lower order than psycho-mental individuation. The former represents a collective, the latter, an individual emphasis. This will be clear if we remember that the beginning of the cycle of humanity (of any cycle, in fact) is a *creative act* releasing collective elements, which have only the potentiality of individual selfhood. To repeat ourself: The Seed-being of the end of the preceding cycle emanates creatively at the beginning of the human cycle a prototypal form (or structure). This form, plus the energy with which it is endowed, is the exteriorization of the quality or Idea which, within the Seed-being, conditioned the creative act. This quality is the monad of the *genus homo*: the noumenon-archetype thereof. It is exteriorized in the creative act as both energy and structure. The structure remains unchanging, as the blue-print does during a building operation. But the energy undergoes a process of differentiation and transformation; that is to say, the money (social energy) put aside for the building at the beginning of the operations *becomes* wood, brick, plumbing and the salary of the builders.

In other words, the idea of the building is the archetype. It conditions the building-operations—the creative act. The latter involves the exteriorization of the "idea of the building" as a blue-print; and also the release of a sum of money—energy—to pay for the construction. When the building-operations are completed, the blue-print has become *substantialized into a concrete body*. The energy has become transformed into work and the gathering of materials; but as the building (let us say an apartment-house) is rented, the money expended in building it will, at the end of the cycle of business, return to its source, with a profit (if everything goes well!).

This illustration shows that the "creative act" releases collective elements (that is, money—a strictly collective value), but with the potentiality of individuality (the blue-print, as an exteriorization of the "idea"). The finished apartment-house will have a certain amount of generic selfhood. It will have a certain quality, in terms of the amount of money (energy) expended as well as of its structure. It will thus call to itself a certain class of people as tenants. These tenants, by living together and interacting, will (if we are allowed to force a point) build up a community of interests, of thoughts and behavior—which might be described as the psycho-mental entity of the apartment house. Within the generic structure of the house will develop a psycho-mental individual structure. The latter will of course be moulded somewhat by the former. Yet this house-structure will have been "created" by the owner-architect *with a view to attracting by special features a certain class of people.*

If you would add that the owner-architect may be a co-operative group of persons building the house in order to live in it, you might have a more complete picture, from the spiritual point of view. That co-operative group represents now the Seed-being of the preceding cycle. It is its own energy-money which is being spent for the house in which, as a group, it will live, and from which it will draw new benefits and a further sense of integration. The house can be said to be built during the summer time, when the co-operative group is having a vacation from the city; or perhaps the whole group is living still in another city, while the house in the new city is being built. The fact is, at any rate, that the group does not move into the house, as tenants, until it is completed—even though minor alterations and the interior furnishing of the several apartments follow their taking possession of the apartments.

The illustration is obviously only an illustration, not to be taken too literally; but it may help to focalize (we hope not crystallize) some of the abstract ideas previously stated. We may pursue it further by considering the behavior of the co-operative group as tenants. The structure of the house, i.e., the way apartments are laid out, determines a great many of their daily activities, such as going from bed to bath, and from bath to breakfast room, etc. These activities are unconscious: they depend on the generic structure of the house. They are powerful and set, determined by unchangeable structure, by "primordial images," that is, by the original blue-print of the house (prototype of *genus homo*) which in turn was the exteriorization of the "idea" of the building, which again was conditioned by the former habits, consciousness and wealth of the co-operative group projecting this "idea." In other words, they are the end-results of a very, very long past.

On the other hand, the type of thinking which the men do at desks in their studies and all the emotional activities that go on between the tenants in their respective apartments, or as they visit one another, are not very much bound or conditioned by the plan of the house. Many different things can be done in the living room or in the studio—from making love to serving tea and playing bridge, or having a recital. The more psychological and conscious activities of the tenants are relatively free from the house-structure; whereas their physiological and quasi-unconscious movements are more regulated thereby.

The illustration becomes quite awkward at this point; but it may still serve some purpose. What it attempts to convey is the difference between permanent structures which are generic, in man, and impermanent structures which are more personal. The former refer to the unconscious; the latter to the conscious. The generic is the collective inasmuch as it represents features and attributes which are the common properties of the many. On the other hand, these generic features can be traced, not only to common experiences and reactions under the same prolonged geographical and environmental conditions (as Jung claims, being a modern scientist); but must be said, from the spiritual viewpoint, to have their origin in the creative act of a "Greater Individual," the "God-of-the-end" of the preceding cycle.

Thus "generic unconscious" would be a better term insofar as elements involving basic common structures are concerned, such as "primordial images." On the other hand, the term "collective unconscious" would mean more specifically the results of the process of civilization, on the psycho-mental plane—the slow-forming ideals of mankind which, step by step, integrate the souls or minds of all men into the Seed-being of the end of the cycle—at the psycho-mental level. "Generic" refers more to that which results from physiological structures common to all men; whereas "collective" applies more strictly to those psycho-mental elements which in the course of human evolution are being released by creative individuals, and, after having been assimilated by many generations, become the common inheritance of all mankind.

Generic and Individual Structures in the Body

Lest we be too severely accused of separating the physiological from the psycho-mental, the body from the psyche, we shall differentiate within the body the individual and the generic structures, and briefly show their relationship, which parallels at the physiological level the psychological relationship between conscious and unconscious upon which Jung's psychological method is founded.

Such a differentiation is of course relative, not absolute. Any part of the body can present features which are characteristics of a particular individual and of no other. All physiological functions are basically generic, yet the total functioning of every body could be described by a formula which would present a certain character of uniqueness. Here

149

we come again upon the fundamental idea that elements are collective, but combining in complex ways each of which is to some extent individual. In any such basic dualism—as *Yang* and *Yin*, positive and negative, individual and collective—we witness always a process of combination of the two polarities. This process may mean a ruthless conflict, or it may mean a harmonious adjustment based on the law of compensation and cyclic permutation.

Considering the dualism of collective and individual, we find a constant shift of emphasis between: 1) faithfulness to the generic type; and 2) stress upon individual variations. Between these two attitudes the pendulum of life swings constantly—as a study of past civilizations obviously shows. The swing manifests first in relation to the physiological nature of man. As this body-nature becomes relatively set, and a race-type is produced which exteriorizes in physical bodies the "creative" archetypal "idea" to a degree of relative perfection, the principle of individualization (i.e., the stressing of individual differences) increases in power. Then it is as if "Life" attempted to extract from the smallest individual variations in the generic physiological structure all the possibilities there were to release individuality in another direction, or at another level. For instance, while the structure of the skull was relatively set, racially, there came the possibility of developing brain-convolutions *in depth*, or inwardly. The brain grew in importance within the relatively set bone-structure: the brain, the medium through which individual differences could be stressed, against the bone-structural conformity to the generic type. Thus the conscious elements, based on the brain and on the cerebro-spinal nervous system, became more and more emphasized; while the unconscious elements, based on the ganglions of the sympathetic nervous system (the solar plexus, principally) and the cerebellum, were placed somewhat in the background.

The Great Sympathetic system, with its nerve-plexuses, is

essentially the seat of generic physiological behavior (instinct) and of collective unconscious images or impulses. It is the matrix from which or through which the "primordial images" of the unconscious operate. This was stated, as early as 1904 (before Jung's important works), by Edward Carpenter in his book, *The Art of Creation* (Ch. VI to XI). Carpenter, drawing his information partly at least from South-Indian psychology, describes the progressive formation of race-images through the experience of countless generations, and claims that these race-images become associated with the nerve-plexus governing the related instinctual activities and feelings in the human body. He considers these nerve-plexuses as the sources of great instinctual collective emotions. The Great Sympathetic system is then viewed as "a kind of organ of the Emotions, in something the same way as the Brain is regarded as the organ of Thought." This view has been taken by many psychologists; however, we would use the term "feelings" here rather than "emotions."

As we saw already, feeling-judgments are like instincts, immediate information as to the vital value of a situation or relationship. Feelings in the more or less individualized man are strongly related to thoughts, but they are, just the same, most obvious developments of the collective instincts. Feelings may thus be called individualized instincts. They are individualized in proportion as the cerebro-spinal system dominates the Great Sympathetic; especially as the cerebrum dominates the solar plexus, which is the brain, or center of the Great Sympathetic system—and is thus the gate for the "messages" of the collective unconscious and its more or less individualized primordial images.*

---

* Thus concentration on the solar plexus is practised where man is willing to become a more or less passive agent to a "primordial image" or "god." The solar plexus is ruled astrologically by Jupiter, which symbolizes religious worship, contact with the "gods," and in general is the reflection of the universally collective—*Parabrahman* or the *Para* condition of consciousness in Hindu philosophy.

The cerebro-spinal system and the brain are the seats or organs of the conscious ego—the individual factor *per se* in man. The ego is, according to Jung, "a complex of representations which constitutes the centrum of my field of consciousness and appears to possess a very high degree of continuity and identity. Hence I also speak of an *ego-complex*" (*Psychological Types*). It is defined by S. Radhakrishnan (quoted by Alice Bailey in *The Soul and Its Mechanism*) as "the psychological unity of that stream of conscious experiencing which constitutes what we know as the inner life of an empirical self."

The ego is the "principle of separateness," symbolized in astrology by Saturn. It is that which says, "I am this particular unique entity and no other." It is the organ of variability from the generic type. It rules over the first phase of the process of individuation. Generally speaking we can divide the process of individuation into two phases: The phase of *differentiation* during which the potential individual emphasizes his own differences from the generic norm, and the phase of *assimilation* during which the differentiated individual assimilates the contents of the collective unconscious, very much as the body grows by assimilating the food-stuff provided by the "collective" earth.

These two processes operate to some extent synchronously, but the emphasis upon the one or the other characterizes the "age" of the individual selfhood. The stage of assimilation presupposes an advanced development of the psycho-mental nature of man—that is, in fact, a vast *collective memory* in the human race, the inherited memory of all the achievements of many and varied civilizations.

Here again we find a reason for differentiating between the generic collective factors and those psycho-mental attributes which are the accumulated products of civilization after civilization, and constitute the collective inheritance of later mankind. It may be said, in passing, that the nerve-plexuses of the

Great Sympathetic system (and cerebellum) are the gateways or agencies for the influx of generic energies (instincts and the most primordial of "primordial images"); whereas the brain's lobes (which are the cotyledons of that human seed: the head) are potential storehouses for the collective fruits of past civilizations. In other words, what is called in its totality the brain has to be subdivided into two basic sets of parts: those that are (figuratively speaking) store-houses of the past, and those that take out of these store-houses the collective elements, and re-combine them into individual formations. A third set may even be mentioned (according to Oriental traditions), which refers to the later stage of individuation and to the final integration of all life-factors. This was called in China "The House of the Creative," and seems to refer to such parts as the pituitary and pineal glands and the Fourth Ventricle—and other "cavities." The book, *The Secret of the Golden Flower*, deals with some of the "occult" processes which are said to occur at the very center of the head and back of the root of the nose. Likewise books on the Hindu *Kundalini Yoga*.

Kundalini Yoga is a system of integration of collective and individual at the physiological level. At least it was undoubtedly so in archaic times, as part of the *Tantrik* system, at the time when mankind was hardly functioning at all at the psycho-mental level. Integration could therefore not be a really psychological, and still less a mental process. Yet it was a reality just the same. The energies of the collective (locked in the *chakras* or centers of the Great Sympathetic system) were progressively assimilated, by means of special breathing exercises and postures, by the center of individual will in man (presumably at the center of the head, or "between the eyebrows"). All the generic energies and instincts of the bodies were drawn to the head and made subject to the individual will of the ego (or perhaps even more, of the monad). This was called the "turn-back process"; the differentiated monadic energies were, as it were, re-unified by an act of will.

The more recent type of *Kundalini Yoga*, since 600 B.C. or later, emphasizes psychological integration of collective elements by the individual ego. But much still depends upon the physiological factors. This is, however, in India, pervaded as yet by the devotional attitude which preserves, by spiritual will and concentration upon absolute unity, the living memory-image of the God-of-the-beginning. But it seems that a new technique of integration is developing (or about to develop in the West in preparation for the "new era") which will throw the almost complete emphasis of the process at the psycho-mental level. In a series of lectures given in student classes by Jung on *Kundalini Yoga*, an attempt was apparently made to interpret the system strictly as a technique of psychological individuation—or as a system of symbolism. In Blavatsky's *The Secret Doctrine*, and still more in Alice Bailey's books on meditation and the treatises on *Cosmic Fire* and *White Magic*, much invaluable information is given about the *new* location of the *chakras* (*now* connected with the spine, because of the new individual and psycho-mental emphasis); also about new methods of development in what might be called "occult" psychology.

Whether we speak of the oldest form of physiological *Tantrika*, of the more psychological type of *Kundalini Yoga*, of the process of individuation in Jung's psychology, or of new forms of meditation used in various "esoteric schools"— in every case we are dealing with interpretations and techniques of integration, which usually mean the same thing at different levels: the assimilation of collective elements by the individual, toward the building of the perfect Self, or Soul-body, the "Temple of Solomon," or the "Christ-Body," or the "Diamond-Body." Thus always the process of individuation, the working out of the essential relationship between individual and collective.

Individual, Collective, Creative and the Cyclic Process

This process consists in a gradual shifting of the center of gravity of the human "personality." *Kundalini* is raised from the lowest sacral plexus (*Muladhara chakra*) to the center between the eyebrows (*Ajna chakra*): the seat of the conscious ego. Each *chakra* represents a stage of the process. Through the intermediary of the heart, the solar plexus (and the lower plexuses it synthetizes) and the conscious center in the head are integrated. This is the "mystical marriage"; not so much of the "man" and "woman" within each person—rather of the "individual" (ego) and the "collective" (the generic self in the solar plexus).

In the Chinese *Secret of the Golden Flower* the union is between "essence" (individual) and "life" (collective). The essence without the life is pure abstraction—the "I" devoid of qualities. The life without the essence is mere instinct, or perfectly adequate generic behavior. The essence must therefore assimilate the life. The Empty must be filled by the Waters of Life. This is the synthesis. The true individual does not stand against the collective, as a conscious ego opposing with his will the generic energies. The true individual is the flowering and the fruition of the collective, which finds itself fulfilled in and through him. He is the collectivity become conscious and significant. He is the drop who has assimilated the wholeness of the ocean's characteristic being, and thus is a *perfect exemplar* of "sea-water-hood."

This is "operative wholeness"—wholeness operating as and through a particular whole. An individual man acting as the agent of Man-the-whole—acting, however, according to his own particular destiny as an individual. The path of operative wholeness is *Tao*. It is the path of relationship; the "middle path" integrating individual and collective, thinking and feeling, esthetics and ethics. It is the path of *Kundalini*—which is "serpentine," because cyclic. It is the *Via dolorosa* of Christian mysticism, each station of which is one of the spinal *chakras*, up to the "Mount of Skull"—Golgotha. In the lower

155

chakras, the collective dominates (as in sex); in the higher, the individual, until the Cross is reached, at the base of the cranium (where the nerves actually cross). Then Iesous is crucified between the two thieves in the center of the head. But after the Third Day (or ventricle) He rises and is seen in his "Risen Body"—in the glory that is the Thousand-petalled Lotus, above the crown of the head, the *Sahasrara chakra*, the "Halo" of Western Saints as well as of Oriental Buddhas; the radiance of operative Wholeness.

The Nature of the Personality

We may now ask: What is the fundamental difference between the "occult" approach and the "psychological" (in Jung's sense)? It is that the latter occupies itself solely with the "life-process," with the development of the "personality"; while the former deals with this "process" mostly in terms of its being a creative (or disintegrative) interlude between the "beginning" and the "end" of the cycle, of which the "process" is the middle—as we saw in the first part of this chapter.

We shall define the term "personality" as the exteriorization of the ever-changing pattern produced by the interplay of collective and individual in the whole human entity (body and psyche). It represents the daily "balance-sheet" of the "process" of living—a balance-sheet which, with many of us, remains in the red most insistently! The personality is therefore the human being as it appears from day to day, with its behavior, thoughts and feelings. It is the "front" which the total man presents to the outer world. Back of it are the numerous currents and conflicts of unconscious and conscious, the bodily as well as psychological tendencies; all of which are more or less amalgamated in that complex of representations, the personality. Many cases are possible according as the emphasis is laid on this or that factor in the life-process of the total being. The center or ruler of the personality may

156

be the conscious ego, if and when individual values dominate; but it may just as well be a "primordial image" of the unconscious, or a powerful instinct. Fear or sex can and often do rule our personality; or the yearning for utter surrender to a "primordial image," or a "god"—or a spook.

The personality, near the end of the true process of individuation, is fully integrated by and centered around the Self. At the very dawn of the process, the personality is normally divided into two parts: the physiological part ruled by instincts and inherited impulses (or the power of the environment), and the psycho-mental part, which is potential rather than actual, and one with the monad and "primordial images." This stage is that of primordial man, a bodily animal and a "spiritual" psyche. Thus we find in him both the finest devotional aspirations and the most violent instinctual passions— natural, not individualized or neutralized passions. At a later stage, and for various reasons, the personality may split off into "partial souls": we have cases of double or multiple personality operating in and through one body.

The process of development of the personality is analogical to the *Kundalini* process, insofar as we deal in both cases with the progressive shift of the balance of individual and collective forces, toward integration or disintegration. But strictly speaking, the *"raising of Kundalini"* is an occult process—in a sense, a forced process; hence, the great danger involved in it. In the new psychological sense, the process is that of individuation (in Jung's sense); and it presupposes at the start a conscious development of the psyche, a relatively strong emphasis on the individual ego. For this ego is the *focal point* for the assimilation of the collective energies. Without such a focal point, and a strong one, the inflow of collective energies would overwhelm the consciousness, and the splitting off of the personality would undoubtedly occur. It would be a case of putting a dynamite-like gasoline into a weakly built automobile engine. The engine would explode. It is therefore necessary to build first a strong individual engine, steel-like in its resistance and resilience, before pouring in it collective energies. In other words: one does not feed meat to babes!

We shall interpret this astrologically when we study the effects of such planets as Uranus, Neptune and Pluto, which symbolize collective or unconscious forces. Unless the individual ego of the native is strong, these forces are bound to be destructive of the unity of the personality. Otherwise they act as high-powered gasoline in Rolls-Royce engines. The functioning is formidably enhanced. We shall see also that the pattern constituted by all the planets represents the personality—the balance-sheet of the collective-individual relationship. This balance-sheet is not a static one: thus the idea of "progressions"—in this case, *secondary* progressions. These measure the movements of the balance-sheet throughout the life. The progression of the axes of the chart refers to the development of the individual factors; the planetary "transits" refer to the strictly collective factors. But of this, more later.

Complexes and in general what Jung calls "the personal unconscious" (the Freudian "unconscious" also) are the manifestations of a balance at least temporarily "in the red," the results of the inability to relate integratively and properly to adjust collective and individual. (Inherited tendencies toward such maladjustments are shown in *retrograde* planets. The relationship between the planetary pattern—especially the Sun—and the two axes of the birth-chart indicate future potentialities of successful or unsuccessful adjustment.)

The adjustment of collective to individual, and vice versa, is the psychological "marriage." The individual *per se* is solely an abstract structure—a formula. It must be filled with life and light—with collective elements. In the first stage of the process of development of the personality, "life" flows in; viz., the generic energies of the physiological nature. As psycho-mental growth really begins and the conscious ego asserts itself, it is "light" that should flow into the abstract structure of individual selfhood. By "light" is meant the essence of civilization—in the spiritual sense of the term; the synthesis of the gift of all truly creative individuals to mankind as a whole.

Out of this "light" is built the permanent psycho-mental organism of the individual human being: the synthesis and Seed of a whole cycle of life-development—the "Diamond Body." This strictly individual body (which is presumably what theosophical teachings call the "Causal Body") is what we would call the "Soul." The vast majority of men are only *potential Souls*. The structure or form is there inasmuch and insofar as they function as "individuals"; but there is usually very little in this structure; and so we would say that the Soul is only potential. It does not function as an "organism." There is no real actual vitality in it. The Light does not shine, because the mystic "Circulation of the Light" (cf. *The Secret of the Golden Flower*) does not yet operate.

It is only when the monad (the God-in-beginning)—which had, in a sense, become the life-process (or personality)—is reborn within the structure of the individual conscious ego, that the Soul begins to function as an actual organism. Before that, it was only the remembrance or reminiscence of the monad,—the ancient and primordial Archtetype, "watching," as it were, from the deepest within or the highest above— which seemed to be the Soul. But it is only as the Monad-of-the-beginning is reborn within the ego as the Self-of-the-end that the Soul becomes an actual organism of psycho-mental substance, vibrating with light—as the physiological organism pulsates with blood.

As this occurs the ego "loses itself" into the Self. But this is obviously no loss. The ego was merely the center of the phase of individual differentiation—somewhat like a scaffolding. As the Self assimilates fully the collective energies it becomes the whole of the psyche. The distinction between unconscious and conscious ceases (at least as far as this cycle is concerned). Man becomes totally conscious: an Awakened One—a buddha (figuratively speaking). He need not give himself up to the unconscious in sleep, or even in death. The body may disintegrate; but as the individual has now built his "body of immortality" made out of psycho-mental substance, he will not lose his individual selfhood—*as long as mankind lives*. For, remember, this psycho-mental substance is made up of the essence of human civilization; it is made up of the "light of Man-the-whole" and can last only as long as Man-the-whole lasts.

Thus the merely-individual ego becomes the individual-plus-collective Self, a focalized expression and an agent of Man-the-whole. The light of Man-the-whole is the very substance of his being—and it may even radiate as a particular vibration down to and out of the physical body. But this light becomes differentiated according to the type of individual selfhood structurally conditioning and focalizing it—which, in turn, depends on the original monad. Thus the occultist speaks of "Seven Rays": seven large groups of monads in the beginning (and Souls or Selves after individuation) which are to the spiritual reality of Man-the-whole what colors are to the white light.

What must be stressed is, first, that the *fundamental structure* of the individual selfhood is not changed as the ego becomes the Self and individuation is reached. It becomes filled with light. Then, we must grasp the difference between, on one hand, the personality who becomes ruled by an entitized "primordial image" or "god," and acts as a mere medium; and on the other, the individuated being who becomes, as a Self, an *individual focus* for Man-the-whole—an operative agent with a *work* to perform in terms of the activity and the need of the whole. The wisdom of the former is always more or less separative (even where it appears to unify); the wisdom of the latter is a focalized expression of the wisdom and civilization of the whole of past and present mankind, *differenti-*

ated only for a particular and conscious use. The realm of the conscious is that of opinions and of theories. The realm of the unconscious is that of instincts, of the immediate and incontrovertible feeling-apprehension of needs. The realm of Self is that of consciously self-evident truths, perceived unanimously by all those who are fully one with the ultimate Whole:—The Seed-men (in Sanskrit, *Shistas*) who constitute in their sum total the God-of-the-end; not a single entity, but a unanimous Host, to whom some fifteen years ago we gave the name of *Synanthropy.*

Summing-up

It may be well at this point to go over the ground which we have covered so far; after which it will be easier to draw this chapter to a close with a very brief sketch of some of the possibilities of extension and application of our cyclic Formula.

First of all, we inferred that, as the philosophy of Time, which is the necessary background to a vital and holistic presentation of astrology, finds its expression essentially in two factors: viz., the Moment and the Cycle; and as, moreover, we had already discussed in the two preceding chapters the creative essence of the moment—therefore our task was to study the Cycle. We then stated that, in past civilizations, formulas defining the essence and structure of the Cycle had been produced; and that such formulas, based as they were upon the respective characteristic world-viewpoints of the civilizations considered, served as quasi-algebraic means of integrating all the knowledge possessed by such civilizations. We analyzed briefly the essence of the Cycle, and isolated the three terms which in their trinity constitute its wholeness: *beginning, middle, end*—or the One-that-is-in-the-beginning, the process of becoming, the Seed-Synthesis of the End. We found that three basic types of world-viewpoints could be determined, each of which emphasizes one of the three components of the Cycle, and we studied briefly the cyclic Formulas which expressed the typical world-viewpoint of Hindu civilization, with its devotional emphasis on the monad or original One, and of the Chinese civilization, with its ethical emphasis on the dualistc process of becoming which, under the condition of equilibratedness, becomes the "conscious Way" that is *Tao*, the Way that leads to fulfillment in and through perfect Harmony.

We then defined the three terms of the new cyclic Formula: *individual, collective and creative*; and their inter-relationship at the various stages of the cycle. We emphasized especially the view which considers the Cycle as a process leading from the "lesser individual" to the "Greater Individual" through the operation of the creative, releasing collective elements which become integrated into the larger synthesis which is the substantial foundation of the "Greater Individual"—who in turn projects creatively the monadic structures of the future "lesser individuals."

Complexity arises because the creative operates in several ways according as this or that phase of the total Cycle is considered. Thus it may refer to various subsequent factors, which may not appear at first to be analogical. In order to bring the matter of the creative to a psychological focalization, we discussed various types of "creative integration," through which the conflict between individual and collective is solved. The concept of "personality" as the balance-sheet of individual and collective tendencies, also as the creative whole of the harmonized human being; the concept of *Kundalini* as the physio-psychological process through which the generic or collective centers of the body and the individual or conscious centers of the cerebro-spinal system are integrated;— the concept of "individuation" as presented by Jung, viz., as a series of assimilations by the conscious ego of unconscious life-contents . . . these and many others refer to the basic term: the creative.

Whereas we spoke of the end of the cycle as the moment of summation and synthesis, we must also realize that it is the phase of the greatest manifestation of the creative. In another sense the creative is that factor which links the end and the beginning of all cycles. And as cycles are within cycles, *every moment can be considered as that creative moment when the end of a cycle gives birth to the beginning of a new cycle.* This is the Creative Now—living in which, man becomes god-like, an agent for the creativeness of the "Greater Individual" who, at the limit, is the universal God—the Supreme Wholeness of the absolute Whole.

We may bring this chapter to a close by adding that the three terms of the Cyclic Formula (individual, collective, creative) as well as the three phases of the Cycle (beginning, middle and end) can readily be correlated with three basic types of human beings—and also with three fundamental types of attitude to the universe and its problems, i.e., three fundamental types of knowledge.

The typical *devotee* looks back to the One-that-is-in-the-beginning. He yearns for unity; but this yearning takes the form of a longing for the glorious and spiritual past, for the Golden Age which is the first period of the cycle, when the "first-born"—the divine Ancestors—lived, still bathed in the glowing remembrance of the One. By worship and concentration the devotee preserves the Image of this One. Thus he keeps alive not only the memory of the Original Source, but, as a result, also the fact of the life-process being a monistic, because rooted-in-a-One, process.

The *scientist* and the *psychologist* (also the philosopher of the Bergsonian type) study the process and attempt either to bring order into its apparent confusion or to help men to go safely through it until the end is reached—the nature of which they only surmise by general inference. The occultist, if he be a true one, is a combination of devotee and scientist. Because he knows in varying degrees the reality and form of the One-in-the-beginning or Monad, he can also know the result of the process which will have for its consummation the integrated sum total uniting in an organic synthesis the successful fruits of the entire process.

The *artist* and the *philosopher*, in different ways, are operating in terms of this ideal of consummation; the former by producing works of art which are prophetic symbols of the organic synthesis of the Last Day; the latter by presenting to men pictures of the goal, purpose and significance of the whole life-process.

The devotee merges with the original One—who is the "Greater Individual," his Creator, his Father-Mother; this merging, when not direct, is accomplished through the intermediary of *guru*, spiritual teacher, priest or hierophant—who are supposed to have accomplished such an identification with the original One. The scientist—in a positive, analytical way—and the ordinary toiler—in a passive, helpless way—deal with the process of becoming; the latter being truly immerged in and a tool of it. As for the creative personality—whether creative of forms or creative of meanings—such a one gathers into and within himself the needs and the yearnings of the collective and fulfills them creatively, uttering prophetically that which will become the seed and archetype of the next phase of the cycle—the next "Dispensation."

The Three Great Approaches to Knowledge

A similar analysis can be made concerning the three basic approaches to knowledge. Usually such approaches would probably be defined as religion, science and philosophy. We believe, however, that in the future the new—and undoubtedly to most people very puzzling—classification should be: the *astrological*, the *psychological* and the *esthetical* approaches. We shall define these terms as follows:

The astrological approach deals with the beginning of all

things and of all cycles. The psychological approach refers to the study of the life-process—the so-called "middle" of all cycles, the world of change. The esthetical approach deals with the ultimate significance and ultimate synthesis of all that is.

Such a new classification may be justified by the fact that during the last thirty years religion, science, philosophy have experienced deep and vital transformations. Religion, insofar as it is a practical approach to life based on unity and identification with the life of "God," should refer to the Monad, to the beginning and principle of all things. Science is of course attempting to analyze and discover the laws of the world-process of change, of universal life and its myriads of transformations. We claim, though this is not the place to try to substantiate such a claim, that science will have to use more and more psychological methods as it finds that atoms and universes behave more and more like personalities. Psychology, by the use of scientific methods, is being prepared for the task of "assimilating" the collective data of modern science. As for philosophy, we believe that its real function is to reveal the ultimate significance of all things and all processes, and to lead to the great synthesis of the end of the cycle—to the Wisdom that is the sum total, quintessence and perfume of all civilization—to the Beautiful. For Beauty is the supreme "body of significance," the body of glory and perfection.

By the foregoing we do not mean that astrology will turn into a "religion of the stars." Far from it—we hope! What we mean is that in its search for the "first Cause" (that is, for the God-of-the-beginning or the universal Monad) religion will use a method and a basis of thought not unlike those on which a revaluated astrology will be founded. The birth-chart of Humanity may eventually be a known fact; and when the cycles of precession of the equinoxes, and other large cycles are really studied, man may be able to behold the symbol of his generic being and destiny—the Archetype of Man. To behold this Archetype has always been held to be one of the experiences of that mysterious process called by the true occultists "initiation." But even initiation may become an experience of Man-the-whole; and as this occurs "the old-fashioned religion" will evidently become worthless. *A symbolic intuition* of the reality and destiny of Man, and perhaps of our entire solar system (at least from the human standpoint) may then become possible. This would be "religion"—and at the same time the highest possible form of astrology. Our work is polarized toward this distant goal. First, we must learn to know the archetypal symbol of every human being and destiny. Then, our children or great-grandchildren may glimpse some day the Archetype of Man-the-whole—not in mystical ecstasy or through occult initiations, but in the clear and individual consciousness of a mind fully awakened to the reality of symbols and one with the Self. A mind "pellucid as crystal," the mind of fully individuated Personalities—of Seed-Men.

In closing, we shall add that the dualism of individual and collective—and its reconciling operative principle, the creative —can be traced at the roots of most, and possibly all, philosophical and psychological problems. Our claim is that it could serve as a basic formula underlying the more specialized formulas of all branches of knowledge, and thus as the keystone of an attempt at universal integration.

The relationship of individual to collective is obviously the foundation of all the branches of the science and art of social organization—including politics, sociology, jurisprudence, and, we would add, economics. In all of these fields the goal is a satisfactory adjustment of individual and collectivity, of the respective rights and duty of the individual and the State. In economics, the basic specialized dualism is that of production and consumption; but an equally important factor is distribution. Consumption is a species of individuation; distribution, of collectivation; production standing here for the creative. All economic ills come from the undue relative prominence of one or two of these factors; in some cases, as at the present, a crisis is really caused by an over-stimulation of all three factors and their operation at a new level. The advent of machines caused a deep change in the *vital meaning of "production"*—or work. Thus humanity has to readjust itself to a new concept of the significance of work—from the physiological-muscular to the mental level. To grasp this is, we believe, to grasp the whole pattern of social changes since the eighteenth century.

Democracy was of course a novel emphasis on the individual factor in human society; but because the creative duty and responsibility of the individual was not properly stressed, the individual factor dominated unduly in the attitude of "rugged individualism" and individual profit at the expense of proper collectivation (distribution of goods); thus trusts and monopolies came to exist. In reaction against the individual's predominance, we see, in Communism, Fascism, Nazism the stressing of collective and generic factors.

The emphasis on the creative is found in such movements as those for the use of leisure, for community music, and for all those activities which reconcile individual and collectivity. Modern law is also being founded on a new concept of the relation of the individual to the collective, shifting to the collectivity much of the guilt which once belonged exclusively to the individual, and emphasizing the value of the creative—even in jails.

In the study of history the same shift is clearly recognizable, and individual heroes give way to collective trends, to economics and to the significance of this or that type of work and production. On the other hand, the collectivating tendencies of later years react in mass psychology by making biographies the most popular among books. The study of past cultures shows an alternation of individual and collective emphasis. Alexandria follows Athens, Christianity the Greek culture. From the broadest possible standpoint we might say that in old Asia, India represents the individual focus; China, the collective; Indo-China (Khmer civilization especially), the creative.

Such generalizations are evidently dangerous; but they may bring to man a sense of order and a broad vision which are of great value psychologically, and which are needed to compensate the attitude and mentality of the man lost in the analysis of minute phenomena within the endless and apparently formless tide of change. Form comes only from the perception of beginnings of cycles, and from the intuition of their ultimate goal and significance.

Perhaps the most fascinating instance of the application of the principle of relationship inherent in the trinity of individual, creative and collective is, however, to be found in the new physics. We refer especially to the dualism of wave and particle which seems to be the essence of light as well as of matter (photons and electrons). We consider light as representing the creative. Time-Space-Light parallel Individual-Collective-Creative, as we have already seen. The unit of light, the photon, acts under certain conditions as wave, under others as particle. The photon is the unit of release of energy —which refers obviously to the creative. Interestingly enough, all occult philosophies speak of the primordial Light, and of the human monads as sparkles within this Light. Thus photons. "*Fohat*," in Tibet, is the name of the universal Creative, whose primordial emanation is Light.

The atom is constituted by a nucleus and circling electrons. At first it was thought that the nucleus was strictly positive and the electrons negative. But this old *Yang-Yin* dualism is giving way to a new kind: the nucleus represents the collective, the electron, the individual. The photon is the creative, and the quantum the law of creative emanation. Once released, the unit of energy deteriorates into various types of rays, just as the emanated image, or idea, becomes a collective element assimilated by other units. It may be that such a formulation is not the correct one, and that intra-atomic physics is still to a large extent *terra incognita*. Yet we believe that the basic dualism which we present can find its place as a philosophical (ultimate) interpretation of atomic structure.

Another important point is that the new physics seems, at least, to lead us to infer that no science of the individual is possible, only statistical science of groups. It may even be better to say, science of the interaction of individual and group—which is what we called the life-process. All empirical science, we believe, deals with, and deals only with, the life-process—and the essence of this process is the constant adjustment of individual and collective. In this sense, the life-process deals always with "personalities"—that is, balance-sheets. Our universe is a credit universe. Death is bankruptcy. Entropy and the "running down of the universe" are concepts of the Depression!

We could go on and on dealing with similar philosophical interpretations; but space (the collective preoccupation!) forbids us this (individual) pleasure. As a last thought, and as a fitting *coda* to a study which dealt primarily with the establishment of a universal Formula of the Cycle, we shall refer the reader to the beautiful archaic invocation heard throughout Tibet: OM MANI PADME HUM. This "magical formula" is a formula of the whole life-process, as sketched out in this chapter. OM is the monad of the beginning—the Original Impulse of the cycle. MANI refers to the creative mind, to that central "jewel" which is the creative principle. PADME means "lotus," and symbolizes completion, synthesis, individuation, the brotherhood of the end from which emanates "perfume" or the quintessence of the life-process—in a sense, consciousness. HUM is the emanated perfume, the withdrawal of the completed body into the quintessence and the abstract. In all 14, or twice 7 letters; 7 being the number of the life-process—which is twofold.

Thus: *OM, the Jewel within the Lotus, HUM!* That is: In the One arises the Creative; and through the operation of the Creative, the collective is gathered into the synthesis; and from the synthesis, emanates the quintessence, the Idea, whose energy is again the One.

IV. A Key to Astrological Symbolism

AS WE come to consider more specifically and practically the field of astrological symbolism, as we study the significance of its many elements, we shall find that the concepts presented in the preceding chapters will enable us to interpret in a consistent, logical and natural manner the sequence of astrological factors. Especially shall we find that the opposition between individual and collective is the most wonderful key to the vital and practical understanding of astrological elements, which are usually produced in pairs of opposite polarities. At first, astrology may appear as a thoroughly dualistic system, very much like the Chinese system of the *Yi King*. But it will be easy for us to point out that behind this obvious dualism there is always to be found a third term, integrating the opposites. And this is perhaps the most important point in this re-formulation of astrology: That it consistently reveals a way to integration, a factor of individual significance which, if creatively used, can lead us to see the wholeness of any whole, the flash of creative light which alone can integrate the opposites, and thus make them significant.

Signatures and Significant Facts

"To make significant" is to visualize each and all situations or entities which one meets as signs of the workings of Spirit. In each of the smallest details of the world-pattern one may see at work the Wholeness of the whole; one may sense all the basic forces which are the warp and woof of the life-cycle, of any life-cycle. In any situation, in any organic entity, all

171

these forces operate; just as every moment is the synthesis of all past moments and the source of all future moments. The whole is active everywhere.

But how to see this action? How to penetrate the "veil of illusion" which covers every separate entity and seems to make of it something unrelated to all the rest? How to get at the interior pattern, the *particular arrangement of universal elements* which is the "real" being? What is implied in this is the power to deal with situations or living entities as wholes; a power to which we have already referred. It is instinct at the unconscious level. It is intuition, or holistic perception, or "clair-seeing" (*not* ordinary clairvoyance!) at the conscious level. It is the power to see universal life-patterns at work in the functioning of particular organisms or processes.

In every man—for instance—individual, collective and creative operate, but of course in most varied proportions. An ordinary onlooker is attracted by the apparently unique outer result of the blend. He is unable to analyze the forces at work, to grasp the significance of their combination. The man is just Mr. So-and-So. The "seer" sees in this man a special focalization of a number of basic life-principles, and he is able to "place" every life-principle where it belongs, tracing back his ancestry by implications, grasping at once the sum total of the man's connections with the universal whole. He sees thus the significance of the man; and besides, he sees also the significance of the man's relation to him.

Instinct gives all this knowledge to the animal who acts accordingly—yet does not know why he acts. Everything for the animal carries a life-significance. It is the sign of some basic fact of life. These facts are few, yet where they are concerned the animal is "clair-seeing." Every feature of a situation or of a person is read as a "Signature" of the life which is focalized in and through it.

The medieval alchemists laid a great emphasis upon this theory of Signatures, following in that the old Chinese tradition—if not the universal tradition of archaic mankind. The form and features of plant, rock, tree, animal, face, etc., were considered as a Signature of the indwelling spirit. The alchemist was supposed to be an expert graphologist deciphering at once the Signature; from the Sign going straight to the life; from symbol, to reality.

The signature of a man is usually not legal unless it contains the *individual* first name, and the family (*collective*) name. It also contains usually some other characteristic or line which refers to the rhythm of the individual—that is, to the *creative* factor in him.

This, of course, is only an amusing symbol—many will say. Truly, but why "only" a symbol? It is by perceiving the value of such symbols that life is made significant. Every object and every situation become signs of the sum total of connections relating object and situation to the universal whole. The attention given by man to such an object at once focalizes in it the whole life-process. The drama of universal life is seen performed on that tiny stage, which thus becomes a microcosm—an image of the whole.

Again, it is the same thing that occurs in a truly instinctual action. The actor is not merely one puny little animal. It is the whole animal species, and behind it the whole planetary being, that acts. The whole of life is focalized in an instinctual performance: depth and depth of significance—but no consciousness *to see it as significant*. It is natural—but not significant, until man arrives on the stage and "sees" in it the Signature of eternal and universal principles.

As we shall see, time after time, an astrological birth-chart is a true Signature—and must be read as such. One must find in it the individual and the collective names—plus the sign of the creative. But now we have not yet come to the point of discussing chart-interpretation. There is, before we reach this point, another Signature to decipher: the Signature of the Earth-being.

The Earth is the Signature of that planetary Whole in which men "live and have their being" as mere cells of a vast body. All collective—or rather generic—values in man come from the Earth. It may be that the Earth is the body of a cosmic Spiritual entity, the Planetary Logos (as occultists call Him). But for all that we know and as far as we can ascertain facts, the Earth is to be considered as the vast matrix of Man-the-whole. Mankind spreads all over the globe. To understand the Earth is to understand mankind. As every single human being is a representative of mankind, then the first thing to do, before we can hope to understand a particular man in terms of universal connections and principles, is to understand the Earth. The Earth as a Signature. We must read every letter of the names and understand all the facts of the Earth. They must become significant to us. How the Earth moves, its positions, its speed, its connections with all that moves around it, its relation to the Sun whence it apparently came: All these things must become Signatures. Astrology is to be made of all these *significant facts* of the Earth. It cannot leave the Earth, for that would be leaving the realm of facts. And *astrology deals only with facts*—but facts that are seen as Signatures of the life of the Earth.

There are evidently many kinds of facts. The astrologer, being *originally* a "seer," will be able to see clearly what facts have life significance, what facts are purely superficial. Moreover, astrology being only one of many possible systems of life-symbolism can operate only through a certain category of facts. These facts are first of all those which affect or are experienceable by human beings living on the surface of the globe. No fact is susceptible of being a Signature for man unless man can experience it and actually see it, directly or indirectly. For instance, Uranus and Neptune had no value as Signatures until men *saw* them. If there are planets besides those we know now, they have no meaning for us, as long as they are not facts to be experienced, whether with the naked eye or through a telescope. Nothing can be a symbol unless it has become the object of a significant experience.

This being understood, we shall begin to study the category of facts of the Earth-life which are the most significant to mankind. These facts—such as seasons, climates, etc.—are all the results of the various motions of the Earth. These motions will prove to be the material on which astrology draws for its symbolism. Each motion will be seen as the Signature of one of the most fundamental principles of life and being.

Motion: Subjective and Objective

We have repeatedly established the proposition that astrology is the algebra of life. What may as yet not have received enough attention is the fact that essentially *life is cyclic motion*. In preceding chapters we spoke of the trinity of time, space and light; and under the term "light" we included all energies which essentially constitute "life." Light and life are, philosophically as well as practically, synonymous. Underneath both we can perceive, by a further process of abstraction, the element of motion. Motion, space and time constitute an old metaphysical trinity, which is as fundamental as can ever be conceived. "Being" is the synthesis of all three. But what we call more particularly "life" is symbolized by the element of motion. In ancient symbolism, this motion that is Life was referred to as the "Great Breath," the in- and out-breathing of Brahma, the Creator. But in our present astrological symbolism we are dealing with another kind of dualism of motion.

All motions necessitate actually space and time. Yet, philosophically speaking, it is necessary to distinguish between two types of motion: Motion which does not involve displacement of the center of the being, and motion which does involve such a displacement. These two types are simple to recognize, when thus described, as we find them exemplified most obviously in the behavior of celestial bodies. Every planet rotates around its axis (first type) and circles around the sun (second type). These two types give us a new dualism of life-direction, and it fits in most logically with our dualism of individual and collective.

The first type of motion can be called "*motion in time*," or "*subjective motion*," as it does not create any change of location of the body as a whole. It is motion within the confines of the self; thus, by extension, interior or subjective motion. It symbolizes inner changes, and what Bergson calls real time or duration—the series of modifications of interior states of consciousness. It refers to subjective being, to the individual.

The second type of motion, on the other hand, is definitely "*motion in space*," or "*objective motion*," as it brings about change in location and displacement of the center of the being. It is visible, tangible motion through space. Space, as we saw in a previous chapter, is a framework for the interplay of relationships of parts within a whole. It is the substratum for all relationships, for all interchanges. Through motion in space, through actual displacement of one's own center, one relates oneself to others, one gains concrete, objective experiences of others, one also becomes aware of the reality of the larger collective whole of which one is but a part.

Thus we have exemplified in the main motions of celestial bodies our dualism of individual and collective. Our "algebra of life" will use these two types of motion as the very foundation for its symbolism. Axial rotation and orbital revolution will be the two pillars upon which the temple of astrological symbolism will rest—a temple of Doric simplicity, once it is understood in its balanced wholeness and in the logic of its construction. Astrology is *a study in significant motion*. It symbolically interprets the motions of celestial bodies and relates them to the movements of the life-force within all organisms and all cycles. These movements of the life-force are represented both by a series of states of consciousness and by a series of organic events; by what happens within the individual, and by occurrences having significance in terms of the collective.

The basis of this study in significant motion is of course the Earth; the Earth not so much as a material object, but rather as the symbol of Man, the interpreter and symbolizer. Astrology, as we present it, is necessarily "anthropocentric," that is, centered around Man. It is an effort made by Man to reduce the bewildering maze of life-appearances into complex series of ordered and cyclic motions. Astrology in its deeper aspect is that effort of Man to give to Nature, within as well as without, the meaning of order, of cosmos. All sciences, of course, work toward this goal. But astrology, which very likely antedates them all, pursues the goal in a broader and more structural way than any other method of thought, because it is not a mere science, tabulating facts; but is also a philosophy interpreting these facts in terms of ideas—and an art applying the interpretations to individual cases.

Every type of creative interpretation must be centered around the interpreter. The individual is the foundation for all creative interpretation. In astrology everything consequently is referred to the point, in time and space, of the observer, or of the native. A birth-chart is the universe seen from the point, in time and space, of the birth-event. The native whose birth-chart is interpreted is seen at the center of his own universe. The fact of birth, its position in space and its moment in time, creates a universe around itself. Every factor of interpretation revolves around this birth-fact.

As men live on the whole surface of the Earth, and not merely at one spot on the globe, the Earth as a whole has to be considered the symbol of Man. The rhythms of the Earth motions will be used to symbolize the rhythms of the *generic* human being. On the other hand, an *individual* man is born at a particular point of the Earth surface; and therefore, while generic mankind is not affected by the axial rotation of the Earth, the individual selfhood of a particular man will be determined in function of this very axial rotation. In other words, there is no day or night (the results of axial rotation) for mankind as a whole, as it is always day for one half of mankind and night for the other half. But there is day and night for a particular man occupying a particular place on the surface of the globe. On the other hand, the relationship (aspects) of the Earth to the other planets of the system have exactly the same significance for collective Man and for any individual man, except that the position of the individual man on the globe's surface will focalize these aspects in a section of *his own* heavens either below or above the horizon, and more precisely in what astrology calls one of the "houses."

Thus all values which deal with the individual and his problems of consciousness as an individual will be referred symbolically to the axial rotation of the Earth and to the astrological factors created thereby, mainly the circle of houses and its two axes, vertical and horizontal. On the other hand, collective values which pertain to the behavior of man as a racial and generic being will be referred to the orbital yearly revolution of the Earth around the Sun. It is this orbital revolution which constantly alters the relationship of the Earth to the Sun and to the planets. As the latter also revolve around the Sun, a complex pattern of planetary motions and of consequent relationships is produced. It is in order to be able to chart such a constantly changing pattern that the idea of the "zodiac" originated, or at least is to be used in an astrology reformulated at an abstract and symbolic level. The zodiac becomes thus a series of points of references which enables us to plot accurately the position of all planets and of the Sun *in relation to the orbital motion of the Earth*. It is this motion which creates the cycle of the year.

A Key to Astrological Symbolism

Day and Year—Individual and Collective

The collective meaning of the year-cycle will be more evident if we realize that because of the inclination of the Earth's axis (which is not perpendicular to the Earth's orbit) the angle of incidence of the Sun rays varies throughout the year, causing the change of seasons. Seasons and climates affect the collective being and consciousness of human races and groups. They affect the growth and development of bodies and of all physiological elements—which belong to the collective realm.

The year-cycle is truly of great importance in the development of the individual; but it is so mostly in terms of the physiological growth or decay of the earthly body, in terms of periodical modifications of the vital forces of the body. The vegetable and animal energies in man are subjected to it —especially the former, as the latter are even more strongly connected perhaps with the lunar tides. The Great Sympathetic nervous system dominated by the solar plexus is strongly influenced by this yearly rhythm, which also affects the inflow of the energies of the "collective unconscious" into the conscious.

It could be added that, as the Bible says, a day of the Lord is like unto a human year. This means that the Lord (the collective Race-spirit: Jehovah) finds his unit-cycle of individual selfhood in the year. For the collective consciousness of Man-the-whole the orbital revolution of the Earth around the Sun means a "day." The "day" is always the unit of selfhood. The self of collective Man operates through a basic unit: the orbital cycle. The self of an individual man operates through a basic unit: the axial-rotation cycle.

The Great Polar Cycle

Besides these, there is another basic cycle: the cycle of the precession of the equinoxes. It should rather be called the "Great Polar Cycle." It is created by a peculiar gyrating mo-

179

tion of the Earth's axis, which can be compared to the motion of a schoolboy's top. This gyrating motion changes very slowly the direction of the polar axis, and consequently the points where the Earth's equator cuts the plane of the ecliptic (the apparent yearly path of the Sun). Thus on one hand the North Pole points successively to a series of stars, describing a complete circle in about 25,868 years; on the other, the vernal point (Spring Equinox) shifts backwards among the constellations (thus the term "precession of the equinoxes") along the circle of the ecliptic.

The important fact, however, is that the polar axis of the Earth points to one star after another. The Pole Star changes: now it is Polaris in the constellation Ursa Minor, but in 5,000 years it will be Alpha Cephei. According to astronomical-telluric facts, the North and South poles of the earth represent respectively the ingress and egress of cosmic magnetic energies. Interpreting this, esoteric tradition has always referred to the North Pole as the gates through which cosmic Power flowed into the Earth, and as the symbol of divine Consciousness. In this, very likely, a simile was established between the polar axis of the Earth and man's spine, which is the "rod of power" through which the energy of spirit operates within man. The North Pole corresponds then to the top of the head, to the mysterious center which, when fully functioning in perfected men, is surrounded with a sort of halo—not unlike the Northern Lights at their best.

To say that this "rod of power" of the Earth alters its direction is to say that the *quality* of cosmic power received by the Earth changes cyclically, following the gyrating motion of the Earth's axis. Now, the interesting point is that this gyration does not mean a displacement of the center of the Earth. It belongs thus to our first category of "motion in time" or "subjective motion." But the "subject" here involved is the Individual whose physical center is one with the center of the Earth, that is to say, the great planetary Whole already spoken of. The polar axis, symbolically at least, is the "I AM" of this great planetary Whole. As it moves about, it changes its relation to stars with which it appears to be connected. In other words, the very selfhood of the planetary Whole modifies itself, attunes itself to different cosmic tones. These changes of planetary selfhood constitute the reality of what we call "Piscean Age," "Aquarian Age," etc., by reference to the precession of the equinoxes—a secondary effect, not a cause.

Thus the "day" is the unit-cycle of individual man, a denizen of the surface of this globe which must rotate to have all its points illumined daily by the noon-sun (save the polar regions). The "year" is the unit-cycle of collective Man, an aggregate of beings spread all around the surface of the globe. The "Great Polar Cycle" is the unit-cycle of the planetary Individual, whose center is one with the center of the Earth.*

With this last cycle we deal with what might be called the cosmically Creative. Every "Age," such as the Piscean Age, starts with a release of cosmic creative powers which become the collectivated materials which men will use for the building of civilizations. It is by considering this that we may better understand the two ways in which this gyration of the Earth's axis operates. Changing the Pole Star means changing the direction of the axis proper—which is one thing. Another

---

* The following is a clear scientific statement of the causes of precession (and of polar gyration):

"This peculiar behavior of the earth's equator (precession) is due to the gravitation of sun and moon upon the bulging equatorial belt or zone of the earth, combined with the centrifugal force at the earth's equator. As equator stands at an inclination to ecliptic, this attraction tends, on the whole, to pull its protuberant ring toward the plane of the ecliptic itself. But the earth's turning on its axis prevents this, and the resultant effect is a very slow motion of precession at right angles to the direction of the attracting force, similar to that exemplified by attaching a small weight to the exterior ring of a gyroscope. Three causes contribute to produce precession: if the earth were a perfect sphere, or if its equator were in the same plane with its path round the sun (and with the lunar orbit), or if the earth had no rotation on its axis, there would be no precession."

A New Astronomy by David P. Todd

thing is changing the zodiacal location of the equinoxes. The former refers to the polar axis—axis of spiritual integration; the latter refers to the equator—circle or belt of physiological vitalization. This dualism of polar axis and equator is a most important one, and will be studied presently.

These two factors are ordinarily not clearly separated, and this may account for much of the confusion concerning the beginning of the "Aquarian Age." It may be that the polar axis in its motion has already become connected with the "new star" (or whatever it may be!) which symbolizes the *spiritual creative impulse* of the new era. And yet the Sun may not have yet reached, by precessional movement of the Equinoxes, the constellation Aquarius—which would refer to the *physiological vitalization and manifestation* of the creative impulse of the new era. In other words, while the spiritually creative impulse is already upon us, it may take a few more centuries before the vital forces building the outer structures of the new era operate fully.

For some peculiar reason (yet quite representative of the development of present-day mankind) we lay all the emphasis on the aspect of physiological manifestation—that which deals with the relation of the equator to the ecliptic—and we forget the spiritual creative aspect—that which deals with the motion of the polar axis. What we should study, and what the future occult astrology will study, is the circle described by the poles during the 25,868-year period—our "Great Polar Cycle."

Centers of Motion

In the foregoing we have dealt briefly with the three fundamental types of Earth-motion. One more important point must be made clear, which is that all cyclic motions (the only ones considered in life-symbolism) must gain their significance from the meaning attributed to the center of such motions. The daily rotation of the Earth has the polar axis of the Earth as its "center." The yearly revolution of the Earth is centered around the Sun.* As for the gyrating motion of the Earth's axis, it is actually centered around the *pole of the ecliptic*; that is to say, the exact perpendicular to the plane of the earth's orbit—an abstraction, but a significant one.

The abstract line connecting the two poles of the Earth is the axis of rotation of our planet. This axis is thus to be considered as the "center" of the daily-rotation cycle. As already mentioned, this polar axis symbolizes the line of power of the planet, just as the human spine represents the line of power of the human being. This "power" is the power to be an individual self, an "I." The polar axis is the line of manifestation of the I AM of the planet considered as a cosmic being. Through this line flows the power to be an individual self. In a general sense, it refers to the cerebro-spinal nerve-system. *Therefore* the cyclic motion of the Earth's globe around this axis *must* refer to the cyclic development of the individual selfhood of all beings living on the Earth-surface, or within the Earth's globe, and susceptible of being "individuals." This needs to be so because of the very principle of "holistic logic" —the logic of symbolism—which we discussed in our chapter "Astrology Faces Modern Thought."

In astrological symbolism this axial rotation of the Earth is charted by means of the circle or wheel of houses. The twelve houses are twelve phases of this daily motion of the Earth. As we said that such a motion should be considered as "subjective motion" or "motion in time," it follows that the circle of houses should be understood more specifically as the *dial* of a clock. This "dial of houses" refers thus more particularly to a sequential development—the development of man's individual selfhood throughout his life.

We must keep in mind that, philosophically speaking, what

---

* The orbit of the earth is elliptical. Thus the sun is only one of the two foci of the ellipse. One might attribute a symbolical meaning to the other focus, even though no physical entity is found there. But this would be too abstract for our present consideration.

makes this daily rotation necessary is the fact of the Earth being a vast globe of solid and opaque substance. As men live on the surface of this globe, they find their awareness of the universe (and of life in general) restricted to a half of its wholeness. The solid Earth shuts from our eyes half of the world of being. This fact at once becomes interpreted symbolically as the need for normal physical man to experience alternately a period of manifestation and one of non-manifestation. In terms of daily living this means waking consciousness and sleep.

Because the Earth shuts out from man's self half of the universe, the Earth must rotate in order to bring to every creature living on its surface each day a whole vision of the world. Thus at the moment of birth the wheel of the horoscope will represent a projection of this basic fact of consciousness. The lower half of the wheel will refer to what is below the Earth surface, the upper half to what is above. The horizontal axis of the chart is then actually the horizon—dividing the world of the living into two realms—visible and invisible; and, by extension, objective and subjective, exterior and interior.

This horizontal line of the birth-chart represents thus the fact of a necessary division of consciousness into two realms, for any individual living on the Earth's surface. But there is something else to take in consideration. Individual selfhood and consciousness are dependent for their very existence upon life and light. It is true that the universe is filled with stars whose rays penetrate the Earth. But unless one of these stars had become a focalized center of life and light for the Earth—a Sun—there could be no individual selfhood or consciousness upon the Earth.

Thus it should be clear that while the horizon and the horizontal line in the chart are expressions of the dualism of consciousness, there must be a point which will refer to the fact of the focalization of life and light through the Sun; for life and light are the necessary *sustainment* of consciousness. This point is obviously the noon-point. If the Earth rotates around its axis it is not only (from the anthropocentric point of view) so that every day man can be aware of the whole of the universe; but also so that he may be energized, every noon, by the direct inflow of solar life and light. As the Earth rotates, noon comes to every point of the globe, which is thus vitalized and illumined.

From this point of view one might say that what is involved in the fact of axial rotation is the impossibility for any whole to have all its parts energized at once by the life-force. Therefore there is need for succession or time. An illustration might make this more concrete. It takes time for the blood to circulate throughout the body, vitalizing all physiological functions and their organs. Such an analogy between the cycle of blood-circulation and the axial rotation of the Earth is not to be taken too literally; yet it has great significance. For just as it is by means of the blood-circulation that the life-force is *distributed* to all parts of the whole organism, so it is by means of the axial rotation that the life-force emanating from the Sun (symbol of the "heart") is distributed every day over the whole Earth.

We shall, later on, grasp the full significance of this word "distributed," but just now we wish merely to establish the basic meaning of the two axes of the circle of houses: the horizontal, representing the dualism of consciousness (subjective and objective, self and the others)—and the vertical, whose apex stands for the noon-point, the point of solar sustainment; also the point where the particular individual finds himself in the fullest possible connection with the vitalizing forces of universal being symbolized by the Sun.

At the horizon man sees himself as a purely *particular* being; but as he relates himself to the Sun, he absorbs life and becomes a partaker in *universal* being. The horizon (and especially the Eastern horizon: the Ascendant of the birth-chart) defines, limits, particularizes. The meridian or zenith (the Mid-Heaven of the birth-chart) vitalizes, collectivizes, universalizes.

This leads us to the study of the second motion of the Earth, its yearly revolution around the Sun. This motion is what gives birth to what is called the zodiac. As every cyclic motion takes on the significance of the center around which it occurs, it will be seen that the zodiac has the same fundamental meaning as the Sun—just as the circle of houses has the same fundamental meaning as the polar axis of the Earth. The significance of the Sun can be formulated in different ways, according to the level of interpretation. It is to be based, however, on these essential facts: It is the source of life and light for man; it is the father-mother of the solar system as a whole, the center of which it occupies.

On the first ground, the Sun represents the life-force. It is the vitalizing, integrating power which makes man whole, on every plane of being; which fructifies everything and brings every living organism to a point of creative fulfillment. On the second ground, the Sun represents the force that holds the entire solar system together. All inter-planetary relationships are thus made organic and significant in terms of the Sun; just as, in another way, the mutual relations between brothers and sisters are essentially significant in terms of their common origin—the mother and father. We might say also that as the complex pattern of inter-relationship linking all the glands and organs of the body is made significant in terms of the blood-stream—so the complex pattern of planetary relationships is made significant in terms of the circulation of the solar force, or by reference to the Sun, center of the system and lord of gravitation.

The zodiac gives us therefore first of all a picture of the cyclic unfoldment of the life-force, both in nature and in man; then it also provides us with a background for the development of the complex pattern of inter-planetary or intra-systemic relationships. In the first instance it represents the ebb and flow of the universal life-force throughout the year cycle. In the second instance it constitutes a system of co-ordinates which enables us to formulate at every moment the configuration of all the elements of the solar system . . . but always, of course, *from the point of view of the interpreter*, of man on this Earth—a point the capital importance of which will be revealed in the next chapter.

In early times, as we saw in our first chapter, the zodiac was simply a kind of agricultural calendar solemnly drawn by Initiate-Priests by order of the King or Emperor, charting the changes in the season. The apparent movement of the Sun was tabulated by checking it up on the permanent pattern of reference provided by the constellations. As the quality and intensity of the solar rays changed throughout the year, and it seemed that these changes corresponded with the successive conjunctions of the Sun with stars and groups of stars, the imaginative astrologers probably came to believe that the stars *did something* to the Sun which made it alter the quality and intensity of its rays. Thus when the Sun "entered" a constellation of the zodiac, its energies took on something of the nature of the constellation. The Sun came to be seen as a lens through which the mysterious power of constellations became focalized. Twelve great types of cosmic energies were thus described, and the solar life-force partook of the characteristics of each of these successively, month after month.

To the modern mind, however, it is clear that the solar force itself does not change because of the "influence" of constellations which in themselves are mere visual configurations linking stars whose distances and characteristics are often so varied as to preclude any possibility of there being a group-significance *to the constellation as such*. The zodiac is merely a symbolic device to define and measure the cyclic unfoldment of the life-force as it streams from Sun to Earth throughout the cycle of orbital revolution. What it helps to chart is the cyclic modifications of the relation Sun-to-Earth (that is, particular-to-universal; individual-to-collective). The significance of the zodiac is the significance of orbital motion. As already said, orbital motion in the solar system represents that type of motion which requires displacement of center; objective motion, motion which involves change of relationship in space. It is the motion of parts within an organic whole. Every whole is composed of parts which move in relation to each other and, in the most perfect systems (such as solar systems and atoms), in orbits around a common center.

Orbital motion is thus the rhythmical motion of relationship; whereas axial rotation represents the cycle of self-unfolding. The development of relationship requires displacement of center. But the unfolding of individual selfhood *per se* requires a process of, let us say, meditation or introspection. We compared, a while ago, the axial rotation of the earth to the cycle of blood-circulation. The circulation of blood does not involve displacement in space of the human organism as a whole. But all the activities of a man as he goes through his life in his home town involve displacement in space, because they refer to the working out of his relations to his fellow-men. These relationships cause him to move about, to go to his office, his club, his parents' home, etc.; and all these displacements could be plotted out on the more or less permanent background of the city's streets and buildings.

Likewise, the Earth's revolution around the Sun can be said to be motivated by the need to work out varying relationships between Earth and Sun, and Earth and other planets. Such a revolution can be plotted out on the more or less permanent background of the fixed stars, mapped out as constellations (city-blocks and streets of the universe!). When an astrologer says that the Sun is in Aries, he means that the relationship Sun-Earth can be located in reference to certain points of the skies. This location gives the relationship more or less accurately known characteristics; as, for instance, the fact that two business men meet in their office defines their contact in terms of business transactions, whereas if the contact occurred in a ballroom it would have another significance.

Stars are thus points of reference enabling the astrologer to plot out the curve of the changing Sun-Earth relationship, and of all planetary relationships. In the case of the Sun-Earth relationship the seasons might serve to define the phases of the relationship; but the position of the Sun with regard to the stars is a much more accurate way of determination—provided the phenomenon of the precession of the equinoxes is taken into account. This phenomenon shows that not only do men move about within the city, but the city itself alters its topography—for instance, a residential district becomes a business center, slums give way to mansions, or *vice versa*.

This illustration is obviously far from perfect; yet if it is not taken too literally it brings out something of the relative values of the three types of Earth-motion which we have studied. It remains, however, in order to complete this part of our work, for us to indicate the nature and significance of the "center" of the gyrating motion of the Earth's axis—the cause of the "Great Polar Cycle," or cycle of the precession of the equinoxes.

All that it will be necessary to say is that the Earth's axis gyrates around the *ideal axis* of the Earth: the line of the poles of the ecliptic—that is, a perpendicular to the plane of the Earth's orbit. The axes of the planets are inclined on the plane of their orbit, and they must all gyrate more or less as the Earth's axes do. When we deal with planetary axes we deal with something which is of opposite polarity to the Sun. The Sun is the collective center of the system. It relates all planets together. And the Sun's power is felt especially at the equator. The plane of the equator is the plane of the Sun's greatest action, the plane therefore along which the integrating forces of the Sun penetrate the Earth. It represents the maximum intensity of the collective energies of life. In man it refers to the Great Sympathetic nerve system dominated by the solar plexus, the center of racial instincts, and largely of the emotions.

On the other hand, the polar axis represents the most individual energies of the planetary life. Thus equatorial plane and polar axis symbolize opposites. It may be that the significant reason why the equatorial plane of the Earth does not coincide with the plane of the Earth's orbit (ecliptic) is in order that the collective power of the Sun may not be overfocalized and over-strong. But as a result of this, the polar axis is no longer perpendicular to the plane of the orbit, and therefore (in a philosophical sense) it must gyrate. It must direct itself successively to various stars; and it may be that by so doing the individualizing cosmic forces connected with the polar axis are strengthened and better able to balance the collective pull of the Sun.*

The pull of the Sun is to the Earth as the pull of the blood-consciousness and of the race-self to the individual attempting to function as an individual. It is like the mother-love which binds, and which often thwarts the unfoldment of the individual factors in the children. Thus, perhaps, the Earth is orientating its axis of individualization to stars, as the youthful individual to teachers beyond the circle of his family and home. Then, as there is no longer the unique dominating pull of the mother, there come in succession various teachers and inspirers who, each in his turn, awaken a particular quality or

---

* The angle formed by the plane of the Earth's equator and the plane of the ecliptic is not constant. It varies within about 2½ degrees limits, and the cycle of the variations appears to encompass approximately 40,000 years. This, of course, means also a change in the inclination of the Earth's axis; which also modifies the circle traced by the gyration of said axis. There are still other cyclic motions of the Earth and cyclic changes in the Earth's orbit. The eccentricity and the position of the lines of apsides of the latter are susceptible of cyclic variations of respectively about 250,000 and 21,000 years. All these slow motions refer to the planetary Being as a whole and to the progressive development of Man as a life-kingdom.

phase of individual selfhood. And this may be the meaning, in terms of the unfoldment of Man-the-Whole, of the "Great Polar Cycle." The polar gyration does not involve displacement of the center of the Earth. It is thus a subjective motion, but "subjective" in a planetary sense.

Before leaving this fascinating phase of astrology, we wish, however, to discuss briefly the problem of the division of this Polar Cycle. Here we have a complete cycle of motion of the Earth's axis, and the question arises: Shall we think of it as divided into twelve sections, as if it were a sort of "polar (i.e., spiritual creative) zodiac?" In all probability it ought not to be so divided. More likely, it should be divided into seven or seventy sections. The concrete reason for such a segmentation is that there is a natural division of the path of the poles, due to what is called "nutation." Nutation is a small and periodic swinging or vibration of the Earth's poles north and south, as they travel around the poles of the ecliptic. It is due to the periodical changes of position of the Moon, slightly altering the direction of the Moon's attraction upon the equatorial protuberance of the Earth. These periodical changes correspond to those of the Moon's nodes, which complete a cycle in an average of 18.6 years. Thus there are close to 1400 polar oscillations due to nutation within each Great Polar Cycle. The circle of polar motion is not a simple curve, but a wavy one. There being on an average close to 1400 such waves, this fact may help us to establish a natural segmentation of the circle of polar motion.

The number 14 is of course significant, being the number of days between new and full Moon, at least theoretically. It is twice 7, and occultists refer repeatedly to 7 Rays or phases of cosmic manifestation; also to 7 Races, sub-races, family-races—and similar planetary cycles. It seems logical to propose, then, a division of the Great Polar Cycle into 7 periods (and perhaps 70 sub-periods) to serve as a background for such septenary cycles, which all refer to the creative differentiation of planetary and generic types or qualities.

We would thus divide the Great Polar Cycle into 7 periods of close to 3700 years each. Each of these periods would cover 200 nutations and 200 complete cycles of the Moon's nodes. There is also, however, another alternative, which is hinted at in H. P. Blavatsky's *Secret Doctrine*, and which refers to the Kabbala. In *The Book of Concealed Mysteries* (*Siphra Dizenioutha*), which is the foundation of the Kabbala, we read the following (section V):

> "31. The tree which is mitigated resideth within. In its branches the birds (*souls and angels*) lodge and build their nests. Beneath it those animals which have power (*human personalities*) seek the shade.
>
> "32. This is the tree that hath two paths for the same end. And it hath around seven columns (or palaces), and the four splendours whirl around it on their four sides.
>
> "33. The serpent which rusheth forth with 370 leaps. 'He leapeth upon the mountains and rusheth swiftly over the hills' like as it is written (in the Bible). He holdeth his tail in his mouth between his teeth. He is pierced through on each side."

Blavatsky comments upon the last stanza by saying that:

> "When mention is made of the cosmic 'serpent which runs with 370 leaps' it means the cyclic periods of the great Tropical Year of 25,868 years divided in the Esoteric calculation into 370 periods or cycles, as one solar year is divided in 365 days."
>
> *The Secret Doctrine, II,* p. 531 (third edition)

The "tree" referred to above is the axis of the earth—at least according to one level of interpretation; its branches are currents of planetary magnetism which, we might say, constitute as a whole the "vital body" or "aura" of the planet. The "7 columns or palaces" would refer to the seven mansions of the Pole, i.e., seven divisions of the great polar cycle of gyration. The "four splendours" *might* refer to the four most brilliant stars on the cyclic path (Polaris and Wega; Alpha Cephei and

Alpha Draconis). The North Pole pointed and will point to these stars respectively about 2700 B.C. (Alpha Draconis), 2100 A.D. (Polaris), 7500 A.D. (Alpha Cephei), 13,000 A.D. (Wega).

As for the "serpent," it refers to the great planetary life-wave, the ascending and descending energy which passes through the "planetary spine," the planetary "I am": the earth-axis. It might be called the "planetary *kundalini.*" It is hard to say if the Kabbala means to convey the idea that the total cycle of the polar motion (which would naturally control the serpentine *kundalini* motion) is to be divided into 370 periods of about 70 years each (as Blavatsky suggests), or that each of the 7 "columns or palaces" is to be divided into 370 periods of 10 years each. Various possibilities of division come to mind, but somehow the numbers 7 (or 70) and 370 (or 3700) appear to be the basic ones.

The important point remains, however, that the path of the pole, because of the secondary movement of nutation, is actually a serpentine path ∿∿ circling around with "its tail in its mouth" (or nearly so, as the pole never returns exactly to the same spot of the celestial sphere, so complex the motion actually is). It would seem logical, then, to have an exact number of the smaller curves at least in each great division of the whole cycle, which would give, as a result, either 7 great eras, each divided into 370 ten-year periods; or better still 70 and 700 sub-periods of respectively 370 and 37 years each. This division into 7, 70 and 700 periods may be the planetary key to the "mystery of the 777 incarnations" to which Blavatsky refers; also Alice Bailey in *A Treatise on Cosmic Fire.**

---

* In a curious and well-known book, *A Dweller on Two Planets*, written supposedly under the dictation of an invisible entity called Phylos, the Tibetan (around 1886), a diagram is reproduced (p. 382) purporting to be a symbolic picture in the "Holy Place" where one comes face to face with the living Christ (the perfected I AM). This would be symbolically the "North Pole," the "Undying Land" of each human being. The figure represents a broad circle on which appear 7 seven-pointed stars, while on each side of this circle are seen a row of smaller stars describing a path

There remains, however, the great problem of how to select a beginning for the Great Polar Cycle. Two possibilities seem particularly attractive to us. The first is to begin the cycle as the polar axis of the Earth comes exactly to point to the present Pole Star, Polaris in the constellation *Ursa Minor*, which should take place between 2000 and 2100 A.D. The second is to begin the cycle as the polar axis points as close as possible to the great star Wega in the constellation *Lyra*.

The first solution is recommended on two grounds: 1) Polaris is probably the most brilliant star exactly on the circle described by the prolongation of the Earth's axis; 2) We believe that ideas always come to be accepted *about* the time when a crucial point in the working out of that to which the idea refers is occurring. In other words, the imminence of an occurrence calls for an adequate interpretation thereof.

The second solution is attractive inasmuch as Wega has always been considered as a star of special significance, and may possibly be close to the point to which the *solar system as a whole* is moving.

The significant fact, however, is that the arc covered by the North Pole's motion between Wega and Polaris is about four times 51° 43', that is to say, it is the space between 4 points of a seven-pointed star—representing a time-interval of about 14,800 years (4 × 3700). We might write down the following dates and correspondences, not as a definitive computation but as a suggestion for further study:

1. Polaris—Pole Star—23,800 B.C.
2. Cepheus—polar constellation—20,100 B.C.
3. Alpha Cygni—Pole Star—16,400 B.C.

representing or at least suggesting the nutated path of the North Pole. Cutting the circle diametrically is a *rod of power* whose inclination is almost exactly the inclination of the pole on the ecliptic. Four great symbols (an Eye, a Star, a Leaf and a Book) are seen inside of the circle. On the two pages of the open book 10 key words are given (Order, Justice, Truth, Mercy, Wisdom—Beauty, Love, Fraternity, Power, Use). The whole picture is typically Kabbalistic and most suggestive.

4. Wega—Pole Star—12,700 B.C.
5. Hercules—polar constellation—9,000 B.C.
6. *Draco*—polar constellation—5,300 B.C.
7. *Draco*—polar constellation—1,600 B.C.
   then again *Polaris*—Pole Star—2,100 A.D.

One should never forget, however, that these dates are at the most approximate, and that other polar motions (such as the cycle of variations in the inclination of the earth's axis) introduce rhythmical alterations. It may also be that after a couple of thousand years of scientific and precise observations we may discover factors at present unexpected. If, for instance, an electron appears to jump from orbit to orbit as it circles around the atom's nucleus, according to the quantum law, why could a planet not have sudden changes of orbit, sudden variations of rhythm—which might obey laws as yet undiscovered? H. P. Blavatsky refers to that in one of her letters addressed to Sinnett, when she remarks that the lengths of the Patriarchs' lives in the Bible were symbolical of the lengths of the year as they changed over vast periods of time. The Earth, according to this, would move regularly closer to the Sun, and thus the length of the year would decrease. This may explain the enormous periods given to the history of the planet in Brahminical records.

However, the important point, symbolically and philosophically, is for us to think of this polar motion as the essential manifestation of the creative factor in astrology—just as we think of axial rotation as an expression of the individual factor, and of orbital revolution as an expression of the collective factor. But by the term "creative" we refer here to a cosmic creativeness, to the cyclic outpouring of archetypes and primordial ideas which mark the beginning of all new planetary cycles. Later on we shall see that there is another astrological factor which also stands for the "creative" but in a more personal sense. This factor is the "Degree of the zodiac"—the product of a combination and integration of axial rotation (individual) and orbital revolution (collective).

The creative is always the result of a synthesis and integration of elements. Thus the gyration of the Earth-axis is the synthesis of various factors which involve on one hand the gravitational pull of Sun and Moon upon the Earth's equatorial belt (gravitation being the force responsible for orbital revolution and thus related to the collective), and on the other the axial rotation of the Earth. (Cf. footnote, page 181.)

196

v. *A Classification of Astrological Viewpoints*

Three Types of Astrology

THE foregoing study of the three basic types of planetary motion and of their relative significances in terms of astrological symbolism will enable us to bring order into a confused situation which disturbs the minds of most students of astrology. The reason for this confusion is the fact that astrology stands at a turning point; that a generalized attempt is being made to reformulate it in terms of values acceptable to the modern mind; and that in such an attempt no line of demarcation has been established between normally conflicting points of view.

Every phase of life and every type of knowledge can be approached from at least three basic directions, emphasizing respectively the individual, the collective and the creative attitude—the latter being again susceptible of at least a two-fold interpretation. Each of these attitudes, corresponding to definite human types (psychologically and physiologically), stresses its own particular point of view, and forgets about the others or denies their validity. Especially as we enter the realm of such unorthodox types of knowledge as astrology and, we might say in general, occultism or esoteric philosophy, do the conflicting points of view appear still more irreducible, because there is less common experience and common evidence to transform ideas into facts, hypotheses into laws. It is therefore particularly necessary, if chaos is to be avoided, to have recourse to some sort of classification of points of view which will leave room for everybody and somehow relate all individual or group efforts in terms of an all-inclusive pattern inherent in the nature of the things studied.

The realization that astrology deals essentially with the motions of celestial bodies will help us to evolve such a classification. If we recognize three basic types of planetary motion, then we may so extend their respective significances as to be able to characterize in terms of such motions three essential approaches to astrology. One type of astrology will function primarily in terms of axial motion, and stress the individual factor in a man (natal astrology) or in a situation (horary astrology). Another type will emphasize every element connected with orbital revolution, with the Sun and the ecliptic, and stress the collective factor in the behavior of man and in the influence determining this behavior. Still another type—very little developed as yet—will be of a more occult character and deal with vast planetary factors, with the cosmic (spiritual and creative) influence of stars and Divine Hierarchies,—or else with occultly perceived symbols revealing the creative significance of every astrological factor.

Each type should normally and logically evolve its own technique of interpretation, its procedure in the application of general principles to particular cases, its tables of data; and it would naturally stress its own basic factors, even to the point of practically recognizing no significance to the special factors which are strictly the products of the other types' emphases. There is nothing absolutely wrong in such a focalization. Nevertheless, someone ought to have enough philosophical understanding and a broad enough vision to grasp the total situation, and to state, for the benefit of all, the relative significance of the diverse methods, techniques, and theoretical emphases or exclusions.

We cannot hope to achieve this result in a complete and fully satisfactory manner, any more than we could in our distressingly brief survey of the historical background of astrology (Chapter One) produce an adequate picture of the growth and evolution of astrology in the past. At the same time, we hope to be able to convey in the following a sketchy, yet inclusive idea of the most fundamental characteristics of those branches of present-day astrology which seem consistent, fruitful and valid.

1. *Astrology of the Individual*

This includes especially the astrology of the individual human being (natal astrology) and the astrology of the individual situation (horary astrology).

In a way, this is the most inclusive type, at least potentially. As "horary astrology" it can be applied to any kind of situation, and as "natal astrology" it can refer to the "birth" of any entity, atomic, human or cosmic. But more specifically, what we mean by "astrology of the individual" is a type of approach which stresses individual characteristics and an individual interpretation thereof. It will stress values which are related to the axial motion of the earth.

"Horary astrology" is the type of astrological practice in which the astrologer judges the elements of a particular situation, their probable development in the near future, and thus is able to advise his client as to what is the best solution of any problem involved in the situation at hand. It means casting a chart for the time the situation is brought to the attention of the astrologer. The chart is interpreted primarily from the point of view of the "houses" (products of the axial rotation of the Earth), of the planetary rulership thereof, and mostly according to an individual technique. The factor of individual interpretation is all-important. Horary astrology depends for its validity entirely upon the "personal equation" of the astrologer. It is the most strictly individualistic type of astrology—even though it obeys rather rigid rules of interpretation.

The Astrology of Personality

"Natal astrology," in the strictest sense of the term, refers to individual birth-moments. It demands as a prerequisite absolute accuracy in the knowledge of the moment of the "first breath"—the moment when the human being reaches the condition of individual or at least independent existence. Such absolute accuracy is necessary to establish beyond doubt the frame-work of the houses,—the very frame-work of the native's *individual selfhood and unique destiny*. It is true, of course, that collective factors, derived from the position of Sun, planets, zodiacal signs, etc., are used; but even those are specifically related to the development of an individual situation: the native's life. Besides, natal astrology presupposes to a large extent a knowledge of the collective environment and nature of the individual studied (just as horary astrology presupposes a "question" establishing the general situation under consideration). For, without such a knowledge, the astrologer has no way of telling whether the natal chart refers to a man or an animal, to a creature of the slums or to a highly cultured aristocrat. Therefore without a general knowledge of the species, race and class of the native, natal astrology can be only very vague, and does not fulfill its function, which is to *release and increase the significance of an individual destiny and of a unique personality—thus enhancing its individualness and its uniqueness*.

Such a true natal astrology is therefore based essentially on psychological understanding. It deals with subjective interpretation of objective facts. It is a system of creative life-interpretation and creative symbolism applied to an individual personality. Theoretically, it stresses factors derived from the rotation of the earth around the polar axis, just as it studies a human being as a complex of attributes and tendencies centered more or less adequately around an individual axis, the "I am" or ego, the spine and cerebro-spinal system of this human being.

A Classification of Astrological Viewpoints

It is this type of astrology which we shall especially study in the remainder of this book.

2. Astrology of the Collective

This is, generally speaking, "natural" or "mundane astrology," the type which was associated with the birth of human cultivation and culture. It gave birth to an Agricultural Calendar based on a study of the modifications of the life-force—especially of the influences of Sun and Moon. It later became the symbol of an ethical and spiritual Law. As "natural" astrology it refers to changes in seasons, climate, weather; as "mundane" astrology it deals with the rise and fall of kingdoms and nations, and with the determination of vast influences moulding the temper of groups and collectivities.

Two points are outstanding in an evaluation of such a type of astrology: 1) It deals with actual influences, with rays and magnetic currents which are said to emanate from Sun, stars and planets, and to produce changes in all Earth-beings. These changes are at first physiological, but they react at once on the psyche—mainly on the emotions. 2) Its approaches is thus essentially objective, which makes it amenable to "scientific" treatment. That is to say, it is largely experimental. It develops by means of statistical judgments, and can be checked up by objective tests of a sort and by measurements. Its mode of operation is not essentially different from that of sciences dealing with telluric forces, earthquakes, weather, and all more or less cyclic changes of conditions affecting all biological species on Earth. It deals with the collective moods of men and nations, just as other sciences deal with the secular growth of trees, rocks and continents. It deals with human collectivities, or human psychological changes in the collective.

As already mentioned, the most clear-cut manifestation of such an astrology is seen in the work of T. O. McGrath, in his studies of the cycles of business in correspondence with

Sun-spot cycles (11.2 years), with the Moon nodes cycle (18.6 years), and with two other cycles of 40 months and of 56 years respectively. He does not call his work "astrology," because it deals with the heliocentric positions of the planets— which are seen much as triggers releasing solar operations, and because in general, the approach is purely statistical and concrete. Sun, stars and planets are huge magnets; their motions release electrical forces. The solar system as a whole, and the surroundings of each planet in particular, are seen as vast, magnetic fields, interacting upon each other. The whole science is that of "cosmic electro-dynamics."

Edward Johndro, a radio engineer, was perhaps the first to develop this approach to a point of great complexity. He does not entirely leave the field of natal astrology. But even when dealing with individual nativities, he apparently stresses almost exclusively the play of collective and concrete factors within the individual. For instance the geographical location— the place of residence of the person—is made to be of paramount importance: man is seen almost completely as product of an environment, as a mere unit in a vast system of planetary and celestial relationships, a particular example of the genus *homo sapiens*. Another Kabbalist and astrologer, Paul Counsil, is following the same line of approach; and a number of other workers in that field are developing it steadily.

They specialize, however, in mundane problems: In the determination of earthquakes, the "birth-charts" of cities and nations, and all matters affecting human collectivities. They are usually very proud of being "scientific" or "mathematical" —though, as a matter of fact, they are not "mathematical" in the deepest sense of the term, but rather exponents of an extended system of electro-dynamics, which considers the push and pull of planets upon each other as very real and concrete, even if stated in terms of electrical forces rather than as Newtonian gravitation. They are dealing not with "symbols"—as the most recent type of atomic physics is wont to do—but with "vital forces" emanating from stars and Sun.

In such a type of astrology the Sun occupies normally a most strikingly conspicuous position as the source of the life-force of the whole system. The approach is logically, in most cases, heliocentric. What is studied is, first of all, solar emanations; and the planets act largely as reflectors or stimulants to solar discharges. In the old Ptolemaic astrology the Sun was seen as the focal point of the zodiac, a band of the skies extending over 23 degrees each side of the ecliptic. The zodiac was the realm of the Sun. Within its boundaries all planets appeared to move. Projected on the Earth globe, it was the equatorial belt—also the realm of the Sun. Thus while "astrology of the individual" refers more especially to the polar axis, "astrology of the collective" deals primarily with equatorial forces. In man these forces are those acting through the Great Sympathetic system and mainly the solar plexus (and other centers). In Hindu *yoga*, these centers are the "lotuses" or *chakras*. But two systems are to be differentiated: the system that deals with these "lotuses" which are foci of collective consciousness and being; and the system that deals with centers in the spine. A third system of "centers" can also apparently be found within the head—giving us again our three basic terms: *collective, individual and creative*.

In the new type of "astrology of the collective" the problem is more complex. The Sun is even more the focal point of the study; but a planetary zodiac and a solar zodiac have apparently to be used in order to make matters logical and coherent—defining respectively the magnetic field of the Earth enveloping the Earth, and that of the Sun encompassing the entire solar system. Ptolemaic astrology, nevertheless, still dominates the ordinary present day astrology; and it is obvious that it must do so because of practical considerations as well as because of the level at which most human beings still live—a physiological, equatorial and collective level. First, for the purpose of quick and professionally cheap astrological interpretation, it is evident that nothing more than "Sun-sign readings" can be offered: solar-plexus, emotional-vital, equatorial readings which deal with *twelve basic types of racial instincts and of collective focalizations of energy*. Then, very few persons know their exact birth-moment, which makes an accurate reading in terms of axial-rotation factors (Houses, Ascendant, Parts, etc.) impossible. Thus the strictly individual factor remains in doubt; very often it is a mere potentiality and can be seen only in terms of "pattern of fated circumstances." Collective-equatorial astrology is the one befitting persons who live a purely collective life.

Collective life, in our age of racial and cultural disintegration, means ordinarily a chaotic, hectic life driven at the mad tempo of city-hehavior. But in ancient times it meant harmonious earth-growth, a growth not unlike that of plants and trees. The great man was the flower and fruition of his tribe or race, a collective expression brought to the point of structural perfection. He was a perfect man inasmuch as he manifested perfectly the qualities of his racial collectivity. As he did that, he was seen as the conscious focalization of a higher collectivity—the collectivity of perfected ancestors in one sense; a vast Celestial Hierarchy, in a still more remote (yet also "ancestral") sense. Such a man became a Mediator between heaven and Earth. Which leads us to a third type of approach to astrology.

3. *Occult Astrology*

Occult astrology should not be considered entirely apart from the two preceding types, any more than one can ever consider the creative apart from the individual and the collective. We have seen that the gyration of the Poles is determined by a combination of factors: mainly, the rotation of the planet around its axis and the gravitational pull of the Sun (and the Moon) upon the bulging equatorial belt (which bulging is again a result of the axial rotation and the centrifugal forces it generates). Likewise the occult approach to astrology—or to anything, for that matter!—is determined by the quality of the individual's approach and the level of the collective instincts (inherited vitality) which the individual focalizes.

In archaic times the consciousness of men was centered essentially at the physiological level. Intelligence was then organic instinct made conscious, then progressively abstracted from particular conditions and endowed with universal significance. This process was really what was meant by Initiation. As the result of Initiation man was able to project his conscious and universalized instincts upon the celestial sphere —the Body of God (Macrocosm and Macroprosopus in the Kabbala). But also he was able to receive the Body of God within his own earthly organism. In other words, the universal became particular, inasmuch as the particular had become universal. And the reverse was also believed to be true: Because the universal—God and the Celestial Hierarchies of Builders—had projected Itself upon the Earth, out of this Earth had ben evolved a creature made into the likeness of the archetypal celestial world and of its Hierarchies—into the very likeness of God; a microcosm, in potentiality however, not in actuality—until by following the first mentioned process of initiation, the potential "likeness of God" became energized by the creative will of the "I am" latent in every man, and appeared as an actual spiritual fact—the so-called Christ-body.

To explain this double process fully would require an entire volume, which in fact would mean very little until the process itself had been experienced; but the main thing to grasp is that it involves: 1) a *structural focalization* of the universal as a prototype latent within man's earthly body; 2) an *expansion of consciousness* from the particular ego-consciousness into an *organic* universal consciousness. These two processes may be called involution and evolution. Involution means here the building by the Celestial Hierarchies of an "astral" proto-type within the earthly man as man's potential form of divin-ity. On the other hand, evolution refers to the expansion and universalization of man's consciousness, through the efforts of his own individual "I am," until this "I am," having assimi-lated the power of all the divine "virtues" or Rays, becomes self-identified with and an avatar of God.

Occult astrology (when properly understood!) clears up much that is confusing and intricate in these two processes. *The involutionary process refers to the equatorial realm and the zodiac; the evolutionary process, to the polar axis and its motions.* So far, there has been practically no direct mention anywhere of the astrological factors involved in this occult evolutionary process. All that has been mentioned has been the change of *instinctual level of mankind* coinciding with the entrance of the Sun, by the precession of the equinoxes, into zodiacal constellations. This, however, is only one half of the story, a consequence rather than a cause. Again let us repeat that the cause of the precession of the equinoxes is the gyration of the polar axis.

The zodiac, in the Ptolemaic system, is a belt of creative fire surrounding the earth, this fire being focalized upon our planet by the disc of the Sun—the Sun being a mere lens through which the zodiacal Whole focalizes its twelve-fold energy upon the Earth. The zodiacal Hierarchies are hier-archies of Builders—*Cosmocratores* as they are called. They constitute together the Cosmic Formative Power (*Mahat* in Sanskrit). In music they are symbolized by the Cycle of 12 Fifths, which rules over the sequence of "tonalities," the cycle of 12 "lyus" which constitute the basis of Chinese music. They are the series of Great Ancestors, the Patriarchs of the Bible and of Hindu cosmogony, the Twelve Gates of the "Holy City" within man's "Christ-body," etc. They refer to the Great Sympathetic system and its "lotuses" (two Hierarchies for each "lotus," as well as two zodiacal signs ruled by each planet—Sun-Moon being symbolically one planet). Most particularly do they refer to the solar plexus and the diaphragm: the equatorial belt within which "tropical" passions, above (heart) and below (sex), centralize. In and through the zodiac, earth-substance becomes Man. But along the path of the polar axis, the "tree" of the "I am," Man *polarizes* himself in turn to the seven great Rays of the Logos or God. He identifies himself with the seven Rays and the seven Avatars of the Cosmic Christ (or Vishnu)—and *becomes the eight*—Krishna, the Human Christ, the Living God, Ishvara-in-the-body.

Thus while the zodiacal Hierarchies are, in cosmic symbology, the Builders of the human bodies or vehicles (represented allegorically in the Bible by the "Tabernacle in the Wilderness" and the "Temple of Solomon"),* the Stars of the Eternal Abode (North Pole) symbolize the Spiritual Teachers and Avatars who, one by one, according to the principle of the *Permutation of Rays*, arouse and energize Man's "I am." It is they who personify the great occult energies of the Dragon of Wisdom (the constellation Draco) whose head points to Wega, whose tail separates the Great Bear from the Little Bear, and whose fore-body curves around the pole of the ecliptic—the Great Empty. This is the "Central Palace" of Chinese cosmogony, *Tien-ki*, whose color is purple.

While on this subject of Rays, which esotericists have so badly mistreated, we may be allowed to quote from *The Secret Doctrine*, where the teaching apparently first appeared in its modern theosophical form:

"The star under which a human Entity is born, says the Occult teaching, will remain forever its star, throughout the whole cycle of its incarnations in one Manvantara. *But this is not his astrological star*. The latter is concerned and connected

---

* Cf. *A Treatise on Cosmic Fire* by Alice A. Bailey, p. 934 and elsewhere.

with the *personality*, the former with the INDIVIDUALITY. The 'Angel' of that Star, or the Dhyani-Buddha, will be either the guiding or simply the presiding 'Angel,' so to say, in every new rebirth of the monad, *which is part of his own essence*, though his vehicle, man, may remain forever ignorant of this fact. The adepts have each their Dhyani-Buddha, their elder 'twin Soul,' and they know it, calling it 'Father-Soul' and 'Father-Fire.' It is only at the last and supreme initiation, however, that they learn it when placed face to face with the bright 'Image.' . . . There are seven chief groups of such Dhayan Chohans, which groups will be found and recognized in every religion, for they are the primeval SEVEN Rays. . . . Hence the seven chief planets, the *spheres* of the indwelling seven spirits, under each of which is born one of the (seven) human groups which is guided and influenced thereby."

The Secret Doctrine, Vol. I, p. 572. First Ed.

The seven "Rishis of the Great Bear" are also often correlated with the seven cosmic Rays and the seven "sacred" Planets; but it is worth noting that the constellation of the Great Bear is *outside* of the circle described by the North Pole. The symbology of these constellations around and partly inside this circle is in itself a fascinating subject for study. Of all, Draco is presumably the most sacred and mysterious. The body of the Dragon cuts the circle of polar gyration about the place where the North Pole was in 3102 B.C.—the beginning of the great cycle of *Kali Yuga*, in Hindu cosmogony. This is perhaps to be considered, if not as the beginning of the whole polar cycle, at least as that of one of its main divisions.

In *A Treatise on Cosmic Fire*, written down by Alice Bailey, there is a great deal which is given out concerning the occult approach to astrology. However, the subject is not studied as a whole, and only somewhat puzzling hints are given concerning such constellations and stars as the Great Bear, Sirius, the Pleiades, etc. We hope that the above may shed some light on a field of symbolism as yet practically untouched.

One thing, however, must be added. For the occultist these constellations and stars are not apparently symbols, but are the manifestations of cosmic Beings, Who influence our planet and mankind. In this, therefore, occult astrology is linked to mundane and vitalistic astrology—which deal with life-force, solar and cosmic Rays, and the like. At the same time, *A Treatise on Cosmic Fire* is based entirely on the Law of Correspondences—as are all occult works, including the Kabbala and *The Secret Doctrine*. But to use the Law of Correspondences is another way of using symbolism! If there is a "Correspondence" between macrocosm and microcosm, between the hair of man and the hair of the Great Man of the Heavens (as in the Kabbala)—then either one or the other of the "corresponding" objects can be considered as a "symbol" of the other; or both may be said to be equally symbolic of a purely subjective, un-formulatable reality. Thus "occult astrology" is, actually and especially for all philosophically inclined students, a system of cosmic symbolism linking the equatorial and the polar natures in Man to related zones of the heavens around the Earth.

Another form of occult astrology, this time symbolical in a dramatic or actional manner, is that which has brought forth series of symbolic pictures, one for each degree of the zodiac. We shall discuss this phase of astrology at length in a later chapter. Suffice it to say here that it follows in the footsteps of the *Yi King* and of the whole of Chinese and Tibetan esotericism; and before them, of what is often spoken of as the Primeval Revelation of mankind. We have already considered this matter in the chapter on the "Cyclic Process" when speaking of Primordial Images and Archetypes. All of these are manifestations of the cosmic Creative—as is occult astrology. For the whole Sky itself is but one of the first and most potent Primordial Images. And it can be considered as the Creation of the One Individual, whom some call the Great Architect of the Universe, and others worship as God.

The Astrology of Personality

Basic Elements in "Harmonic Astrology"

After having discussed the "logical" foundation of astrological symbolism, and after having isolated the three great approaches to astrological interpretation, the three basic types of astrology, we shall now study this astrological symbolism in relation to the "astrology of the individual." More particularly, we shall show how the universally accepted elements of astrology—such as houses, zodiacal signs and planets—are to be interpreted in a type of astrology which emphasizes psychological values. We have often called such a type of astrology *Harmonic Astrology*, because it provides a basis for the harmonization and integration of the human psyche. It considers the birth-chart *as the life-chord of the individual being and destiny it symbolizes*; also we might say, as the true *Name* of this individual being. It realizes that most human beings are living only in parts of themselves, living fragmentary, incomplete and sadly unfulfilled lives. The wholeness that they essentially are, as complete Individuals, is there —potential, archetypal, but expressed or manifested only in bits. This wholeness is the true Chord of their individual selfhood; but only a few notes of the chord are sounding at a time, some never vibrate at all, and there is no intensity or fulness in their whole life-performance.

To help man fulfill the wholeness of his being and perform the total score of his Destiny—such is the purpose of Harmonic Astrology. The birth-chart is the key to the wholeness of an individual and of his outer manifestation—his Destiny. It is the score of the symphony which a living man is. It is the archetypal pattern, the symbolical formula, the Signature of the whole being. It is the blue-print of the building that is his perfected selfhood—and it also contains the time-schedule according to which the various phases of the building-operation will proceed in ordered sequence—what we call the Destiny of the man.

A Classification of Astrological Viewpoints

Astrology is not merely the study of an interesting system of symbolism; nor is it essentially fortune-telling to satisfy personal curiosity. It is a practical study with a very definite—even if usually not understood—purpose. A vital purpose. It is, at least potentially, the foundation of a new technique of living, of a new principle of conduct (or, we might say, a new *yoga*)—implied already more or less in the technique of analytical psychology (Jung's technique) and hinted at in a previous chapter when we studied the dualism of ideals characterized by the terms *ethical* and *esthetical*.

As we then take such an attitude toward astrology we have to confine ourselves largely to the realm of psychological values. It is true that we cannot really separate the psyche from the body. Physiology and psychology are closely interrelated. The ancients knew this fact, but worked out the correlation in terms of *subtler bodies* (vital and astral, mostly). Modern science is tending to accept the idea of "magnetic field" and "electrical emanations" which—when fully worked out—will probably fulfill exactly the same function—a function of correlation—as that which gave value to the archaic or "occult" concepts.

At present, however, and considering the practical difficulty there is in applying astrology to physiology and medicine, it seems much wiser to focalize astrological interpretation at the psychological level, merely indicating the possibility of physical-organic correlations when such seem particularly obvious and of paramount influence upon psychological development.

We therefore face the human being through his birth-chart mostly as a psychological entity. He is a particular, unique being. There is no other being *exactly* like him. Yet we realize also that this unique being is a compound of elements which are found not only in him, but in a multitude of other beings—especially those constituting collectively his space-time environment—that is, his surroundings and his ancestors.

This unique being is a particular chord, or combination, of collective elements. What is individual therefore is the *structural framework* within which the collective elements are organized more or less adequately. It is the form of the self. The substance, on the other hand, is of a collective nature. The body of man is made up of molecules which are parts of the vast storehouse of this Earth. The psyche of man likewise can be seen as composed of psychic elements—may we call them *psychons?*—which are parts of the vast reservoir formed by the collective unconscious of mankind as a whole or of definite groups within mankind (races, tribes, nations, families, churches, etc.).

We saw in the last chapter that the *houses* of the birth-chart, and all the elements originating from the axial rotation of the Earth, refer to the individual factor in man—to the structure of his individual selfhood. On the other hand the *signs of the zodiac*, and all the elements originating from the orbital revolution of the Earth, refer to the collective factor, the substance of his being. We shall now add that the *planets* refer to the energies which are generated by the constantly changing relation of collective to individual factors.

The zodiac is the realm of the Sun and of its planets. It is the general symbol of life-relationships, which can be expressed as gravitation. Gravitation is the symbol of relationship, of attractions and repulsions between members of a group. It is a factor which belongs symbolically to the category of "equatorial." For, as we already saw, the terms equatorial, orbital, solar refer to the same basic factor: the collective. The zodiac is thus truly a background for and an expression of the various orbital motions of the planets. It is a convenient way of patterning and recording the complex inter-relationships between planet and Sun, and planets and planets.

Planets are thus, in terms of their zodiacal positions, focal points for collective energies. On the other hand, they represent in terms of their house positions (that is, by reference to the horizon and the meridian) centers of activities within the individual structure of the entire being (and destiny). Thus, as they can be interpreted according to two basic sets of reference (signs and houses) they represent the centers of forces and of activity, whose character, intensity and mode of operation are determined by the constantly changing balance of collective to individual: i.e., the personality.

For instance, Jupiter in Aries refers to a certain type of energization and activation of the type of organic substance and organic function represented by the zodiacal sign Aries. Jupiter in the seventh house refers to the fact that whatever in the consciousness and in the destiny of the individual is symbolized by the seventh house will be affected by a Jupiterian type of activity. As the seventh house refers to relationships and sensations, these will operate according to an expansive Jupiterian rhythm; and the native will have associates and partners who will expand his viewpoint and his sphere of action.

What we call today "personality" is a synthesis of patterns of behavior. It is the sum total of all the outer motions and emotions of the human being: The total rhythm of his life-operations—from the way he walks and twitches his lips, to his behavior on the battlefield or on a concert platform. It is a complex of activities. Without activity there could be no "personality." And personality behavior is obviously a blend of inherited and environmental influences operating within an abstract structure of selfhood—the individual factor. Likewise, the planets are characterized as to their nature by their zodiacal positions, and they operate in particular ways according to their positions in the structure of the houses. The sum total of the planets including the Sun and Moon—the *planetary pattern*, as we call it—represents thus the personality as a whole.

The reader will probably infer from the preceding that the

planetary pattern stands therefore for our third basic term: the creative. It does, but only potentially. It represents activity, first of all. But activity need not have the significance of creativeness. Everybody is active, but how many are creative? *Creativeness is the significant activity of a relatively individuated personality*. The element of significance is there to be emphasized; and, as we shall see presently, this element is to be revealed by the symbols of the *degrees* which are energized and brought out by the activity of the planets located thereon. The planet, however, need not, and very often does not, bring out the symbolic significance of the degree, in which case the type of activity represented by the planet *is not creative*. The human personality has not reached the point of even relative individuation, and the individual has not yet the power to give to his life and destiny a creative significance.*

---

* We are no longer mentioning the gyration of the poles and the factors associated with it, for those refer to the *planetary* Creative and to generic changes affecting Man-in-the-whole, not a particular personality.

SECOND SECTION

VI. *The Dial of Houses*

AT THE beginning it may be well to try to clear up a point which has puzzled students of astrology. If we look at an ordinary birth-chart, at its simplest stage (p. 232), we find a wheel divided by twelve spokes into twelve geometrically equal sections of 30 degrees of arc. Then we see that, on the circumference, where the spokes end, signs and degrees of the zodiac are written—giving the longitude of these spokes—i.e., their ecliptical or zodiacal position. The question is then: What is to be considered exactly as a house?

We said that the houses referred to the individual factor— and yet every chart has these same twelve angular divisions, the same obvious frame-work. The astrologer may consider the question as one of little meaning; but it has a philosophical aspect which deepens the significance of the term: "individual." Briefly stated, all human beings are as variations upon one theme, MAN. The generic structure of all human individuals is fundamentally the same. This is what is implied in the fact that, although the structure of houses is the symbol of individual selfhood, this structure is geometrically the same for all individuals. What brings a relative uniqueness to an individual is the way this twelve-fold framework is correlated to the zodiac. And this correlation is indicated by the degrees and signs of the zodiac written at the beginning (or *cusp*) of each house. The inclination of the Earth-axis on the plane of the Earth's orbit introduces greater variations according to the latitude of the birth-place. As a result, usually more or less than 30 degrees of the zodiac are inscribed within each house.

Even so, there are obviously a limited number of possibilities, and therefore every individual is not unique in his so-called individual house-characteristics. This again refers to the fact that there are a limited number of individual pattern-types. But the point is that every pattern-type operates as an *individualizing factor*. When we speak of "individual" we do not mean the "absolutely unique"; we refer to that which assumes the position and significance of uniqueness. There might conceivably be another entity exactly alike; but in the houses we shall still see that which, in each of these identical "uniques," forces upon them the consciousness and inner realization of their own, to them, unique "I am." And this is what matters, psychologically.

The Significance of the Twelve Houses

Considering now the twelve-fold structure of the houses, we shall recall what was written in the last chapter as to the significance of the horizontal and vertical axes of the birth-chart—horizon and meridian. What is below the horizontal axis is made invisible by the Earth. Whatever there is below the Earth must reach us *through the Earth*. It is the interior subjective realm. What is above, reaches us *through the air*. It is the outer, objective realm. If emanations there be, in the former case they reach us through the feet; in the latter, largely through the head (an occultly important fact). This explains why the zodiacal sign symbolizing the head, Aries, deals with the beginning of objectivity; whereas Pisces, symbolizing the feet, refers to subjective interior consciousness.

One can understand the genesis of the meanings of the houses in two ways. In the first, the whole wheel is considered as a static structure operating all at once. The two axes mentioned above represent the structure of space, of the particular space of the new-born entity. They form his cross of incarnation. He is universal Life quartered in Space and thus taking form as a particular being. Within and through this

The Dial of Houses

frame-work collective human nature operates in a particular way which characterizes man as an individual being. The two axes divide the chart into four quarters, traditionally called East-North, North-West, West-South, South-East quarters. These work out respectively the meaning of the Ascendant, the *Imum Coeli* (Nadir), Descendant and Mid-Heaven; because in astrology every division of space or time carries the significance of its point of origin. So the East-North quarter (first three houses) carries out the significance of the Ascendant, the South-East quarter that of the Mid-Heaven, etc. Each quarter is divided into three secondary "houses," for each operation of life is basically threefold, including action, reaction, and the result of both (either consciousness or disintegration)—also, self, not-self and the relation-between. The cross of particular selfhood for man generates four basic modes of being, four fundamental operations in the process of living as an individual. These can be described (using C. G. Jung's nomenclature) as: Intuition, Feeling, Sensation, Thinking.

But one should more logically consider the houses as the dial of a watch, a mere projection in space of a set of pointers (or numerals) recording a periodical motion which occurs really in time. In this case we must imagine the line of horizon moving counter-clockwise, as the hand of a clock. The cusps of the first and seventh houses represent the position of the horizon as it actually is at the time of the first breath. The line of the cusps of the second and eighth houses represents the position of the horizon *two hours afterward*; the line of the cusps of the third and ninth houses, the position of the horizon four hours afterward. Each house represents a two-hour interval. The house-cusps give the successive positions of the Ascendant (the Eastern half of the horizon) every two hours; just as one can see from the figures on a watch the points to which the small hand will point successively during a 12-hour period. The astrological "dial of houses" is a 24-hour dial with only one hand.

We shall see the significance of this conception presently as we come to study the 28-year cycle of unfoldment of the individual self. For the time being, it will be simpler to consider the houses as a segmentation of the space around the new-born child into twelve sections of 30 degrees generated by two fundamental axes, horizon and meridian. The emphasis in this case must be put upon these two axes. The cusps of the intermediary houses may be calculated in several ways, but with horizon and meridian we have two basic factors of individual being from which every other secondary element derives. The two axes represent then what can be named the space-quadrature—the cross of individual existence.

The horizon is the *line of awareness*. It is so according to the most obvious logic of symbolical significance; for it differentiates the two most fundamental types of awareness. Above the horizon is everything that can be perceived by the senses; below the horizon is the realm of this interior awareness, which Jung rightly calls "intuition." Intuition is the faculty of awareness through which we perceive inner facts. Sensation is awareness of the not-self, of others. As the Ascendant is the seed-point of the lower hemisphere, it takes on necessarily the meaning of *pure self-awareness*; the Descendant, being the seed-point of the upper hemisphere, is the symbol of *awareness of others*. Thus intuition and sensation are seen as two complementary factors, related respectively to East and West.

One becomes aware of one's own existence as an "I" by an interior process which is intuition, whereas sensation is the result of an awareness of outer causes attributed to sense-impressions. A true sensation is not a mere impression, but is rather the result of the combination of a sense-impression and of our particular sense of self. A photographic plate receives impressions similar to those received by our retina; but the visual sensations which correspond to these impressions contain, besides the latter, our own particular capacity to react to stimuli. All sensations involve, therefore, a relationship between object and subject. Thus sensation is truly ascribable to the Descendant, which, traditionally, rules over matters of relationship, partnership, marriage, etc.

Through intuition we become aware of that which we essentially are. On the basis of that awareness—"I am this and this"—we begin to pass immediate judgments on those changes which we experience within our psyche. We feel for or against these changes—spontaneously, instinctively. Thus a new mode of operation arises: *feeling*. Likewise from sensations and their correlations is born a new process: *thinking*. Thought is the result of sensation, just as feeling is the result of intuition. What was abstract as intuitive awareness becomes concrete as feeling. What was vague, fugitive, impermanent as sensation, becomes established, relatively permanent as thought. More than this, what was a mere matter of awareness becomes an actual concrete experience, having form and purpose—thus significance. Feeling involves experience, and experience manifests either as feeling (if the basis of it is *subjective*) or as thought (if the basis of it is *objective*). To experience is not merely to receive an impression or be aware of something. It is to go out into the thing (or the self) and establish the significance thereof, through feeling or through thinking.

Thus we grasp the significance of the vertical axis, which refers to *concrete experience*. Horizontal awareness becomes focalized at the vertical points as concrete experience. The receptive becomes the active, as horizon becomes meridian. The horizontal axis referring to awareness is, to use Jung's term, the *irrational* axis; whereas the vertical axis relates to the *rational* operations of the self. Awareness, whether of self or of others, involves no rationalization. It is a direct fact of life. An impression is not rational of itself. It just *is*. Then we begin rationalizing it. If it is an inner experience we pass immediate judgment upon it at first by feeling. Feeling is not rational in the same way as thinking is; yet both have a value as judgments, on the basis of which we act subsequently as bestowers of significance. Thus we may call them rational because of the particular operation in consciousness which they involve. We must emphasize, however, the fact that these terms are used according to their strict psychological sense, and not as commonly used in everyday language.

If, then, we wish to interpret psychologically a birth-chart in which we find Scorpio ascending, Taurus descending, Leo in the Mid-Heaven and Aquarius at the *Imum Coeli*, we shall begin drawing our conclusions as follows: The intuition operates on a Scorpio basis. The native will "find himself" *naturally*, by using methods fitting the characteristics of Scorpio. These Scorpio characteristics will provide him with the best, because to him most natural, path toward a full awareness of what he essentially is. Through sex, through the use and control of life-energies, through a steady release of power, he will reach full self-awareness. The same type of reasoning would apply to the four angles.

The goal of Harmonic Astrology is to lead men to the fulfillment of their whole nature and being; fulfillment, correlation, integration—and thus sublimation. What is necessary, then, is to enable the person whose chart is analyzed to do the things which, if his *instinct* had not been frustrated by family and society, he would have done in pure spontaneity. The sign (and degree) of the zodiac at the four angles indicate thus the natural path toward the fulfillment of the activity symbolized, the best way to function intuitively or through feelings or thoughts as the case may be. It represents what essentially *is*—but in many cases what has been obliterated by social and intellectual living; thus it indicates how to go, underneath the superficial and acquired characteristics, to the basic qualities which are really our own.

The signs of the zodiac provide us with a set of twelve characteristic life-substances, or qualities of being, or attitudes to life, as we may wish to consider them. Where they appear in the frame-work of the selfhood of any particular person shows the qualities which are to be attributed *congenitally* to the various faculties and modes of activities of the person. They indicate, to use an Oriental term, the *dharma* of this person. The *dharma* of the fire is to burn, of the tiger to be ferocious, of a man born with an artistic nature it is to create, etc. Reading the angles of a chart is thus to read the total *dharma* of the native.

This will be supplemented by an interpretation of the signs on the cusps of the other houses. The "succedent" houses (second, fifth, eighth, eleventh) signify the reaction to the action expressed in the "angular" houses (first, fourth, seventh, tenth). This can refer to either a positive or a negative reaction. If the reaction is positive, what is signified in the "angular" house becomes *consolidated* and *focalized* by means of limitations and contrasts. If the first house means awareness of self, this awareness becomes consolidated by the limitations imposed upon it by past inheritance (physiological and psychical); or at a later stage, by possessions of all sorts. But if the reaction is negative, then this inheritance or these possessions stifle the awareness of self, weigh upon the intuition of the "spiritual" I with all the inertia of materialism.

Likewise, the fifth house may either consolidate the experiences and feelings represented by the fourth house, as for instance home (fourth house); or else, its contents may mean the loss of the fourth house matters, as pleasure and speculation may lead to the loss of the home. Too much pleasure and foolish self-assertion dulls the feelings; but teaching and art-expression enhance and focalize these feelings by forcing them to face and to give form to the materials involved (children or esthetic materials—fifth house). The same line of thought applies to the interpretation of the eighth house (consolidation or loss of the power of relationship) and the eleventh house (consolidation or loss of professional and public life; friends or chimerical hopes which take one away from reality).

With the "cadent" houses we face either the result of the loss implied in the succedent houses or the workings and expression of the psychological mode of operation (angular) after it has been focalized (succedent). Thus the third house symbolizes matters dealing with the workings out of an integrated psycho-physiological inheritance. The substance of our body becomes really our own through the nervous system relating the abstract self to the racially inherited cells. These atavistic influences of the second house manifest in the third as brothers and sisters, or rather as our mode of relation to them. Every possible type of intimate connections (in one's own body, or one's family circle, or the area reached by small journeys) is here characterized. On the other hand, if the second house meant the loss of self in one's atavistic nature (or in acquired possessions, in the latter cycles of life), then the third means neuroses, family jealousy, envy and perhaps insanity.

In the sixth house we reap from others as service the consequences of a constructive fifth house, or else illness and the obligation to serve others follow our wastefulness and self-indulgence in matters of self-expression, home education, etc. In the ninth house the loss of sensations or the power of relationship (death, bankruptcy, etc.) forces us to take a "long journey" over the border . . . of our country or of this plane of existence. But if the house of relationship and marriage has proven positive, the new power we get from the consolidation of the opportunities accruing from human contacts enables us to extend our operations, whether through physical trips or mental expansion of consciousness. At the descendant we find the index of our power of sensation. Sen-

The Dial of Houses

sations focalized and consolidated through the power that flows upward through the spine (Scorpio-Kundalini) become ultimately abstract thoughts and religious at-one-ment with universal ideas (Sagittarius—ninth house).

The twelfth house signifies negatively the vanishing of our social ideals and our hopes—self-questioning as to the meaning of life. The prison of our dreams and illusions keeps us confined until we emerge with a new vision, or are forced back unenlightened into a new cycle of bondage. Or else it signifies the closing chapter of a period well lived and the transition to a new birth at a higher level of selfhood whose foundations will have been our altruistic work for society and our friends, inspired as it was by noble and magnanimous ideals.

In order to make the foregoing more graphic the following diagram may be useful to the student, paralleling the conventional and the psychological-philosophical meanings of the houses:

DIAGRAM*

HOUSE	TRADITIONAL INTERPRETATION	PHILOSOPHICAL INTERPRETATION
I.	Bodily form; personal appearance and outlook on life.	Awareness of self; subjective viewpoint. "The Sower." Form-principle. The particular destiny.
II.	Health; possessions; gain or loss.	The life-substance to be used by the self; the material to be redeemed. "The Soil." The heredity. The social substance disposable to work out the destiny (wealth, possession). The chemical substance of the body. Food. Metabolism.
III.	Brethren, n e i g h b o r s, short journeys, letters; lower mind.	Relationship of personal self to physical substance, of Sower to Soil: the Seed. The formative intellect synthetizing sense-impressions and bringing together individual destiny and social elements. The environment.

IV.	Home and the parents; the father; end of life. Affairs regarding land and estates.	Concretization of self; the Soul. Its base of operation. The father whose seed carries the astral pattern, the plan of the body.
V.	Offspring, children, artistic creations; speculation, amusements.	Exteriorization of self. Creative and procreative activity. Recreations.
VI.	Sickness. Servants and dependents. Private enemies.	Conflicts resulting from exteriorization of self. Enmity of other personal selves, including the cells of one's own body. Sickness. Relation between master and slave, employer and employees.
VII.	Marriage and partnership.	The sense of human relationship on a basis of giving and taking. Interchange of vital energies and of ideas.
VIII.	Death and legacies.	Destruction of personal limitations as a result of human interchange. Enlargement of viewpoint. Regeneration and death. Practical occultism.
IX.	R e l i g i o n, philosophy. Science, writings, distant travels.	The abstract mind and the sense of relationship between relations. World-wide contacts; mental adjustment to racial ideas and collective needs.
X.	H o n o r, preferment, fame; public position; also the mother.	Concretization of relationships. Base of operation in human society. Business, state affairs. The mother in whom racial consciousness and the national Soul are concretized.
XI.	Friends; w i s h e s and hopes. Flatterers.	Exteriorization of social position. The circle of acquaintances and the friends. New ideals of human and social relationship. The Reformer's dreams and efforts.
XII.	Hidden enemies. Fate. Imprisonment.	Conflict with the inertial forces of society. The limiting power of the race's level of consciousness; and the rising above it by indi-

vidual efforts of will occultly
exerted. Karma, and the fatality
of rebirth in a limited form of
selfhood, either to neutralize failures, or in compassionate sacrifice.
Forces which brought the self into
incarnation. The overcoming of
Karma. Liberation.

Such a charting of the meanings of the houses does not,
however, exhaust the possibilities of significance. These possibilities are in fact infinite, just as the possibilities of applications of any complex algebraic formula are practically infinite.
Every one who really understands the meaning of charting
the twelve basic operations of selfhood will readily see that
new sets of meanings will arise each time we consider a *new
level* of selfhood. The wheel of houses is a universal formula.
Wherever the polar oppositions of self and not-self, of awareness and experience, of abstract and concrete, apply—there
the wheel of houses can be used most efficiently in bringing a
pattern of order to the apparent confusion of phenomena,
whatever they be. Wherever any agglomeration of substantial elements can be considered as an organic entity, as a relatively closed circuit of life-energies, there the wheel of houses
and its four-fold and twelve-fold differentiation of *viewpoints*
apply. This is so because the fact that life-energies move in a
closed circuit (metabolic action) makes of the collectivity of

---

* The attribution of father to the fourth house, and of mother to the
tenth house has been very strongly disputed. In medieval times the son
followed nearly always his father's profession, therefore as the profession is
always related to the tenth house the idea of father seemed also connected
with the tenth house, especially where sons were concerned. Also many
astrologers relate the signs of the zodiac to the houses thus: Aries corresponds to the first house, Cancer to the fourth, Capricorn to the tenth.
As Cancer is "ruled" by the Moon (which symbolizes the mother) and
Capricorn by Saturn (which symbolizes the father) it has seemed logical
to relate the mother to the fourth house and the father to the tenth house.
We would be inclined to believe that these co-relations are interchangeable, according to the level of being at which one establishes itself.
A co-relation which is true physiologically may have to be reversed at the
psychological level. The mother may dominate the physical home (fourth
house); but the father may form the psychological home: the soul.

cells which these energies vitalize an organism. Every organism is, to some extent, an individual entity. Inasmuch as it is an individual entity, there will arise in it a certain type of awareness (of self and of other selves) and a certain type of concrete experience (subjective—as feeling or instinct; objective—as acquired groupings of sensations, or thoughts).

It is true that in all kingdoms below man there is very little awareness of self, if any; and very little sense of a particular formed ego as a basis for individual self-expression. In other words, the subjective, below-the-horizon realm of selfhood is not developed in the separate individual entity. But we may be willing to say that such a realm is developed in the vegetable or animal species as a whole—constituting what Bergson calls the "Genius of the Species."

In man only, as far as we know, every specimen of the human species is, potentially at least, a complete individual. The "Genius of the Species," that is, the archetypal reality of MAN (what the Hindu calls the "Manu"), *can* become the center of the personality when the latter is duly "individuated." As it does so it becomes the living Christ, the God-within. In other words, a man ceases to be a creature of the Earth-surface—an animal. He begins to live both above and below the horizon, objectively and subjectively. His own center becomes identified with the center of the Earth. He thus becomes a planetary being—a microcosm.

The lower hemisphere of the birth-chart refers therefore to the potential formation and expression of the God-within. There, at the nadir point (the "Midnight Sun" of Masonry), man's conscious ego is born in the manger of the "feelings." Then, after having been regenerated by the trials involved in all human relationship and in social living, this ego eventually becomes more and more inclusive. The center of collective being, which is symbolized by the zenith and the noon-point, is assimilated by the individual ego! This in turn gives food for a deeper awareness of self and others. Ultimately the four "angles" of the chart become integrated at the center of the chart—or in another sense in a third dimension, as the apex of a pyramid built upon these four "angles." The point of integration—or individuation—is what Jung calls: the Self.

In Rosicrucian symbology, the Self is the Rose that blooms at the center of the cross. It is also the fire that surges from the whirling center of the Swastika. It is the apex of the Egyptian pyramid—which was a chamber of initiation.

The Unfolding of the Individual Self

From the foregoing it will be evident to the student of astrology that the wheel of houses is inherently to be interpreted in terms of becoming rather than of static being. It is a time-pattern; a pattern of unfoldment, recording essentially a *process*. And this process is the great psychological process of individuation: the alchemical "Great Work"—the Biblical "building of the Temple." MAN—the universal Archetype or "Manu"—is crucified into the physiological entity (the perfected human animal) and after *three days* arises as the Christ —the perfected human "Individual."

The symbolism of these "three days" is susceptible of an infinite number of applications—just as is the symbolism of the "seven days" of creation. The latter refers to the building of the physiological entity; and in a larger sense to that of the planetary Being (thus the sevenfold division of the Great Polar Cycle). The former refers to the building of the human "individual," as a psycho-mental being. Astrologically speaking, we can use the wheel of houses to chart this building of the human individual. We shall see that each "day" is in reality a cycle of 28 years. Thus the entire process will last theoretically 84 years—which is the cycle of revolution of Uranus around the sun, a significant fact which will take on added meaning as we study presently the Uranus-symbol.

The two processes (physiological and psycho-mental; or generic and individual) are closely related; and this is curiously apparent when one studies "kabbalistically" the number 7. If one adds all the digits that come up to this number (Kabbalistic addition process) one gets the number 28; for $1+2+3+4+5+6+7=28$. But if one carries the process to each number up to 7 we have as a sum-total the number 84. That is to say we get the following figuration:

1	which gives Kabbalistically				1
2	"	"	"	$1+2=$	3
3	"	"	"	$1+2+3=$	6
4	"	"	"	$1+2+3+4=$	10
5	"	"	"	$1+2+3+4+5=$	15
6	"	"	"	$1+2+3+4+5+6=$	21
7	"	"	"	$1+2+3+4+5+6+7=$	28
28					84

The meaning of the "Kabbalistic addition" can be intuited perhaps from a geometrical illustration of the process, which has a particular significance in this case.

From this figure made up of 28 equal and tangent circles, it is clear that the number 28 reveals by such an analysis that it refers to *three realms of being*.

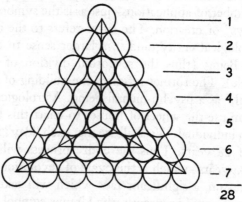

The outer realm is marked by the 18 outer circles; the middle realm, by the 9 middle circles; and the inner realm by the 1 central circle.

The Dial of Houses

The only preceding number to give a symmetrical figure centered around one circle is the number 4;—kabbalistically equal to 10. The number 10 refers to the cosmic; but number 28 is the number of *triune Man*: Man as spirit, soul and body. Spirit is 1; Soul is 4; Body is 7. The number of the perfected individual is therefore 28. But the fully worked out process of individuation requires that each component factor (or number) be also fully developed; and thus the duration of it is 84 years. By developing *only* the basic numbers (1, 4 and 7) we have a total of 39; that is, 1 + 10 + 28. At the age of 39 man reaches a condition of particular significance in his spiritual development—the fortieth year being also the seed-year of the decade 40 to 50, which is the *fifth* decade. MAN is also symbolized as a five-pointed star. The fifth section of the star is the head—the organ of the creative. During this fifth decade a man finds his work of destiny. Indeed, in this sense, "life begins at forty"!*

After this brief excursion into the realm of numerical or Kabbalistic symbolism, we return now to the astrological analysis of the 28-year cycle. Such a cycle, then, is one of the "days" of which Jesus spoke when he said: "Destroy this temple and I shall raise it again in three days." Each day represents, not a literal cycle of rotation of the Earth around its

---

* The formula implied in these paragraphs can be used to determine the archetypal significance of all the main turning points in the cycle of human life; but it needs to be applied with care and understanding. We might give more instances to clarify the matter.

If we consider 15 circles arranged in the way above described we see that they constitute two series—an outer triangle of 12, an inner triangle of 3. The number 15 is the "kabbalistic sum" of 5; but if this sum is fully developed, following the above procedure, it gives the number 35. As we shall see presently, 35 is the point in life which brings symbolically the Marriage of Heaven and Earth. It is the working out of number 5—the number of the Great Initiator. The 15-circle figure is symmetrical, but contains only two series: the inner spiritual circle is still missing. This inner circle will appear in the figure developed from the number 6, giving the years 22 and 56 (cf. left and right columns of figures above). These are years of spiritual arousal; but the figure lacks foundation with only 22 circles. It will acquire this foundation and become symmetrical with 28 circles—the full number of individuation.

axis, but a cycle of rotation of man's individual self around its spiritual axis, its real "I am" overshadowed by the spiritual Pole Star—the monad or "Father in Heaven" watching over every human being.

This 28-year cycle can be plotted out on the birth-chart. In other words, the birth-chart is not only to be used as a space-pattern revealing the blue-print of the completed self-

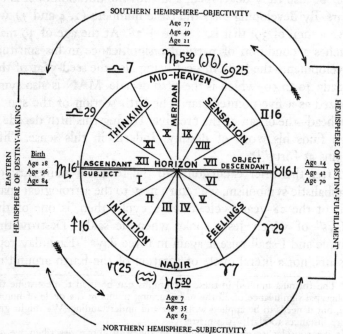

A Symbolic Interpretation of The Dial of Houses

hood, but the time sequence of the operations of the building can be discovered also by starting from the Ascendant, the beginning of the building, and following along the circumference of the chart in counter-clockwise motion. When the Ascendant is reached again the first cycle of twenty-eight years is closed, and the second begins, ending with the 56th year; the third 28th year cycle follows, coming to a close at the age of 84, which marks the theoretical and symbolical completion of man's *inner temple*. This is the end of the process of Individuation.

However, the temple may never be completed, and in almost every case at present is *not* completed. Just the same, whether fulfilled or not, the curve of unfolding is there as a potentiality. Together with the *blue-prints*, the Great Architect (the God that dwells in the Pole Star, according to the Chinese) gives man a *time-schedule of operation*. The space structure is to be completed within a certain span of time, and the building operations are to proceed in a definite order; this part of the blue-print first, then that one, then the next, etc. The foundation, the first story and the second story including the great Dome covering all. Thus three periods: from physical birth to the age of twenty-eight; then from what ought to be the psycho-mental birth (28) to 56; finally, from this potential third or spiritual birth to the end (84).

This again corresponds to the age-old tradition that the nature of man is threefold: body, soul, spirit. Moreover the three great 28-year cycles form the true basis for the ancient idea of first-born, twice-born and thrice-born. But popular Brahmanism accelerated the occasion of the second birth for easily understandable, practical purposes. During the first 28 years, man perfects (always theoretically) his physio-psychological body, or better, his *race-self*. He fulfills his ancestry and the past of his family and race. Then he emerges as a new-born *individual self*. Having discriminated, selected, rejected and chosen, out of what the past of mankind offered to him, the foundation for his own individuality, he builds on the foundation of this past (for every temple must have a foundation) the structure of his individual selfhood.

Finally, if this structure is at all completed, he reaches at the age of fifty-six the point where the universal Spirit is born within him—the third or spiritual birth. This is symbolized by the building of the dome of the temple—a replica of the vault of the sky, itself a symbol of the Universal Self, or God. When that also is completed man passes to other spheres; consciously and without loss of personal identity, if he has built for himself a "vehicle of immortality." The first cycle sees potentially the completion of the body of *earth*; the second cycle, that of the body of *sound*; the third, that of the body of *light*. Out of the physical mother's womb an organism of flesh and bones is born. At the second birth, a *Tone* sounds forth, the *Ishwara* or Logos, the Voice of the God-Within. At the third birth, *Light* pours upon the consecrated Self—as Wagner symbolizes it in the Grail consecration of the last act of *Parsifal*.

Each cycle represents a complete revolution of the entire "pattern of selfhood," i.e., of the axis of the birth-chart. This *symbolical* revolution is timed in such a manner that every seven years one arm of the cross comes to the position which the succeeding one occupied originally. In other words, at the age of seven, the Ascendant comes to the position occupied at birth by the *Imum Coeli*, the latter to that of the natal Descendant, etc. At fourteen, the Ascendant comes to the birth-position of the Descendant; at twenty-one, of the Mid-Heaven. At twenty-eight it reaches its own natal position; and a second cycle begins, in the same way.

Theoretically, it is the entire axial cross which rotates in 28 years. For practical purposes, the revolution of the Ascendant is usually the most valuable to study. For the ascendant symbolizes the very essence of self, man's attitude and path toward himself. It represents that particular viewpoint on life, that particular quality of life of which the man, as an individual identity, is to be the representative. It is man's standard of values as an individual self. Thus it is the very center of the whole consciousness. As it is seen to revolve throughout the 28-year cycle, one gets a most valuable graph of the sequential unfoldment of man's original or central attitude toward life.

In the same manner, one can trace also with a great deal of value the successive transformations of the three other basic points of consciousness. The change in man's attitude toward others, toward the outer world in general, will be plotted out by the revolution of the Descendant. His fundamental attitude in thinking and feeling can be deduced from the symbolic motion of the vertical axis of the birth-chart. Extremely valuable indications will be given in each case, provided one does not expect to find exact accuracy in terms of the occurrence of concrete events. In this entire discussion we do not deal with the mapping of outer life-happenings, but with changes in the inner operation of the individual self; that is, with changes of psychological points of view and of inner attitudes toward the whole of life, subjective and objective. These may be related to outer events; but, even then, what matters is the direction of the subjective changes rather than any exact date to which one might "pin it down." The type of approach befitting an analysis of these cycles of unfolding is purely psychological.

Such an analysis serves also to check up and interpret mathematically the general findings of psychology concerning the progressive development of the human psyche and of its functions or modes of activity. It also verifies the ancient "occult" idea of the division of human life into 7-year cycles, each of which marks the unfolding of one particular aspect of the individual's character and means of self-expression. The first seven years see the development of the power of self-awareness, or intuition—as understood by C. G. Jung. The young child sees everything in terms of personality. It is hard for him to differentiate between objective and subjective, inanimate and animate, because he lives so completely in a subjective world. He has an "intuition" of things rather than objective perceptions. He has not yet succumbed to the "heresy of separateness" which creates a chasm between subject and object (or other subjects), between *I* and *Thou*. Thus the mystic, who strives to reach complete at-one-ment with the All, is urged to become again "as a little child"—a stage which is related theoretically to the period after the third birth, between fifty-six and sixty-three. This first septenate corresponds also to the infancy of mankind, when man saw in every object a psychic entity or "spirit," when the wall between the unseen (subjective) and the seen (objective) was almost non-existent. In a general sense it represents the type of approach to life called *animism*.

From the age of seven to that of fourteen, the feelings mature. By "feelings" is meant, we must repeat once more, the direct judgments placed upon experiences on the basis of the previously unfolded awareness of self. The abstract self, intuitively apprehended, becomes around seven a concrete soul, or ego. This ego enables the child to have strongly subjective experiences. It is the age of creative self-expression, as every progressive educator will say (the fifth house period around the ages of nine and ten). The result of this is often illness, the crisis of puberty, at any rate (sixth house period).

At fourteen, true contacts with the outer world begin. The objective world becomes definitely separated from the subjective. This means sexual development: facing the other sex, the enemy and the mate. This means fear, not knowing how to "fit in," not feeling secure in a world that confronts one dangerously and with which somehow—but how?—one must become adjusted. At twenty-one, mind, which had been maturing out of the play (or drama) of objective relationship, becomes consolidated by public life, by outer experience on the basis of social responsibility. Man comes of age.

Then mind has to prove itself and to find its own ideals, its own friends. This is the twelfth house stage. At the middle point of this 7-year cycle, that is, at the age of twenty-four and a half (theoretically at least), man faces the great crisis of discrimination between various types of ideals and companions. He has to "make up his mind" about what he is going to be. Usually this determines the nature and character of the "second birth" at twenty-eight; not, however, before a period of readjustment is passed through, perhaps at the cost of deep suffering, the twelfth house stage (around twenty-six and twenty-seven).

What this second birth is to be depends on the results of the entire first 28-year cycle. The new cycle will see, like its predecessor, a progressive differentiation and development of the four basic faculties of the Self and their subdivisions; but now at the level of truly individual selfhood—*if such level can at all be reached*; which of course depends on what occurred during the first cycle (that of racial selfhood). Racial, individual, universal selfhood—three cycles; one certainty, and two potentialities. If the level of individual selfhood is not reached, at least in seed, at twenty-eight, then the human being merely conforms to the race-pattern of consciousness, and goes on living as one among countless thousands. He is one of the thousands of seeds which drop to the ground, yet do not take root.

This does not mean that a youth of twenty-eight will become a real individual, but that he then begins the stage of truly individual development. Before, he fulfilled the past (of his race, and of his own Self, if reincarnation is accepted). Now, he is building the present. After fifty-six, he will mature and become the seeds of the future (of his race and of his own Self) . . . if he can. The year thirty-five sees the revolving Ascendant at the *Imum Coeli*. This corresponds at a higher level (if the second birth is a success) to what occurred at the age of seven. From about thirty-seven to forty is again the stage of self-expression (fifth house stage) at this psycho-mental level. New ideas are born, new departures initiated; the truly individual work of the Destiny becomes clear. It will manifest objectively around the year forty-two, when man again faces the outer world and his work. This is a turning point again: a new type of adjustment is demanded, often very hard to make. The psychoanalyst recruits most of his patients from this period of life, because a definite mental psychological reorientation is then imperative. It is the "change of life," the second puberty—a most interesting time, at least for the psychologist!

Then comes forty-nine, often the time of greatest social activity. Man becomes a power in human society, on the basis of whatever individual accomplishment he can produce. At fifty-six, the third cycle begins. It is the time for man to face the Spirit, and perhaps to become transfigured by the Spirit— or by his Work. Man becomes orientated toward death or immortality. Death, if he has been unsuccessful. Immortality, if successful. In what, successful? In building his own vehicle of immortality. Which means one or more of three things:

1) Success in building a family and having become an "ancestor" whom his posterity will physically and psychologically perpetuate. For instance, the direct descendant to Confucius, by male descent, is now living, a young man—after close to eighty generations, if we are not mistaken. This *is* physio-psychological immortality.

2) Success in building a Work, which will be remembered generation after generation. This is the case of all great geniuses in religion, art, literature, science, politics.

3) Success in building a "spiritual body" in which the Self may continue to function consciously after death. This is spiritual immortality.

At sixty-three we see the combined culmination of the cycles of 7 and of 9 years. In one sense at least spirit and matter, or individual and collective (7 and 9) can then be fully harmonized. At seven, thirty-five and sixty-three the conscious ego is stirred to its depth by a new life. Then seventy sees the "third puberty" with the entrance into the new relationship—which often means death. And so tradition speaks of the life of man as being normally "three score and ten." What is meant is that at the age of seventy the last stage begins, when man relates himself to a new life. Usually the body cannot stand the strain of this new type of relationship, and this means death. But if the organism (physiological and psychological) can repolarize itself according to a new rhythm of life-contacts, then the real inner world *may* open; and man learns to be familiar with the rhythm of the "other world," with entities or energies of the "beyond"—whatever may be meant exactly by the term. He becomes the wise old Sage in whom the collective acts in a new way, bringing to earth visions of a world of pure and serene significance. If this happens, a further change of magnetism occurs at seventy-seven (7 times 11)—because 11 is the number of the Sun and of the circulation of solar energy throughout the solar system. Then, at eighty-four, a "fourth birth" occurs, which takes man altogether into a new realm of significance and destiny: which means disintegration of the personality or (relative) immortality.

Thus the cycle of individual destiny—as it *archetypally* is. Every personality weaves its particular patterns within this framework, often obliterating outwardly the big structural outlines. But the more significant the destiny, the more true to the essential cycle as outlined here: likewise the more significant the individual, the more true he is to the archetypal form of Man within a particular planetary era. This is the great paradox. The supremely individuated personality reveals the most perfectly in its outline of character, consciousness and destiny the form of generic Man. The most individual becomes the most universal, just because of being the most individual. This is because he becomes an absolute manifestation of the creative. He becomes a "solar Hero"—an Exemplar or Avatar, whose deeds and whose personality are universally significant.

VII. *The Signs of the Zodiac*

What Is Actually the Zodiac?

WE COULD easily proceed with our study of the significance attributed to the signs of the zodiac, singly and in their traditional groupings; but to do so would be taking things for granted and shrinking, in fact, from facing serious problems concerning the zodiac and the place it occupies in any coherent and holistically *logical* system of astrological interpretation. Thus we must again return to foundations and try to fathom what are the facts really involved in the establishment of a zodiac.

The Ptolemaic zodiac has been already described as a belt of creative fire surrounding the Earth, and focalized upon the Earth mainly by the Sun and secondarily by the planets. The center of this belt of fire is the ecliptic, the apparent path of the Sun. The signs of the zodiac are identified with the constellations (at least in pre-Ptolemaic astrology) and as well with celestial hierarchies of Cosmic Builders. These hierarchies constitute collectively the Universal Mind, the operative creative energy of the macrocosm. The zodiac as a whole is a vast cosmic lens focalizing upon the earth the combined powers of the hierarchies, thereby making of the Earth as a whole, or of Man-in-the-whole, a microcosm.

As the Sun passes in turn in front of the twelve zodiacal constellations the operative processes of life on Earth are started and pushed to completion. Spring and Fall are logical starting points as, in the temperate zone, they mark definite changes of season, and alter the physiognomy of the Earth-surface through the season's effect upon vegetation. This obvious fact is made more precise by measuring the changes of location of sunrises and sunsets. The Sun sets at its southernmost point at the winter solstice; then "moves northward" (and also closer to the zenith) until it reaches its northernmost point at the summer solstice. Thus the solar year normally divides itself into two halves: "when the Sun moves northward" and "when the Sun moves southward." The first half is spiritual, the second material—in most occult-mythological systems. The equinoctial points, on the other hand, being the time when the Sun seems to stand still, represent points of balance.

In these ancient systems the whole year is seen as a great *symphony drama of integration* under the supreme leadership of the Sun, and with secondary work being performed by the celestial soloists: the planets. It is a drama of *collective* integration, affecting the race as a whole, the planet as a whole. There is no real *astrological* individual integration. Individual integration is then reserved to secret initiation; and, in a sense, it is not individual "integration," but rather the assumption of an earth-body by a super-earthly entity—a Star. And so initiation is then related to star-cycles; as can be seen from studying what remains of the process of Egyptian initiation that took place in the pyramid, with telescopic orifices pointing at certain stars connected with the initiatory process.

There is then no astrology of the individual and no public knowledge of the fact of the axial rotation of the Earth. The definite public discovery of the Earth's rotation corresponds with the beginning of the age of individualism, the Renaissance—another "proof" of the correctness of our symbolism! The Pythagoreans in Greece knew about the Earth's rotation, but it was with them a more or less sacred and secret matter— just as was the process of individuation, then purely a matter of secret initiation.

Now, this fact of the public discovery of the Earth's rotation around the polar axis and of its revolution around the Sun upset completely the basis of astrological symbolism. At any rate, it brought about a cleavage between nascent astronomy and traditional astrology. What astrologers did not see, and even now have not yet seen fully, is that the sphericity of the Earth and the fact of its rotation introduced an utterly new sense of space, which necessitated a revaluation of the zodiac. In Ptolemaic astrology there was no *fundamental* difference between the revolving motion of the sphere of the fixed stars and of the various planetary heavens. But now that the Earth rotates around its axis, a dualism of motion is made obvious: the dualism of axial rotation, which, as we saw, gives birth to all individual factors, and of orbital revolution in which all planets partake.

In other words, the unity of the zodiac is broken up: that which was the symbol of the simple operation of life as it builds forms, bodies, and souls, becomes a complex system of motions with at least two basic types of meaning. *And we must face that fact.* We must either stick to a Ptolemaic world and say that we are dealing purely with a system of life-symbolism based on apparent motion and on the concrete data given by our *senses*, or else we must produce new evidences and new theories to explain the zodiac in an intellectual, scientific way. The difference between the Ptolemaic and the modern system is the difference between direct sense-perception and intellectual knowledge. Astrology must choose which it wishes to follow.

Our point of view is that if we adopt our modern astronomical outlook, we must cease to consider the Ptolemaic zodiac as the basic factor in astrology; and instead we have to emphasize the circle, or dial, of houses. For with the latter we are doing, in our new way, what the ancients did when they spoke of the zodiac as the symbol of the yearly drama of integration—collective and planetary.

As we wrote a moment ago, there was no conception of a

real type of *individual integration*, except insofar as the secret process of initiation was concerned. Individual integration is what C. G. Jung calls "individuation." And what we ought to realize is that this process of individuation will in time take the place of the process of initiation. It is no longer the Sun that turns, focusing the stellar spaces of boundless life upon the collective Earth. But the Earth now turns, and this rotation has an individual significance for the individual man. It becomes, in a larger sense, the symbol of the process of individuation.

We studied this process actually when we dealt with the three 28-year cycles of human life—measured along the dial of houses. Thus this dial of houses can be considered now as the basic factor, instead of the solar zodiac; as a pattern of integration or life-fulfillment. The individual can experience his own cycles of consciousness through such symbolical cycles of Earth-rotation: for he is now centered, at least potentially, in his own Pole Star—and is no longer a creature of the Sun, with open solar plexus through which the formative energies of life pour.

The zodiac remains, of course, the pattern of collective development and universal life-functioning; but as we emphasize the psychological process of individuation, we must also emphasize the houses as a set of points of reference, i.e., as determining the basic cycles of selfhood. And yet the beauty of the symbolism is shown in this: That nothing actually is changed *except the point of view*. This will be made clear at once in the following way.

"The year is the day of the Lord." But who is the Lord, astrologically? It is the North Pole, the integrative end or head of the planetary "I am" (polar axis). And we all know that, theoretically at least, at the North Pole the year is divided into *a 6-month day-time and a 6-month night-time*! Truly the year of the North Pole is a "day"; and we find thus that here our dial of houses applies in a modified manner: 6

months, the Sun is below the horizon—6 months, above the horizon: a planetary day-and-night cycle, and thus the possibility for a dial of houses measuring the twelvefold process of consciousness during this "day" of the Lord!

This is most logical, if we realize that the solar year is originally a record of the changes of season. But these changes of season are due to the fact of the inclination of the Earth's axis; which is also the cause for the 6-month day-time, and 6-month night-time experienced (again relatively speaking) at the poles. This shows that what is a year cycle (*collective*) in relation to the temperate zones, is a day cycle (*individual*) in relation to the poles. We may interpret this by saying that what is the collective for cells within an entire organism, is individual in reference to this organism as a whole. Individual and collective are relative terms. Relative to what? To the point of view taken.

As the Bible and all occult books say, men are cells in the body of the Lord. Polar astrology deals with the planetary Individual (the "Lord"), and *his* cycle of individuation is the year. He functions solely through the polar axis, and the facts concerning this polar axis (inclination, gyration, etc.) are the bases for the symbolism of a planetary-polar astrology. The fact of axial inclination, coupled with that of revolution of the whole planet around the Sun, constitutes the basis for the polar "day"—just as the fact of rotation of the surface of the globe around its axis causes the "day" of us, men . . . cells of the planetary body.

However, being cells, we relate ourselves one to the other constantly—and it is this relation, this collective interchange, which is pictured symbolically in the zodiac. In this case we may consider the Earth as a huge body in which men-cells "move and have their being." If the zodiac is a picture of the motions and relations of these men-cells within the Earth-body, then it follows logically that *the signs of the zodiac represent anatomical divisions of the Earth-body*. However, it is not the material planet which is to be considered, but the planet *as a field of relationships*. This field is really created by the rotation of the Earth and the magnetic currents generated by the Poles. It is also connected with the *ionosphere* (above the stratosphere), influenced by the ultra-violet rays of the Sun. In brief, the zodiac is what astrologers-scientists call the "magnetic field" of the Earth, what occultists call the "aura of the Earth," or the auric egg of the planetary Being.

Abstractly, it is the realm where all relationships between all living beings on Earth are interwoven. It is the great matrix of the collective, energized and stirred rhythmically by the solar radiations and presumably also by cosmic rays and the like. It is a magnetic field—but it can be pictured less scientifically as an envelope of fire or electricity *within which the Earth rotates, but which itself remains constantly polarized in the same direction: toward the pole of the ecliptic.*

This line of the poles of the ecliptic is the ideal axis of the Earth around which the actual axis gyrates in 25,868 years. The zodiac can thus be conceived as the *ideal Earth*, the archetypal body of the planetary Whole in which men live as cells and groups of cells.

It is probable that such a statement will seem to conflict with our previous ones indicating that the zodiac was the result of the orbital revolution of the Earth around the Sun and a background for the orbital movements of all planets. But we must also remember that we added: Always in relation to the Earth!

Remembering this, we can say that the zodiac is the solar system in relation to the Earth. One step further: It is the whole of the planetary-solar relationship projected upon the solar, or spiritual, envelope of the Earth. Or again: It is the zone around the Earth where the collective emanations of the Earth integrate with the collective emanations from Sun and planets. And it may very well be that this zone corresponds actually, in the regions surrounding the Earth, to the equatorial belt on the surface of the globe. As a matter of fact *it does not matter* from our standpoint what definition or formulation one adopts.

The zodiac, as Western astrology uses it, is both an idea and a fact. *As an idea,* it is an expression of the combined movements of and relationships between Sun, Moon, planets, and the Earth. It is an expression of collective being and of relationship between the parts or organs which together constitute an organic whole. It is the expression of organic wholeness. As everything has to be related to the observer on Earth, we may project this "expression" around the Earth and call it an "auric egg" or "ideal Earth," or whatever indicates the wholeness of life in dynamic operation. We may even project the zodiac-idea on the Earth surface and so determine which locality belongs to which sign of the zodiac—as Johndro and Counsil have done, each starting with a particular "world-basis" for the projection. In every case, what is being done is a charting of collective elements and of organic interchange.

This is made even more evident by the traditional projection of the zodiac upon the human body—or, which is less usual but better, the human "aura" or auric egg. Here we see a particular sign of the zodiac assigned to every part of the body. Indeed, the zodiac is then a pattern of organic interchange, a charting of the circuits of the life-force (Sun) as it energizes the various parts and organs of the integrated collectivity of cells—which we call a body. The zodiac is thus seen as the ideal pattern and the formative mould of every "body."

As a fact of practical astrological application the zodiac, as we now use it in the Western world, has to be considered as the "magnetic field" of the Earth, this being the only way to justify our astrological measurements from the point of view of a heliocentric scientific solar system. This is explained most lucidly in Alan Leo's *Casting the Horoscope* from which we shall quote the following:

The Signs of the Zodiac

"The zodiac that we use is really the Earth's Aura. It is a sphere or ovoid, the poles of which coincide with the poles of the Ecliptic and its middle or equatorial plane is the Ecliptic. . . . For some reason at present unexplained, this sphere is polarised in one direction; that is to say, it remains always in one position whatever the place of the Earth in its orbit, in this respect being comparable to the ordinary mariner's compass, the circular card of which always floats with its North Pole pointing in one direction. This sphere is divided into twelve parts like the sections of an orange, and it is these sections which constitute the "signs" of the zodiac. We are, however, chiefly concerned with its equatorial plane, for it is this which we measure in signs or degrees, and which determines the zodiacal position of a planet.

"Now it is clear that since this sphere or aura remains constantly 'floating' in one position while the Earth journeys round the sun, the sun's rays will successively pass through each one of the signs. If you place a lamp in the middle of a table, and walk once round the table, always facing one particular corner of the room, the rays of the light will have shone upon each part of the head in turn—the nose, left cheek, back of the head, right cheek, and so on. . . .

"It need hardly be mentioned that this 'aura' does not turn round each day with the rotation of the earth on its axis, but that the Earth spins round *within* it, like the wheel in a gyroscope."

In other words, this "aura" represents the collectivity of the whole solar system in relation to the Earth. The Earth spins around within it, *just as any individual moves within his own environment*, which environment represents for the individual the collective, that is, the sum total of relationships this individual can experience. The zodiac is the collective environment of the Earth, and thus of mankind as a whole. All cosmic relationships in which the Earth can ever enter, all outside radiations which can ever penetrate the Earth's atmosphere, and thus the lungs and blood of every breathing organism on Earth—all must pass through the zodiac. In another sense, then, the zodiac is the placenta of the embryonic

247

Earth-body. All the building energies which produce the growth of the embryo must pass through the placenta. The placenta is the formative zone, the zone in and from which the building energies and substances of the macrocosm vitalize the microcosm just as the mother's energies vitalize the embryo.

As the solar and planetary rays pass successively through each one of the zodiacal signs, the growing microcosm accordingly receives "nourishment" or stimulation—until eventually it reaches the state of perfect development. The Earth is not perfectly developed, neither is the human race. So year in, year out, the Earth, the human race and all other life-species on this globe receive more "cosmic substance," more "macrocosmic food"—the very substance of the Celestial Hierarchies, in occult symbolism; the celestial Bread and Waters of universal Life.

The reader who has thoroughly grasped the foregoing will then see readily that *it does not in the least matter whether the*

Earth is said to revolve around the Sun, or the Sun around the Earth. What we deal with in astrology are three factors: the microcosm, the macrocosm and the relation between the two. This means, in other words, the particular, the universal, and the sum total of agencies by means of which the universal becomes focalized as a particular organic whole. The sum total of these agencies constitutes the zodiac. And as far as we men are concerned, the whole universe revolves around us, *just as the mother's life revolves around the child.* Egoism? Not at all; just common sense. Modern science in trying to be very impersonal and objective does not yet realize that, when all is said and done, it is impersonal and objective only insofar as *individual human beings* are concerned. All that science does is to give us a knowledge valid for all men *on this Earth.* Philosophically, nay, even practically speaking, scientific knowledge is utterly conditioned and limited by the Earth's boundaries. The Earth is like an embryo within the placenta. The embryo can only know directly what occurs to and around him, and this in terms of life within the womb. And so, the zodiac is actually what the theosophists call the "Ring-Pass-Not" of the Earth.

In scientific terminology the viewpoint and knowledge of all inhabitants of the Earth are absolutely limited to what occurs within the magnetic field of the Earth. They can know the outside only through disturbances in this magnetic field. We know, of Sun, planets and stars, *only* their effects upon the magnetic field of the Earth. We have absolutely no way of knowing whether the rays of the stars are not regularly deflected by the magnetic field of the Earth. All we can do is to measure accurately disturbances in this magnetic field or "Earth's aura." There is no philosophical and theoretical possibility of ever knowing *directly* what actually is beyond the boundaries of this field. We can know only "by inference." In other words, to use terms which the new school of idealists especially among English physicists has popularized, our knowledge is valid only in terms of the "intellectual framework" which we have adopted. This "frame-work," which is perhaps man's greatest objective creation, is relative to man. Modern science acknowledges the fact of its being "man-centered"—an interpretation of collectively experienced facts, collectively valid for mankind on Earth.

The zodiac symbolizes the frame-work to which every

astrological phenomenon must be referred. It is thus man-centered and Earth-centered. It *is* an abstraction and a symbol, just as the Holy City with its twelve gates—in the Biblical allegory—is an abstraction and a symbol. The zodiac is the Wall that separates all inhabitants of the Earth-surface from the universe. Symbolically, this Wall has twelve gates, twelve signs of the zodiac, twelve channels through which universal energies flow. We speak of the "wall" of an atom, but mean only the limits of a magnetic field; and we now shoot high-powered particles through this wall and so release from the atom's "Holy City" one or more photons.

Why do we speak of "gates" in a "wall"? Why not an open field? Perhaps because: 1) the boundaries of a magnetic field differentiate sharply enough the inner from the outer to appear as a solid wall—just as the surface of a table appears as solid as a wall, though it is nothing more than a magnetic field; 2) because energy, coming from outside in and going from inside out, can only either enter or exit in lumps called in modern physics "quanta." And it may be that the way these "quanta" behave can be accurately, yet of course symbolically, expressed by the concept of "gates"—which open and close rhythmically *like the valves of the heart*.

However this may be, the fact is that the zodiac which we use in modern astrology is to be considered as surrounding the Earth, but not a creation of the Earth's as a rotating globe. It is the expression of the relation Earth-to-universe, and more particularly Earth-to-Sun. This is made evident by the fact that this postulated or symbolical sphere around the Earth is orientated to the ecliptic and the pole of the ecliptic. It does not partake in the axial rotation of the Earth, or the inclination of the Earth's axis. It is thus in every way the same as the Ptolemaic zodiac!—only seen through the spectacles of modern astronomy. It is the "celestial sphere" of the astronomers, but limited to the neighborhood of the Earth—using the term "neighborhood" as in modern physics.

Many astrologers, however, often for the sake of simplicity, more often still because they do not consider attentively the logical foundations of the system they use, refer to the zodiac as if it were a vast sphere centered in the Sun and encompassing the entire solar system. Then, there are some who deliberately speak of it as the "magnetic field of the Sun." There is, of course, nothing wrong with this last idea, only it does not correspond either with the factual, practical reality or with the philosophical idea of the zodiac, as we apply the term "zodiac" today.

The simplest illustration of this is contained in the following fact: If the signs of the zodiac are a twelve-fold segmentation of the space around the Sun, and the Earth passes through one of these segments each month as it revolves around the Sun, then it remains during, let us say, April in the sign Libra (and the Sun appears thus to be in Aries). But if so, the Moon revolving close to the Earth remains in this sign Libra about as long as the Earth does, that is, a whole month! In other words, the whole fabric of astrology as we use it today falls very much to pieces. We have to think of an Earth zodiac through which the Moon moves (the lunar zodiac of the past perhaps ?); we have to give up the idea of retrograde planets. In other words, we have to have an entirely new astrological frame of reference. The idea, however, is attractive to the scientific type of astrologer. From our standpoint, it does not fit in with the basic principles of astrological symbolism. For it involves the idea that we can legitimately imagine ourselves on the Sun and that we can interpret life and planetary relationships from there. To us this is not philosophically acceptable. As we said, we are dealing in astrology with the interpretation of facts of experience. Thus, as long as we experience in and through Earth-born and Earth-conditioned bodies, we cannot assume the imaginary viewpoint of a being with an actual Sun-born and Sun-conditioned body. We know actually nothing about the Sun, except as a center of radiations which affects us. We call this center "Sun." And symbolically and theoretically everything works *as if* the Sun were what we make it be. But we do not experience the Sun from the Sun's viewpoint. We experience it only from the Earth's viewpoint. And, as already said, astrology—or any type of life-interpretation—deals *with experienced facts made significant.*

We are not in this contradicting previous statements. We can well accept modern science's interpretation of the relative motions of Sun and planets, yet take the attitude just defined. The astronomical concept of the solar system is a system of interpretation of observed facts—a very convenient and intellectually wonderful one. But what count for us are the facts. On the basis of these facts, astronomy establishes a model of the solar system. On the basis of these same facts, astrology establishes a symbolism of life-interpretation. Both are equally logical. And if the former appears to work more accurately than the latter, it is probably because the latter deals with a realm of being which is more exact in terms of significance than in terms of events; a realm in which the "principle of indeterminacy" operates strongly.

The Meaning and Classification of the Signs of the Zodiac

In ancient astrology based on the Ptolemaic conception of the universe, the houses were static divisions of the space above and below the flat Earth. Not being an expression of planetary motion, they could not be an expression of Life. They dealt thus purely with outer circumstances, establishing set departments for the activities of Life. Therefore the basis of all classification of life-operations was the zodiac and the cyclic course of the Sun through its signs. The equinoxes and solstices served most naturally to effect a division of the zodiac into four great quarters corresponding to the seasons. This division is based precisely on the relation of the equatorial plane of the Earth to the ecliptic, the apparent path of the Sun. Where these two planes intersect, there are the equinoxes; where they are the farthest apart, the solstices. This gives us the four *cardinal* signs of the zodiac: Aries and Libra, at the equinoxes of spring and fall—Cancer and Capricorn, at the solstices of summer and winter.

These four signs were seen as the crucial times of the year, as periods of special activity of the life-force and of special release of power. It was clear, however, that the types of release that occurred during these four crucial periods were of different natures. At the equinoxes came the times of greatest momentum of life; at the solstices, of least momentum; just as if we watch the oscillations of a pendulum we see its motion being the fastest when it crosses the point of equilibrium, and the slowest when it reaches its end-positions.

For the ancients, the ecliptic appeared to oscillate southward and northward in relation to the Earth, completing a full oscillation every year. For us moderns, it is the poles of the Earth which perform the oscillating motion with regard to the Sun, turning themselves to and away from the Sun. When the North Pole places itself face to face with the Sun, this is summer in the northern hemisphere; when it hides its face from the Sun, it is winter. The same pendular oscillation, but seen either from the point of view of the equator-ecliptic relation, or from that of the pole-Sun relation.

The result, in both cases, is that the equinoctial signs of the zodiac, Aries and Libra, are signs of great positive momentum; whereas the solstitial signs, Cancer and Capricorn, are signs of negative momentum. On the other hand, at the solstitial points the polarities of life (the *Yang* and *Yin* of Chinese philosophy) are to be experienced respectively in their purest quality. The purest *Yang* (with the least admixture of *Yin*) is experienced by the Earth at the summer solstice; the purest *Yin* (with the least admixture of *Yang*) is experienced by the Earth at the winter solstice; while at the equinoxes the two polarities are equally blended.

Thus we have two sets of factors. At the equinoxes the momentum of life is greatest. At the solstices the qualities of the polarities of life are to be felt in the purest way. This gives us the meaning of the characterization of the four crucial periods of the year in terms of four "elements": Fire and Air, Water and Earth. Fire (Aries) and Air (Libra) are expressions of momentum; Water (Cancer) and Earth (Capricorn) are expressions of life-qualities, or polarities. At the equinoxes we have extremes of *motion* and activity (either toward or away from the Sun, positive or negative in direction); at the solstices we find potentially extremes of *realization* (either of the *Yang* or the *Yin* polarities).

The terms *Yang* and *Yin* must, however, not confuse us. They really mean in this respect objective and subjective, outer and inner; thus, according to ancient customs they referred to man and woman. From Aries to Libra: this is the period of living objectively, the period when vegetation is manifest. It is the realm of *leaf*. From Libra to Aries: this is the period of living subjectively, the period when vegetation is latent, hidden below the crust of the earth. It is the realm of *seed*. Leaf and seed are two great symbols of outer and inner, of objectivity and subjectivity.

Aries represents, therefore, the extreme of momentum toward the leaf-condition, toward the extreme of realization in and through objective reality, which is Cancer—the plant fulfilled in the fruit: objective maturity.

Libra, on the other hand, represents the extreme of momentum toward the seed-condition, toward the extreme of realization in and through subjective reality, which is Capricorn—the birth of the Christ-consciousness within: subjective maturity.

Thus Fire (Aries) is motion toward objective manifestation:—the primordial desire for manifestation, the thirst for life in a body: *Tanha*—the will to live as a separate self—in Buddhistic philosophy. Fire is fulfilled in Water (Cancer):

254

the urge-to-be is fulfilled in the sap of plants, the lymph and milk that sustain all animal life; the personal soul also.

Air (Libra) is motion toward subjective realization—the yearning for the God-within, the thirst for "Liberation" or for *Nirvana*. Liberation from what? From the bondage to the body and to separate selfhood. It is motion away from the physical sun and toward the beyond. Air is fulfilled in Earth (Capricorn): The longing for God is satisfied in the birth of the Christ-body within—the spiritual Earth, the New Jerusalem.

In terms of our previous nomenclature—individual, collective and creative—we have the following diagram:

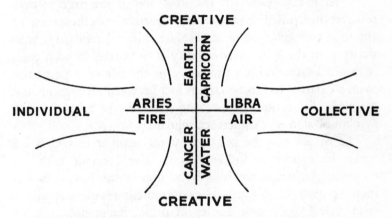

This might seem to conflict with what we said of the zodiac referring as a whole to the collective. But we must realize that individual and collective are purely relative terms. The body is "collective" to the individual self; yet it is a whole, therefore an individual organism. When we speak thus of "individual" with reference to the zodiac, we speak of these cosmic energies which are building the wholeness of any whole. Wholeness and individual selfhood are almost synonymous—the same fact looked at from two different points of view.

Fire is individual, because it is the animating principle of all individual selfhood. It is that which rises out of the Earth toward the Sun. It is the fire of germination that propels the nucleus of the seed Sunward, toward the God-that-is-everywhere.

Air is "collective," because it is that which brings every separate individual and body into the subtle communion of the breath. Air links the lungs and blood of every breathing entity. It is that which rises out of the Water toward the all-encompassing Space. It is the emanation of all bodies, the perfume of all lives. In and through it, all lives reach unity in the all-embracing seed that is the God-of-the-Mystery: SPACE.

Water is the "creative" manifestation of the urge to be a separate individual. Earth is the "creative" manifestation of the urge to reach a stage of absolute spiritual *solidarity*. Solidarity is to the spirit what solidity is to matter. In both cases it means Earth. Within the scope of the life of a particular man, solidarity has to be established between all organic and magnetic life-centers before the Christ-body takes form—a symbol or sign of this perfect solidarity.

The reader may be puzzled by the manner in which we make the opposition individual-collective coincide with the equinoxes, whereas we found the opposition *Yang-Yin* coinciding with the solstices. The contradiction is more apparent than real. The Chinese duality of principles or polarities referred to *concrete facts*, whereas we are dealing, when speaking of individual and collective, with *principles of motion*, or let us say, with trends of consciousness. In other words, we place ourselves at an abstract level, which, obviously, changes our focalization. Practically speaking, there is very little difference. Cancer traditionally rules the "home" and Capricorn, the "public life" or "profession"—truly the sphere of individual creativeness and that of collective creativeness.

Much confusion occurs in the application of astrological symbolism because the various points of view of interpretation are not clearly enough differentiated. When the ordinary textbook lists all the things Cancer is supposed to represent, it is, in fact, piling up a mass of "meanings" which are the results of several types of interpretation. Cancer means one thing from one point of view, another thing from another point of view. This fact justifies our present attitude which aims at a clarification and classification of meanings. One may try to interpret the signs of the zodiac from several points of view, each giving a particular set of meanings; but, unless one realizes the way each set is produced and *the logic of its production*, much confusion is bound to ensue.

So far, we have dealt with the most general and archetypal foundation of zodiacal interpretation, considering the four basic moments of the cycle of the year. It is evident that further differentiation is advisable, in fact necessary, and there are two essential ways in which this can be done. The fourfold structure of "cardinal" signs (Aries-Libra; Cancer-Capricorn) gives us four sections of 90 degrees each. Each section can be divided into two sub-sections of 45 degrees each; or into three sub-sections of 30 degrees each. The latter procedure is the usual one; but it loses much of its meaning when it is not correlated with the former, which, unfortunately, is very little understood.

Energy-differentiation: The four-fold division of the zodiac which we have studied so far gives us four basic types of cosmic *substance*: Fire-Air; Water-Earth. This is the most fundamental zodiacal differentiation inasmuch as the zodiac as a whole symbolizes, as already said, the building of a microcosm. Substance is the most fundamental thing in any building. But "energy" and "form" are just as important. Therefore we shall see that the zodiac is, most logically, susceptible of two other types of differentiation, referring respectively to energy and form.

Energy is not very different from substance. It is substance activated and released, as modern physics has shown most definitely. Thus we can expect the principle of "energy-differentiation" to be similar to that of "substance-differentiation." Both are based on the principle of polar dualism; of action and reaction. The *energy-zodiac* will thus be eight-fold, while the *substance-zodiac* is four-fold.

According to T. O. McGrath (*Timing Business Activity and the Sun*, p. 12):

> "It is known that all bodies such as the sun and its satellites are charged bodies and are surrounded by a magnetic field;— that in any magnetic body having two poles (the sun and its satellites are such bodies), the magnetic currents circulate from the north to the south pole, become neutral at each 90 degrees, and reach a maximum intensity at each 45 degrees."

If such is the case, it is evident that the points of maximum release of energy are to be found mid-way between equinoxes

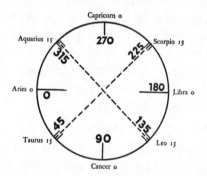

and solstices. These points are thus on the following degrees of the circle: 45-135-225-315; or in terms of the usual zodiacal nomenclature: Taurus 15; Leo 15; Scorpio 15; Aquarius 15. These points are not unknown to some occultists. They correspond to what has been called: the Four Gates of Avataric Descent. As an "Avatar" in ancient terminology is in fact a *release of cosmic energy*, the meaning of the phrase is quite evident. These Four Gates are symbolized by the four symbolic creatures: the Bull—the Lion—the Eagle—the Angel. Each of them depicts a particular type of dynamic release, a particular type or Ray of Power—and of power-releasing "initiation."

The Bull and the Lion represent *individuating* power, power rooted in the planet, i.e., in concrete selfhood. On the other hand, the Eagle and the Angel symbolize *collectivating* power; power that expands the individual into the collective and the universal. We might add that the Bull is power toward the formation of the individual being, while the Lion is power emanating from the individual being. The Eagle is power toward the formation of the universal being, while the Angel is power emanating from the universal being.

In the cycle of the year the four "avataric" points occur approximately on May 6; August 8; November 8; February 5. At these times the energies or realizations which were gathered in at equinoxes and solstices are released and made effective. It might interest the numerologist to consider the fact that the figures in the number of each of these eight points of the circle add up to the digit 9: (45, 90, 135, etc.). Baha'u'llah, the great Persian prophet, whom many consider as the Avatar of the new Aquarian Age, was born on November 12, very close to the Eagle-point—a very fitting time for one who preached the gospel of a "universal religion," and in general of an all-inclusive planetary synthesis. He took the number 9 as the symbol of his message.

Form differentiation: Energy operates on a polar rhythm of action and reaction; thus any type of energy-differentiation is based on theoretically equal divisions and sub-divisions: 2 — 4 — 8. In ancient symbology 8 is the number of the Sun; 888, the number of the Christ, the triune Sun. The number 9 thus represents Him who wields the 8-fold power. But how is one to wield power, unless one has a form-of-power—an engine—in which to *hold* and from which to *release* power at will? We cannot go fully into a discussion of the meaning of the term "form-of-power."* Suffice it to say that there can be no controlled and rhythmical release of energy unless there is some sort of "engine" through which this release is effected. All engines are "forms-of-power;" that is, forms which control the generation, concentration and distribution of power.

Three operations always: generation, concentration and distribution. Therefore the basic number of all forms-of-power (and we probably could say of all types of engineering) is 3. The engineer uses push and pull. Push and pull are two things; but "uses" involves a third principle. Action and reaction: such is the pure energy-rhythm. But a third term is necessary: interaction, if the energy is to build an organic body. A body is not a pipe through which tides of energy have their ebb and flow. It assimilates substance. It holds energy. It transforms power. It uses ebb and flow to step up the level or potential of the energy. And this is "organic living"—which always involves three basic faculties: self-maintenance, self-reproduction, self-realization.

We could go on almost indefinitely enumerating trinities of principles in all realms of being and becoming. But here, with the zodiac and with all "equatorial" elements, we deal mainly with power—with the power that builds and regenerates organisms or bodies. And the most satisfactory formulation of the trinity of elements which enters in this building operation is the one already mentioned: *generation, concentration* and *distribution.*

We saw that at the four crucial points of the year's cycle there was a generation of power. The results of this generation are four basic types of "substances": Fire-Air, Water-Earth. *Through* these four "substances" or cosmic elements power will operate according to the triple rhythm above mentioned. This will give us the following scheme of operation:

---

* This point has been discussed in our book, *Art as Release of Power* (1929).

The Signs of the Zodiac

At the spring equinox: Fire-power is   generated   *Aries*
                        then concentrated   *Taurus*
                        lastly distributed   *Gemini*
At the summer solstice: Water-power is generated   *Cancer*
                        then concentrated   *Leo*
                        lastly distributed   *Virgo*
At the fall equinox: Air-power is   generated   *Libra*
                        then concentrated   *Scorpio*
                        lastly distributed   *Sagittarius*
At the winter solstice: Earth-power is generated   *Capricorn*
                        then concentrated   *Aquarius*
                        lastly distributed   *Pisces*

Zodiacal signs of generation of power are called: *Cardinal* signs.

Zodiacal signs of concentration of power are called: *Fixed* signs.

Zodiacal signs of distribution of power are called: *Mutable* signs.

They can be referred respectively to spirit, soul and mind— *all three operating within the total "body," or "auric egg": the microcosm.* This microcosm can also be called, using the term in its most inclusive significance: personality. Personality, or perhaps, better still, the Living Person, is the synthesis of spirit, soul and mind operating within a body (or bodies, if one accepts the occult concept of several distinct vehicles for spiritual, animic and mental energies centered around the visible physical structure).

Spirit—or Life—generates. Soul concentrates. Mind distributes. Personality manifests—or hides! The work of life-development for every human being is to reveal in the operation of personality the generations of spirit, the concentrations of soul and the distributions of mind.

In order to make the symbolical picture complete we have only to relate the four-fold and the three-fold classification. We shall then try to understand how:

Fire-power (Aries)	concentrates through Earth (Taurus), is distributed through Air (Gemini).
Water-power (Cancer)	concentrates through Fire (Leo), is distributed through Earth (Virgo).
Air-power (Libra)	concentrates through Water (Scorpio), is distributed through Fire (Sagittarius).
Earth-power (Capricorn)	concentrates through Air (Aquarius), is distributed through Water (Pisces).

This may seem rather involved and disconcerting; and so we may try another way of stating the zodiacal "formula:"

Spirit-Fire (Aries) is generative Fire: Electric Fire.
Soul-Fire (Leo) is concentrative Fire: Solar Fire.
Mind-Fire (Sagittarius) is distributive Fire: Fire by friction.

This means that:

When Fire generates it is operating in terms of spirit.
When Fire concentrates it is operating in terms of soul.
When Fire distributes it is operating in terms of mind.

In other words:

Generative Fire is the starting-point of individual selfhood (Aries).

Concentrative Fire refers to the creative release of self, by means of which the soul knows itself whole and god-like (Leo).

Distributive Fire is that fire which blends, synthetizes and universalizes all elements and energies prior to the Christ-birth —the birth of the universal being (Sagittarius).*

The same procedure will bring out more clearly the significance of the other elements:

---

* We shall not attempt here to explain more in detail what these three Fires represent; but in H. P. Blavatsky's *The Secret Doctrine* and in Alice Bailey's *A Treatise on Cosmic Fire* much is said concerning these three Fires that operate in and through all living organisms. It will be relatively easy to work out the correspondences if one is endowed with the type of mind necessary for such a performance. If not, the accepted astrological formulation can be used or the formulation which we shall introduce presently and in which the signs of the zodiac are interpreted in terms of the pattern of houses previously studied.

Generative Water (Cancer) operates in terms of spirit. It is the power that gives birth to concrete selfhood, that creates a concrete basis of operation—a home—for the individual self.

Concentrative Water (Scorpio) operates in terms of soul. It concentrates and sustains the collectivating urge of spirit-Air (Libra), the impulse toward "re-birth in Christ."

Distributive Water (Pisces) operates in terms of mind. It effects the synthesis of energies that were brought to creative focalization in Capricorn, and vitalized in Aquarius.

Generative Air (Libra) operates in terms of spirit. It is the power that gathers and communalizes the emanations of individuals.

Concentrative Air (Aquarius) operates in terms of soul. It gives vitality and momentum to the spiritual Earth (Capricorn). It is the breath of the collective soul.

Distributive Air (Gemini) operates in terms of mind. It exteriorizes and interprets the individual impulsion of Aries, once focalized and insubstantiated in Taurus.

Generative Earth (Capricorn) operates in terms of spirit. It is the power of incarnation, the power to assume a body—from the point of view of the involving spirit.

Concentrative Earth (Taurus) operates in terms of soul. It gives substance and depth to the Aries impulses.

Distributive Earth (Virgo) operates in terms of mind. It spreads the creative release of self of Leo through space, where it is seen as a mass of polar energies (The Virgin of Light). Discrimination is aroused in the mind as the problem of dealing with polarities, with light and shade, arises.

From this, we can see how each cosmic element is susceptible of assuming three distinct functions, somewhat as a man can act, feel and think at the same time: 1) as a father to his son; 2) as a husband to his wife; 3) as a comrade and coworker with his associates and friends, thus (roughly speaking) generating, concentrating and distributing the energies of his own being.

The Zodiac as the Cycle of the Planetary Individual

So far we have considered zodiacal signs mostly from the point of view of their being a series of cosmic energies projected as it were by the Macrocosm (the Twelve Hierarchies) upon the microcosm; in other words as a series of formative operations, or phases of the building of this microcosm. This is the equatorial-collective viewpoint. But we can also think of the zodiac as the cycle of houses of the planetary Individual Who "dwells at the North Pole," and for Whom a year is as a day, with six months of sunlight (Aries to Libra) and six months of darkness (Libra to Aries), at least theoretically speaking. From such a standpoint the zodiac becomes interpreted in terms of *consciousness* rather than in terms of energy.

Such a consciousness-interpretation is most valuable, as it brings the signs of the zodiac in relation to the houses, and thus an interpenetration of meanings is shown which helps one to understand much of the confused traditional statements as to the significance of both houses and signs. Besides, a sort of algebraic formula is thus evolved which can easily be shown to be the sub-structure underneath all dramatic and mythological interpretations of the zodiac known to students of astrology and occultism. The most remarkable of these interpretations is undoubtedly the one detailed in Sampson's book *The Zodiac*. Alice Bailey gave another traditional interpretation when relating, in a series of lectures, the story of the Twelve Labors of Hercules. Hercules is the Sun, and his Twelve Labors are the twelve cosmic operations of the zodiac seen from a regenerative, rather than a formative, standpoint.

In ordinary astrological works the zodiacal signs are presented as the basic factors of significance, and the houses model their meanings after them. But from our standpoint we find in the twelve-fold pattern of the dial of houses a basic formula of individual unfoldment; and it is this pattern—a purely abstract one—which establishes the most universal series of meanings. It is of course purely a numerological pattern dealing with the significance of the numbers from 1 to 12 inclusive; but the numbers are made significant by being projected, as it were, geometrically. This projection is the wheel or dial of houses. Aries becomes thus significant because of being an equatorial-organic projection of No. 1; Taurus, of No. 2, etc., up to Pisces, as No. 12. The axis 1-6 represents the dualism of self and not-self, of "I and Thou." The axis 4-7 represents the dualism of experience: subjective experience and objective experience—or of private and public behavior. We hope that the following table will make the matter clear. It should be studied in connection with the table of meanings of houses on page 225. Modern astrological textbooks, such as those written by Alan Leo, C. E. O. Carter,* A. G. Libra, Parker, etc., are full of valuable added references to the meaning of the signs of the zodiac, singly and in groups. As Carter writes:

> "The task of interpreting the zodiacal script has been attempted by many writers, each approaching the work from his own standpoint. It is far from my desire even tacitly to differ from their conclusions or to seek to supersede anything written before. The contents of the Circle of Zodiacal Wisdom are inexhaustible, and present all-various aspects of the integrality of Truth."
>
> *The Zodiac and the Soul*, p. 14.

The last sentence of this quotation gives us the clue to much that could be developed at length; especially the term "contents." The zodiac represents, we said, the element of "substance." But substance means also contents. The zodiac gives us a knowledge of the life-contents of every living entity.

---

* Read especially, in *The Zodiac and the Soul*, the chapter "The Signs and Planets as Cosmic Ideals."

The houses tell us the manner in which these contents are distributed in a form of selfhood and destiny. The Planets are focal points for and symbols of all life-activities. The Degrees give us a clue to the inherent creative significance of all activities and all focalizations.

THE ZODIACAL FORMULA

Signs of Zodiac	Abstract Meaning	Concrete and Traditional Meaning	Parts of the Body Ruled
ARIES 1	The Idea of self. The primordial archetypal structure of the individual. The Will-to-be-manifest.	Desire, pioneering, initiative, courage. Forceful entrance into things. Rashness and impulsiveness. The male power.	Head: The cerebro-spinal system.
TAURUS 2	The primordial substance of manifestation for the self. The synthesis of the past, as inherited tendencies. All basic possessions.	Inertia, practicality, concreteness, bondage to the Earth and to the energies of the Earth. Determination, Energy, Fruitfulness. The female power.	Neck: Cerebellum and ears.
GEMINI 3	The relation between self and substance. The function of linkage and the urge to integrate through rhythm and form.	Intellect, sensation and nerve-action. Changeability, Duality. Restlessness. Cleverness. Literary and artistic ability. Skill.	Nerves, lungs. Hands, arms and shoulders.
CANCER 4	The concrete foundation for the expression of the I AM. The living organism and its power of growth.	The home and all domestic feelings. The soul and all psychic feelings. Imagination. Receptivity. Sensitiveness. Mediumship. Suggestion.	The chest cavity; the breasts and the stomach; the mucous membranes.
LEO 5	The power to express the I AM. All modes of self-expression and creative activity. Man, the Actor and Performer.	Imperious self-expression. Assumption of authority. Love of pleasure and luxuries. Speculation. The Arts. Child-bearing. Intuition. Dynamic intensity.	The heart and the spine.
VIRGO 6	The judgment of self and of life upon all creative activities. Discrimination through a critical analysis of the fruits of action. Adjustment.	Critical discrimination of the mind. Analytical faculties. Susceptibility. Readiness to serve or to be served. Selfishness. Orderliness. Fastidiousness. Utilitarian outlook.	The small intestines and the general food metabolism. The solar plexus. The spleen.
LIBRA 7	The realization of the Not-Self. Meeting "the others." Objectivation of consciousness through association and partnership.	Social consciousness. Affableness. Love of beauty. The longing for comradeship. Sympathy. Equipoise. Justice. Spiritual devotion. Operative wholeness.	The kidneys and perhaps the liver.
SCORPIO 8	The substance of association and marriage. Manifestation of the urge to unite with others. Regeneration of the attitude of self-centeredness.	Sex. Occultism. All types of power and magical operation. Regenerative function. Will. Obstinacy. Revengefulness. Jealousy. Driving force.	The sex-organs. The lower intestines. The bladder.
SAGIT-TARIUS 9	Expansion of relationship. The relation between relationships. Abstract linkage and integration through perspective.	Open-mindedness. Vision. Honesty. Tendency to generalize. Compassion. The will to conquer new fields. Passion for ideas. Love of outdoor and travels.	The thighs and the pelvic region. The ovaries. The sciatic nerve. The muscular system.

The Signs of the Zodiac

THE ZODIACAL FORMULA

SIGNS OF ZODIAC	Abstract Meaning	Concrete and Traditional Meaning	Parts of the Body Ruled
CAPRI-CORN 10	The concrete foundation for relationships. Life in the social organism. The sustainment of marriage.	Ambition, perseverance, political genius. Reserve. Strong reliance upon social factors and all permanent structures—including spiritual ones. Industry. Stability.	The skeleton. The knees and all joints.
AQUA-RIUS 11	The power to express ideals and to create in terms of social behavior. The creativeness of relationship and of marriage.	Idealism. Humanitarianism. Self-expression through collective movements, brotherhoods. Group-feelings. Sensationalism. Dramatic sense. Creative genius, as a mouthpiece of the race.	The legs and ankles. The sanguineous system.
PISCES 12	The judgment of society upon ideals and their modes of operation. Relationship judging itself and "the two" withdrawing, each in his or her own self-meditation.	Openness to life. Resignation. Psychism. Mysticism. Memory. Conventionality. Devotion. Introspection. Self-abnegation. Inferiority complex. Other-worldliness.	The feet. The lymphatic system.

267

VIII. *Planets and Personality*

WE DEFINED "personality" as "a synthesis of patterns of behavior; as the sum total of all the outer motions and emotions of the human being: the total rhythm of his life-operations—from the way he walks and twitches his lips to his behavior on the battlefield or on a concert platform." We said that, as without activity there could be no "personality," we can speak of it as a complex of activities. Such statements are sufficient proof that we do not give to the term the rather pejorative meaning which theosophists and students of esoteric philosophy ordinarily affix to it.

We do not consider personality as representing the "outer" being in contradistinction to the so-called individuality or "inner" being. We feel that this opposition or dualism is not particularly fruitful at our present stage of human development. Rather, it tends to focalize human behavior in a way which is more devotional-ethical than integrative and esthetical—the latter term being used as previously defined. Personality, to us and presumably to men like General Smuts and most modern psychologists, is *the whole human being in operation.* It is not the whole human being in essence or abstractly, but in actual manifestation and to the extent to which it is perceptible to other personalities functioning *at the same level* of operation.

No astrologer—and as well no psychoanalyst—can interpret a life and destiny at a level higher than that at which he himself functions. A narrow-minded clerk in a small town office cannot know the personality of a great saint or genius as it is. He will, of course, pass judgment upon it or possibly worship it, but he is not in a position to know it and to evaluate it as a personality—even though he may react most sharply to some features of it. Personality signifies wholeness *in actu*. And there is no real perception, or at any rate no understanding, of personality unless the totality of its components is apprehended, consciously or through intuitive feelings. And no one can apprehend this totality unless he be at the same level of human development, or, if at a higher level, to be still able to put himself temporarily at the lower level.

These remarks are necessary, because people often speak of personality as if it were an absolutely obvious thing similarly apprehended by everyone. Reacting to some phases of a personality, and understanding or even being aware of the reality —that is, of the human wholeness, which is the personality itself—are two very different operations. Personality, as a synthesis of patterns of behavior, may encompass many phases of activities most difficult to apprehend. We are not referring here to an exaggerated *dédoublement* of personality which produces two absolutely distinct types of behavior in relation to one physical organism, but merely to the fact that personality may involve series of activities which transcend the normal conscious development of mankind as it is today. Personality is a "balance-sheet" showing the ever-changing relationship of conscious to unconscious, individual to collective factors, in the whole human being. Men whose inner beings are flooded with projections from the deeper layers of the "collective unconscious" are, as personalities, complex and hard to fathom. Only their peers can know them, can know the total pattern of their behavior at all levels. For, as Walt Whitman wrote, with cryptic beauty of utterance:

"Only themselves understand themselves and the like of themselves,
And souls only understand souls."

Undoubtedly one of the greatest achievements of astrological technique is the power one acquires, through mastering it, to see in a birth-chart the blue-print of a total personality. We have already seen how one can isolate and interpret the individual and collective factors which constitute, as it were, the warp and woof of personality. But the pattern of the tapestry is to be apprehended only by studying those astrological entities which are foci of color, foci of activity, foci of significance. These entities, considered in their infinite correlations and not as isolated dots, make all together the design of the life-tapestry. They reveal the personality as a pattern of multifarious behavior, symbolizing from the most matter of fact to the most exalted or transcendental modes of physio-psychological activity.

These astrological entities come under two general categories. First, the planets themselves, including Sun and Moon; second, abstract points derived from the relationships between either the orbits of the planets (nodes) or the positions of said planets in reference to horizon and meridian (parts). This chapter will be devoted to a brief analysis of the basic significance of planets in terms of personality-analysis; the next, to a study of the nodes and of the most important among the parts.

We shall, however, once more have to divide our field of study, and to classify the planets in at least two essential manners. The first type of classification deals with the motivating power and the source of the activities symbolized by the planets. We shall distinguish between *planets referring to the conscious* and *planets referring to the unconscious*—using the terms "conscious" and "unconscious" as used by C. G. Jung, and as defined in a previous chapter (Cf. p. 66, *Astrology and Analytical Psychology*). Outside of these two categories we shall place the Sun as the symbol of the integrating energies of the Self, which is described by Jung as the "center of the totality of the psyche." The psyche includes both unconscious and conscious contents. To integrate these contents—that is, consciously to assimilate the contents of the unconscious—is the essence of the process of individuation, of which the Sun is the active symbol.

The Sun as Integrator

Astrology, being a system of symbolic interpretation of significant astronomical facts, must obviously differentiate strongly between the Sun—a life- and light-giving star which is the center of the astronomical system to which we belong —and planets which are merely reflectors or transmitters of light, and of which the Earth itself is one. If we refer to the ego as "a complex of representations which constitutes the center of my field of consciousness and appears to possess a very high degree of continuity and identity," it is clear that the astrological symbol thereof is the Earth itself *as seen from the birth-place of the native*. The continuous field of consciousness of any man is what is contained within the boundaries of his horizon, and by implications what, though below the horizon, will emerge into the field of his consciousness.

In other words, the quadrature of the astrological chart (horizon and meridian—and especially Ascendant and Mid-Heaven) represents the form of the field of consciousness. The ego may be considered as the birth-point itself, the center of the chart—or, in an even more accurate symbolization, the apex of the pyramid built on the four angles of the chart. The ego is not the integrator—because it is only an abstract point. Neither are Ascendant nor Mid-Heaven integrating factors, for they too have only structural implications. They determine the *form* which will have to be taken by the process of integration. They do not symbolize the *quality of energy* by the release of which this process will, or may, ultimately be completed.

Building the field of consciousness *as a clearly formed structure centered accurately in the ego* is like building a perfect eye with the power of precise focalization through the lens and the eye's muscles, so that the image reflected upon the retina falls exactly on the "yellow spot" of the retina which alone is endowed with full sensitiveness to light. It is what the great eye specialist and philosopher, Dr. Bates, called "central fixation"; and this operation requires muscular practice and visualizing or imaging practice, including relaxation.

In a psychological sense, "central fixation" refers to the use of the intellect—the mechanism of conscious focalization—according to the laws of logic and formal thinking. Much, if not all, of classical and post-classical Greek philosophy (especially since Aristotle) and all Western science (especially since the Renaissance) and modern scientific philosophy (for instance, Bertrand Russell) constituted and still constitute a vast collective training in mental "central fixation." In the psychic-spiritual realm certain types of esoteric practices, some derived from the Buddhistic world-viewpoint in the East, others from the Pythagorean philosophy, aimed at a similar "central fixation" of the soul-energies within a formed structure of "I Am-ness." As already said, it was around the sixth century B.C. that this problem of mental focalization began to dominate the outlook of the élite of mankind. This process of "central fixation" in the field of the conscious has been going on throughout the European cycle (especially since Abelard), and has produced the Western man, with what Jung called so graphically his "cramp of the conscious."

Just as Dr. W. H. Bates asked his patients to relax their eyes by imagining a perfectly black spot, so Dr. Jung asks his to relax their conscious intellectualism by "letting things happen" and by practices of psychic relaxation, such as the use of spontaneous creative "phantasy."

If thus the chart-axes represent the structure of the field of consciousness—the structure of the "eye," symbolically—the Sun stands for the "light" releasing the energy (the photons) by means of which vision is made possible. In a real sense the eye as an organ of vision is molded structurally by the nature of the light. Likewise the ego—the conscious "I"—is moulded by the power emanating from the Self. Fittingly therefore, it is said that the Ascendant and the other "angles" of the chart

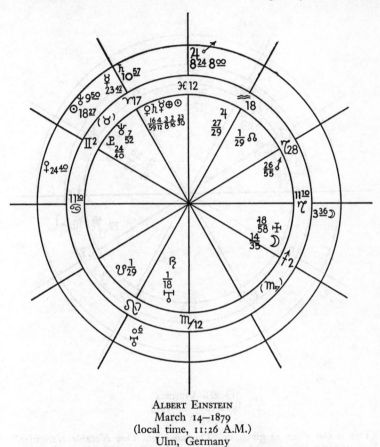

ALBERT EINSTEIN
March 14–1879
(local time, 11:26 A.M.)
Ulm, Germany
Planets in outer circle are progressed for early April, 1935.

distribute the power of the Sun, as we shall see in the next chapter. The Sun is the life-energy. The chart's axes are channels for the distribution and "transformation" of this solar energy within the field of consciousness.

The Sun, however, should not be considered as the symbol

of the Self. It represents the *power* of the Self; but the Self itself is not only power. It is power in relation to form. It is

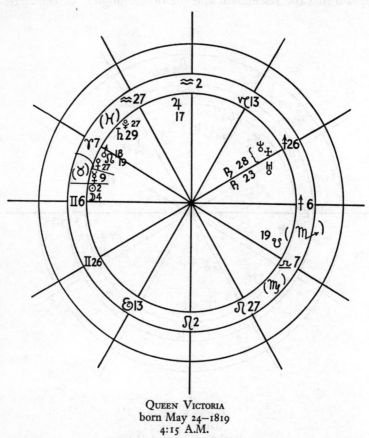

QUEEN VICTORIA
born May 24—1819
4:15 A.M.

(This is the chart as given in *"Thousand and One Notable Nativities."*
For a slightly different one read *American Astrology*: "The Victorian Era as
Seen through Queen Victoria's Birth-chart," by D. Rudhyar.)

power operating through a form and regenerating substance.
In other words, the Self, if its nature can at all be ascertained
astrologically, is the relation between the Sun and the axes,
horizon and meridian. More accurately still, it is the relation

between the significance of the zodiacal positions occupied by the Sun and the four angles—significance in terms of zodiacal signs (or sign subdivisions), of degree, and of angular relationship between these positions. The latter refer to the aspects between Sun, Ascendant and Mid-Heaven; but even more so to the house-position of the Sun.

This house-position of the Sun denotes the phase of individual selfhood and the period of the life in and through which the integrative power of the Self will be the most strongly operating. By referring to our previous tabulation of the meanings of houses, and to the schedule of the 28-year cycle, these two elements of personality and destiny can be easily ascertained—provided of course the exact birth-moment is known. The zodiacal position of the Sun (and its degree position) will show the quality of this integrative power in itself.

Take for instance Einstein's chart. The Sun is in the twenty-fourth degree of Pisces in the tenth house. Therefore the quality of the integrative power of his Self will be: synthesis, consummation, meditation and introspection. But the Sun being in the tenth house of public activity, profession, and of thinking (as a function of the individual selfhood), this power will operate through these tenth-house characteristics. The Sun's position also indicates that an intensification of the significant power of his destiny occurred when Einstein was in his twenty-second year, i.e., in 1901. Then he became inspector of patents in Berne, Switzerland; and it is probably about that time, a little after Planck's papers on the quantum theory were published, that at least the rudiments of the theory of relativity were developed. It was brought to the attention of the scientific world in 1905—when Einstein's "point of self" came in conjunction with Pluto. Moreover the Sun's degree, which, as we already said, "gives a clue to the inherent creative significance of all activities and all focalizations," carries this most fitting symbol: "A small island in the midst of the ocean; its happy inhabitants have created a world of their own." What could be more significant in the chart of the man who even wrote of "island universes" and did create new cosmic vistas!

As another illustration we can give Queen Victoria's chart, which symbolizes not only a personality, but, by implication at least, also the era which carries her name. The Sun had just risen at birth and it was about an hour after the new moon in Gemini. Here we have a personality of rare intellectual gifts (Gemini), an era which had all the rigidity and narrow viewpoints of over-emphasized intellectualism; which, moreover, saw the amazing growth of means of transportation and of travel—and of nervous disturbances. The twelfth-house meaning is shown in the fact that after her husband's death Queen Victoria lived in practical seclusion for most of her long life, and that she acted best when behind the scenes and through some great Prime Minister, as for instance Disraeli. The symbol of the Sun's degree gives the meaning of aristocracy and efficient strength of individuality. We may say that the whole Victorian era is a typical twelfth-house manifestation—a summing up, a period of karmic precipitation, the tail-end of a cycle prior to a strikingly new beginning, perhaps now about to manifest.

The most significant moment in her life came when, at the age of 56, plans were definitely made for the consecration of the British Empire and as an initial gesture her son was sent to India. Then her "point of self" had come to her Sun, and her personality had truly become a world-wide symbol, fully manifesting the power of her destiny—thus of her true Self. Her consecration as "Empress of India" came a year later, as the "point of self" was trine Jupiter, and in her first house. This and the Diamond Jubilee of 1897 (when "point of self" came to conjunction Jupiter in the tenth house) were the outer gestures of power. But the Queen's true selfhood is not to be found in them, but in the more concealed "backstage" moves which the twelfth-house lunation so aptly symbolizes.

Planets Referring to the Conscious

We are now considering the realm of the particular ego, which is the field of consciousness centered around the realization: "I am this or that." This realization by the conscious "I" that he is that particular being and no other is the first basic factor in the conscious life. Every living entity must first *be* itself as a definite exclusive form. This is the Saturn aspect. Then it must *maintain* itself, and such a factor of self-maintenance works out through the principle of compensatory action which is the foundation of all organic life. This is the Jupiter aspect. Finally it must *reproduce* itself through some sort of creative action—which refers astrologically to Mars.

These three planets (Saturn—Jupiter—Mars) are to be considered as the three positive or "masculine" planets, and for reasons which we shall consider later on, are paired with three other planets which are considered as negative or "feminine" planets: respectively—Moon, Mercury and Venus. The terms "masculine" and "feminine" are not particularly fortunate. It would be better to say that Saturn, Jupiter and Mars initiate life-processes. They act as *causal agents*; while the Moon, Mercury and Venus establish or vivify, complete or bring to fruition these same processes. We shall therefore consider these six "planets of the conscious" as being three pairs, each pair being connected with one of the three basic life-operations above mentioned. The reason for this procedure will be explained more fully later, as to do so now would complicate matters unnecessarily.

Saturn-Moon. Saturn, in Greek mythology, is the ruler of the Golden Age, the first age of childhood and innocence. It refers to the first process whereby the universal life-force becomes differentiated, limited, particularized as a living cell —as the initial seed. Such a process of differentiation is the absolutely necessary condition for individual existence, that is, existence as a separate self-sufficient entity. Psychologically speaking, Saturn symbolizes, therefore, that process which leads to the realization: "I am." This may not be, however, such a simple realization as it may seem and has seemed to many. Thus the modern psychologist speaks of the "ego-complex," as previously defined: "A complex of representations which constitutes the center of my field of consciousness."*

Within the "field of consciousness" life flows; in other words, changes take place, energy is released in actions and re-actions. This "psychic energy" which is contained and operates in the field of my consciousness (within the boundaries of my ego, set symbolically by Saturn) is represented astrologically by the Moon. The Moon is that portion of the Sun which is enclosed by Saturn—if such an astronomically peculiar sentence may be allowed. It is that portion of the life energy of the total being which I am aware of as myself, as the conscious ego which I am. Saturn refers to the abstract structure of this ego. The Moon pours into this structure "psychic energy"—and the result is a conscious entity, a particular living entity. The relation Saturn-Moon is therefore the relation: form-to-energy. Form conditions energy, though there is really a deep reciprocal action, which would be too long to discuss in such a brief survey.

Jupiter-Mercury. Jupiter is a much more mysterious symbol than most astrologers seem to believe. Its reputation as a sign of unalloyed good fortune does not appear to stand the test of psychological analysis, even though, in an abstract sense and ultimately, the process it symbolizes is always leading to an increase and expansion of consciousness—but at times through very dire ordeals. Jupiter is ordinarily opposed to Saturn as expansion is opposed to contraction. Saturn differ-

---

* *Psychological Types,* p. 540.

entiates the particular entity out of the universal matrix of life. Jupiter brings to the bound ego that which will compensate its one-sidedness, and thus will make it once more whole and universal.

Jupiter's function can be best expressed in practical or analytical psychology by the term "compensation." The self-compensatory character of the psyche, as an organism, has been mentioned in our chapter dealing with analytical psychology. Jupiter refers thus to the *anima* and *animus* of Jung's theory. But it means more. It is the function of compensation in all its possible aspects. Marc Jones defines Jupiter as "the point of the soul's precipitation out from itself into tangible life and definite being." It shows "the point of expression of true selfhood, of the purpose of incarnation." This means also "compensation" in a metaphysical sense. Because the soul may be regarded as that which constantly strives for harmonization and integration, and the "purpose of incarnation," as the neutralization of past disharmonies and failures—toward the establishment of harmony at a fully conscious level.

Jupiter is thus the power in us of right action, the voice of our true Destiny. Our conscious ego (Saturn-Moon) is the result of our past, the synthesis of our limitations and our ancestry. It is the present as the sum total of the past. But Jupiter is the future, pulling this present onward. It is the destiny which is to be ours, the destiny which will balance our past inadequacies, and fulfilling which we shall become whole. The soul and the ego are the two poles of a relation which operates by compensation. Thus for a masculine consciousness the soul, if projected as an image, is normally a woman—the Muse, the Eternal Feminine drawing us onward, etc. For a feminine consciousness the soul is the hero, the Christ-image, the Adonai, Siegfried the victorious, etc. It is always that which completes us, which makes us whole. It is also, for the devotee, the incarnate God, the savior, the spiritual teacher or *guru*: that divine personage who comes to us as representative of the Whole, however we may imagine this wholeness. Therefore Jupiter is God's path toward men. It is religion. It is ceremonial. It is also the King, as a symbol of the wholeness of the State; he whose justice and strength (ideally) compensate the weakness and failures of the citizen. In a Democratic state it is the Constitution.

Mercury makes the Jupiter function operative. And therefore it is intelligence, the vehicle of the soul. But alas! a vehicle which often throws off the divine Personage it carries and runs amuck, goaded by the moods of the Moon, or dominated by the separative crystallizing power of Saturn. Mercury as ruler of the nervous system brings sensation to the ego, that the ego may learn the lesson of relationship to the objects of the outer world. It unifies the reactions of the body. It is the servant of Zeus-Jupiter—but so often an unworthy messenger and a thief. The Moon, the feminine pole of Saturn, has moods and constantly changes. Mercury, which holds a similar relation toward Jupiter, is ever restless and molding itself upon the object of the sensation or the thought. Hindu *yoga* is largely a system of concentration by means of which the Jupiter function subdues the Mercury function.

If Jupiter assumes the position of an avenging God—if there is no other way to counteract Saturn's crystallizations—Mercury is likely to turn equally destructive and to shatter the Moon's tides; for Mercury is always more or less inimical to the Moon—unless Saturn has turned subservient to those functions of the unconscious which we shall presently study.

Mars-Venus. With this pair we deal with the centrifugal and centripetal forces of experience. Mars "shows the tendency of the life in expressing itself, moving from itself outward without particular regard for external conditions." It is "the first impulse of being in all outer revelation of self" (Marc Jones). In other words, it is the desire to move away from the center, the primordial Eros, the *libido*, as it flows outward through the psyche. It symbolizes all beginnings, all initiating impulses; self-projection as a release of sheer energy.

That which goes out from the psyche as Mars, returns to it as Venus. Venus is the effect experienced as a result of the way in which the outer world reacts to our Martian outgoing. The Martian impulse returns home filled with experiences, probably with bruises and possibly with wisdom. Venus is the end of the experience and what we have gathered as a result of it; thus it is the purveyor of consciousness, of knowledge and wisdom to the ego. It is symbolized by bees, because bees bring back to the hive the honey gathered from the flowers which are also the last product of the plant. It is therefore the symbol of all arts, of all social wisdom, of all that is matured out of experience. It also means emotions; because we get emotions, or effects, as a result of our outer contacts. Out of relationship arise joy or pain, songs or despair, art or sensuality. The soul of relationship is love. Mars-love is the love that is desire, self-projection, brute force toward self-reproduction in and through others, but with no regard for the others. Venus-love is the love that is wise, the love that arises from true interchange, from altruistic companionship: love-wisdom.

This, then, is the outline of the conscious trinity of basic life-powers, each active and reactive, which astrology symbolizes as Saturn-Moon, Jupiter-Mercury, Mars-Venus. Every living entity must first *be* itself as a definite form (Saturn); then it must *maintain* itself as a self-compensating system (Jupiter); finally it must *reproduce* itself through creative action (Mars). "Being" manifests through feelings (Moon); "maintenance" operates through intelligence or instinct (Mercury); "self-reproduction" is demonstrated in the power to bear children or ideas (Venus).

Thus the sphere of the conscious. We come now to the process whereby the conscious transcends or destroys itself.

The Astrology of Personality

Planets Referring to the Unconscious

A. THE PERSONAL UNCONSCIOUS

The way in which the planets Neptune and Pluto have been discovered serves as a symbolical illustration of the relationship between conscious and unconscious. It was found that certain anomalies in the behavior of Uranus could be explained only by postulating the influence of another planet beyond its orbit. Such an influence was carefully measured, and the place of Neptune was approximately determined; after which astronomers were able to find this planet at the place thus analytically discovered.

The existence of many psychological anomalies, neuroses and supernormal states likewise led some psychologists to attempt to chart an unknown psychological realm the existence of which we have apprehended so far mostly by the way it upsets conscious behavior. It is apparent that our conscious ego is not always master of its house, that at times powers which seem to well up from nowhere or from some ancestral mist overwhelm our consciousness. Gone are our small categories and barriers; forgotten are our sense of self-preservation and our social training—and we move bewildered, swayed by deep commands, which are voiced by unrecognized forces.

C. G. Jung was perhaps the first of modern psychologists to recognize that the realm of these unknown forces was really a twofold one. In this he was merely following (unconsciously, perhaps) the ancient Kabbalistic tradition which speaks of a "memory of Nature," an "astral light" which is also twofold, lower and higher, deceitful and ensnaring in its lower portions, celestial and pure in its higher. Jung's interpretation of the personal and the collective unconscious is naturally very different outwardly from the occult teaching concerning the astral light; yet the latter may prove necessary some day to sustain and deepen the former.

282

Planets and Personality

As we have already seen, the personal unconscious is the sum total of repressed or submerged contents of a man's psyche. Freud began a study of this realm in which are hidden the seeds of neuroses, and to which we relegate all the feelings, thoughts, impressions which we refuse to admit to the shrine of our conscious being, and from which we shrink in fear, disgust or suppressed hatred. Life brought to us these psychic facts and filled them with vital energy; but instead of allowing this vital energy to spend itself in correlation with our ego, within the sphere of our conscious thinking, feeling and behavior, we turn back, as it were, the flow of this energy and push the disturbing thoughts or feelings, impressions or intuitions into dark caves where memory can no longer call them to the light of the conscious. There they may fester and decay, sending poisonous emanations into the conscious; or the subterranean pressure they exert may lead us unaware to deeds and thoughts bewildering to our conscious ego.

Astrology has probably no way of checking up these hidden and repressed contents of the personal unconscious, yet it contains in its symbolism certain factors which enable us to discern and analyze the action of the repressive tendencies which twist and dam up the normal flow of psychological functions. In other words, it can detect the backwash of the psychic energy from the conscious to the unconscious as it occurs in the psyche. It can determine the polarity of psychological functions, some of which act in a repressive and inward direction, others which operate in the normal way, from the center outward.

Here we come to the factor of planetary retrogression. Due to the fact that on the Earth we see the solar system from a somewhat peripherical point and not from the center, the other planets of the system move in apparently irregular manner. At times they appear to stand still, at others to move backward in the direction opposed to that of their normal course around the Sun. In the first case we speak of a stationary planet; in the second case, of a retrograde planet. Otherwise the planet's motion is direct. These geocentric characteristics of the planets (Sun and Moon not included, for they are always direct) are of great importance psychologically. Direct, retrograde, stationary: This trinity of modes of planetary motion corresponds to some very basic elements of what we may call *psychological dynamics*. Back of these types of motion we find the still more general factor of *planetary speed* (apparent speed, in this case). From the point of view of the earthly observer, the speed at which the planets move across the sky is constantly changing. These variations of speed correspond to variations in functional intensity of the psychological factors symbolized by the planets. The functional intensity varies as a result of many causes; but the speed-variations are at least one of these causes, symbolically speaking. This is especially demonstrable when we consider the speed-variations of Mercury and the Moon, but it applies to all planets.

The faster the speed, the more rapid the flow of psychic energy in and through the function considered. When the planet becomes stationary, the speed, of course, equals zero. The function symbolized is shown to have extreme stability. A peculiar kind of doggedness may well describe this condition. That particular factor in the conscious make-up of the person will not let go. It will resist change. It will offer a tremendous power of inertia. As it was in the beginning, so will it be ever after. Persons born with stationary planets will always present a characteristic of this nature. This of course will be emphasized if the stationary planet is also the ruler of the chart, or strongly placed. The corresponding psychological factor will quietly but stubbornly hold its own within the consciousness, whatever may happen.

Many examples could be given, but the difficulty is that usually the psychological characteristics depicted by a stationary planet are not obvious, except from the point of view of psychological analysis. The Saturn stationary in Richard Strauss' chart is a good illustration of strong egocentricity and of an equally strong sense of form. Its being in Libra gives an added artistic significance.

A stationary planet is said to be "stationary direct" or "stationary retrograde" according to the direction of its subsequent motion. In psycho-astrological analysis a planet can be considered stationary within a few minutes of the exact point at which it changes the direction of its course. The speed factor here involved is purely relative, and practically all that is required or useful to consider is whether the planet's speed is above average (in which case it is fast moving) or below average (slow moving).

Retrograde planets symbolize the turning back of the libido (psychic energy or life-force) from the conscious into the unconscious. If a planet is retrograde, the function it represents is not activated for conscious operation. The psychic contents related to this function, instead of emerging directly in the conscious and thus influencing directly our behavior, are thrown back temporarily into the unconscious. This does not mean necessarily that they are divested of their energy. They merge with other unconscious contents, then reappear later in the consciousness through the agency of one of these functions of the unconscious which we shall study presently. The latter correspond to the planets Uranus, Neptune and Pluto.

We may consider at first the planet Saturn, builder of the ego-complex. Through differentiation and isolation Saturn sets apart a certain amount of life-energy and binds it into a form. It builds walls to protect and differentiate the particular entity thus conditioned and isolated from its surroundings. Saturn, in other words, sets up a system of defense against the outside world by emphasizing the separate characteristics of the ego. "I am this particular attribute, and no one else is, or can touch it."

If Saturn is retrograde at birth, the native will not naturally and spontaneously experience or feel this. He will not feel it to be true especially with regard to the outer world. His Saturnian defense-mechanism will not be directed against the encroachments of the outer world—at least, not immediately and spontaneously. He will not feel himself fortified against the outer world—because the pattern of his conscious being is not very rigid. He will yield easily to external influences which will constantly tend to blur this pattern of his consciousness. He will be somewhat defenseless with regard to external contacts, and will appear shy, introverted, uneasy, un-self-assertive—or else he will take an arrogant attitude to shield his weak stand. His manners may then be abrupt and explosive.

Saturn retrograde will direct this pattern-crystallizing and wall-making power inward. Self-assertion will be against inner influences. The person will yield outwardly, but show a great power of resistance against inner, unconscious suggestions. He will fortify himself spontaneously against impacts coming from the collective unconscious, from race tradition and collective standards. He will develop a sense of destiny, separating him inwardly from his fellowmen, while he will often be unable to resist the pressure of demands made upon him by friends and foes alike. He will be obdurately self-centered in his innermost self, while he may be unable to resist anyone asking favors or gifts.

It may also be that a man with Saturn retrograde finds himself mostly preoccupied with building or strengthening his growing individuality. The differentiating function then works inward, strengthening the magnetic field of the Self and crystallizing its contents into a form as yet unconscious. He will yield without, only to be better able to endure within. Such an astrological factor is found in persons who have to guard their individuality against psychic or religious or racial influences which are particularly strong in their im-

mediate family environment. The enemy is in the unconscious, pressing from within. The past is menacing the present. The first psychological task is therefore one of *inner*
self-protection and self-assertion. Thus the Saturn function operates inward, and its effect will usually be felt only indirectly in the consciousness and in the behavior, blended with
other unconscious elements. Nicholas II, the last Czar of
Russia, had Saturn retrograde. Ramakrishna, the great Hindu
mystic, and the seer, Swedenborg, furnish other examples.

In such cases the Moon (polar opposite of Saturn) finds
herself, as it were, unprotected. The Moon can never be retrograde; but because of moving around the Earth she is *either
within or without the Earth orbit.* When within (nearer a
solar conjunction), she operates more in connection with the
solar energy of the Self. When without (nearer a solar opposition), the feelings are more "extraverted" or dominated
by the objective mind. It might be said also that outside of the
Earth's orbit the Moon follows the centrifugal pull of Mars,
the planet of all beginnings; when inside, she gives in to the
centripetal attractions of Venus, the planet of consummation
and fulfillment. If the Moon is inside the Earth's orbit and
Saturn is retrograde, the feelings are directed inward; we have
a clear case of introversion. Love goes to an inner image
rather than to actual and real persons. The feelings are in any
case somewhat unprotected when Saturn is retrograde. They
are not firmly anchored in, or they may cause much trouble
to, the conscious ego.

When Jupiter is retrograde the function of soul-compen-
sation is turned inward, affecting the consciousness almost
exclusively through the unconscious, that is, by means of
dreams and similar projections. If at the same time Uranus is
strong, these projections from the unconscious can become
extraordinarily vivid. If Jupiter is weak by sign position, this
may mean that the compensation-function is endowed with
little energy; but if at the same time it is strong by house

position, the compensation, though weak, is brought out constantly to the consciousness by the power of circumstances. This remark applies more or less to all planets. Aspects to other planets may, however, introduce other and contrary factors. Jupiter in an angular house (first, fourth, seventh, tenth) is typical of strength by house position. If direct, the native is consciously ruled by his Destiny, usually for a group-purpose. He may experience this inner power in the form of some great Personality leading him to appointed ends. This may be so especially if Jupiter is retrograde. If stationary, the native is almost wholly subject to this ruling power. The Emperor of Austria, Francis Joseph, whose rule seems to have been the very center of precipitation of the karma of Europe, had, according to Alan Leo, Jupiter retrograde in the fourth house, square Mars on the Descendant. His was altogether an extraordinary chart. Bismarck also had Jupiter retrograde. Aristide Briand, the famous French Premier, had Jupiter and Saturn retrograde conjunct in his fourth house.

Mercury retrograde symbolizes a mind inwardly turned, either because of a mystical trend or because of a congenital slowness of perception and an inability to project thoughts outward. According to Marc Jones, the position of Mercury before and after the Sun represents respectively mental eagerness or deliberateness. "Mental chemistry" can be shown by linking these positions of Mercury together with the speed of the Moon's motion. Paul Clancy traced a parallelism between quickness of mind and the speed of Mercury's motion. Outwardly a retrograde Mercury may give a slow mind; but by no means necessarily so. It may just as well be a mind preoccupied mostly with the collective unconscious, the mind of a seer. Abdul Baha, whom the Bahai consider as a divine Personage, had Mercury and Saturn retrograde and in trine. Mercury was in Gemini six degrees ahead of the Sun; the Moon, in conjunction with the great star of Persia, Regulus, also trine Neptune in Aquarius. In other cases, we have the basis for peculiar mental complexes. An example of a vacillating mind is given by Louis XVI, the French king executed by the revolutionists. He had Mercury retrograde in exact conjunction with the Sun, also Saturn and Uranus retrograde.

Mars retrograde indicates that impulses to action do not flow outward from the ego into spontaneous expression, but move back to the unconscious where they become united with some unconscious contents (often collective images). It is the power inherent in the latter which really impels the native to action. Action does thus not arise from spontaneous, clearly conscious impulses, but from a more or less unconscious motivation. Among the several retrograde planets in the chart of Annie Besant, late leader of the Theosophical Society, we find Mars. Her acts often arose from motives hidden in the unconscious, whether personal or collective.

Such a condition may affect the sexual forces. They may be thrown back into the unconscious, forming complexes and neuroses. On the other hand, we may deal with a definite attempt to sublimate the desire-nature, as in the various *yoga* disciplines. In the case of Annie Besant, we note also that she became known first as an apostle of birth control.

With Venus retrograde we get a condition in which the fruits of experience are not brought to the conscious ego and normally assimilated or released through various types of emotions. There is often a strong lack of adjustment to the conditions of outer living. The emotional life is unsatisfied, and unconscious contents disturb the natural flow of consciousness and love. At times a strong emphasis on artistic creation is found, but this is usually colored by abnormal feelings. A desire for intoxicants may be connected with this. The romantic poet Alfred de Musset had Venus stationary retrograde.

Retrograde planets must not be asked to tell too much, for the reason that they indicate only the direction in which some psychological functions operate, but not what happens as a result of this backward flowing motion, which is to be judged on the basis of the chart as a whole. A boy and a girl instead of going to work at the factory, take the train and go to the city. We may know they have gone to the city; but that will not tell us how they will behave and what they will encounter in this city. Likewise we know that when a planet is retrograde the function it symbolizes does not operate in the so-called normal way. The psychic energy used by this function goes in the direction of the unconscious. What will happen to it there depends upon all the other factors of the chart.

B. THE COLLECTIVE UNCONSCIOUS

In the planets studied so far we have found a means of analyzing the make-up and constitution of the individual human being as he functions in the midst of the collectivity of which he is a part. Family, nation, race, religious group, club, trade union and factory are various types of collectivity. The individual acts in their midst and may help to create or transform them. But they also act upon the individual. If he shrinks from contacts and experiences within the collectivity, he becomes inhibited and acquires complexes or special attitudes which retrograde planets, together with other astrological elements, help us to analyze.

If the individual faces normally his group and society in general, then society influences him. The collective in him, that which is identical in all the men of his group, imposes upon the individual its ageless standards. Society gets hold of the individual through his instincts and traditions. Primordial images beat upon the inner walls of his consciousness, asking admittance. These images may be divine or they may be devilish. They are the voice of wholeness compelling the individual parts of the whole to take heed. The undertones of this collective voice are dark and possessive; its high overtones are vibrations of light, songs of liberated souls that draw upward toward the final goal of Man.

This voice of the collective, insofar as it acts upon individuals, is symbolized by the trinity of remote planets: Uranus, Neptune and Pluto. It is significant that these have become *publicly* known at a time when humanity is breaking through isolating barriers of creeds and dogmas, and, materially if not yet spiritually, all men flow into the ocean of a common humanity. Uranus became known as the American and French Revolutions broke the weight of feudalism and medievalism; Neptune, as humanitarianism and a rebirth of the religious spirit (or of its opposite pole, materialism), swept the world; Pluto, as mankind is getting on its way toward new structures of social relationships.

In the life of the individual these planets act in various ways and in widely varying degrees of intensity. The more universal or "wholeward" the consciousness, the more constructive and effective the action of these planetary agents of wholeness. In the unregenerate they may either remain individually ineffective, or else become symbols of the destruction of the en-shelled ego. In any case they come to the individual ego as forces from the beyond of consciousness, bearing messages, striking blows, or causing in him whom the gods have condemned spiritual blindness and insanity. They may symbolize the spiritual apex of collective humanity—whether it be called the Church Triumphant, the assembly of the Blessed, or the White Lodge of Initiated Adepts. They may also stand for what the newspapers call "society," or else for the power of the mob. They may be the agents of those collective forces which men learn to know under the name of religion. They may even speak of cosmic events beyond our solar system, and bring to the initiated tidings from our galaxy and forebodings from the spaces beyond. In any case they are wholeness speaking to the individual particles.

If we limit ourselves to the psychological approach and the relationship of the collective unconscious to the particular ego, we say that Uranus is the *projective* power of the unconscious, Neptune, its *dissolving* power, and Pluto, its *regenerating* power. Uranus brings to the conscious symbolical representations and impulses. This may occur in dreams or in waking consciousness. Under Uranus come the inspirations of the poet, the artist, the inventor, the scientist, the statesman, the religious reformer. Uranus is characterized by its image-forming power. It regenerates the conscious by bringing to it vistas of the whole, images and ideas of the universal Mind. Strictly speaking, it does not "regenerate." Instead, it projects images and ideas which have the power to *transform*, which are seeds of the new consciousness. Transformation and creation are key-words of this revolutionary planet which constantly pours new dynamic quanta into the heart of the ego—upsetting, stimulating, stirring, disrupting, the soul of divine discontent, the madness of the anarchist and of the lawless. Genius or insanity; inspiration or perversion.

Neptune acts in more subtle and mysterious ways. It eats up like a strong acid the crystallizations of the ego, ever calling the particular and the bound to the limitless state of the universal. It is the insistent, compassionate, overflowing love of the whole for the separate part which may not even know it is a "part"—a love which can be most tender, yet which usually is so filled with cosmic horizons and universal dispassion that our limited, narrow feelings recoil before it in subtle awe. Neptune is the man transfigured by the Christ within; but he may be also the man lost in an "artificial paradise," asking of drugs that he be led beyond the jail of normal perception and daily routine into the realm of dreams and visions.

Every force which denies limitations and tends to make us whole, which saps the strength of the particular viewpoint and injects into it the fluid of unearthly desires; every agency which dissolves crystallizations and puts the lens of the ego out of focus, which stirs us with divine longings through days of second puberty and enravishes us away from family and home into the snow-white peace of convents or to the living fermentation of the jungle—all belong to the Neptune symbol.

Physiologically speaking, the bodily part ruled by the zodiacal sign in which Neptune is posited lacks differentiation and focalized growth. It appears undeveloped. The life-energy did not succeed in making itself concrete enough. Where Uranus is placed we often find, on the contrary, abnormal growth, overfulness of a sort; not so much an abundance of life-force as a peculiar tension of energy which creates genius or freaks. Neptune is the symbol of the sea, of the undifferentiated, of cosmic matter in the prenatal stage, or of *nirvana* and infinite compassion. It shows how society acts upon the individual; whereas Uranus indicates more the fecundating power of the individual, how he acts upon society, constructively or destructively. Neptune's keynotes are redemption, universalization, or un-focalization.

Pluto is the planet of the second birth, ruler of the Mysteries—of every type of group-assembly, of parliamentary organization in which new policies are decided upon for the collectivity, or of ceremonial through which the individual and society are readjusted according to the outworking of a new law of being. Jupiter deals also with governing bodies and with religious ceremonies—but *within the limits set by Saturn*. In other words, Jupiter symbolizes racial gods and religion based upon kinship and blood-relationship. It stands for hierarchy and autocracy—political or religious—this, because Saturn has first of all set the ego, the One, as a ruler within certain boundaries. Jupiter acts within these boundaries. The rule of Zeus follows that of Chronos-Saturn. Jupiter as the *guru*, the spiritual teacher or religious guide, involves elements of personal relationship.

On the other hand, Pluto is strictly impersonal and recognizes no personal God or King; only an elected chairman, as it were. Its King is the Law. It is ruthless and absolutely just—but just in terms of a Law which often transcends our limited understanding, and may seem cruel. Pluto relates the ego to a greater center of being, part conscious, part unconscious. It leads to what C. G. Jung calls the Self, the totality of the being. It symbolizes the final stage of the process of individuation, the second birth, the "making perfect," initiation, the "birth of the Living God." For Pluto is God-in-the-depths, God made concrete and actual within and at the center of personality. Thus the personality becomes transfigured into a Living Person. In this sense Pluto is the symbol of the Incarnation of God, of the Apostolic Brotherhood, reflection of the cosmic zodiacal order; of the White Lodge on Earth.

Pluto represents the Law of the whole-Self in opposition to the law of the particular ego (Saturn-Jupiter). His reign comes after this ego has been impregnated with Uranian seed-ideas and archetypes, and has lost all its resistance and its pride through the Neptunian baptism. Then Pluto, having judged the ego in the scales in which are balanced conscious and unconscious, concrete and abstract, particular and universal, initiates it into the Company of the Perfect. His keynote is therefore *rebirth*; also the concretization of the All into the universal One.

Of all the astrological signs which have been suggested as symbols (or causes) of the Great War, only one seems valid. Pluto was in conjunction with the summer solstice in June, 1914, and had apparently come to his first conjunction for a brief time during September, 1912, at which time the Balkan War was being planned. The summer solstice is the point of cosmic fecundation. Life becomes concrete in the womb. The mystery of the "shedding of blood" may also accompany vast cosmic fecundations—or initiations.

Pluto was entering Aquarius around 1777. It was close to the time which Swedenborg mentioned as being that of the descent to earth of the "New Jerusalem." From this time on the American Revolution was taking shape. In 1937-38 Pluto will enter Leo. This will definitely mark the beginning of the new era. According to the Pyramid number-symbolism this era began September 16, 1936.

The fact that the coming upon the astrological scene of Neptune and Pluto corresponded to the time when different aspects of the unconscious gained public recognition is interesting. Pluto was discovered exactly 84 years (the cycle of Uranus) after Neptune (1846). In 1848 Europe witnessed a great revolutionary upheaval. It is the date of Marx's Communist Manifesto. It marks the beginning of the spread of Spiritualism. The great spiritual movement, Bahaism, was initiated in 1844. In every way it was a time of religious enthusiasm and of humanitarian ideals—truly a Neptunian time. Likewise, Uranus became known in the midst of the revolutionary era that aroused all the Western world to a realization of new archetypes of social relationship. Pluto was sighted January 21, 1930, as the Sun entered the sign of Aquarius. The decade thus ushered in promises to vie in importance with those which made Uranus and Neptune known. The ideals of the New Deal are typically Plutonic, insofar as we have in this New Deal an attempt at including all social classes in an integral type of organization in which the two factors of individualism and collectivism will be harmonized. Neptune makes whole, but it also leads to formlessness. Pluto brings the message of concrete form, of organization. If often we see it as disorganization, it is because we can discover only the first stage of the process. The Great War meant disorganization; yet it tested the power of men to organize on a scale never dreamt of before. It taught efficiency and precision. It created the machinery which man may use constructively if he so desires.

It is not at all improbable that under the régime of Pluto, as Paul Clancy suggests, concrete and scientific proofs of human immortality will be forthcoming. Alice Bailey announces the same; and there is no doubt that Pluto deals with all the concrete manifestations of the new order.

Uranus, Neptune, Pluto symbolize processes which bring the unconscious and its subliminal powers to the threshold of the consciousness and the ego. They are thus intermediaries between the Solar system proper and the galaxy. Comets are also intermediaries, but of a more fleeting quality. We can conceive the unconscious in terms of an accumulation of both personal and collective conscious contents; in fact we must do so, if we consider consciousness as bound to physical organisms. But the occultist will of course claim that the collective unconscious is the product as much of superhuman and superterrestrial Beings as of the past generations of men. He will consider the fixed stars astrologically as symbols of such cosmic entities as the awakened intuition may dimly sense beyond the realms known to human minds. Uranus, Neptune, Pluto are thus links between the stars and the intra-Saturnian planets—between the "gods" and men.

There remains one more point to be touched upon: What is the significance of the three remote planets when retrograde? It is probable that what is indicated is a return-action of the collective element to the collectivity, but with the added power of the individual to make it effective in a new way. To put it more clearly: Sooner or later races and groups always degenerate. The individuals composing these collectivities fail to act in accord with the deepest instincts and the archetypal truths which belong to mankind, biologically or spiritually. Out of all the sum total of these particular failures comes a general perversion or decadence of the collectivity. A race or nation or religious group falls into evil ways, crystallizes or disintegrates. What individuals caused, individuals must readjust. Reformers arise who proclaim the ancient forgotten truths, probably under a new garb. These men are led by the living spirit of collective humanity to reform the sick body of the collectivities of which they are parts. This reforming action of the collectivity by the collectivity, through the individual, is symbolized by the retrograde motions of Uranus, Neptune, Pluto.

Uranus "direct" reforms or rather transforms the conscious ego; when "retrograde," what is symbolized is the reform of the unconscious, of the hidden depths from which the ego emerges. In some cases it may mean that all the dark closets are being aired and family skeletons are being thrown out; in others, it means that the man is actually the agent for some sort of reforming impulse which is to change the mind of his race or group. The Uranian images he projects are impregnated first of all with an iconoclastic energy. They will not only challenge the conscious of the race, but generate storms in the unconscious. Neptune retrograde is found often where religious shams are unearthed and denounced; where inner subconscious pride is subtly annihilated. Mystics often have such a factor prominent in their charts, especially if they stand positively against beliefs of their day. A good illustration of this is Bo Yin Ra, the great living German mystic-occultist, who has only one retrograde planet, Neptune. As for Pluto retrograde, one can only surmise that it would tend to let loose organized destruction—this, in an individual chart, might be connected with a peculiar protest against the established order of society.

The Solar System As Personality

Our approach so far has dealt with purely psychological factors, and we have considered planets as symbols which would enable us to chart the three main types of activity characteristic of any life-organism: activities determining what the organism is, how it maintains itself, how it reproduces itself. Then we studied problems arising from the repression of natural organic activities as symbolized in retrograde planets. Lastly we analyzed the three modes of activity by means of which the particular ego is able to transcend itself and to partake of the character of universality. The

Saturn-image which is the foundation of particular ego-hood then fades into a type of representation Plutonic in character. The Jupiter mode of compensatory activity gives way to a Neptunian process of sublimation. The Mars type of self-reproduction is superseded by Uranian creativeness.

If, however, we approach the subject from a reverse direction, that is, starting from an analysis of the solar system as a whole and projecting the result thereof into our physio-psychological experience, we get a more logical and more ordered picture. Our concept of personality broadens and assumes cosmic perspectives. The whole solar system, seen as a complex life-organism, becomes a cosmic personality. However, we must carefully avoid the mistake of losing our base of operation: the Earth. "Cosmic" as we may be, we are always and forever rooted in the Earth. The only solar system we know is that which is seen through the Earth-atmosphere and by means of earthly senses and instruments. We know nothing in fact beyond the Earth and the reactions which the Earth experiences from outside. We must always remain Earth-centered, because as long as we operate through Earth-born vehicles of consciousness, refined as these may be, all our experiences are conditioned by the quality of our planet, and all the *vital* symbols which we may conceive, being necessarily interpretations and extensions of these experiences, must be grounded in the viewpoint of the Earth and of Man as a planetary being.

If, therefore, we speak of the solar system, it is as it appears to the scientific investigator, spreading on each side of the path described yearly by the Earth. There are celestial bodies within the confines of the Earth's orbit and there are some outside of it. It is true that the Sun is demonstrably one of the foci of this elliptical Earth-orbit, and also of all other planetary orbits. But all it means is that we, human observers, are not at the center of the system to which, we know enough now to realize, we belong as a mere planet. This fact of our knowing that the Sun is the center of the system, and not the Earth, does not make a truly heliocentric point of view legitimate. We know this fact intellectually, yet all our experiences are necessarily Earth-centered. In other words, I, the ego, know now that the field of my consciousness (my own Earth) is not the center of my total being. I assume that there is a Self which, Sun-like, is the center of this total being. Yet I do not *experience* as a Self, but only as an ego. I postulate the possibility of an identification of this ego with the Self. But if I *did* experience such an identification I would no longer be an ego-centered personality. I would be a divine Personage—with a solar vehicle of consciousness—whatever it may mean. It may be that there are divine Personages operating through an Earth-born body, but if so, the personality rooted in that body and perceived by ordinary man is not their true Personality. And thus we cannot profitably discuss a "Solar Personality" which we as Earth-beings will never experience fully; neither is there any validity in assuming a Sun-centered point of view as the basis of a system of symbolical life-interpretation. Our cosmic flights must start from and end on the Earth—or else they must remain dreams and speculations without vital meaning.

Let us, therefore, consider the solar system, from the point of view of the Earth and of Man, as a planetary whole. We shall divide the solar system into that part which is contained inside of the Earth-orbit and that part which is outside of the Earth-orbit. *Inside* the Earth-orbit we find the inner planets Venus, Mercury and the Sun; *outside* of it, the outer planets Mars-Jupiter-Saturn and Uranus-Neptune-Pluto. The relative positions of these planets within these two celestial realms will give to each planet its essential symbolical meaning; for, let us repeat it again and again, the basic meanings of the planets belong to them *by the logic of their positions in relation to the Earth and by virtue of their astronomical characteristics*, such as speed of revolution and rotation, mass, color, number of satellites, etc. In other words, Venus has a certain basic meaning simply because it is the first planet between the Earth and the Sun. Likewise there can be no doubt as to the basic meaning of Pluto, because this meaning is derived from its position, orbital characteristics, etc. Of course such a meaning is both very basic and very abstract or general—as abstract or general almost as the meanings of the numbers 2 and 3. Therefore, in applying this meaning to the interpretation of particular nativities, statistics and accumulated experience are absolutely invaluable. They do not, however, give birth to the basic meaning.

This is particularly important when we consider the Moon as an astrological factor. For the ancients, the Moon was the handmaid of the Sun, the secondary "light" that shone by night. The entire symbolism of Sun and Moon was built on these data of experience concerning the light of Sun and Moon, and the physio-psychological correlations established between sunlight (day, warmth, etc.) and moonlight (night, mystery, fear, etc.).

Such correlations are no longer the main generators of significance in terms of modern scientific knowledge and behavior. For one thing, artificial light has changed night into day, and modern city living has made of office-days a sort of night. But deeper than this, the attribution of meaning to the planets (and to all astrological factors) must now be established upon what, to us modern men, is our basic knowledge—scientific, intellectual knowledge.

From this astronomical point of view, the Moon occupies a special place indeed as the satellite of the Earth. Revolving monthly around the Earth, it is found half of the time within the Earth-orbit, half of the time outside of it. As a result of this the Moon is the *link* between the inner and the outer realms of the solar system; between the inner and the outer planets. Because of this function of linkage it appears constantly changing in its aspect. It has phases, waxing and waning tides; a definite dualistic rhythm. At New Moon, the Moon is at its innermost point within the Earth-orbit. At Full Moon, it is at its outermost point outside of the Earth-orbit. Subjectivity and objectivity.

Previously, as we studied the planets in pairs, we said that the Moon was the feminine counterpart of Saturn. But such a statement, while true in a certain sense, must not be taken as definite. There *is* a "mystery" connected with the Moon, and it has to do with the change which took place (potentially at least) at the close of the archaic ages (around 600 B.C.). If, now, we study the solar system from the point of view of the Earth-orbit, and if we proceed to pair the outer and the inner planets, we shall have the following result:

Mars and Venus standing on each side of the Earth become polar opposites; so do Jupiter and Mercury; then Saturn and —the Sun. Before we discuss what the Sun signifies here, let us repeat that the outer planets are positive in the sense of referring to the *causes* of the activities represented by the pairs; while the inner planets refer to results, and are thus called negative. Mars symbolizes the initiating and impulsive power that starts all life-activities; Venus, the consummating, concluding, fruit-bearing energy which closes up all cycles of activity. Jupiter symbolizes the power of circulation within every organic whole and that which expands them from within and which makes them whole. Mercury is the nervous system, and later the power of thought which consolidates and becomes the vehicle of the Jupiterian power. Saturn is the original power which starts every life-manifestation by isolating from the undifferentiated ocean of life a particular fragment thereof, and which, by building a wall around this fragment, enables it to be a separate independent entity.

Then what of the polar opposite of Saturn? Logically it ought to be the Sun. But there has also been a great deal of talk about, even an ephemeris of, an intra-Mercurial planet, Vulcan. We do not know whether or not Vulcan exists. But one cannot base astrological significance on merely possible astronomical facts. Vulcan may exist. But, whether it exists or not, what it stands for, as significance, can be attributed much more satisfactorily to the *photosphere of the Sun*. Occultists have said that we do not know the real Sun, that what we see is only, as it were, the light that comes through an open window. This light constitutes what may be called the surface of the Sun, the actively radiant part of the Sun. Actually it is all that we know of the Sun, sensorially and physically. It is the source of "solar vibrations;" and those mean to us, life and light. Saturn sets the boundaries of every particular living organism and thus helps to focalize within these boundaries, as if through a lens, the diffuse light of interstellar or galactic space. The Sun is, in a sense, the lens itself. The photosphere is the totality of the light and heat rays which are focalized and which fill in the boundaries of the living organism. Saturn differentiates. The photosphere makes the differentiated entity alive.

Thus we have a two-fold trinity of inner-outer planets. Each of these planets stands for a polarity of triune life: three positives and three negatives. What is the "seventh"?—for, we are told in all philosophies, the great number of all life-manifestations is 7. The seventh is that which correlates the opposite polarities. It is that which, moreover, collects these polar energies and distributes them through a cyclic tidal process to the living organism. It is the Moon.

Without the Moon, there would be no interchange, no relationship between the inner and outer planets. There would be no flow of energies within and through the Earth. On each side of the Earth, the planets stand. But it is the Moon which collects their energies as it shuttles back and forth between innermost and outermost. Having collected and blended them, it distributes them to the Earth. It feeds the Earth with these energies.

Thus the Moon is the womb and the mother of the Earth.

It is the lymphatic fluid. It is the watery flow, the sap within the plant. It collects all cosmic forces and distributes them to the embryo within its womb. It collects all mineral salts of the soil and distributes them to the entire plant. It is the placenta orbitally surrounding the Earth, as the placenta surrounds the embryo. The Moon may indeed be called "she" —the mother. She is the mother-force, the waters of life. But she is also the possessive mother-love that stifles and enwombs the child, drawing him back to the cradle, psychologically:— the mother-complex, the thralldom of feelings and sentimentality.

Yet we have touched only the fringe of the garment. Is there only one inner planet and one outer planet? Here the "mystery of the Moon" begins to open. For there must, of course, be one "Moon," one linking agency, for every polar duality. We saw that there are three pairs of planets, three basic powers of life (being a self; maintaining oneself; reproducing oneself) in every living organism. Then there must be three "Moons," and our physical Moon is only the agency which links the closest planetary pair, that of Mars and Venus. Because it is the closest it is the most visible, the most obvious, the most outwardly and consciously compelling; the source of our most patent desires and feelings. But there must be also a "Moon" to correlate the couple Jupiter-Mercury and distribute their harmonized energies to the Earth; and again a "Moon" to distribute to us the correlated energies of Saturn and the photosphere.

But where are those "Moons"?—the reader may ask. Perhaps there are no *actual* celestial physical masses of substance which would fill the office of the two "higher Moons" above mentioned. Perhaps they exist in an invisible state, reflecting light too much toward the infra-red or ultra-violet to be visible. Perhaps it is these "higher Moons" which "clairvoyants" have seen and have taken for planets revolving around the Sun. Perhaps the "mystery-planet" behind the

Moon is the next "higher Moon." There are many "perhapses." But what of it?

What we are speaking of are *cycles of motion and of distribution of energy*. One of these cycles is operating with or through our visible Moon, and is approximately a 28-day cycle. Another of these cycles is beginning to be known as a 40-month cycle, affecting financial changes and the heat of the Sun. Another cycle is the well-known "sun-spots cycle" of eleven years plus. All such cycles are really cyclic paths of circulating energy (or abstract correlations of motion—if one prefers to be more abstract). Whether they operate through the agency of a physical body such as our Moon, or through some flow of magnetic particles tidal in its effects—there is no difference *as far as astrological symbolism is concerned*. What counts in the cyclic activity is the flow of "something" that the astrologer can relate symbolically to a life-function (collective and social as well as individual). What the "something" is, whether a solid planet or a tide of electric particles, or even an abstraction pure and simple—this should be but of slight importance to the astrologer. It belongs to the astronomer to find out all the scientific facts about it.

The following sketch may help to make clear how and where—schematically of course—the "Moons" operate. The first (our physical Moon) links the orbs of Mars and Venus, and has a period of approximately 28 days. It refers to the realm of physical action and physiological procreation. It represents all the "feelings" connected with that realm. It vitalizes all things, even those most remotely connected with sex, and all creative activity insofar as such activity has a material concrete basis of manifestation through bodily motions (all fine arts, as they involve muscular activity of one kind or another). It vitalizes therefore, almost exclusively, the man and woman functioning at an instinctual and physiological stage. It operates, moreover, in and through the cycle of growth and decay of all biological organisms.

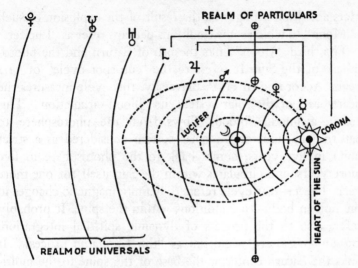

The second "Moon" links the orbs of Jupiter and Mercury, collects and distributes their energies to the Earth. The period of this activity is probably 40 months. The number is significant and links the cycle with the gestation cycle of 40 weeks. This number 40 is found most frequently in Biblical symbolism, and refers to a period of tribulation and interior formation (as the gestation period is, of course). Even of late, Abdul Baha, leader of the Bahai cause, is said to have been imprisoned in Akka (which means "womb") for 40 years: a symbol of the formation of the new spiritual era entered in after his death, or at his birth.

It seems that the 40-month cycle has two meanings, just as Jupiter has two meanings: 1) *spiritual*—referring to processes of Soul-growth and psycho-mental development or "initiation"; 2) *financial*—as a mean cycle of 20 months up and 20 months down, accounting for movements in prices and volume of transactions (Cf. T. O. McGrath, "Solar Radiation and Business Activity," in the *Bulletina* April-May-June, 1934). Interestingly enough, the Jupiter symbol ♃ is really a number 4 figure. It might also be added that the asteroids between

Mars and Jupiter might be the result of the explosion of such a "Moon" to which some traditions perhaps refer as "Lucifer."

The third "Moon" links the orb of Saturn and the photosphere of the Sun. It refers to the "sun-spot cycle" of 11.2 years. According to H. P. Blavatsky, this cycle measures the heart-beats of the solar system, its "blood-circulation." This cosmic-magnetic "blood" flows from the photosphere to Saturn (the limit of the solar system considered as a strict unit) in five years; comes back to the photosphere in five more years, and circulates within the Sun itself for one more year. The 11-year cycle refers to definite magnetic changes in the human body—to conditions within the spine. It probably refers also to the process of dynamic spiritual integration, known in Eastern occultism as "the *Kundalini* process." It links the Saturn center at the base of the spine to the multi-petalled "lotus" on the top of the head—the "halo" of saints and buddhas—truly a photosphere or corona of the "spiritual sun" within the head.

We must come now to consider the outermost planets, Uranus, Neptune and Pluto. If we still take the Earth orbit as a hinge, we shall see that these universalistic planets are balanced only within the very "heart of the Sun."

In our previous discussion, "The Sun as Integrator," we wrote that the Sun represents the power of the Self—not the Self itself. This integrating power of the Self operates first of all, during the development of Man's psyche, within the Saturn-defined boundaries of the conscious. Saturn plus Sun-power (photsphere) constitute the "I am"—Saturn is "I" and Sun-power is "am"—always considering our Earth-centered solar system as a "cosmic personality."

Then the Saturnian "I" becomes transcended through the triune life process symbolized by Uranus-Neptune-Pluto. These three planets represent what Jung calls the "Not-I," that which must be assimilated by the "I." As this assimilation takes place, the "cosmic personality" expands; better still, it experiences a repolarization or "conversion." Within the "heart of the Sun" arises a transfigured "I," and this "I" finds his "am" in the power of the trinity Uranus-Neptune-Pluto. This planetary trinity constitutes the process by means of which the "cosmic personality" finds itself *linked* to the vaster astronomical whole, let us say, the *galaxy*.

One might ask: But what is really meant by the "heart of the Sun"? It is the Self. And the Self is the wholeness of the fulfilled and integrated personality—an abstraction. And yet even this abstraction is susceptible of being concretely symbolized in terms of the next vaster whole. We might thus say that the "heart of the Sun" in terms of the (Earth-centered) galactic whole is the star which (within our galaxy) is located exactly behind the Sun. This, however, has hardly any practical significance for us, ordinary men!

What has significance, however, is the idea that there is a cycle of linkage between the Uranus orb and the "heart of the Sun," a fourth "Moon." This cycle is the 28-year cycle of individual selfhood, which, repeated three times (once for each of the three outermost planets), gives the time of the symbolical "building of the Temple of Sol-o-Mon" (the Sun of Man): 84 years—the period of Uranus' revolution around the Sun. Two 28-year cycles (one 56-year) constitute, according to Mr. McGrath, the major business cycle. This cycle equals three nodal cycles of 18.6 years each and five sun-spot cycles of 11.2 years each. Such correspondences throw light upon the significance of Neptune, when fully understood; as the sidereal period of Neptune equals three 56-year periods.

All these cycles, which can be considered as higher "Moons," are most important in the study of "cosmic personality," for they symbolize "functions of linkage" between the soul-energies which, when fully integrated, are the substance of this "cosmic personality," so conveniently symbolized for us by the complex pattern of the solar system as understood from the Earth. Such "functions of linkage" were held esoteric and mysteriously sacred in archaic cosmo-psychology. Thus the "mystery of the Moon."

This mystery, for the ancients, resided in the attribution of the Moon as a polar opposite to Saturn. When mankind was functioning purely at the physiological level, and mind was hardly an *independent* factor or a basis for the focalization of life-energies, then it was indeed the Moon which, as the Mother-force, animated the egos (the Saturnian boundaries) of men. Men are still, psychologically, within the womb of the Mother—and this at the physiological-instinctual (Mars-Venus) level of operation. But as men become mentally polarized and rise out of the psychological Mother-womb into the realm of pure energy and independent thought, then they become progressively filled with the power of the solar photosphere. Their Saturnian egos become illumined, and the "higher Moon," Lucifer (i.e., Light Bearer), "bears light" to them, the light of the correlated Jupiter and Mercury. A next step in spiritual development will make them illumined by the power of the *Kundalini* Moon (Isis?) linking Saturn and the solar photosphere; another step will see them vitalized by the correlation Uranus-Sun (Osiris?). We believe that the "mystery-planet behind the moon" was no planet, but this second "Moon" which we called Lucifer—the Jupiter-Mercury link. The asteroids are the remnants—or are they not rather the prenatal condition?—of this Lucifer. May not the myriads of asteroids be a symbol of the scattered state of men's psychomental energies, or soul-forces? The Great Work of the spirit is the integration of these scattered soul-forces into a spiritual organism, a "temple of the living God." Thus every man must integrate within himself these "asteroids" and make them into a "Moon" through which the power of soul (Jupiter) and the power of mind (Mercury) will be correlated and made cyclically operative.

After this preliminary work of psycho-mental integration, concentration, or *yoga*, will come a further stage—symbolized by *Kundalini*—Isis. The veil of Isis is then to be lifted by the candidate to initiation. Man finds himself surrounded by the halo of the living God, by the multi-flamed radiance of the Corona. Finally man himself becomes a Sun. His heart beats in unison with the "heart of the Sun."

The physical moon represents normal mankind today. The three "higher Moons" stand for the three stages of Masonic initiation: Apprentice — Companion — Master. These stages symbolize ritualistically the three basic phases of the process of personality-integration—of the gestation of the "Living God," the Christ-child, within the psyche.

IX. *Planetary Interweavings*

THE study of the higher "Moons" and of the "functions of linkage" which they symbolize has prepared us for further considerations along the same line of thought. In this chapter we shall re-interpret traditional astrological elements which are known as "nodes" and "parts." The former have been used for ages in India, especially in reference to the Moon. The latter seem to have been the special feature of Arabian astrology. Both these factors serve to establish points of relationship between the planets and the Earth. They refer to the operation of personality as a unified whole and as a unit in the infinitely complex interweavings of social relationship.

Planetary Nodes

The nodes of a planet are two opposite points where the plane of the orbit of the planet intersects the ecliptic. As the ecliptic is not only the apparent path described by the Sun on the celestial sphere (i.e., among the constellations), but "a plane through the center of the Sun through which the average orbit of the Earth lies," it follows that the planetary nodes represent the points where the line of intersection of the plane of a planet's orbit and the plane of the Earth's orbit meet the celestial sphere (i.e., the "dome of the skies"). The Sun is naturally at the mid-point of this line of intersection.

What is involved, therefore, in the idea of nodes is a type of relationship existing between the planes of the planetary orbits and the plane of the Earth's orbit. The sizes of the various angles of inclinations of the planets' orbits to the ecliptic might be taken as representations of these orbital relationships; but this would give us only numerical values as symbols—which could fit into a system of astro-numerical symbolism, but not into astrology; for all measurements of astrological relationship must always be referred to the factor of zodiacal position. The line of planetary nodes ends in two points on the celestial sphere which have zodiacal longitude; thus these points are taken as symbols of the relationship between the orbits of planet and Earth.

The reason why the orbits of planets are considered important is that, with the orbit, we are dealing with values of motion. The plane of an orbit is the plane of periodical motion. And, as we saw already, all true astrological factors can be abstracted into factors of motion. Astrology is an algebra using cyclic motions as its symbols. (Cf. the chapter: "The Key to Astrological Symbolism" p. 175). Thus the planes of orbital motions can indeed be considered as significant, the significance being revealed to us by the zodiacal position of their line of intersection.

The orbit of a planet represents the total cycle of dynamic activity of this planet in relation to the Sun. The Sun stands there as the integrator of the whole system, that which holds it together and represents its ultimate total significance. The planet, of itself, symbolizes a particular and to some extent independent mode of life-activity. But its orbit is a representation of this characteristic activity, not as a thing in itself, but rather in relation to the Sun. The orbit signifies therefore the integrative aspect of the planetary activity, viz., this activity as it operates definitely within the organic whole and for the fulfillment of the central aim of integration of personality.

What the relationship of the planet's orbit to the Earth's orbit will indicate is the part which the life-activity represented by the planet occupies, at any time, in the scheme of development of Earth-born mankind. If Uranus symbolizes the regenerative force which tends to bring to humanity as a whole universal images that will supersede the Saturnian stereotyped formula of separative egoism, then the nodes of Uranus will tell us the manner in which this regenerative force is operating at present. The indication given will be broad, and it covers a large span of years or centuries, for the planetary nodes move very slowly along the zodiac, seemingly with alternately direct and retrograde motion. At present, Uranus' line of nodes extends from Gemini 13.40 to Sagittarius 13.40; and what it thus stresses is the fact that the regenerative force of Uranus is operating, and has been operating for centuries, through the mind of man.

A closer analysis of the nodes' meaning will attribute opposite and complementary significances to the two terminals of the lines of nodes, the North Node and the South Node. This nodal dualism is logical, for every type of life-activity in relation to the center of integration of the organic system may take on a positive or a negative value. Integration and disintegration go ever hand in hand. Every life-element can operate as a destructive or as a constructive agency, such being the universal law of life.

The North Node is the positive pole of integration; the South Node the negative pole where disintegration of some sort (it may not be "evil," however) takes place. The former is a point of ingestion and assimilation; the latter, a point of release and evacuation. We shall study this polarization of life-activities in greater detail when we shall consider the Moon's nodes. In the meantime these brief remarks will suffice to indicate the general opposition of meanings manifest in the two nodes.

If, therefore, we refer again to the present position of Uranus' nodes, we shall see that its North Node, being in the fourteenth degree of Gemini, signifies that positive regeneration comes to mankind at present by the use of the concrete intellect, and through the establishment of spatial connections —which are two of the essential characteristics of Gemini; also that there is an integrative Uranian emphasis on the development of the nervous system, of postal communications, etc.

On the other hand, the Sagittarian qualities of religious idealism, of obedience to authority, etc.—even of metaphysical abstractedness—are seen as negative from the point of view of the planetary Uranus action. They constitute the "line of least resistance;" they result largely from past habits of integration, and thus constitute most often "mechanisms of escape," from the psychological standpoint. Nevertheless powerfully creative and Uranian releases may come along Sagittarian lines through individuals who act as the culmination of traditional impulses to activity, as the "last word" in a realm of achievement which, having been thoroughly developed for millenia, may have nothing compellingly vital to offer—yet is able to produce absolute formal perfection.

The symbol for the present degree position of Uranus' North Node is: "Two people, widely separated, are communicating telepathically."* This is most significant, if we are to believe the statement often repeated in Alice Bailey's books that the development of the telepathic faculty is the most important task now confronting the spiritual pioneers of the race. On the other hand, Uranus' South Node is on a degree symbolized by: "The Sphinx and the Pyramids are glorious vestiges of the past"—which emphasizes the fact that now all the glorious past of mankind is being synthetized, recorded, brought to a culmination through many types of human activities—from archaeology to occult metaphysics. Yet this suggests also that dependence upon these past glories, national or religious, is most often the result of shrinking from the task of the future, and is a form of escape based on fear.

The following table gives the zodiacal positions of the

---

* Cf. the following chapter for a study of the significance of Degree-symbols.

planets' nodes for 1935. The yearly variation is in every case less than a minute.

	North Nodes	South Nodes
Mercury	Taurus 17° 33'	Scorpio 17° 33'
Mars	" 19° 3'	" 19° 3'
Uranus	Gemini 13° 40'	Sagittarius 13° 40'
Venus	" 16° 5'	" 16° 5'
Jupiter	Cancer 9° 47'	Capricorn 9° 47'
Pluto	" 19° 25'	" 19° 25'
Saturn	" 23° 5'	" 23° 5'
Neptune	Leo 11° 3'	Aquarius 11° 3'

The way the nodes are distributed in the zodiac at present is most interesting, for they cover an area of less than 90 degrees North or South—in fact 84 degrees, which recalls the Uranus cycle and that of the "building of the Temple." It is especially interesting to see that the summer solstice is at present almost exactly at the center of the configuration. This solstice is the time of most intense solar manifestation (in Chinese philosophy, domination of the active principle *Yang*); while the winter solstice is the point of lowest solar vitality (domination of the passive principle *Yin*). The positions of the combined planetary nodes are thus correspondent with points of solar dynamism exactly analogical. This would tend to show that the integrative power of the solar system as a whole upon the Earth is at its apex now (or close to it); for the maximum of integrative activity of the planets is, as it were, synchronous with the maximum of activity of the Sun, the integrator. A study of the symbols of the degrees on which the planetary nodes are found, as outlined in our preceding example (Uranus), will be of deep interest to the student of contemporary planetary trends.

To the foregoing we must add that as planets, in their monthly or daily course, reach the degrees of the zodiac on which their nodes are located, a definite stressing of their positive or negative characteristics is apparent. When planets pass their North Node they operate positively, actively; while at their South Node point they are receptive and passive—that is, the quality or function they signify operates in a passive (yet strong) manner. In an individual chart, a planet situated over its North Node is very dominant psychologically; its effect is stirring up the consciousness, in the sense that all the integrating life-energy received by the native has a tendency to relate itself to the particular quality expressed by the planet. On the other hand, a planet situated over its South Node may refer to a definite type of psychological escape. The native may tend to evade the issue represented by the planet, or else to be passive and "let things happen" in the sphere of activity which the planet denotes.

A very definite result is also usually to be noticed (more definite probably in the more developed type of personality) when important planets in a chart are located on degrees which are the nodal points of other planets. The characteristics of the latter *undertone* as it were the activities of the former. The late King George V of England, for instance, had his Sun over Uranus' North Node. Undoubtedly his reign has been full of Uranian happenings. Franklin D. Roosevelt's chart is also characteristic in this respect. His Jupiter is on Mercury's North Node, and Uranus' North Node corresponds to his Mid-Heaven. Moreover his Sun is on Neptune's South Node. If Neptune represents the power of collectivities, Neptune's South Node would symbolize that power disintegrated and left to follow the line of least resistance. Roosevelt's Sun would then shine in the midst of such a condition, and add solar power to the Neptunian element. His own Neptune placed between Saturn and Jupiter (closer to the latter) is symbolically between, on one hand, darkness and Saturnian "rugged individualism" (to be regenerated, as it is in the eighth house), on the other, Jupiter and the power of expansion and circulation of energy.

An even stronger effect can be expected where the line of

nodes of a planet coincides with the horizon or the meridian in a birth-chart; or even with the line of the cusps of two opposite houses. In these cases the quality of the planet is strongly, yet subtly, influencing all the matters related to the two opposite (and complementary) houses.

The Moon's Nodes

While the Moon's nodes are also produced by the intersection of the lunar orbit and the ecliptic, and while, because of this basic fact, the significance of the line of nodes, and of the two nodes, follows the general principle already stated, nevertheless they differ from the planetary nodes in many ways. First of all they are purely geocentric, and not heliocentric—being the nodes of a satellite and not those of a fellow-planet of the Earth. The Moon's nodes are actually the points where the Moon, as a celestial body, is seen from the Earth, passing from a northern to a southern latitude, and vice versa. In other words, they are critical points in the relation of planet to satellite—as critical, let us say, as the equinoctial points on Earth, which—by analogy—might be called the "nodes of the Sun" (in relation to the celestial equator and *not* to the ecliptic) and which are definite moments of change in the relation Sun-to-Earth.

Other critical moments in the relation Moon-to-Earth are those which mark the Moon's entrance into and exit out of the realm of space figuratively bounded by the Earth's orbit; moments which correspond approximately to the last and first quarters of the Moon. But these refer more particularly to the general subject of "aspects" between celestial bodies—a subject which we shall be able but barely to touch upon in this present work; or else to that of the "functions of linkage" integrating the activities of astrological factors inside and outside of the Earth's orbit—as mentioned in the preceding chapter.

As we study the Moon's nodes, we are considering a relationship established between the plane of the Moon's orbit and that of the Earth's orbit. The latter is centered around the Sun, like all planetary orbits. But the former is centered around the Earth. Thus the relation Moon-orbit to Earth-orbit translated in terms of the relation between these two orbits' centers becomes the relation Earth-to-Sun! But this is a new type of Earth-to-Sun relationship, one which refers to the innermost meaning of the possibility of adjustment between, on one hand, the Earth-centered ego and his will, on the other, the solar Self and His will.

What is seen therefore through the Moon's nodes is the relation between the "human" will and the "divine" will, between the conscious efforts at integrating an ego-centered personality and the super-conscious guidance or motivating urge which is working toward the realization of the total "cosmic" or divine Personality. The former is largely the result of the individual's conditioning by heredity and environment; the latter is the true factor of Destiny. By Destiny we mean the ordered plan by the actualization of which as perfect a personality can become a fact of life as was potentially contained in the seed-moment of the individual's birth—viz., in the "monad."

At the Moon's North Node we see Destiny at work; at the South Node, human will. The lines of nodes show us the directives of Destiny, the purpose of Destiny—and what is back of this purpose, in the past. More than anything else, it tells the "Why" of individual life. Why the particular ego was projected out of the ocean of universal Life—why we are born and what for. The line of nodes is a sort of "line of cleavage" which represents the first polarization of being. At one end of this line we see the past (South Node), at the other, the future; what the personality emerged from, what it is meant to accomplish; these things will not be determinable in terms of concrete events, but a general direction will be made clear—inasmuch as the line of nodes points at two houses in a chart and thus at two definite phases of selfhood. A positive and a negative *pole of Destiny* will be determined.

The way in which the individual will orient himself along this line of Destiny will largely determine whether his life will be a success or a failure; or, more correctly, whether his accomplishments can be tabulated as positive or negative ones. By negative accomplishments I mean those which really belong to the soul's past, which are either a repetition of things so learnt that they have become almost automatic, or the breaking down of psycho-mental crystallizations. Positive accomplishments, on the contrary, are things which constitute a constructive step forward, the birth of a new faculty.

This problem of orientation along lines of cleavage touches the very roots of astrological symbolism. We can never understand an astrological chart save on the basis of those diametrical relationships which link opposite houses, and, to a lesser extent, signs. The essential quadrature of a chart, the vertical and horizontal lines formed by horizon and meridian, is the key to all the deeper types of astrological interpretation; for here we deal with the most primordial process of cell-segmentation and multiplication. Every growth, every manifestation of life, takes place along certain axes; and while the conventional axes of space (North, South, East, West, Zenith, Nadir) form the structure of the development of *individual selfhood*, the nodal axes (or lines of nodes) give us the directional forces of *Destiny*.

This is true, above all, of the Moon nodes axis; but also, in a less obvious way, of all planetary nodes. Every planet represents a particular quality of the whole life-process, and thus a psychological function. The nodal axis of the planet stands for the main *line of stress* in the development of that quality. In more trivial terms, things will happen along that line— insofar as this quality is concerned. The characteristics of the two houses affected by this "line of stress" will indicate what departments of life, what phases of individual selfhood, will experience the strain.

The axis constituted by the Moon nodes deals most directly with the very process of *individuation.* Here we see at work the forces which try to integrate the particular "I" and the greater Self; the faculty of assimilating new substance of living and of rejecting the values which are no longer useful because they have been shorn of all that was of vital necessity for the individual personality. We may even go so far as to say that there we have a line of metabolic action, not unlike that tubular channel which stretches from mouth to anus. At the North Node life is being absorbed, the substance of experience is being ingested and reduced to assimilable material; at the South Node we assimilate the contents of life, automatically, effortlessly, and eliminate the refuse.

In this physiological illustration the Earth stands for the diaphragm. Above the diaphragm is the North Node realm, below, the South Node realm. The former represents the new foodstuffs and the active process of digestion; the latter the old food now digested and being assimilated, turned into automatic instinctual activity—plus the rejection of unassimilable residue. Marc Jones calls the Moon's nodes axis the "fate axis." But undoubtedly the digestive axis, including stomach, bowels, etc., is the "fate axis" of our body—a real fatality for most of us!

This illustration, however, is not altogether perfect. In a more general sense the North Node represents the point where a particular entity absorbs or receives the substance of life. It is the channel through which the power of integration (which is Life) enters the Earth and her inhabitants; for there the Moon becomes a vase into which this power is poured and from which it flows to all planets. The South Node is, on the contrary, the point where the Moon becomes the automatic distributor (and ejector) of the Earth-assimilated force that was once solar. At the South Node the Sun and the Moon are absolutely unrelated. The Moon scatters at the South Node, and focalizes at the North Node. Thus integration (at the North pole of the axis) and disintegration (at the South pole): or indrawing and distribution. *Progress* is made at the North Node through exertion. *Habit* is established at the South Node through automatism, based on repetition.

If we should lie along the nodal axis we would look into the future facing North, and accept the past facing South. The North Node deals, therefore, with the work to be done, the new accomplishment, the new faculty to be developed; and if we are willing to *exert* ourselves in that direction, from it we shall receive power in abundance. The South Node represents the work that has been done, the well-known accomplishment, the routine performance already gone through many times, perhaps—the easy way out. Thus the opposition between, on one hand, self-integration, individuation, effort, the line of greatest connection through exertion; and on the other, self-undoing, automatism, inertia, the line of least resistance.

The South Node is always in any chart a wonderful index of the line of least resistance, especially through its house-position. For what do we mean by the line of least resistance, if not that of easy performance? Ease, in turn, depends on prior repetition of similar performances, which repetition built as habit, or on instinct. What is easy to do is that which we, as reincarnating individual souls, or as the end-point of a long chain of hereditary transmission, have done before. It represents thus a past achievement. It indicates that an adequate and efficient instrumentality has been built in the past, that a faculty or tendency has been inherited at birth, for the acquirement of which we have not had to struggle consciously.

It must be clear that such an inherited gift or instinct is not evil, and therefore that the South Node in a chart does not have of itself an evil or destructive significance. If it has been called the point of "self-undoing" it is because we have so often a way of following the line of least resistance, that is of keeping to the thing already well known, to the performance in which we can display ourselves most advantageously. By so doing we refuse to progress, to move on to new achievements. We become slaves to our great natural gift. Instead of *using* this natural ability in terms of a new type of development, it "runs away with us"—and leads us to our own undoing. If we are controlled by our inborn abilities instead of controlling them, we miss the main purpose of our life.

If the North Node is a point of reception of spiritual power, the South Node is by no means a symbol of impotence. It is, however, a symbol of maladjustment to new conditions. It signifies inborn faculty, but usually we find that life to some extent forbids us the use of that faculty. It belongs to the past in some way, and unless we make it subservient to a new purpose and rather rigidly control it, it will hamper the correct growth of a new vital faculty, one which represents our next step.

On the other hand, when we consider the type of faculty characterized by the North Node's position, we find that life forces us in many ways constantly to develop it. Life calls for that power—and is willing to shower it upon us if we exert ourselves in this direction; if we open up a channel. Every effort made in that direction will be usually well repaid—unless we stick stubbornly all the while to the attitude represented by the South Node. We may do it unconsciously, if we take care not to do so consciously. If so, a psychological complex is bound to develop. The present will be hopelessly torn between past and future. Then impotence will be the result. And we shall experience the tragedy of "fate." The past will have to die before the future may live. And we shall find ourselves deprived of our inborn gift by some stroke of

Destiny, because we had become identified with it, lost in it, "undone" by it. Thus truly our "self-undoing."*

One of the simplest examples we could give is that of the nodes in the fourth and tenth houses. Here we have an opposition between home and profession, private and public life. If the North Node is in the tenth, public life and the profession will be the channel to self-integration. The South Node in the fourth house will indicate that the native has a congenital pull toward the building of a home, and this may cause him to shrink from public life. If he shrinks too much, his home life will turn destructive. It will disintegrate in his hands even though he runs back to it yearningly, hopelessly. If, on the contrary, he works intently on his professional ideal, he may be able to make of his home (in the largest sense of the term) and of his own concrete basis of selfhood the true foundation for his public life.

There is, however, another possible interpretation, according to which public activity and professional efforts are seen as generators of the energy which is then *released* into the sphere of the home or of the soul (fourth house) of the South Node. This second interpretation is the more positive or spiritual one. It explains for instance why a great genius like Wagner had the South Node in his tenth house. He released publicly through his creation the energy generated through his feelings and his home or inner life (fourth house).

The operation of the nodes is not always easy to detect by merely being acquainted with the native. Most of us hide carefully the fact that we are following the line of least resistance. We hide it mostly from ourselves. And the ap-

---

* The South Node may also refer to what Jung calls the "persona," which is the result of the efforts made by the individual to integrate his behavior in terms of a social pattern, or of some "image" which at best satisfies only a part of his total being. The individual crystallizes his behavior in the shape of this "image" and thus assumes a part, which he maintains either by egocentric will-force or under the compulsion of social traditions, or social necessity. This "persona" is a false personality, because the total Destiny of the individual cannot operate in and through it.

parent ease with which we may perform certain types of actions may lead us to believe that we should keep on performing them. In some cases we should; but then the meaning we attribute to them would have to be different. Here, as in every case dealing with a spiritual appreciation of behavior, what counts is not the act itself, but the motive or will behind or within the act.

A study of the Moon's nodes helps us greatly to probe our own motives as well as those of others. For, confronted with many situations, we may put our actions and reactions to the acid test of nodal polarities. Did we follow in this situation the line of least resistance or the line of greatest integration? The nodes will tell us when we have the most chances of "fooling ourselves." Possibly even, in horary charts, we may be able to find quite accurately what is our true motivation in a particular instance. But the reading of horary charts in such a psychological way is a rare art indeed, which but a very few will ever be able to master.

The "Ascendants" of Planets

This often confusing subject, which introduces us to the still more general concept of "Parts," can be readily understood if we re-state in a slightly different manner ideas often repeated in this book. We know that the Sun represents the individuating, integrating, vitalizing power, which makes man whole on every plane of being. As for the spatial cross formed by the line of horizon and the line Zenith-Nadir at birth, we saw that it constituted a symbolical framework for all operations of our individual being, within and through which human nature operates in a particular way which characterizes us as an individual being. This Cross represents, in other words, the exteriorization—in a structural, functional pattern—of that spiritual "quality" which is the supreme essence of man's individual selfhood. It defines the particular way in which the life-force of the Sun operates.

This is easily understood when once we realize that the zodiacal position of the Sun at the moment of the first breath represents the exact point of the Earth's orbit around the Sun where the native is born; whereas the Cross of the birth-chart determines the exact moment of the day at which the birth occurred; thus, the exact stage of the daily rotation of the Earth around its axis.

The Sun in a nativity represents the dynamic emanation of the essential quality of man's individual selfhood, because it is the motion of the Earth around the Sun, involving actual displacement in space, which, symbolically, generates such "essential qualities." Each of these "qualities" represents a particular aspect of life, a particular relationship between human nature and the source of all life in the solar system. The Earth's orbit (the zodiac) is the sum total of all such possible relationships, therefore of all the different types (or Rays) of human individualities.

But while the Earth moves about one degree on its orbit, it rotates around its axis, presenting successively all parts of its globe to the light of the Sun—in other words, vitalizing all parts of itself by bringing them to be fecundated by the significance of that particular Sun-Earth relationship. It will be seen thus that any point on the globe (unless too close to the poles) receives this fecundating impact from the Sun about 365 times in a year. This constitutes (with a slight discrepancy, the meaning of which will be discussed later) the spiritual reality of the degree as a division of the zodiac.

The point we wish to convey is that there are only 365 (or 360) basic types of individual selfhood on Earth, each the result of a particular and *full* relationship between the Earth and the Sun, symbolized by the zodiacal degree of the natal Sun. This full relationship is not instantaneous, because it requires, in order to be total, a complete rotation of the Earth around its axis. This rotation brings all parts of the Earth successively in direct contact with the Sun's emanation (at noon). The axial Cross in a birth-chart defines a particular phase of this motion *which distributes the Sun's power through the whole being (psyche and body) of the native.* In other words, it shows the hour and minute of the day at which birth occurred. Moreover, it determines the structure of this whole being; for what constitutes the particular individual being is the particular way in which this solar life-force is distributed through his entire organism. This "particular way" manifests as the structure of the organism.

The two axes of the chart—and especially the Ascendant, which symbolizes more precisely the "uniqueness" of the individual—determine thus the essential structure of body and psyche alike. Moreover, the relation Sun-to-Ascendant represents the relation of the vital, individuating force in man to the structural type of activity which characterizes his individual selfhood. This relation can be estimated not only by the position of the Sun in the houses, but also more precisely by the distance, measured in zodiacal longitude, between the Ascendant and the Sun. When this distance measures to especially significant values (as for instance the half, third, fourth, fifth, sixth, eighth of the full 360 degrees of the circumference) astrology says that certain "aspects" are formed between the two factors considered—a matter which we shall discuss briefly in another chapter.

We can extend this principle of the relation Ascendant-to-Sun to other planets, because planets symbolize differentiated modes of life-activity. The planetary power is distributed by the axial rotation of the Earth to its entire surface, just as is the solar life-force. The house-position of the planets has reference to the manner in which this distribution is effected. But if we wish to know more precisely and significantly *the unique character of this distribution as a factor of the native's individual selfhood*, we shall have to determine points which bear to the planet under consideration the same relation as the Ascendant bears to the Sun. In other words, we shall have to determine, by analogical inference or by a sort of symbolization of the "second degree," the "Ascendants of the planets."

What this procedure leads to, when generalized, we shall see presently, but for the time being we shall take it for granted and see how it operates in the most important case: that of the Moon. Our aim will be to define the manner in which the Moon-power is distributed through the organism. In order to do that we shall then erect a symbolical "Cross," which will be in relation to the Moon's zodiacal place as the cross formed by horizon and meridian is in relation to the Sun. Especially, we shall calculate the point of the zodiac which stands in the relation to the Moon as the Ascendant is to the Sun. We may refer to such an abstract point as the "Ascendant of the Moon." This point has been used for a long time in astrology under the name *Pars Fortuna*: the Part of Fortune. It is found by adding the longitudes of Ascendant and Moon, and subtracting from the sum the longitude of the Sun.

If the Ascendant represents the characteristic activity of the individual selfhood, the Part of Fortune will thus symbolize the characteristic activity of the ordinary ego-centric personality largely conditioned by feeling-reactions and "lunar" moods. In the "Sabian System," "the Part of Fortune indicates in any chart that department of life in which or through which the native either expresses himself to the best advantage, or is forced by life as a whole to express himself."* To the term "native" we would merely add, "as a conscious ego." The Part of Fortune represents a man's congenital activity, as a merely conscious ego—and discounting all his deeper intuitions and unconscious or super-conscious motives. It deals with his strictly personal reaction to life, the spontaneous reactions of the conscious personality which he has built, or which life has forced upon him.

* Marc Jones' *Professional Astrology*, Lesson XII.

In medieval astrology the Part of Fortune was said to represent the native's "wealth." According to E. Parker, where the Part is found, in such a department of life will the native find his happiness; this especially in terms of house position. The three interpretations are quite definitely related. For man is happy in functioning according to his spontaneous personal reactions, and both happiness and spontaneity of personal reactions are usually much involved in money, or at least in social cooperation and credit (of which money is the symbol).

The value of the Part of Fortune will become very clear for instance to anyone who has observed individuals having it in conjunction with Jupiter or with Saturn. Here you have two types of basic conscious reactions to life: optimism and pessimism—modified as they may be by other factors. Here also you have on one hand a tendency to get credit and social cooperation for any personal venture; on the other, a tendency for the native to be thrown back upon himself constantly, as if a foreigner in a strange land, whose natural conscious reactions to life are perhaps unfamiliar and bewildering to the collectivity in which he lives.

The same procedure, described in reference to the Moon, can be followed in reference to all planets. The "Ascendants" of all planets are significant and worth studying in a refined type of astrological analysis. One of the most valuable, practically speaking, is the "Ascendant" of Uranus, to which we have given the name "Part of Imaging." It indicates how the image-projecting power of the unconscious operates within the individual's being and Destiny. It symbolizes the creative genius of the individual, its mode of contact with the deepest sources of his being, and his reactions to such a contact. The Moon's "Ascendant" reveals conscious reactions to outer situations conditioned by heredity and environment. Uranus' "Ascendant" characterizes unconscious, creative reactions to situations affecting the entire field of consciousness.

The Astrology of Personality

The General Theory of Astrological "Parts"

The "Ascendants" of the planets are determined by calculating the "arcs" (or differences of longitude) between the Sun and the planets, and by adding the value of these arcs to the longitude of the actual Ascendant. This procedure can be followed in the case of any two planets—or even of any two astrological points previously determined. As the result of such a procedure, if carried out to its limits, we can locate on the zodiac an almost infinite number of symbolic points. These are the "Parts," used so extensively by Arabian astrologers.

The procedure involves two factors: First the factor of *distance* between two planets, measured in terms of zodiacal longitude. Such a distance is considered as establishing a significant relationship between two planets, or any two astrologically valid points of reference. This is the factor on which all astrological "aspects" are founded. However, "aspects" are constituted by only a few significant values of distance determined by dividing the whole circumference by the use of simple denominators (2, 3, 4, 5, 6, 8, 10, 12 mostly)—such as 180°, 120°, 90°, 72°, 60°, etc. Yet theoretically, any distance is significant, and this distance-factor is made even more significant if it is connected with the Ascendant.*

This is just what constitutes the reality of the Parts. *A Part is the distance between two planets, referred for its significance to the Ascendant.* The Ascendant is the point of individual awareness. Therefore a Part gives significance to the relationship between two particular modes of life-activity (planets), in terms of the individual's intuitive perception of life and Destiny. Thus the Part of Fortune shows how the

---

* Marc Jones has used this factor of distance in a most original manner in a system of interpretation studied under the name "Pythagorean Astrology" which deals partly with the degree of completeness or approximation of the "aspects." Cf. Chapter on "Form and the Pattern of Planetary Aspects," (p. 394).

relation between solar and lunar energies operates in determining the individual's attitude to himself and to his Destiny. The Part of Imaging indicates the manner in which the integrative (Sun) and regenerative-transforming (Uranus) factors of his being cooperate in enhancing the creative individuality, the uniqueness, of the native.

Put any other planet in place of the Sun, and the same principle will be working out. Special meanings are released when the two planets considered form a positive-negative pair: Saturn-Moon, Jupiter-Mercury, Mars-Venus. Others, where antagonistic life-activities are concerned; the most significant being the case of Jupiter and Saturn. Not only planets, but such astrological points as the "New Moon before birth," can be paired, and their distance related to the Ascendant, thus constituting Parts. Parts reveal meanings in terms of their house, first and foremost, and also their sign and degree position, in terms of their conjunctions with other planets. They are "sensitive points" in a chart. Only, so many of them are possible that their number detracts from their significance.

This number is increased tremendously by the fact that the distance between two planets can be related (added) not only to the Ascendant, but also to the Mid-Heaven, Descendant and Nadir (or *Imum Coeli*). Each of these four points represents a function of selfhood, and therefore is entitled to become a center of reference for combinations of planetary activities. And this is not all! When considering the distance between two points of the zodiacal circumference, one can obviously get two arcs of measurement. Supposing that we measure the distance in the direction in which the signs of the zodiac increase (counter-clockwise), then we can measure the distance from the Sun to the Moon; but just as well that from the Moon to the Sun. In the following illustration we count 25 degrees from Sun to Moon, and therefore 335 degrees from Moon to Sun. If we add these 335 degrees to the longitude of the Ascendant (or, which is the same, if we *subtract* 25 degrees from its longitude), we get a new Part of Fortune as far *above* the horizon as the original Part was *below* the horizon. And if we operate likewise with regard

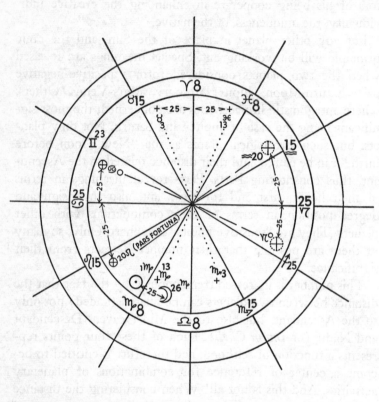

The eight possible points interpreting as "Parts" the relation Sun to Moon
—in two directions and applied to each of the four angles.

to the four angles, we find *eight* symbolic points created by the relationship Sun-Moon!

The astrology of Parts is indeed a kind of "group-algebra" working out nearly endless correlations and permutations between the original elements of the birth-formula. Its complexity makes it, of course, most unwieldy; yet there is no doubt that it represents the ultimate and most abstract type of astrological thought—that by means of which we come most closely to life itself and its multifarious network of relationships. Think for a moment of the myriads of nerve-tracts in a human body, each one establishing a path of linkage between cells of various kinds. Sensations, reactions, volitions, feelings, instincts, thoughts, all travel along this unbelievably complex web of life-threads. Personality is the result. And if we are to approximate with our tools for analysis the infinite variety of the connections to be analyzed, it is obvious that nothing short of the multitudes of Parts can do the work. The vistas open are vast almost beyond comprehension, for personality is ubiquitous. Astrology studies the personality of every minute of life, of every situation; of nations as well as of individuals. It is indeed the algebra of multitudinous and protean Life.

x. *Degrees of the Zodiac and the "Sabian" Symbols*

THE Degree is not merely a subdivision of the zodiacal sign, or of the whole zodiac. It stands, as an astrological element, alone and in a position of supreme (though little understood) significance. The Degree is the most mysterious element in astrology, and indeed the key to all deeper astrological interpretation. For in the Degree come to a point of synthesis the two motions of the earth—and, symbolically, the two great principles of all life: collective and individual, universal and particular. In the Degree we witness the operation of the creative within an individual personality, or a particular situation. Here "meaning" stands revealed—for whosoever knows how to read symbols.

Ignoring for the time being the numerical discrepancy existing between the 365 days and the 360 Degrees, we see that the Degree is the space covered by the Earth in its orbital revolution while it effects a complete axial rotation. The Degree is thus the projection in space of the time-unit, the day. In the Degree, time-value and space-value are integrated, and the two motions of the Earth are combined. Every complete axial rotation *distributes* all over the Earth some phase of the Life-function related to the zodiacal sign (or segment of the Earth-orbit) in which this particular rotation occurs. Because the Earth moves on its orbit while rotating around its axis, there can be only a limited number of axial rotations within the yearly revolution around the Sun. Each rotation generates thus, orbitally, a Degree. These Degrees are *not* mere subdivisions of the zodiac; for the fact of their existence is not dependent upon any intrinsic differentiation caused by the nature of the zodiac itself, or of the universal Life-force. It is dependent solely on the axial rotation of the Earth. The Degree partakes thus of two natures. It is an orbital element conditioned by the axial rotation. It must stand therefore for that factor in life which "reconciles the opposites."

What this function of reconciliation of the opposites is can be ascertained from our previous study of Jung's analytical psychology as well as from the contents of our chapter "Individual, Collective, Creative," etc. In the "day" we see operating successively all the phases of consciousness—from the waking state to the deepest sleep. All the stages from clear consciousness to the deepest unconsciousness are theoretically present. But if a "day" is a basic cycle of being, there must be something which integrates all these stages, a function of relation between conscious and unconscious. This function manifests in various ways; mainly, on one hand in dreams, on the other in creative phantasy. In the former, the unconscious predominates; in the latter, the conscious. But in both cases we find a linking or integrating process at work; and this process manifests through the projection of images, which are symbols. Dreams, or the greatest inspirations of the genius, are alike the products of an integrating process linking conscious and unconscious. In a sense, they are more often conditioned as to form by the state of the conscious—as the Degree is conditioned by the axial rotation of the Earth—but the *energy* with which they are endowed comes from the unconscious—the Degree *is* a part of the zodiac.

It might be said that the planet Uranus (and, in another way, also Jupiter) symbolizes this activity of the unconscious in relation to the conscious; but what a planet represents is pure activity. Whether the individual extracts out of the activity the "jewel of significance" or not, the planet *of itself* does not reveal; nor does it indicate the particular quality of the meaning that the individual at best *could* extract from the completion of this activity; that is, the nature of the "jewel of significance."

What is seen in the Degree is the archetypal "quality" of whatever occurs within its boundaries; the potential selfhood of any life-manifestation focused therein. The zodiac, considered as a complete cyclic series of Degrees, becomes much more than a representation of collective energies. It becomes the universal womb of significances. It becomes Time in its highest sense: A cyclic series of creative moments which are "wombs of souls," each of which releases a "quality" that becomes the "monad" of every entity reaching independent existence within that moment. Time, thus understood, is identical with the great Chinese concept of *Tao*.* The Degrees are units of creative Time. They reveal the boundaries of the great creative "moments" for human beings on this Earth.

That there are 360 of such Degrees means that there are, *from a planetary viewpoint*, as many basic types or modalities of individual selfhood on Earth; as many "meanings" incarnate as "groups of human beings." It is a planetary number. There is a different number for each planet, and it is determined (archetypally rather than phenomenally, as we shall see) by the relationship between the durations of the planet's revolution and of its axial rotation. This relationship between the two durations is the mystical and creative meaning of Time, as we understand the term. It is the operative number of *Tao* on Earth, we might say—very much as, for instance, the number *Pi* (3.14159) is the operative number of life, universally considered.

From the foregoing it may have become clear that the reality of the Degree, being of such a transcendental nature, can be considered and studied only in terms of a particular

---

*These ideas have been developed in the first part of this book: Cf. p. 63 and p. 93.

symbolical representation attached to it. Each Degree of the zodiac must therefore carry a symbol; and this symbol will reveal the meaning—the potential selfhood—of whatever is found located in this Degree; whether it be a planet or a cusp or any other abstract point.

How can one perceive or visualize these symbols? The answer is not so easy to give. To perceive symbols that are "wombs of significance" one must have a faculty of spiritual perception; moreover, the power to make the images visualized explicit and self-revealing. The term "clairvoyance" does not elucidate much, but we must use it in this connection. Space forbids us to explain what type of "clairvoyance" we are referring to. It certainly is more akin to real intuition than to mere "psychic" gifts. It can be said to be a special type of "holistic perception"—but one which is of planetary scope. Also we must add that the revelation of the symbols may reach the public only through several stages of transmission. Those who actually have such a planetary "holistic perception" may transmit the symbols to disciples, who in turn record these for general use.

Be this as it may, we find that, in the Alan Leo Astrological Manuals series, the booklet entitled *The Degrees of the Zodiac Symbolized* gives two sets of symbolic interpretations of the Degrees. The first, by Charubel, is quite valuable; the second, from a medieval source, seems completely useless. Marc Edmund Jones has given out another set which is by far the best; which, in fact, actual practice has proven, to those who know how to use symbols, absolutely invaluable. The symbols are presented as quite modern pictures, thus in a garb more significant to the average student of today; but they are said to be derived from very ancient Egyptian sources. We are adding to this chapter, with the special authorization of the recorder, our own condensed formulation of these symbols. We believe that they constitute a momentous astrological revelation, the significance and import of which may loom larger and larger as the years pass.

In this "Sabian" cycle of symbols we have something similar to the cycle of the *Yi King* as interpreted by the King Wen some 3000 years ago. The Chinese seer used pictures and scenes taken from nature and from the simple agricultural life of his day in order to convey through the instrumentality of images otherwise inexpressible meanings. He had to use such pictures and scenes because unless they were familiar to, and easily experienced by, men of his time, these men would not have been able to extract the *vital* significance locked therein. The same thing is true today. Therefore the "Sabian" symbols, recorded by Marc Jones, present to us moderns pictures and scenes which are relatively familiar or at least within the scope of our vicarious experiences. It is possible that the formulation of these 360 symbols is not yet perfect; that in some cases the scenes depicted as symbols are not sufficiently deeply rooted enough in the common experience of mankind, and not universally or vitally compelling. But in the main we believe that such a series of symbols goes to the very root of planetary significance for our present era, and that, after being refined here and there, and after its structural rhythm is made clear through interpretative studies at various levels, it will stand with a significance comparable to that of the 64 symbols of the *Yi King* series. At any rate its practical value in astrological practice is, to us, absolutely beyond doubt. It has proven itself in hundreds of cases; in fact, practically whenever it has been tested, both in natal charts and in important horary charts.

We might add, for the sake of a fuller understanding of the matter, that there are very plausible reasons why several valid symbols recorded in more or less the same way by persons of different spiritual "qualities" could be attached to each Degree. We must realize that in the realm of pure significance values are very different from those encountered in that of intellectual or scientific analysis. First, the individual element is paramount; second, it is connected with the factor of time. A symbol may be valid now, which may prove valueless a few centuries hence. The matter is not one of truthfulness or correctness, but one of value. And values are cyclically changing. A set of values may be "true" or rather vitally significant now; also it may have been as significant 5000 years ago. Yet it may have had very little or no validity 1000 years ago. For the same reasons, cultures and art-expressions change periodically. There are cycles of significance within cycles. Each race, each cycle, is the symbolic image of some vast planetary or cosmic meaning. Some men who strive after *real* spiritual values refine their inner awareness to the point at which they can become the recipients, the "grails," into which flows, and into which alone may flow, the "wine of significance." They are the "seers," the creative geniuses of the race—the avatars of Time, and themselves seeds of significance to the monadic group to which they belong by spiritual right.

These monadic groups can be discovered by means of astrological analysis. They are, in a sense, hidden behind the zodiac. But not the ordinarily understood *zodiac of signs*; rather, the more mysterious *cycle of 360 Degrees*. The key-number in such a cycle is not 12, but 6. The cycle is one of awareness, awareness being the vehicle for significance. As such, its first division is one which corresponds to the concept of *horizon*; and also to the theoretical division between day and night; which refers to the division between conscious and unconscious, outer and inner, man and woman, sensation-thinking and intuition-feeling. The concept of *meridian*, on the other hand, refers to the element of "power." The birth-chart of the individual uses both axes, because birth means crucifixion in space and the number 4 is the number of formation. The ordinary zodiac, symbolizing also as a whole the universal "power of formation," had therefore to be divided into 4 sections, which by trisection, gave the twelvefold division—or by bisection, the eightfold one.

Significance is based on the type of spiritual activity which constantly "reconciles the opposites." It is, in an absolute sense, the source of this activity; in a relative and concrete sense it is the result thereof. Its keynote is thus 2 multiplied by 3; the number 3 referring to the principle of essential manifestation, or individuation. In other words, in terms of significance, we find the cycle divided into 6 phases. Each phase is the spiritual reality of what the occultist-theosophist calls a "Ray." Each Ray, as it manifests *concretely*, has to subdivide itself into 4 parts: the crucifixion of the Ray. Thus we have the 24 Elders of the Bible, standing around the throne of God. In ancient times, as manifestation was more potential and energic than concrete and actually embodied, each Ray was rather trisected, giving the number 18—the 18 chapters of the *Bhagavad Gita*. Krishna was the nineteenth, just as in the first phase of the Bahai movement, the Bab (the Herald of the Avatar-to-be) and his closest companions formed the 19 "Letters of the Living"—because they constituted the group before the concrete manifestation of the "Glory of God"— Baha'u'llah.

The 24 Elders represent the 24 hours of the day, for the day is the unit of Time and the reality of the Degree, which in turn is the unit of significance. Each "hour" stands therefore in the complete *zodiac of significance* for 15 degrees; just as each Ray stands for a two-month period—or two successive signs of the zodiac (which are traditionally referred to as a masculine-feminine pair; for instance, the pair Aries-Taurus).

In his interpretation of the "Sabian" cycle of symbols Marc Jones refers to these "hours" as *spans*, and divides them each into three five-degree sections: "In each hour the first five degrees express the factor of the habit realm in man; the second five, the emotional realm; the third five, the mental realm—the order of all trisection in . . . evolution from matter upward towards spirit." (*Symbolical Astrology:* Lesson II.)

At this point, however, it seems necessary to answer two questions which probably have presented themselves many times to the reader's mind while reading the last paragraphs. The first is: If there are over 365 days in the year, why only 360 degrees?—The second: Are there not seven Rays, rather than six?

These two questions can be answered simultaneously, the two answers deriving from the same principle. We can state this principle briefly by saying that there is always in Nature a value of indeterminacy where two fundamental polarities are to be interpreted in terms of each other. The axial rotation of the earth is a cosmically subjective and individualistic time-factor. The orbital revolution is an objective and universalistic space-factor. And the former cannot serve as an exact unit of measurement to determine the latter. We cannot measure one set of values by a unit belonging to another realm of value. The collectivity is not an exact sum total of individuals. There may be 360 individuals in a group; but the value of the group is not the exact sum of the values of each individual. There is in any collectivity an increment of growth, a *plus*; a mysterious quantity which, in a sense, is not a quantity—at any rate never a *rational number*.

The process may be reversed, and one may say that the individual is not an exact fraction of the group-value. Life is not as mathematical as we might think; and modern physics has discovered this while investigating the behavior of electrons. The result has been Heisenberg's principle of indeterminacy: You cannot know accurately and at the same time the position and the speed of an electron. Likewise no two planetary motions of different orders can be related quantitatively by rational numbers. Perhaps the most universal symbol of this law of cosmic relationship is to be found in the value of *Pi* which measures the relation of circumference to diameter; 3.14159. It would seem logical that the circumference should contain 3 diameters or 6 radii. But it contains more than 6 radii, just as the year contains more than 6 x 60 days.

The "more" represents the coefficient of indeterminacy in all integrative processes. It represents the freedom of the Soul, the Seventh Day of Creation, the *Atman* of Hindu philosophy: the Imprevisible. Occultists speak of the Seven Rays. But the seventh is not really a Ray; it is a bridge between two sixfold scales of being. Musically speaking, it is the "leading note" of the major scale. It is the irrational value by which the length of the circumference is more than the sum of the lengths of six radii; that is .14159. . . . It represents the freedom of all Rays; that by which they can be more than they are. Likewise if one divides 365¼ by 360 one gets a decimal value which represents symbolically that by which, each year, the individual may grow to a higher state of selfhood. This value, curiously enough, gives again the number 14—being .014+.*

In another sense, the extra days mean also that the Earth's orbit is not perfect nor the Earth's pace steady. This might be referred to the tilting of the polar axis over the plane of the ecliptic. Whichever way one looks at the subject, 360 must be taken as the archetypal number measuring the relation of individual to collective on Earth: the creative number of the Earth as an archetype of significance. The realm of significance *is* the archetypal realm; and *no* concrete manifestation is ever a perfect replica of its archetype. Likewise, no astronomical cycle can be calculated in whole numbers; and, we might add,

---

* The number 365¼ refers to the *solar* day but there are 366¼ *sidereal* days in a solar year. One can take either of these two values according as one considers (1) the motion of the Earth along its orbit, that is, in reference to the Sun; or else (2) the cycle of axial rotation of the Earth in reference to the fixed stars (sidereal day). The difference is subtle, philosophically speaking. The sidereal day refers to the individual as an individual; the solar day, to the individual in relation to its spiritual source (symbolically, the Sun).

no actual life is ever absolutely and rigidly true to the pattern offered by the birth-chart; no group of prognostications can ever be absolutely accurate. Somewhere, at some time, some discrepancy will always occur. Otherwise the universe would already have reached a point of static perfection. The fact that life *is*, is the surest indication that spirit and matter, significance and form, can never be perfectly adjusted, and their opposite emphases never perfectly reconciled. Therefore there must always be destruction and regeneration. Out of the "indeterminate," the creative freedom of Shiva arises—the symbol of all transitions, the god of the "First Ray." All creation that is absolutely significant is imprevisible, because it arises out of relative imperfection, out of the perpetual need to find a new form to integrate the unintegrable.

There is a great symbolic truth in the tradition that, in leap years, on February 29, women can propose to men. For that extra day symbolizes the unfulfilled part of any cycle; and in that part the call of substance unmarried to spirit rises to spirit. And it must be heard. And the answer is the Avatar, the Christ-being, the Seventh Who is the First.

———

We now give the "Sabian" series of Degree-symbols in our condensed version. We shall add only these few remarks which are excerpts from Marc Jones' course:

> "Symbolical astrology is a living art and must be studied as such. The symbols connected with the degrees of the zodiac are seldom to be taken literally. They are rather catalytics to the astrologer's higher understanding, the development of which will enable him to add content and implication to every factor of life."

Marc Jones gives a positive and a negative interpretation of every symbol. In the present version, only the positive meaning is usually given, although occasionally both meanings are mentioned. This dualism of meanings is the expression of the fact that all being can orient itself toward spirit or toward matter, and all conditioning is susceptible of two basic types of interpretation—which, in turn, can be related to one of several (at least three) levels of consciousness. Hence the application of symbols to individual cases requires a technique, based on the higher understanding.

Any fraction of a degree is to be considered as a whole degree. Aries 15° 0' is to be read as Aries 15°; but Aries 15° 1', as well as Aries 15° 59', represents Aries 16°. The symbols are the expression of a span of activity, a cycle, the significance of which is released at once, the moment it begins.

ARIES   I. THE SPAN OF REALIZATION

1° A WOMAN HAS RISEN FROM THE OCEAN; A SEAL EMBRACES HER
Potentiality of selfhood: the individual is emerging from the
collective and realizes self for the first time.

2° A COMEDIAN IS ENTERTAINING A GROUP OF HIS FRIENDS
Objective understanding through extracting salient elements of
being. Joy of life's discovery; or escape through humor.

3° A MAN'S PROFILE SUGGESTS THE OUTLINES OF HIS COUNTRY
The individual self as an avatar of greater collective reality; as
participant in the larger scheme of society or life.

4° TWO LOVERS ARE STROLLING THROUGH A SECLUDED PARK LANE
Fullness of conscious participation in life without responsibility.
Closing of a cycle of activity, implying satiation.

5° A WHITE TRIANGLE, WITH GOLDEN WINGS ON ITS UPPER SIDES
Evolution of values in the sphere of inward self, but at a stage
not yet substantiated. Eagerness for a spiritual goal.

6° A BLACK SQUARE; ONE OF ITS SIDES IS ILLUMINED RED
Primal effort toward individual selfhood. First and uncontrolled
interest in any given thing. Great inner restlessness.

7° A MAN EXPRESSES HIMSELF AT ONCE IN TWO REALMS
Conscious duality by which man first really differentiates himself
from the animals. Versatility in work. Self-expansion.

8° A WOMAN'S HAT, WITH STREAMERS BLOWN BY THE EAST WIND
First real attempt at self-exteriorization and embodiment in consciousness. Individualizing Eastern forces are suggested.

9° A SEER GAZES WITH CONCENTRATION INTO A CRYSTAL SPHERE
Direction from within. Taking advantage of all factors in a given
situation, and knowing when to make decisions. Assurance.

10° A SCHOLAR CREATES NEW FORMS FOR ANCIENT SYMBOLS
Deep understanding, beyond normal means. Abstract seership,
integrating the inner and the outer. Interpretative gift.

11° THE RULER OF A COUNTRY IS BEING OFFICIALLY INTRODUCED
Fine stewardship of collective racial ideals. Good and necessary, but unimaginative conformity to standards. Idealization.

12° A FLOCK OF WHITE GEESE FLIES OVERHEAD ACROSS CLEAR SKIES
A soul as yet socially immature and unadjusted; not come down to full and steady concrete expression. Self-discovery.

13° A BOMB WHICH FAILED TO EXPLODE IS NOW SAFELY CONCEALED
Intangible fears of nascent selfhood: the creative stirring up of a new perspective and a new identity suddenly revealed.

14° A SERPENT ENCIRCLES A MAN AND WOMAN IN CLOSE EMBRACE
Power of higher wisdom manifest in the bi-polar nature. Protection by the higher genius of Self. Fulfillment in truth.

15° INDIAN WEAVING A BASKET IN THE GOLDEN LIGHT OF SUNSET
Full and conscious realization of selfhood, through the memory of all the powers acquired in the past. Retentiveness.

ARIES   II. THE SPAN OF EXAMINATION

16° BRIGHTLY CLAD BROWNIES, DANCING IN WARM DYING LIGHT
Relationship between conscious and unconscious sides of life. Invisible assistance often entailing obligation to outer forces.

17° TWO PRIM SPINSTERS ARE SITTING TOGETHER IN SILENCE
Poised and dispassionate outlook, involving either great dignity and integrity of self, or inability to live life fully.

18° AN EMPTY HAMMOCK IS HANGING BETWEEN TWO LOVELY TREES
Rest after some notable achievement. Capacity for consciousness after the act, for reaping fruits of activity. Detachment.

19° A MAGIC CARPET HOVERING OVER AN UGLY INDUSTRIAL SUBURB
Capacity to transform everyday life by the power of creative significance; or escape in idle fancy.

20° A YOUNG GIRL FEEDING SWANS IN A PARK ON A WINTRY DAY
Participation of self in a life larger than any conception of selfhood. Protection, or the need for it.

21° A PUGILIST, FLUSHED WITH STRENGTH, ENTERS THE RING
Complete immolation of self in things purely physical. Intense self-assertiveness, physical and psychological.

22° GATEWAY OPENING TO THE GARDEN OF ALL DESIRED THINGS
Joy and utter lack of inhibitions in objective life. Self-exaltation or bondage to the craving for happiness.

23° WOMAN IN SUMMER DRESS CARRIES A PRECIOUS VEILED BURDEN
First maturity of conscious life in any phase of experience. Sense of value and delicacy—or wastefulness. Innocence.

24° A WINDOW CURTAIN BLOWN INWARD, SHAPED AS A CORNUCOPIA
Good fortune attending upon the putting forth of effort. Rush of spiritual forces into the conscious ego. Protection.

25° A DOUBLE PROMISE REVEALS ITS INNER AND OUTER MEANINGS
Fortuitous cooperation between inner and outer elements of being. A sense of responsibility to self or to society.

26° A MAN, BURSTING WITH THE WEALTH OF WHAT HE HAS TO GIVE
Supreme endowment, and inexhaustibility of resources in all possible life realms. Sometimes obsession by potentiality.

27° THROUGH IMAGINATION, A LOST OPPORTUNITY IS REGAINED
Beginning of mental maturity and slow growth of the creative faculty. Revision of attitude. Mental house-cleaning.

28° A CROWD APPLAUDS A MAN WHO SHATTERED A DEAR ILLUSION
A new light is shed upon cherished ideas. Fearless, constructive and public facing of the facts of existence. Adjustment.

29° A CELESTIAL CHOIR HAS ARISEN TO SING COSMIC HARMONIES
At-one-ment of consciousness with cosmic powers. Harmonic understanding and faith in the order and meaning of life.

30° YOUNG DUCKLINGS DISPORT THEMSELVES MERRILY UPON A POND
Essential social cooperativeness and appreciation of selfhood. Also a sense of inner restriction. Contentedness.

TAURUS   III. THE SPAN OF EXPERIENCE

1° A CLEAR MOUNTAIN STREAM FLOWS THROUGH A ROCKY DEFILE
Purity, excellence and immediate availability of the strength and
power of being. Refreshment. Self-sustainment.

2° AN ELECTRICAL STORM BRILLIANTLY ILLUMINES THE SKIES
A sensing of the power and wonder of nature's forces. Complete
transformation of the implication of all being. Awe.

3° NATURAL TERRACES LEAD UP TO A LAWN OF CLOVER IN BLOOM
The invitation extended by all nature to man for self-expression.
Inspirational possibilities in all experience. Hope.

4° THE RAINBOW'S POT OF GOLD GLOWS AMIDST THE SPARKLING RAIN
Unlimited resources. Overflowing sense of power. Prodigality of
spiritual love showered upon seekers for the highest.

5° A YOUNG WIDOW, TRANSFIGURED BY GRIEF, KNEELS AT A GRAVE
Revelation of meaning behind fleeting appearances. Restless quest
for understanding. Birth from illusion into reality.

6° A CANTILEVER BRIDGE IN CONSTRUCTION ACROSS A DEEP CANYON
Conquest of difficulties and limitations by intelligence. Directed
effort toward solving a problem. Channel-ship.

7° WOMAN OF SAMARIA COMES TO DRAW WATER FROM THE WELL
The gaining of perspective by a return to ancient sources of
being. Introspective approach to collective unconscious.

8° A SLEIGH SPEEDS OVER GROUND AS YET UNCOVERED BY SNOW
Independence of the will of the self from outer circumstances.
Power to mould life upon the pioneer's prophetic vision.

9° A CHRISTMAS TREE LOADED WITH GIFTS AND LIGHTED CANDLES
A symbol of the promise which outer life offers to the pure in
heart; of immortality through giving of self to the race.

10° A PRETTY RED CROSS NURSE HURRIES ON AN ERRAND OF MERCY
Natural, unrestrained pouring of self in service to one's fellow-
men. Self-expression through compassionate understanding.

11° A WOMAN WATERING ROWS OF FLOWERS IN FULL BLOOM
Man's and nature's creative partnership of service and beauty.
Nature's rich response to man's care or lack of care.

12° YOUNG COUPLE WALKS DOWN MAIN STREET, WINDOW-SHOPPING
Inner interest in outer life which leads to whole-souled participation and achievement. Self-projection. Estimation.

13° A PORTER IS CHEERFULLY BALANCING A MOUNTAIN OF BAGGAGE
Joy of effort put forth. Faith in the eventual results of a simple
plunging ahead in things. Extreme of self-reliance.

14° CHILDREN SPLASH IN RECEDING TIDE AMID GROPING SHELLFISH
Need for a realization of life's unity in the multiplicity of its
forms. Unconscious contact with higher stages of being.

15° MAN WITH RAKISH SILK HAT, MUFFLED, BRAVES THE STORM
Supremacy of conscious mind over brute nature forces. Full
appreciation of outer difficulties. Great inner resources.

TAURUS   IV. THE SPAN OF ENJOYMENT

16° OLD MAN TRIES HARD TO IMPART HIDDEN TRUTHS TO A CROWD
Conscious possession of greater knowledge and potentiality than
can be used. Great inner fullness. Spiritual loneliness.

17° A SYMBOLICAL BATTLE BETWEEN "SWORDS" AND "TORCHES"
Struggle between might and enlightenment, physical desires and
higher inspirations. Self-orientation. Divine enthusiasm.

18° A WOMAN IS AIRING A LINEN BAG THROUGH A SUNNY WINDOW
Revolt against musty, dark corners of being. Psycho-analysis.
Self-dissatisfaction. Strong will for self-transformation.

19° A NEW CONTINENT, FRESH AND GREEN, RISES OUT OF THE OCEAN
Potentiality for tangible self-manifestation in all beings. Overflowing originality. Spontaneous, rich creative urge.

20° WISPS OF CLOUDS, LIKE WINGS, ARE STREAMING ACROSS THE SKY
Exalted state of consciousness; lightness and breadth of being and
understanding. Mystical and ecstatic self-expansion.

TAURUS

21° MOVING FINGER POINTS TO SIGNIFICANT PASSAGES IN A BOOK
Symbol of spiritual discrimination, of capacity for getting to the heart of any matter. Good memory. Perspicacity.

22° A WHITE HOMING PIGEON FLIES STRAIGHT OVER STORMY WATERS
Freedom of understanding; strength based on the possession of a real mission. Transcendent activity. Self-extrication.

23° A JEWELRY SHOP FILLED WITH THE MOST MAGNIFICENT JEWELS
Abundance of permanent spiritual values; or social display of traditional racial achievements. Profusion of inner gifts.

24° INDIAN, HUMAN SCALPS HANGING AT HIS BELT, RIDES PROUDLY
Forceful intrusion of elemental energies in over-conscious selfhood. Return to primal values. Conquest of inhibitions.

25° VAST PUBLIC PARK DISPLAYS GLORIOUS AND INSPIRING VISTAS
Social strength of collectivities. Power of traditional culture. Faithfulness to established achievements. Immutability.

26° A SPANISH SERENADER AT THE WINDOW-GRILLE OF HIS BELOVED
Power of well-defined desire which assures success in all life-contacts. Imaginative power that compels manifestation.

27° A WITHERED OLD SQUAW, SMILING BRIGHTLY, SELLS TRINKETS
Dignified offering of fruits of wisdom to exuberant youth. Patient understanding of destiny; or else meddlesomeness.

28° MATURE WOMAN REAWAKENED TO ROMANCE ADMIRES HERSELF
New perspective on life, genuine rejuvenation. The compelling charm of mature experience. Rebelliousness of inner hopes.

29° TWO GARRULOUS OLD COBBLERS WORK SEATED ON AN OLD BENCH
A symbol of discursive reason, the battle of "pros and cons" within the inner being. Analytical, recapitulative judgment.

30° PEACOCK DISPLAYS ITS PLUMAGE ON LAWN OF OLD ESTATE
Personal magnificence or unconscious splendor. Sure retreat for the solitary soul where it can reveal its inmost glory.

GEMINI   V. THE SPAN OF ZEAL

1° GLASS-BOTTOMED BOAT DRIFTS OVER UNDER-SEA WONDERS
Depth of realization in a consciousness constantly in touch with
the sources of life. Sensitiveness to collective images.

2° SANTA CLAUS IS FURTIVELY FILLING CHRISTMAS STOCKINGS
The natural beneficence in any normal human heart. Alertness to
the wishes of others; the often hidden pride of benefactors.

3° LOUIS XIV'S COURT IN THE GARDENS OF THE TUILERIES
A degree of genuine aristocracy and perfection of behavior. Self-
fulfillment in form and tradition. Collective strength.

4° HOLLY AND MISTLETOE BRING CHRISTMAS SPIRIT TO A HOME
Holiday spirit as an attempt to preserve for individuals the wealth
and power of racial background. Social warmth.

5° A RADICAL MAGAZINE DISPLAYS A SENSATIONAL FRONT PAGE
The compelling power of social propaganda. Exteriorization of
emotional sympathy in organized reform. Efficiency.

6° NIGHT WORKMEN DRILL FOR OIL AMIDST NOISE AND CONFUSION
Exaggerated activity in pursuit of material wealth. Capacity to
drive oneself in view of future and speculative gains.

7° AN OLD WELL, FILLED WITH PURE WATER, SHADED BY TREES
Deep and mature relationship between man and the basic life-
giving reality of his environment. Inner assurance; poise.

8° AROUND A CLOSED-DOWN FACTORY STRIKERS MILL DEFIANTLY
A stirring of the collective, unconscious factors of being toward
the repolarization of the conscious ego. Idle protest.

9° A MEDIEVAL ARCHER, WITH BOW AND ARROWS, READY TO FIGHT
Superiority and ease based upon training. Sure markmanship.
Certain self-direction. Preparedness. Invisible help in trouble.

10° AEROPLANE, AFTER A NOSE-DIVE, RIGHTS ITSELF GRACEFULLY
Capacity to plunge into experience without surrendering one's
principles or self-control. Self-expansion through sacrifice.

11° NEWLY OPENED LANDS OFFER VIRGIN REALMS OF EXPERIENCE
New vista of concrete, conscious development. Renewed and enlarged opportunities. Nature's call for the pioneer spirit.

12° A BLACK SLAVE-GIRL DEMANDS HER RIGHTS OF HER MISTRESS
The will to rise above racial conditioning and limitations; or a sense of the need to conform to things as they are.

13° WORLD-FAMOUS PIANIST BEGINS TO PLAY TO A HUGE AUDIENCE
Extreme exaltation of social standing. Reaching of climax in selfhood. Ghastly sense of emptiness at the end of the quest.

14° TWO PEOPLE, LIVING FAR APART, IN TELEPATHIC COMMUNICATION
Conscious mastery of space-time limitations of ordinary existence. Realization of basic realities in all situations.

15° TWO DUTCH CHILDREN ARE STUDYING THEIR LESSONS TOGETHER
Conscious approach to spiritual truth and underlying meanings. Open-mindedness. Clarity of thought along traditional lines.

GEMINI　　　　　　　　VI. THE SPAN OF RESTLESSNESS

16° WOMAN AGITATOR MAKES AN IMPASSIONED PLEA TO A CROWD
Rising of the human soul in demand for the recognition by the outer nature of the needs of inner being. Self-assertion.

17° HEAD OF A YOUTH CHANGES INTO THAT OF A MATURE THINKER
Progression from robust participation in outer things to a realization of deeper realities. Inborn wisdom. Steady growth.

18° TWO CHINAMEN CONVERSE IN CHINESE IN AN OCCIDENTAL CROWD
Alienness, but also independence from environment. Conscious self-sustainment in spite of all conditions. Individualization.

19° LARGE ARCHAIC VOLUME ON DISPLAY IN A MUSEUM'S ARCHIVES
Reserve of collective knowledge and wisdom beyond true individual self-expression. Deference to past experience.

20° A SELF-SERVICE RESTAURANT DISPLAYS AN ABUNDANCE OF FOOD
Prodigal distribution of life-resources. Inner wealth. Satiation, or discriminative use of natural energies. Rich supply.

GEMINI

21° A LABOR DEMONSTRATION THRONGS A LARGE CITY SQUARE
The impetuous onsurge of natural instincts within the field of the
conscious ego. Blind struggle. Compelling power of fate.

22° DANCING COUPLES CROWD THE BARN IN A HARVEST FESTIVAL
Richness of life in associations based on natural instincts. Warmth
of simple living. Normal fulfillment of self.

23° THREE FLEDGLINGS LOOK OUT PROUDLY FROM THEIR HIGH NEST
Conscious self-establishment in the soul and its threefold nature.
Innate self-confidence. Superiority of real being.

24° CAREFREE CHILDREN SKATE OVER A SMOOTHLY FROZEN POND
Capacity to use every opportunity, even in the hardest of environment, for self-recreation or relaxation. Appreciation.

25° A GARDENER TRIMS BEAUTIFUL PALM TREES WITH UTMOST CARE
Capacity in man to control his environment and the impulses of
his most intense nature. Active care for possessions.

26° FROST-COVERED TREES, LACE-LIKE, AGAINST WINTER SKIES
Creative bestowal of significance upon all things. Transforming
power of beauty. Keen appreciation of natural processes.

27° YOUNG GYPSY EMERGING FROM THE WOODS GAZES AT FAR CITIES
Growth of consciousness from the instinctual to the intellectual.
Anticipation and mounting self-confidence. Deep longing.

28° BANKRUPTCY GRANTED TO HIM, A MAN LEAVES THE COURT
Release of self from collective pressure impossible to bear. Determination to regather forces for new attempt. Protection.

29° THE FIRST MOCKING BIRD OF SPRING SINGS FROM THE TREE TOP
Recapitulation of past opportunities at the threshold of a new
cycle of experience. Realization of new potentialities.

30° A PARADE OF BATHING BEAUTIES BEFORE LARGE BEACH CROWDS
Use of individual vanity in raising racial standards. Examination
of intellectual values for use in the soul life.

CANCER   VII. THE SPAN OF EXPANSION

1° SAILOR READY TO HOIST A NEW FLAG TO REPLACE OLD ONE
The nascent desire to align oneself with a larger and more significant life trend. Compelling decision. Repolarization.

2° A MAN ON A MAGIC CARPET OBSERVES VAST VISTAS BELOW HIM
Broadening of perspective. Supremacy of intelligence over circumstances. Conscientiousness. Objective self-control.

3° AN ARCTIC EXPLORER LEADS A REINDEER THROUGH ICY CANYONS
The pioneering, trail-blazing instinct urging man to get out
beyond all things. Plunge into virgin possibilities of life.

4° A HUNGRY CAT ARGUES WITH A MOUSE, BEFORE EATING HER
The urge to self-justification through intellectual sophistry or
social-ethical considerations. Sense of self-righteousness.

5° AUTOMOBILIST, RACING MADLY WITH A FAST TRAIN, IS KILLED
Individual man is brought to account for his obligations to society. Curbed recklessness. Tragic escape from emptiness.

6° INNUMERABLE BIRDS ARE BUSY FEATHERING THEIR NESTS
Instinctive preparation for mature and full expression of the self.
Subconscious planning or dreaming of idle dreams.

7° IN A MOONLIT FAIRY GLADE TWO LITTLE ELVES ARE DANCING
Man's recognition of the elusive play of underlying forces in
nature. Cooperation with the invisible. Unusual good luck.

8° RABBITS IN FAULTLESS HUMAN ATTIRE PARADE WITH DIGNITY
Reaching out to participation in a higher order through imitative
behavior. Willingness to grow; also self-exploitation.

9° NAKED LITTLE MISS LEANS OVER A POND TO CATCH A GOLD FISH
First curiosity of being; innocent reaching out for understanding.
Untiring eagerness. Unsocial or infantile cravings.

10° A WONDERFUL DIAMOND IS BEING CUT TO A PERFECT SHAPE
Spiritual fulfillment or the acme of civilized being. Actualization
of potentialities and outpressing of real selfhood.

11° A CLOWN CARICATURES MERRILY ALL KINDS OF HUMAN TRAITS
Sharp discrimination and understanding of human nature. The
light touch of masterful living; self-control; or frivolity.

12° A CHINESE WOMAN NURSING A BABY HALOED BY DIVINE LIGHT
The promise to all men that God may take birth within their
souls. Personality integration. Illumination; or frustration.

13° A HAND WITH PROMINENT THUMB IS HELD OUT RECEPTIVELY
Strong, active and self-certain will, or persistent yet blind plunging ahead into reality. Freedom from soft illusions.

14° AN OLD MAN, ALONE, FACES THE DARKNESS IN THE NORTHEAST
Fearlessness; and noble, self-perpetuating strength arising from
knowledge. Courage in the facing of spiritual problems.

15° MERRY AND SLUGGISH PEOPLE RESTING AFTER A HUGE FEAST
A turning to superficial things for self-strengthening. Self-
indulgence in sensations. Unintelligent satiation; dullness.

CANCER   VIII. THE SPAN OF INGENUOUSNESS

16° A MAN HOLDS A SCROLL. BEFORE HIM, A SQUARE IS OUTLINED
Underlying tendency to revert to root patterns of being: "squaring" oneself with everyday reality. Control over life.

17° THE ARCHETYPAL SOUL BECOMES FILLED WITH LIFE-CONTENTS
Gathering of all life values and experience in the perfectly formed
consciousness. Spiritually integrated knowledge.

18° IN A CROWDED BARNYARD A HEN CLUCKS AMONG HER CHICKENS
Constructively practical, natural approach to life and its simpler
joys. Concern over things. Child-like group devotion.

19° AN ARISTOCRATIC AND FRAIL GIRL WEDS A PROLETARIAN YOUTH
Blending of the cultural fruition of the past with the impetuous-
ness of new blood. Assimilation of unconscious contents.

20° A GROUP OF SERENADERS MAKE MERRY IN A VENETIAN GONDOLA
Exaltation of social intercourse in the traditional manner. Senti-
mental clinging to old life-ideals. The will to romance.

CANCER

21° AN OPERATIC PRIMA DONNA SINGS TO A GLITTERING AUDIENCE
Elevation and popularization of human values through art as a social factor. Supreme realization of the life-ambition.

22° A YOUNG WOMAN DREAMILY AWAITS A SAILBOAT APPROACHING
A longing to live life as a great adventure. The compelling power of all sustained desire and of the dreaming of dreams.

23° A GROUP OF INTELLECTUAL INDIVIDUALS MEET FOR DISCUSSION
Interchange of ideas among any élite as a basis for the cultural development of the whole. Mental or physical fellowship.

24° WOMAN AND TWO MEN CASTAWAYS ON A SOUTH SEAS ISLAND
The three "souls" in man—actional, emotional, mental—"exiled" in the body. Potential fulfillment. Sense of being lost in life.

25° LEADER OF MEN WRAPPED IN AN INVISIBLE MANTLE OF POWER
Support of unconscious elements in every fearless and positive stand of the ego. Restoration of strength; or self-discovery.

26° GUESTS ARE READING IN THE LIBRARY OF A LUXURIOUS HOME
Emergence of consciousness upon higher levels of being, once life has been fulfilled at normal levels. Conscious fruition.

27° A FURIOUS STORM RAGES THROUGH A RESIDENTIAL CANYON
Intensification of elements necessary to arouse latent possibilities. Rising to the occasion. A descent of cosmic power.

28° INDIAN GIRL INTRODUCES COLLEGE BOY-FRIEND TO HER TRIBE
The human soul as intercessor between primordial natural forces and the intellectual order. Self-integration. Linkage.

29° A GREEK MUSE WEIGHS IN GOLDEN SCALES JUST BORN TWINS
The revelation of latent worth in all things through the power of creative imagination. Piercing beyond appearances.

30° A LADY OF ARISTOCRATIC DESCENT PROUDLY ADDRESSES A CLUB
The will and ability to maintain a social supremacy based on thoroughly established tradition. Inner or outer aristocracy.

Degrees of the Zodiac and the "Sabian" Symbols

1°   UNDER EMOTIONAL STRESS BLOOD RUSHES TO A MAN'S HEAD
A basic symbol of Man: forceful, dangerous entrance into the
Soul realm. Irresistible outpouring of self. Activity *per se*.

2°   THE SCHOOL CLOSED BY AN EPIDEMIC, CHILDREN PLAY TOGETHER
Constructive result of inconveniences of life in developing com-
munal values. Self-sensitiveness. Subtraction from things.

3°   MATURE WOMAN, HER HAIR JUST BOBBED, LOOKS INTO MIRROR
Sense of freedom from age and realization of the value of youth.
Self-creation and independence from fate. Will-power.

4°   ELDERLY MAN GAZES AT MOOSE HEAD ON CLUBROOM'S WALL
Self-development through the culture of masculine activities.
Subservience of individual to social pattern of behavior. Taste.

5°   SUGGESTING FIGURES, GRANITE MASSES OVERHANG A CANYON
Permanence of basic elements in nature underneath temporary
changes and emphases. Endurance. Steadiness of self-knowledge.

6°   OLD-FASHIONED BELLE AND FLAPPER ADMIRE EACH OTHER
Realization of changeless subjective worth beyond changing appearances. Interchange of sympathy. Enhanced self-awareness.

7°   THE CONSTELLATIONS GLOW IN THE DARKNESS OF DESERT SKIES
Sense of primordial wonder and awe before life. Unquenchable
faith in a spiritual being complementing our own. Realization.

8°   PROLETARIAN, BURNING WITH SOCIAL PASSION, STIRS UP CROWDS
Leavening of the inchoate materials of a new order by a forceful vision born of repression and misfortune. Revolution.

9°   GLASS-BLOWERS SHAPE WITH THEIR BREATH GLOWING FORMS
The formative power of the soul in moments of emotional intensity. Controlled self-expression. Art as a spiritual fact.

10°   EARLY MORNING DEW SPARKLES AS THE SUN FLOODS THE FIELDS
Freshness of spontaneous response to life and emotions. Uplifting
lightness in experience; or else superficial glamour.

11° CHILDREN PLAY BENEATH HUGE OAK, SHELTER FROM THE SUN
The sustaining and protective power of ancestral background against emotions. Appreciation of inborn cultural restraint.

12° A GARDEN PARTY IS IN FULL SWING UNDER JAPANESE LANTERNS
Easy intercourse of human souls in moments of relaxation from strain. Examination of, or self-loss in social values.

13° OLD SEA-CAPTAIN RESTS IN NEAT LITTLE COTTAGE BY THE SEA
Reward of growth from outer to inner realms. Serenity through the overcoming of storms. Self-gained mellowness. Retirement.

14° CHERUB-LIKE, A HUMAN SOUL WHISPERS, SEEKING TO MANIFEST
The desire to be, to suffer and to grow which brings Spirit to Earth. Whole-souled self-giving. Yearning for experience.

15° THE MARDI GRAS CARNIVAL CROWDS NEW ORLEANS' STREETS
Spectacular, dramatic release of subconscious energies. Self-exaltation for social approval. Self-indulgence and license.

LEO　　　　　X. THE SPAN OF INTERPRETATION

16° REFRESHED BY A STORM, FIELDS AND GARDENS BASK IN THE SUN
A return to values after a major life-crisis. Cleansing power of suffering overcome. Mastery of strain—or indifference.

17° VOLUNTEER CHURCH CHOIR MAKE SOCIAL EVENT OF REHEARSAL
Utilization of normal human instincts as a foundation to high endeavor. Lay-participation in Mysteries. Joy in faith.

18° CHEMIST CONDUCTS AN EXPERIMENT BEFORE HIS STUDENTS
Practical application of principles to ordinary life. Active enlightenment; or forced awakening to inner potentialities.

19° A BARGE MADE INTO A CLUBHOUSE IS CROWDED WITH REVELERS
The transforming power of pure joy over routine existence. Human fellowship in the effort to make life happier, freer.

20° AMERICAN INDIANS PERFORM A MAJESTIC RITUAL TO THE SUN
Man's instinctive or traditional call upon basic life-energies for sustainment. Sense of fitness in behavior. Worship.

LEO

21° INTOXICATED DOMESTIC BIRDS FLY AROUND IN DIZZY ATTEMPTS
Unsteady first realization of spiritual being. Forced inspiration which the ego cannot sustain. False self-intoxication.

22° A CARRIER-PIGEON ALIGHTS AT DAWN BEFORE HIS OWNERS
The return of the soul-energies to the central Self after a significant experience. Adventuring. Practical enlightenment.

23° THE BAREBACK RIDER IN A CIRCUS THRILLS EXCITED CROWDS
The supremacy given to the man who has mastered his senses and his emotions. Full utilization of inner powers. Audacity.

24° A YOGI, WITH TRANSCENDENT POWERS—YET UNTIDY, UNKEMPT
Spiritual emphasis at the expense of outer refinement. Interior focalization of energies. Self-abnegation. Character.

25° A MAN, ALONE, DARINGLY CROSSES THE DESERT ON CAMEL-BACK.
Superiority of knowledge and will over hostile nature. Mental self-control. Spiritual strength in facing past Karma.

26° AS LIGHT BREAKS THROUGH CLOUDS, A PERFECT RAINBOW FORMS
Promise of conscious immortality after the death of useless things. Spiritual linkage through emotional stress. Blessing.

27° IN THE EAST, LIGHT SLOWLY INCREASES, WIPING OUT THE STARS
Transforming power of creative impulses as they bring ideas to concrete manifestation. Stirring to opportunity. Soul-power.

28° MYRIADS OF BIRDS, PERCHED UPON A BIG TREE, CHIRP HAPPILY
Social nature of experience as man finds sustainment in a larger whole of being. Normal, collective self-expression.

29° MERMAID AWAITS PRINCE WHO WILL MAKE HER IMMORTAL
Pure longing for a new order of selfhood. Critical point in "emergent evolution." Perspective; or a sense of incompetence.

30° AN UNSEALED LETTER FULL OF VITAL AND CONFIDENTIAL NEWS
Basic faith in the goodness of all life. Unthinking trust in, or desire to see to the bottom of all things. Confidence.

1° IN A PORTRAIT THE BEST OF A MAN'S TRAITS ARE IDEALIZED
The shaping power of idea or ideal over outer form and behavior. Completeness of realization. Pure aggrandizement. Intent.

2° A LARGE WHITE CROSS STANDS ALONE ON TOP OF A HIGH HILL
Dominance of environment through individualistic self-realization. Eminence at the cost of struggle. Full self-assurance.

3° TWO ANGELS BRING PROTECTION TO FAMILY IN THE WILDERNESS
Divine guarantee to man of supply of all his needs. Divine help
when human efforts fail. Unconscious sense of strength.

4° NEGRO CHILD PLAYS WITH WHITE BOYS UNAWARE OF RACE LINE
Underlying fellowship of all life underneath social creeds. Stimulating sense of distinctness. Rising above contrasts.

5° IRISHMAN DREAMS OF "LITTLE PEOPLE" BENEATH A TREE
Constructive imagination as it reveals unconscious realms of
being. Creative fantasy. Contact with inner life-energies.

6° EXCITED CHILDREN RIDE ON A BLATANT, GAUDY MERRY-GO-ROUND
The culture of pleasure as a transmuting force. Unfearing plunge
into life. Endless and futile repetition of experience.

7° IN A PALATIAL HAREM BRIGHT-EYED WOMEN LAUGH HAPPILY
Early stage of development of individual soul, with full yet binding life-protection. Freedom from responsibility or restraint.

8° ARISTOCRATIC FIVE-YEAR-OLD GIRL TAKES FIRST DANCING LESSON
Early social conditioning of the superior elements of being. Proper
start in self-discipline. Conventional development.

9° A MODERN EXPRESSIONISTIC ARTIST PAINTS A STRANGE CANVAS
Original genius of every individual soul unconcerned with collective values. Absolute, tradition-less self-expression.

10° A MAN WITH TWO HEADS IS SEEN LOOKING OUT TO THE BEYOND
Consciousness functioning in inner and outer realms. Competence
in understanding. Over-sensitiveness to life-currents.

11° A TYPICAL BOY, YET MOULDED BY HIS MOTHER'S ASPIRATIONS
Efficacy of overtones in life; of ideals in giving reality or depth
to outer material things. Conformity to inner light.

12° A BRIDE, LAUGHING, SCOLDS THE GROOM WHO LIFTED HER VEIL
Disclosure of the hidden fruitions of nature to him who dares
and who loves. Full appreciation of life. Penetration.

13° A POWERFUL STATESMAN WINS TO HIS CAUSE A HYSTERICAL MOB
Power of personality as incarnation of subconscious race ideals.
Sublimation of motives. Transmutation of energies.

14° A SPLENDID FAMILY TREE ENGRAVED ON A SHEET OF PARCHMENT
Importance of ancestral background in all accomplishments.
Power to experience deeply. Cultural sensitiveness. Heritage.

15° OLD LACE HANDKERCHIEF; SOME RARE PERFUME; A MIRROR
Ultimate fineness of material values shading into the spiritual.
Schooled and aristocratic delicacy. Cultured restraint.

VIRGO   XII. THE SPAN OF EXPERIMENTATION

16° CHILDREN CROWD AROUND THE ORANG-OUTANG CAGE IN THE ZOO
The lesson which the very old can give to the very young in all
realms. Vicarious experience. Inertia of instincts. Poise.

17° A VOLCANIC ERUPTION RELEASES POWERFUL TELLURIC ENERGIES
Irresistible outbursting of pent-up impulses, creatively or regen-
eratively. Breaking up of "complexes." Will to wholeness.

18° TWO EXCITED YOUNG GIRLS EXPERIMENT WITH A OUIJA BOARD
Human desire for contact with the beyond. Inquiry. Restless
questioning of superficial facts of being. Immature curiosity.

19° A SWIMMING RACE NEARS COMPLETION BEFORE A LARGE CROWD
Social sustainment of individual accomplishment. Encouragement.
Competition as a means to create group-consciousness.

20° A GROUP OF SETTLERS START ON THEIR JOURNEY IN OLD CARS
Rising to achievement in spite of an inadequate equipment. Joying
in meeting life's challenges. Venturing with faith.

VIRGO

21° TWO TEAMS OF GIRLS ENGAGED IN A CONTEST OF BASKETBALL
Physical wholesomeness as prelude to inner integration. Self-evaluation, or refusal to face self. The rhythm of instincts.

22° A JEWEL-SET ROYAL COAT-OF-ARMS IS DISPLAYED IN A MUSEUM
Preservation of ancient race values for healthy veneration by youthful individuals. Certification of merit. Aristocracy.

23° A LION-TAMER RUSHES FEARLESSLY INTO THE CIRCUS ARENA
Readiness to face the aroused energies of one's nature and test one's moral strength. Faith in self. Valor and mastery.

24° A BOOK FOR CHILDREN PICTURES LITTLE MARY AND HER LAMB
Freshness of viewpoint un-inhibited by social intellectual pre-occupations. Vibrant simplicity. Spirit-born imagination.

25° A FLAG AT HALF-MAST IN FRONT OF LARGE PUBLIC BUILDING
The ability to carry a task through to consummate completion. Deference to past achievement. Cultivation of public spirit.

26° RAPT-EYED, A BOY SERVES IN A MASS READ BY AUTOMATONS
Ability to find inspiration in daily routine. Hope arising in the midst of all deadness of heart. Rejuvenation of spirit.

27° ELDERLY LADIES DRINKING AFTERNOON TEA IN A WEALTHY HOME
Preservation of social and cultural values. Inward, unobstrusive superiority, or else pure smugness. Prestige of position.

28° BALD-HEADED MAN DOMINATES GATHERING OF NATIONAL FIGURES
Driving power of real personality in moments of crisis. Capacity for hard work. Compelling manifestation of inner self.

29° ARCHAIC MS. DISCLOSES TO SCHOLAR THE OLD MYSTERIES
The understanding which is built on patient steady work and persisting aspiration. Fecundative power of ancient wisdom.

30° AN EMERGENCY CALL FREES HOUSEHOLDER FROM ROUTINE DUTY
Joy of enlisting in a task which broadens the life-horizon. Willing rising to the occasion, or escape from narrow destiny.

1°   PIERCED BY A DART OF LIGHT A BUTTERFLY IS "MADE PERFECT"
The symbolical death that is initiation into spiritual reality and
wisdom. Sudden awakening. Craving for inner light.

2°   A SYMPHONY IS PLAYED DRAMATIZING MAN'S HEROIC ASCENT
Inspiration through creative identification with the large sweep
of cycles. Spiritual expansion. Renewed encouragement.

3°   A NEW DAY DAWNS, REVEALING A WORLD UTTERLY TRANSFORMED
Transforming power of periods of silence and darkness, which
lead to stirring revelations. Real touch with cosmic process.

4°   PILGRIMS GATHER ROUND CAMP-FIRE, IN SILENT COMMUNION
Fellowship of higher ideals that sustains the individuals on their
arduous path to Reality. Mellow participation in life.

5°   INSPIRED DISCIPLES LISTEN TO THE WORDS OF THEIR TEACHER
Knowledge and experience put to the test. Greatness calling its
own to itself. Ordered seeking. Distrust of appearances.

6°   IN A TRANCE, A PILGRIM BEHOLDS HIS IDEALS MADE CONCRETE
Inevitable confrontation with the concrete results of one's ideals.
Lessons to be learned from it. Willingness of heart.

7°   WITCH FEEDS CHICKENS FRIGHTENED BY A HAWK SHE HAD TAMED
Control of natural forces by the higher intelligence. Taming the
strong, uplifting the weak. Transmutation through service.

8°   A FIREPLACE BLAZES MYSTERIOUSLY IN A DESERTED FARMHOUSE
Constant presence of unseen, sustaining agencies in every worth-
while activity. Great depth of initial effort. Providence.

9°   THREE "OLD MASTERS" HANG ALONE IN AN ART GALLERY
Efficient cohesion of the three "souls" of man; of mind, feeling
and instinct. Integrated wisdom. Sagacious behavior.

10°   A CANOE LEAVING NARROW RAPIDS REACHES CALM WATERS
The reward of all sincere and daring outreaching of self in life.
A sure Destiny. Reliance upon skill and circumstances.

LIBRA

11° KINDLY OLD PROFESSOR IS TEACHING A CLASS OF YOUNGSTERS
Cooperation of genuinely superior agencies with beings less evolved. Glad willingness to assist and protect. Kindliness.

12° MINERS ARE EMERGING FROM A DEEP WELL INTO THE SUNLIGHT
Depth of participation in the world's work. Whole-souled giving of self to service; or inability to bring self to effort.

13° CHILDREN ARE BLOWING SOAP-BUBBLES AT A YOUNGSTERS' PARTY
Healthy stimulation through play and joy of human intercourse. Creative fantasy; spinning of idle dreams. Relaxation.

14° RICH LAND-OWNER TAKES A SIESTA IN HIS TROPICAL GARDENS
Proper adjustment to the rhythm of nature. Faith in the ordered scheme of things; injudicious dependence upon others.

15° A STACK OF MACHINERY PARTS; ALL ARE NEW AND ALL CIRCULAR
Perfect and effortless participation in the universal order. Smooth approach to self-expression; inert self-satisfaction.

LIBRA   XIV. THE SPAN OF REVELATION

16° A HAPPY CREW IS RESTORING BEACH PIERS WRECKED BY STORMS
Constructive results of apparently destructive forces; stimulation to new accomplishment. Glad response to needed work.

17° RETIRED SEA-CAPTAIN IN UNIFORM WATCHES SHIPS SAIL AWAY
Vicarious or mellow participation in life. Transfer of activity from physical to mental; or self-involvement in the past.

18° TWO MEN PLACED UNDER ARREST ARE BEING BROUGHT TO COURT
Responsibility of individual to society in terms of normal behavior. Return to values. Obligation to face objective facts.

19° ROBBERS ARE HIDING, READY TO ATTACK HEAVILY ARMED CARAVAN
Protest against the perpetuation of unearned social privileges and wealth. Repudiation of bondage. Challenge to custom.

20° OLD RABBI SITS CONTENTEDLY IN ROOM CROWDED WITH BOOKS
Interest in permanent rather than transient values. Accumulation of ancient wisdom brought to use. Competent service.

21° HOT SUNDAY CROWDS DELIGHT IN THE COOL SEA BREEZE
Fundamental popularity of natural values. Communion in objects of real and universally recognized worth. Association.

22° CHILD LAUGHS AS BIRDS PERCH ON AN OLD FOUNTAIN, AND DRINK
Intuitive understanding of simple souls in spiritual matters. Youthful life-enjoyment. Fresh grasp of the soul's needs.

23° CHANTICLEER SALUTES THE RISING SUN WITH EXUBERANT TONES
Capacity for self-refreshment at the inner sources of ever-renewed life. Anticipation of opportunity. Security in Self.

24° A BUTTERFLY SPREADS ITS WINGS, SHOWING AN EXTRA LEFT ONE
Potentiality of new forms and opportunities in every life. Instinctive expansion of self; or submergence in the not-self.

25° FALLING GOLDEN LEAF TEACHES LIFE TO REBELLIOUS SCHOOLBOY
Discovery of deeper elements of wisdom after intellectual knowledge wearies. Growth through awareness of basic meanings.

26° AN EAGLE AND A WHITE DOVE CHANGE SWIFTLY INTO EACH OTHER
Necessary cooperation between mind, will, spirit—and heart, love. Power of psychological balance and compensation. Unity.

27° A SPOT OF LIGHT IN CLEAR SKIES, AN AEROPLANE SAILS CALMLY
Dwelling above the normal stress of existence. Superior mental vision. Calm objective observation; quiet inner strength.

28° A MAN IN DEEP GLOOM. UNNOTICED, ANGELS COME TO HIS HELP
Spiritual sustainment given to him who opens himself to his full destiny. Slow realization of betterment. Unsolicited help.

29° VAST MASSES OF MEN PUSH FORWARD REACHING FOR KNOWLEDGE
Intense desire to overcome the blind life of passion and to uplift others. Intellectual vision. Tense mental outreaching.

30° A PHRENOLOGIST DISCOVERS MOUNDS OF KNOWLEDGE ON A HEAD
Ability to read spiritual meanings in concrete objects. Objectivication of abstract truths. Cleverness in understanding.

1° SIGHT-SEERS IN A BUS STRAIN TO SEE CROWDS AND BUILDINGS
The perspective which leisure gives to everyday affairs. Appetite
for larger things. Seeing life as whole. Social Intercourse.

2° FROM A BROKEN BOTTLE TRACES OF PERFUME STILL EMANATE
The fine scent of deeds well done as it persists in the memory of
men. Stimulating recollection. Spiritual immortality.

3° HAPPY HOUSE-RAISING PARTY AMONG WESTERN PIONEERS
The constructive sharing of experience which builds social values.
Interchange of efforts. Necessity to learn cooperation.

4° YOUTH CARRIES A LIT CANDLE IN HIS FIRST CHURCH SERVICE
Beginning of spiritual participation in the world's work. Sustained
inspiration. Conscious linkage to inner realities.

5° A MASSIVE ROCKY SHORE UNCHANGED BY CENTURIES OF STORMS
Revelation of absolutely stable elements in all life. Strong confidence born of fundamental perception; or spiritual inertia.

6° CALIFORNIAN HILLS: THE "GOLD RUSH" SHATTERS THEIR PEACE
The passionate quest for universal values, destructive of cultural
ease of living. Leaping to opportunity. Avid seeking.

7° DIVERS OF THE DEEP SEA ARE BEING LOWERED INTO THE WATERS
Purposeful, daring plunge into life-mysteries. Fulfillment of individual selfhood through study of unconscious energies.

8° A HIGH MOUNTAIN LAKE IS BATHED IN THE FULL MOONLIGHT
Illumination of the soul by transcendent wisdom. Quiet touch
with cosmic strength; or wayward moody effort at greatness.

9° A DENTIST IS REPAIRING TEETH RUINED BY CIVILIZED HABITS
Mechanical inventiveness and control over nature needed to balance man's emphasis on mind and self. Applied creativity.

10° A FELLOWSHIP SUPPER REAWAKENS UNFORGETTABLE INNER TIES
Companionship rooted in past performance. Group-personality
emergence. Fraternity of ideals uplifting individual efforts.

11° A DROWNING MAN IS RESCUED, BROUGHT BACK TO THE CROWD
Outreaching warmth of human character. Saving power of social
restraint for too emotional souls. Humanitarian ideals.

12° HIGH OFFICIALS ARE GATHERED AT AN IMPORTANT EMBASSY BALL
Social recognition of accomplishment as the substance of a ritual
of human association. Certification of rank. Ambition.

13° IN AN IMPROVISED LABORATORY AN INVENTOR IS NEAR SUCCESS
Driving power toward achievement, as featured in all benefactors
of mankind. Self-sufficient activity. Clever outwitting.

14° WORKERS PUSH A TELEPHONE LINE ACROSS FORBIDDING RANGES
The will to association regardless of time and space. Linkage of
separate realms. Spiritual living "in spite of" nature.

15° LAUGHING CHILDREN PLAY UPON FIVE MOUNDS OF WHITE SAND
The world of the five senses as the playground of God and Soul.
Honesty in self-expression. Bondage to sense-patterns.

SCORPIO XVI. THE SPAN OF APPRECIATION

16° A GIRL WITH ARISTOCRATIC FEATURES SMILES ENTRANCINGLY
Fervent outreaching of self in moments of the purest beauty.
Leaping to meet the potentialities of life. Blossoming forth.

17° WOMAN, FECUNDATED BY HER SPIRIT, IS "GREAT WITH CHILD"
Fullness of self-reliance and individual destiny. Cooperation between spiritual and material agencies. Pure self-revelation.

18° A WINDING ROAD LEADS THROUGH GLORIOUS AUTUMNAL WOODS
The light which transfigures the soul after passions have faded
away. Revelation of inner wealth. Radiant consummation.

19° A WISE OLD PARROT REPEATS THE CONVERSATION HE OVERHEARD
Dependence upon inner or outer environment for the substance
of understanding. Transmission of knowledge. Channel-ship.

20° WOMAN FLINGS OPEN DARK CURTAINS CLOSING SACRED PATHWAY
Courage needed to enlarge sphere of being. Readiness to press
beyond self. The "woman" within, opening the gates to Spirit.

SCORPIO

21° SOLDIER READY TO FACE CHARGES OF DESERTION FOR LOVE'S SAKE
Conflict between old and new perspectives. A willingness to face chaos for the sake of a new order. Yielding to emotions.

22° HUNTERS SHOOTING WILD DUCKS WALK THROUGH A MARSH
Aggressive quest for outer or inner sustenance. Purposeful satiation of desire. Tragic incorporation of ideals. Exercise.

23° PLACID WHITE RABBIT METAMORPHOSES INTO A DANCING ELF
Revelation of unexpected vital urges latent in all beings. Great creative potentialities. Capacity for self-maintenance.

24° CROWDS, STIRRED BY A GREAT MESSAGE, RETURN HOME
The power in well-formulated ideas to become actual facts. Practical inspiration; or else inability to face a vital challenge.

25° THANKS TO A FINE X-RAY DIAGNOSIS, A MAN'S LIFE IS SAVED
Penetrating power of reality. Dependence of outer facts upon basic structures or causes. Sharp and applied discrimination.

26° SWIFTLY, INDIANS ERECT THEIR TEEPEES. CAMP IS BEING MADE
Ability to feel at home in any outer or inner environment. Efficient functioning. Retreating into the familiar and the known.

27° A MILITARY BAND, FLASHY AND NOISY, MARCHES ON POMPOUSLY
Desire to impress upon others the glory of one's social eminence. Materialization of normally subjective values. Show.

28° THE KING OF FAIRYLAND IS SOLEMNLY WELCOMED TO HIS REALM
Necessary respect for symbolic values holding vital forces integrated. Self-realization through devotion to the One.

29° PRINCESS PLEADS BEFORE INCA KING FOR HER CAPTURED SONS
The soul's mediation between spirit and matter. Sustaining power of instincts. Self-awakening to the need for action.

30° HALLOWE'EN GIVES SOCIAL RELEASE TO YOUTHFUL IMPISHNESS
Need for giving free rein to unsocial instincts within the pale of social traditions. Planned release of inner pressure.

SAGITTARIUS XVII. THE SPAN OF RECEPTIVENESS

1° RETIRED ARMY VETERANS GATHER TO REAWAKEN OLD MEMORIES
Cohesive power of social experience. Comradeship, born of collective achievements, which quickens the self. Fervent reunion.

2° WHITE-CAPPED WAVES DANCE RHYTHMICALLY UNDER THE WINDS
Glad response to a vital call to activity. Power to stir and to impress one's own rhythm upon materials. Proud adornment.

3° TWO SEDATE MEN, SMOKING PIPES IN COMFORT, PLAY CHESS
Re-creation of a world of manifestation through symbols and intelligence. Schooled confidence in the judgment of self.

4° WATCHED BY HAPPY PARENTS, A CHILD TAKES HIS FIRST STEPS
Life's kindliness in creating safe opportunities for growth. Full appreciation of opportunity. Crisis in self-development.

5° HIGH ON AN OLD TREE, A SOLITARY OWL IS GRAVELY PERCHED
Poised observation upon the drama of life. Mellow judgment. Ingrained confidence in the situation and worth of the self.

6° A CRICKET GAME IS BEING WATCHED BY A COLORFUL CROWD
Socialization of man's competitive impulses. Instinctive solidarity building race consciousness. Capitalizing on skill.

7° CUPID KNOCKS SMILINGLY AT THE DOOR OF THE HUMAN HEART
The happiness which awaits every man willing to accept its fulness. Rounding out of experience. The call to love's feast.

8° IN THE CAULDRON OF THE UNIVERSE THE METALS ARE FORMING
Irresistible determination to *be*. Infinite capacity for hard work. Crystallization of purpose and will out of experience.

9° A MOTHER IS LEADING HER CHILDREN UP A BROAD STAIRWAY
Conscious advance of selfhood from plane to plane. Real courage in all approach to life. Inner guidance in all growth.

10° A STAGE SYMBOLIZATION OF THE "GODDESS OF OPPORTUNITY"
Power of creative significance, as it transforms mere facts into universal symbols. Exteriorization of inner impulses.

11° AN EVER-BURNING LAMP THROWS LIGHT UPON AN ARCHAIC IDOL
Influence of social mass upon the individual. Power of "primordial images of Unconscious." Activity dominated by fate.

12° A FLAG BECOMES AN EAGLE; THE EAGLE A PROUD CHANTICLEER
Development of consciousness from abstract to concrete, from general to personal. Mounting mastery. Extreme good fortune.

13° A YOUNG WIDOW IS SURPRISED INTO A NEW BIRTH OF LOVE
The eternal call for fulfillment through love which overcomes personal sensitiveness and set patterns. Revision of attitude.

14° SPHINX AND PYRAMIDS STAND, REMAINS OF A GLORIOUS PAST .
Achievement based on past greatness. Power of the countless dead upon the living. Vast resources in selfhood. Antecedents.

15° GROUND-HOG, OUT OF ITS WINTER SLEEP, LOOKS FOR ITS SHADOW
Revelation of basic life-purposes and cycles through omens. Universal patterning of life-relationship. Keen divination.

SAGITTARIUS   XVIII. THE SPAN OF DETACHMENT

16° A CALM OCEAN; A MOTIONLESS SHIP; LAZILY SOARING SEAGULLS
The moments of pause which sustain and presage change. Alert readiness to act; or distress at not knowing what lies ahead.

17° PEOPLE GATHER BEFORE DAWN FOR AN OUTDOOR EASTER SERVICE
Spiritual living in conformity to natural law. Coming out of doubt and despair. Unwavering faith in a near higher power.

18° ON THE HOT BEACH CHILDREN PLAY, PROTECTED BY SUNBONNETS
The protective agency which safeguards the free behavior of individuals. Vivifying contact with collective life-energies.

19° PELICANS, DISTURBED BY MEN, MOVE TO PLACES UNKNOWN
Inward re-emphasis of foundations. Recuperation by retreating within. The introvert's escape. Moving about in reorientation.

20° MEN CUTTING THE ICE OF A FROZEN POND, FOR SUMMER USE
Depth of operation necessary to prepare for next phase of life. Sacrifice of present to future. Thoroughness of action.

SAGITTARIUS

21° CHILD AND DOG PLAY GRAVELY, WITH EYEGLASSES ON THEIR NOSES
Usefulness of make-believe. Rising to situations through the imagination. Assuming a part ahead of natural development.

22° THE SHOP CLOSED, CHINESE LAUNDRYMEN REVERT TO RACE TYPE
Retreat to the inner world of self after outer achievement. Safe return to ancestral patterns of behavior. Easy poise.

23° IN NEW YORK, ELLIS ISLAND WELCOMES THE IMMIGRANTS
New openings that come to all who are willing to risk self for the sake of greater selfhood. Reorientation. Presumption.

24° THE SYMBOLICAL "BLUE BIRD" ALIGHTS UPON A LITTLE COTTAGE
The blessings bestowed upon all those who are true to themselves. Unexpected assistance. Happiness. Sheer good fortune.

25° RICH LITTLE BOY RIDES UPON HIS BRIGHT-COLORED HORSE
Growth through vicarious, imaginative experiences, which life might deny us. Detachment from reality. Self-conservation.

26° FLAG-BEARER DISTINGUISHES HIMSELF IN HAND-TO-HAND BATTLE
Exaltation of physical valor as necessary support to lofty race ideals. Spectacular effort. Endowment beyond realization.

27° THE SCULPTOR'S VISION IS TAKING FORM UNDER HIS HANDS
Mastery of formative intelligence over substance. Sure characterization and understanding. Permanent self-expression.

28° ANCIENT BRIDGE WITNESSES TO THE SKILL OF FORGOTTEN MEN
Enduring elements in understanding as symbols of the community invisible of man, dead and living. Steady coordination.

29° PERSPIRING FAT BOY, EAGER TO REDUCE, IS MOWING A LAWN
Desire for fitness inherent in all living beings. Consciously built, thus dependable determination. Persistent endeavor.

30° THE POPE IS HOLDING AUDIENCE IN A HALL OF THE VATICAN
Wealth of spiritual resources which can be tapped for the glorification of every relationship. Concrete form of ideals.

CAPRICORN   XIX. THE SPAN OF ILLUSIVENESS

1° INDIAN CHIEF CLAIMS POWER FROM THE ASSEMBLED TRIBE
Mastery of a situation through purposeful planning and venturing. Bold rising to opportunity. Extreme of self-confidence.

2° ROSE-WINDOWS IN A GOTHIC CATHEDRAL; ONE, DAMAGED BY WAR
Underlying resistance to change in life foundations. Faithfulness to self. Testimony of beauty against brute force.

3° THE SOUL, AS A HOVERING SPIRIT EAGER TO GAIN EXPERIENCE
Inner and pure motivation. The power to remain superior to physical limitations; to demonstrate free will. Detachment.

4° MERRY-MAKERS EMBARK IN A BIG CANOE ON LANTERN-LIT LAKE
Externalization through individuals of the collective urges of the race. Foolish love for pleasure. Exploitation of self.

5° AN AMERICAN INDIAN CAMP: A FIERCE WAR DANCE BEGINS
Mobilization of latent energies for determined self-exertion. Obsession by elemental forces. Violent awakening to reality.

6° TEN LOGS LIE UNDER ARCHWAY LEADING TO DARKER WOODS
Illimitability of experience, as man moves from completion to ever greater fulfillment. Keenness in knowing. Thoroughness.

7° A HEAVILY VEILED HIEROPHANT LEADS A RITUAL OF POWER
Gathering together of the power of a group to one purpose and into an individual will. "Avatar"-ship. Responsibility.

8° IN A BIG LIVING ROOM FLOODED WITH SUNLIGHT CANARIES SING
The happiness that radiates from an integrated personality. Firm self-establishment in social comfort or respectability.

9° AN ANGEL CARRYING A HARP COMES THROUGH A HEAVENLY LANE
The basic harmony of fulfilled selfhood. Realizing harmony in everyday life through detached and lofty understanding.

10° ON A SAILBOAT THE SEAMEN ARE FEEDING A TAME ALBATROSS
Overcoming of instinctive fears through gentle persuasion. Kindly conquest. Culture of spiritual values. Harmlessness.

11° PHEASANTS DISPLAY THEIR BRILLIANT COLORS ON A VAST LAWN
Latent richness of natural resources brought out through selective processes. Capitalization upon opportunity. Luxury.

12° NATURAL WONDERS ARE DEPICTED IN A LECTURE ON SCIENCE
Piercing through appearances; disclosing the magic splendor of the core of things. A universal living touch. Keen vision.

13° BENEATH SNOW-CLAD PEAKS A FIRE-WORSHIPPER IS MEDITATING
Firm establishment upon immemorial principles. Consciousness of absolute unity. Depth of soul-penetration. Self-conquest.

14° IN DENSE JUNGLE, A PERFECTLY PRESERVED MAYAN BAS-RELIEF
Man's power to leave permanent records of his achievements. Personal immortality. Fecundation of future by past. Assurance.

15° IN A HOSPITAL, A CHILDREN'S WARD FILLED WITH PLAYTHINGS
The goodness of life in the tragic trials of first attempts at self-regeneration. Administered responsibility; or escape.

CAPRICORN   XX. THE SPAN OF DEPENDENCE

16° SCHOOL GROUNDS FILLED WITH YOUTHS IN GYMNASIUM SUITS
Normal dependence upon physical stimulation. Robust enthusiasm in approaching life's contests; or immature impulsiveness.

17° REPRESSED WOMAN FINDS A PSYCHOLOGICAL RELEASE IN NUDISM
Escape from bondage to social inihibitions. Readjustment of relation of spirit to body. Self-purification. Self-confrontation.

18° THE UNION JACK FLAG FLIES FROM A NEW BRITISH DESTROYER
Extreme of objectification of inner resources. Challenge to life. Splendid self-realization. Full awareness of competition.

19° FIVE-YEAR-OLD GIRL PROUDLY DOES HER MOTHER'S MARKETING
Capacity to take place ahead of normal standards. Increased self-confidence. Waiting for conditions to catch up with self.

20° THROUGH THE EMPTY CHURCH, THE CHOIR IS HEARD, REHEARSING
The unrealized fullness of life even in the emptiest hours. Preparation for activity. Ray of hope through all difficulty.

CAPRICORN

21° A RELAY RACE. EACH RUNNER SPRINGS EAGERLY INTO PLACE
Extreme of cooperation and give-and-take in life-relationships.
Full surrender of self to service. Planned group-behavior.

22° DEFEATED GENERAL YIELDS UP HIS SWORD WITH NOBLE DIGNITY
Apparent defeat that spells real spiritual victory. Bowing to custom. Conquest through conformity to established norm.

23° A SOLDIER RECEIVES DECOROUSLY TWO AWARDS FOR BRAVERY
Reward offered by society for the fulfilling of individual responsibility. Recognition of worth; unearned good fortune.

24° A WOMAN WALKING TO THE SURE HAVEN OF A CONVENT
Protective kindness of life to weary hearts. Quiet undercurrent of real existence. Compelled assistance. Timely rescue.

25° LITTLE BOYS FROLIC UPON SOFT RUGS IN AN ORIENTAL STORE
First realization of cultural values through sensuous enjoyment.
Refinement of sensations. Psychological enrichment.

26° RADIANT SPRITE DANCES UPON THE MIST OF A WATERFALL
Transcendence of spirit over body and environment. Lightness of understanding. Inexhaustible soul resources. Effervescence.

27° MEN CLIMB A SACRED PEAK: BELOW, THE WORLD—ABOVE, PEACE
Necessary linkage of above and below in the seeker's personal experience. Balanced dualism of subjective-objective life.

28° THE AVIARY OF A RURAL MANSION, FILLED WITH SINGING BIRDS
Enhancement of personality by familiarity with spiritual values.
Joying in the significance of things; or mental confusion.

29° A GYPSY READS FORTUNES IN THE TEA-CUPS OF SOCIETY LADIES
The quest for inner understanding through all life-conditioning.
First approach to reality. Desire to transcend routine.

30° THE DIRECTORS OF A LARGE FIRM MEET IN SECRET CONFERENCE
Activity of inner formative elements of real personality. Massing of soul-energies in an emergency. Spiritual leadership.

AQUARIUS   XXI. THE SPAN OF DEFENSIVENESS

1° OLD ADOBE MISSION NESTLES IN CALIFORNIA'S BROWN HILLS
Mastery of man over environment while becoming an integral part of it. Recognition of established values. Impressiveness.

2° UNEXPECTED THUNDERSTORM BRINGS RELIEF TO PARCHED FIELDS
Liberation from adverse conditions through violent spectacular developments. Galvanizing to action. Cosmic visitation.

3° A DESERTER SUDDENLY REALIZES THE FALLACY OF HIS CONDUCT
Ability to regrasp past experience and turn it to account. Sharp self-examination. Awakened new fearlessness. Decision.

4° A HINDU PUNDIT REVEALS HIMSELF SUDDENLY A GREAT HEALER
Supremacy of the unsuspected faculties hidden deep within. Conscious utilization of divine potency. Revelation of self.

5° A WORLD-LEADER IS SEEN GUIDED BY HIS ANCESTORS' SPIRITS
The rich ancestral heritage of every individual, which is the potent foundation of character. Direct, real inspiration.

6° IN AN ALLEGORICAL MYSTERY RITUAL A MAN OFFICIATES ALONE
Compelling urge in every soul to express the unknown and the more-than-physical. Sensitiveness to high purpose. Conflict.

7° OUT OF THE COSMIC EGG, LIFE IS BORN FRESH AND VIRGINAL
New actuation of effort by the power of unrealized purposes. Self-expression beyond all expectation. Spiritual protection.

8° WAX FIGURES DISPLAY BEAUTIFUL GOWNS IN STORE-WINDOWS
Need for public presentation of virtues and life standards. Exteriorization of value, that it may be shared with others.

9° IN MEDITATION, A FLAG IS SEEN, WHICH CHANGES INTO AN EAGLE
Process of spiritual realization as it progresses from outer to inner standards. Rebirth, or rebellion against drudgery.

10° UNSPOILED BY POPULARITY NOW WANING A MAN PLANS ANEW
Ability to rise above vicissitudes of passing fortune. Faithfulness to self. Dependence upon native endowment. Projection.

11° ARTIST, AWAY FROM THE WORLD, RECEIVES A NEW INSPIRATION
Creative power in man: its relationship to social behavior. Self-crystallization in a form of power; or else self-exploitation.

12° LIFE'S BROAD STAIRWAY: EACH LANDING, A NEW GRADE OF LIFE
Points of pause and transition, where the soul can evaluate its progress. Graded effort. Necessity for divorcing the past.

13° A BAROMETER HANGS UNDER THE PORCH OF A QUIET RURAL INN
Vantage point in consciousness whence life may be observed and measured in peace. Inner retreat of a soul seeking truth.

14° ON A STEEP CLIMB, A TUNNEL OFFERS SHORT-CUT TO A TRAIN
The way within to outer success. Sure relief to the toiler ready to face facts. Penetration and direct accomplishment.

15° TWO LOVE-BIRDS ON A FENCE SING OUT THEIR PURE HAPPINESS
Contagiousness of happiness in human associations. Revelation of constructive reality. Radiation of spontaneous faith.

AQUARIUS   XXII. THE SPAN OF PERSPECTIVE

16° BUSINESS MANAGER AT HIS DESK STUDIES A COMPLEX PROJECT
The central control of operations needed in all organized enterprise. The head-function. Surety in decision. Management.

17° WATCH DOG ON GUARD AS GOLD-MINER SLEEPS NEAR HIS STRIKE
Nascent protective faculties in all men as they adjust themselves to new conditions. Competent organization of affairs.

18° AT MASQUERADE, THE LAST MAN UNMASKS, URGED BY THE GIRLS
The introvert's desire to protect himself from social judgment. Clinging to self-valuation. Conservation of experience.

19° A FOREST FIRE SUBDUED, THE WEARY FIGHTERS FEEL JUBILANT
Exaggeration of life-problems, which reveals to man his real stature and which expands him. Impatient challenge. Ascendancy.

20° WHITE DOVE CIRCLES OVERHEAD; DESCENDS, BEARING A MESSAGE
The blessing of every effort by the "Holy Ghost" of revealed significance. Exaltation of all individual efforts. Celebrity.

AQUARIUS

21° A WOMAN IS DISAPPOINTED, AS A MAN LEAVES HER BOUDOIR
Capitalization upon misfortune by which spiritual justification is gained. Supremacy over experience. Inward retirement.

22° CHILDREN REVEL UPON A SOFT NEW CARPET IN THEIR NURSERY
Life's warmth and richness given to those who eagerly learn to live. Luxurious self-knowing, or self-appreciation. Comfort.

23° A BIG TRAINED BEAR PERFORMS, SITTING ON A HUGE CHAIR
Need to build an adequate concrete vehicle for cosmic power. Performance beyond native endowment. A striving for balance.

24° NOW FREED FROM PASSION, A MAN TEACHES DEEP WISDOM
Utilization of experience and passion by the intelligence that remains un-involved. Self-conquering. Genuine dispassion.

25° A BUTTERFLY EMERGES FROM ITS CHRYSALIS, RIGHT WING FIRST
Necessary advance of volition over reflex elements. Willing approach to problems of being. Fitting to alien ideas. Choice.

26° A GARAGE MAN IS SEEN READY TO TEST THE BATTERY OF A CAR
Capacity of self to take up and deliver spiritual power. Controlled release of power through the emotions. Measurement.

27° AMID RARE BOOKS, AN OLD POTTERY BOWL HOLDS FRESH VIOLETS
Reality of spiritual or esthetic values, linking generations of seekers for the highest. Addition or commitment to value.

28° HUGE PILE OF SAWED-UP WOOD INSURES HEAT FOR THE WINTER
Rich contribution of nature to all who work with foresight. Intelligent preparation. Calm yet potent faith in Providence.

29° METAMORPHOSIS COMPLETED, A BUTTERFLY SPREADS ITS WINGS
Immortality of the real self. Graduation into a new realm of being. Confident projection of self; lack of self-confidence.

30° MOON-LIT FIELDS, ONCE BABYLON, ARE BLOOMING WHITE
Soul-refreshing inner poetry of being. Spiritually nurtured sentiment which illumines the heart. Voices from the past.

PISCES   XXIII. THE SPAN OF INNOCENCE

1° LATE SATURDAY AFTERNOON: CROWDS FILL THE PUBLIC MARKETS
The social nature of human responsibilities. A last-moment, joyous rallying to a task. Seed synthesis at end of cycles.

2° SQUIRREL, SHOWING HUMAN ACUMEN, HIDES FROM HUNTER
Instinct of self-preservation as a basis for greater realization. Lifting of self to surer foundations. Transference.

3° A PETRIFIED FOREST: PERMANENT RECORD OF ANCIENT LIVES
Mastery of form over substance. Archetypal immortality. Conscious handling of existence. Participation in race impulses.

4° CARS CROWD A NARROW ISTHMUS BETWEEN TWO RESORTS
Linkage in activity of all community values. Free flow from ideas to consummation. Sense of significance in relationship.

5° A WARM-HEARTED CROWD GATHERS AT A CHURCH BAZAAR
Interchange of spirit and understanding on which groups are built. New self-development. Discouragement mastered. Commerce.

6° A PARADE OF WEST POINT CADETS IS HELD AS THE SUN SETS
Self-exaltation through consecration to the task of defending collective values. Self-testing. Perception of high goals.

7° FOG HIDES THE SHORE; BUT ON A CLEAR ROCK A CROSS RESTS
Concentration of values amidst the chaos of outer living. Clear light of high realization. Acceptance of life's limits.

8° GIRL-SCOUT, IN CAMP, BLOWS HER BUGLE TRIUMPHANTLY
Fullness of life as it manifests in service to the whole. Spiritual socialization. Call to participation in the race work.

9° THE RACE BEGINS: A JOCKEY SPURS HIS HORSE TO GREAT SPEED
The capacity of man to throw himself fully into any type of activity. Self-quickening. Premature expenditure of energy.

10° THE AVIATOR SAILS ACROSS THE SKY, MASTER OF HIGH REALMS
Transcendence of normal problems. Gaining of celestial responsibilities. Consummation of the highest ideals. Coronation.

11° SEEKERS FOR ILLUMINATION ARE GUIDED INTO THE SANCTUARY
Introduction of conscious mind to the intuitive soul-realms. Self-dedication. Self-awakening; or surrender to inner fears.

12° CANDIDATES ARE BEING EXAMINED BY THE LODGE OF INITIATES
Inner ordeal before every true seeker. The individual facing collective wisdom. Re-affirmation of purpose. God-revelation.

13° OLD WEAPONS IN A MUSEUM: IN A GLASS CASE, A SACRED SWORD
Courage and fearlessness needed in the quest for spirit and real understanding. Real faith in self; or emptiness of dread.

14° A YOUNG LADY, WRAPPED IN FURS, DISPLAYS SUPREME ELEGANCE
Necessary superficial advertisement of inner worth. Certification of true merit. Schooled esteem. Embarrassing wealth.

15° AN OFFICER IN UNKEMPT CAMPAIGN UNIFORM DRILLS HIS MEN
Subjection of outer appearances to real necessities. Potent compulsion of a great task to be performed. Opportunity seized.

PISCES   XXIV. THE SPAN OF PROTECTION

16° IN A QUIET MUSEUM, AN ART STUDENT DRINKS IN INSPIRATION
Subjective source of strength around all manifestation. Communion with accumulated race power. Deep, vibrant realization.

17° EASTER: RICH AND POOR ALIKE DISPLAY THE BEST THEY OWN
A symbol of "high moments" in life, when man challenges himself and renews his faith in circumstances. Self-improvement.

18° IN A HUGE TENT A FAMOUS REVIVALIST CONDUCTS HIS MEETING
Reinforcement of faith which can open up a new environment. A revision of ideas back to source. Critical survey of life.

19° MASTER AND PUPIL COMMUNE IN STRENGTH IN A LONG WALK
Body-strengthening function of the soul. Release from race karma. Transmutation of everyday facts into intelligence.

20° IN THE QUIET OF EVENING THE FARMER'S SUPPER AWAITS HIM
Encompassing richness of experience whenever a particular ordeal is over. Spiritual nourishment. Ingathering of forces.

PISCES

21° CHILD WATCHED BY CHINESE SERVANT CARESSES A WHITE LAMB
Eager probing of the soul into its many potentialities and higher reaches. Self-expansion: or refusal to grow in Spirit.

22° DOWN A SYMBOLIC MOUNTAIN OF INDUSTRY COMES A NEW MOSES
Man's success in meeting the challenge of a new order. Codification of new values. Holding oneself to highest standards.

23° A "MATERIALIZING MEDIUM" SUMMONS WEIRD GHOSTLY SHAPES
Display of powers which, though physical, transcend our normal awareness. Subjective mastery of, or passivity to life-forces.

24° IN A TINY LOST ISLAND MEN BUILD HAPPILY THEIR OWN WORLD
Adaptability and inherent creativeness of man. Extreme of surety in self-expression. Centralization of supernal forces.

25° AFTER DRASTIC REFORMS A PURIFIED CLERGY OFFICIATES ANEW
Ability periodically to cleanse from all selfish dross the channels for spiritual service. True vision. Soul-reformation.

26° TWO RAPT LOVERS AND A PHILOSOPHER WATCH THE NEW MOON
Polyphony of values as man lives at various levels of consciousness. Inner call to realization. Transmutation of meaning.

27° THE HARVEST MOON RISES IN TRANSLUCENT AUTUMNAL SKIES
The power of creative visualization by which great Dreamers transcend outer reality. Complete dominance of circumstances.

28° UNDER THE FULL MOON THE FIELDS SEEM STRANGELY ALIVE
Normally unnoticed powers released at the fruition of natural processes. Call of universal mind to the heart. Fullness.

29° SCIENTIST IS MAKING TESTS BY MEANS OF SPECTRUM-ANALYSIS
Capacity of mind to transfer its powers to machinery. Enlargement of perception. A closing-in of vision. Subtle analysis.

30° A SEER'S DREAM NOW LIVES: A FACE CARVED INTO HUGE ROCKS
Eventual concrete manifestation of all higher poetic images and enduring truths of the race. Sure culmination of effort.

XI. *Form and the Pattern of Planetary Aspects*

FORM is, generally speaking, the element of being which defines the particular out of the universal. Every particular manifestation of life has a form which essentially and spiritually characterizes it, giving it a determinable significance in terms of the manner in which it relates itself as a whole to universal life. Form is an abstraction. To speak of form as a tangible reality is to misuse the term and to confuse it with "body." One of the most unfortunate practices in modern Theosophy has been to use the term "form" where "body" was meant. The confusion is apparently rooted in an old distinction current in Hindu philosophy, but which is most likely due to a faulty translation of words; or perhaps even more to a misinterpretation or misunderstanding of the concept behind the words. Our Western mind is apt to materialize the metaphysical concepts of the East and by so doing to get involved in an approach to life which is not truly integrative.

Form is an abstraction. It signifies the essential patterning or relationship of parts within a whole by means of which this whole is defined as a particular entity. Form is a complex of relationships: a total formula of relationships of parts to parts and parts to whole. The individuality of this whole is thus totally defined and made significant by this form.

Body is unsubstantiated form and incorporated substance. Form, in itself, has no substantial implications, though it is originally and in terms of life-purpose determined by the *need* of the substantial elements which it correlates and in-

379

tegrates into a body. Body is an agglomeration of substantial elements (atoms, molecules, etc.) which is made relatively permanent and significant by the fact that it has form. Form is abstract. It is the blue-print of the skyscraper defining its structure generally and in all its details of functioning. The completed skyscraper is a body—substantial and tangible.

The form defines the significance and purpose of the body. One can conceive of a realm of pure form inoperative and unconnected with substance or materials: a realm of blue-prints and algebraical formulas. This, in a sense, is the world of archetypes or ideas—except that energy is always associated with what are called archetypes or ideas, whereas there is no energy *ordinarily* connected with the concepts of algebraical formulas or blue-prints. One might say that this is the difference between idea and concept: The idea is vital and charged with potential life-energy; the concept is purely intellectual. The distinction might be the same as that between algebra (a system of abstract symbolism which "works," i.e., which has been useful in interpreting data of experiences) and algorism (also a perfectly logical system of symbolism, but one which as yet has never been useful or applied).

In this sense—which is not universally accepted—an idea is a seed at the psycho-mental level. It is a seed, because it is both form and energy. The idea will eventually germinate and become a body: an individual organism or a social racial organism—a great human movement, an institution that is operative among men. On the other hand, the concept is a mere intellectual structure, form as yet un-charged with life energy. A concept becomes an idea when a being—human, super-human, or divine—identifies himself with the concept and pours energy into it.

Thus we have the basic trinity: energy, form, substance, synthetized by the fourth term: personality. Personality itself is, however, the ultimate manifestation of a more universal term: activity. When activity becomes truly *creative* in an individual sense, real personality is born. But we have previously used the term *personality* as meaning "a pattern of human behavior;" and so, inasmuch as we are considering primarily the psychological aspect of astrology, we can use the term personality as the fourth term, in which energy, form and substance are synthetized.

In the preceding chapters we have studied the four fundamental factors in astrology: the dial of houses, the signs of the zodiac, the planets and the degrees. We pointed out that the first two factors were generated by the two primary motions of the Earth, axial rotation and orbital revolution, and as such, corresponded respectively to the individual and the collective elements of being. The degree, being a synthesis of the two motions, was said to reveal the creative element, the element of significance. We furthermore referred to the planets (considered in their totality as the solar system viewed from the Earth) as indicators of personality.

These characterizations were made in relation to human psychology. But if we wish to broaden them so as to include every possible manifestation of life, we shall have to refer to the four terms above mentioned: energy, form, substance and activity. Using now these latter terms, we can re-define our fundamental astrological factors as follows:

The zodiac represents *substance*. It constitutes the substance of all life-manifestations on Earth, for it refers to the varying relationship of the Earth to the source and origin of all life. The signs of the zodiac symbolize the twelve basic types of life-substance, at every level of being. Substance stands for the collective. Every astrological factor is always referred to the zodiac, just as every individual manifestation of being is born out of, and is a particular combination of, collective materials.

The dial of houses stands thus for *form*, for that which essentially characterizes the "particular combination"—i.e., the individual. While the zodiac is a spatial and objective factor, the dial of houses refers inherently to time and subjective values, to the form of the individual selfhood, symbolized primarily by the "cross within the circle"—the familiar astrological wheel being a further differentiation, by trisection, of the basic *mandala* of the soul (Cf. "Astrology and Analytical Psychology," p. 122).

Form, however, may be considered either from the point of view of the individual selfhood or from that of the active and creative personality. That is to say, it can be represented astrologically by the relation of the Earth to the zodiacal space surrounding it—the Earth's magnetic field; or by the relation of the Earth to the totality of the solar system surrounding it. In other words, my particular orientation to life as an individual is a subjective factor. It is the way I realize, I feel, I sense, I think of myself. It is my point of view on life. It relates myself to life. The *form* of this relationship is given by the houses.

On the other hand, as a human personality involved in actions and reactions, living with other personalities in a vast world of human relationships, I also have a certain *rhythm of behavior*. This rhythm *is* my personality; and it may express exactly my individual point of view on life—or it may not. This, because it is an attempt at adjusting or balancing the individual and the collective factors in my life; thus, a sort of compromise—at best, the integration of opposite tendencies. Astrologically speaking, this complex rhythm of behavior is symbolized by the solar system as a whole, as seen from the Earth; which means *by the related positions of all planets* (including always Sun and Moon) *in my birth-chart*. This we called the "planetary pattern." It gives us a second type of form—form, not in relation to the individual *per se*, but with reference to personality, or to the term "activity."

Thus we have, let us say, subjective form—determined by the relationship between the chart's axes and the ecliptic; and objective form—determined by the relative positions of all the planets, and also by their positions relative to the chart's axes (horizon and meridian). We shall study briefly these two types of form; but there is one more point to dispose of. We have considered the elements of "substance," "form" and "activity." Nothing has as yet been said concerning "energy."

Energy is the factor of motion, implied in all the other factors discussed so far. Motion is the energizing principle in all living. It is at the core of zodiacal substance spread in collective space. It is the power of unfoldment at the center of all individual selfhood born out of the womb of time. It is the vital power in the maze of activities in and through which personality demonstrates itself. Moreover, significance is born out of a combination of motions. It is as the individual interprets the collective substance of all functions and all activities that significance arises. Significance is symbolized by the "degree" which is archetypally the amount of orbital space covered in a day by the Earth, the amount of universal substance (zodiac) assimilated by the individual in his basic cycle of awareness (cycle of the Earth's rotation—day).

Significance is ubiquitous, but only as a potentiality. Every astrological symbol is not only to be interpreted in terms of its position in one or another of the zodiacal signs, but it is located in (or on) a degree. It has, therefore, potentially at least, significance. But the realm of significance is not only "individual," it is "collective" as well. The number of degrees of the zodiac is a finite number. And this number characterizes the spiritual status of the planet as a whole. Significance is thus a planetary factor applicable to individuals. It is the gate through which the individual man enters the being, or be-ness, of the planetary Individual. Conversely, there is an action of the planetary Individual (call it Logos, or God) upon the individual man, as there is one upon collective mankind. The latter is revealed in what we called the "Great Polar Cycle"— ordinarily named the cycle of the precession of the equinoxes; the former might be found in a symbolization of the "degrees" of that cycle. What is meant by "degrees" in such a cycle might be suggested indirectly by the subsidiary motion of the poles (nutation) whose cycle equals the cycle of the Moon's nodes.

It might be added that the Moon, and those cycles of energy which we have considered as "higher Moons," represent a particular aspect of energy in terms of the "personality" factor. The Moon is the visible symbol of those energy-cycles because it is the Earth's satellite. Its revolution around the Earth represents Earth-centered actual motion. Its phases can be seen to affect the processes of life-growth. At higher levels the several "Moons" control the tides of psychic, mental and spiritual energy.

Subjective Form

What is considered under this heading is really the factor of the Earth's inclination upon the plane of its orbit, as it manifests in the birth-charts of individuals. Because of this inclination, a house contains, in most cases, either more or less than thirty degrees of zodiacal longitude. The crowding or spreading of zodiacal space within the fixed framework of the twelve houses creates a certain type of form. The same sign of the zodiac may appear on two successive cusps, or there may be "intercepted signs." This brings out important elements of significance, which cannot be easily understood, however, unless one gives more attention to the matter of cusps, a matter often misunderstood.

Referring to previous chapters, we need hardly emphasize the fact that the "dial of houses" is to be considered as the dial of a watch projecting in space a process that actually occurs in time. The circle of twelve houses charts on a flat sheet the rotation of the Earth around its axis, the successive changes of position of the horizon throughout the day. The two opposite cusps represent a position of the horizon every two hours as the Earth turns around the axis whose ends are the North and South Poles. In the birth-chart, the line formed by the cusps of the first and the seventh houses is actually the horizon at the time and place of the birth. The line formed by the cusps of the second and eighth houses gives the position of the horizon two hours later; the line formed by the cusps of the third and ninth houses, the position of the horizon four hours later, etc. Thus the contents of a house are the sum total of celestial phenomena reaching the horizon during a two-hour period; and each cusp should be considered as the Eastern horizon—the point of awareness of self—at different times and related to successive phases of individual selfhood and destiny.

Each cusp carries the basic significance of "Eastern horizon." It marks the beginning of a new period of awareness, and is a moment of primordial significance in relation to everything that will occur during the period it initiates. Each cusp is a moment of initiation, a birth-moment. What the self of the native, the "I am," becomes aware of during that moment determines the significance of the two-hour period which follows. He becomes aware of a certain section, or degree, of the zodiac—and the whole period (house) is characterized by, "ruled" by, that degree and sign of the zodiac—and, by implication, by the planet whose function correlates with the nature of the sign.

In other words, at each cusp the "I am" is born in one of its aspects. This cuspal moment is a seed-moment, a moment of transition from one stage of being to another. The twelve cusps represent twelve great *life-transitions*, and thus carry the meaning of those critical moments in life in which not only is there a slow passage from one phase to another, but when something occurs which is unique and which partakes of the meaning of "birth" or "seed."

Such "seed-moments" are creative utterances of the whole individual. They are acts of manifestation of the self: creative acts, moments of freedom. The individual is "free" only at his cusps. It is only during these moments of "life-transition" that man is not conditioned utterly by the consequences of past actions, by the effects of previous causes. It is only then that he can truly operate as an "individual;" for at any other time he is bound by the group or collectivity of which he has become a part. He is geared to his group, bound by the initiative he has taken during the cusp-moment and by the environment he has chosen—more or less deliberately—in which to work out this initiative. At the cusp, the individual is, as it were, "in neutral"—able to move into whatever gear or speed he chooses.

For instance, at the cusp of the seventh house the individual chooses, symbolically, his mate or partner. The cusp is the symbol of his initiative and of his creative freedom in this particular seventh-house phase of life-experience. Once he has chosen, he is no longer free; he has to work out the results of this initiative. The cusps of the eighth and of the ninth houses show the secondary moments of choice in relation to this matter of partnership. At the former, self-regeneration is possible within the sphere of human relationship; at the latter, self-expansion and broadening of life-perspective.

The concept of cusp must be extended in practice to that of "cuspal zone." In some lives, the speed of life-transitions is great and changes come suddenly; in others, the transition is very gradual. As a result, it is difficult to determine the exact dimensions of these cuspal zones. But in most cases they should not encompass more than three or four degrees. Planets located within these zones have a particularly creative significance. They emphasize the element of individual freedom, and characterize, according to their own nature, the nature and potentiality of the free operation of the "I am" in relation to the phase of selfhood represented by the house.

Planets located at the very beginning of a house are "rising," from the point of view of the cusp of this house, and represent *initiating impulses*. Planets located at the very end of a house represent *fulfilling qualities*, the gathering-in of the fruits of experience related to a particular phase of selfhood. If within the cuspal zone, these planets indicate that the self will manifest creatively and realize itself powerfully through either the initiating impulse or the fulfilling quality, as the case might be.

This being understood, we can solve the problem of "intercepted signs," that is, the case when a zodiacal sign does not appear on any cusp, but is sandwiched, as it were, inside a house. When a sign does not appear on a cusp, this shows that the individual self of the native does not operate creatively, or does not reach awareness through the life-quality symbolized by that sign. The native, as a spiritual being, does not exercise his freedom by means of the power of that sign; but he exercises it doubly, as it were, by means of the power of the sign which appears on two successive cusps. By "doubly," we mean in relation to two basic phases of his being and destiny.

In other words, great issues do not arise for him positively through the quality represented by the intercepted sign. If, for instance, Aries is intercepted in the tenth house, the impulsive, pioneering quality of Aries is not a life-issue in the native's life. He has no choice as to whether he uses it or not. He does not, as an individual self, express himself through it. What happens is that this Aries quality is, as it were, *taken for granted* in all tenth-house matters. It can be seen operating in the background of all the public and professional activities of the native—*subconsciously or instinctively*. This may mean that the Aries quality operates as a psychological "complex." It may have been inhibited; in this case, perhaps because of the father's social position. It may have become the substance of an "inferiority complex;" and this complex drives the native powerfully, *yet fatefully and perhaps tragically*, toward public achievements.

Thus the Aries quality dominates tenth-house matters; but

the domination may in some cases be an almost neurotic one. It is rooted in unconscious factors, factors over which the individual, as an individual, has very little control, and through which he neither gains real awareness nor expresses himself creatively. This may be because, in past lives (if such are believed in) the individual soul has gained from the quality of the intercepted sign all that could be gained—and in this case the quality is built in in the new personality as an unquestioned instinct. Or else it may be because the personality became formed under an external pressure which inhibited the conscious and harmonious (spiritual) development of the quality, and a "complex" developed.

The outer results will be quite different in each case; yet what can be ascertained astrologically is the fact that there is a certain fatefulness connected with the quality of the intercepted sign—something which is inherent or subconscious, which operates with inevitability, and over which the individual has practically no control. It will be insistent, if not pathological or tragic. It will always mean a sort of disequilibrium, psychologically. But this very disequilibrium may mean a concentration of forces which will drive the native to striking accomplishments. As C. G. Jung often points out, a "complex" is indeed not necessarily "bad." It is often the means whereby the individual rises above the average and the norm. It spurs him on to heights of individual accomplishment— provided a psychological adjustment is effected which is individually significant and steady.

If the quality of the intercepted sign has such a character of unconscious and fateful motivation, on the other hand, the quality of the sign spread over two successive cusps is shown to be one of decisive importance in the conscious and deliberate life of the native. Should, for instance, the sign Leo rule the second and the third houses, matters pertaining to both these houses will be solved by the individual by means of the Leo quality. In dealing with his ancestral possessions, as well as with his close environment, for instance, the native will express himself and find himself through forceful, emotional, self-projective assertion.

We shall study in a later chapter the matter of progressions; but we might say here that whenever the progressed Moon (or Sun) or the "point of Self" passes through an intercepted sign, the rhythm of life (external or internal, respectively) is usually accelerated. The individual faces issues that are deeply rooted in the past and which are compelling. On the other hand, when these moving indices of life-unfoldment pass through spread-out signs, the rhythm of life slows down or becomes freer from compulsion. The individual may seem to take a breathing spell and to go after one type of thing in a quieter and more deliberate way.

Such indications as are given by intercepted and spread-out signs have, of course, to be modified by other, and often more important, indications derived from planetary positions, aspects, etc. But by utilizing all the various elements connected with the cusps the intuitive astrologer may read the spiritual story of the individual in a way which probably cannot be duplicated. It is perhaps for this reason that the exact degree of cusps is so hard to determine! For the spiritual story of an individual's development should ever remain a deep mystery to the superficial investigator.

Objective Form

A. PLANETARY ASPECTS

The first condition to a successful grasp of the subject of "aspects" is a real understanding of sphere, circle and circumference.

It has been said that "all forms reach toward the condition of sphere"—that the circle is the perfect form. If, however, form means the defining of the particular out of the universal, then the sphere and circle (according as one chooses to consider three-dimensional or two-dimensional being) are not to be considered as "forms." They are instead the symbols of universal being. But as it would be a grievous mistake to think of universal being as "formless"—in spite of the fact that this is often done—we may extend the concept of form and say that the circle (or the sphere) is the "universal Form," the summation or culmination of the evolutionary series of particular and thus imperfect forms.

It is truly "universal," by etymological derivation, because every point thereof is "turning toward the one," toward the center. For the convenience of our analysis we may describe a circle as the total of an infinite number of infinitely close circumferences having a common center. Thus we are dealing essentially with circumference and center; and the circumference is a curve every point of which is equally distant from a common center. This symbolizes a state of being in which absolute universality of viewpoints is attained; in other words, the Universal Mind, the Perfect Personality, that men have called *God*. God is not formless, but He is the equilibratedness of all forms, the total harmony or integratedness of all viewpoints. A divine Person is a man who, although operating temporarily within a particular form, yet has so equilibrated his spiritual being that his "body of light" is a perfect sphere of being and understanding. He has reached—not beyond form, but beyond the disequilibrated state that a particular form implies—the condition of "universal Form." In Gnostic philosophy, such a one is called Eon or Sphere. In a sense, of course, he is not only a "one." He is an absolutely centered, integrated, unanimous Host.

But everyone of us is a host of lives. It is so in a psychological sense, and the psychological Great Work is that of harmonizing and integrating the "soul-forces." It is so also in an even deeper sense, for our physical body is a host of "lives" —and in the perfected man (the man of the "third birth") the individual draws to himself, as to a center, this host and makes of it, as it were, the substance of this "body of light"—the perfect and radiant Sphere of spirit-substance.

If we now proceed from the universal to the particular, we shall see that birth as a particular personality means establishing linear or angular disequilibrium within the circle or sphere. A particular being is one in whom some elements (or viewpoints) are emphasized, others subdued. He is no longer a "perfectly rounded" individual, but an angular being, with points of stress and concentration of energy, and zones of relative emptiness.

This particularizing of the universal (which means birth) can be symbolized accurately by inscribing a polygon within the circle. There is an infinity of polygons which can be inscribed within a circle, some regular (with sides of equal length), all others irregular. Regular polygons are geometrical figures such as the equilateral triangle, the square, the pentagon, the hexagon, the heptagon, etc.—having respectively 3, 4, 5, 6, 7, etc., sides. If lines are drawn from the center of the circle to the points of the figures, angles are formed at the center. The triangle produces three angles of 120-degrees each; the square, four 90-degree angles; the pentagon, five 72-degree angles; the hexagon, six 60-degree angles, etc.

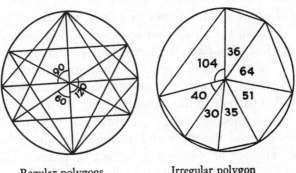

Regular polygons   Irregular polygon

If, on the other hand, we consider an irregular polygon, such as the one in the adjacent illustration, we find it composed of a number of unequal sides subtending unequal arcs which represent unequal angles.

If one should mark on a circumference the twelve signs of the zodiac, considered archetypally as equal segments of the circular magnetic field surrounding the Earth, and further divide each sign so as to mark the degrees on the circumference; if, moreover, one connected by lines each one of these 360 degree-marks—one would then have a regular polygon with 360 sides. This, symbolically, would represent the perfect form of a being still identified with an Earth-body. He would be a particular being—but one in which every "life-quality" possible on our planet would be equally represented.

The "God" of our planet (what the Theosophist calls the "planetary Logos") would have to be conceived, however, not as such a complete polygon, but as the circumference (or circle) itself, considered as a complete series of arcs, each having a universal significance. This would symbolize the universal quality of His total being. From this standpoint, we can see that the symbols of the degrees of the zodiac are attempts at bridging this gap between the very small side of a 360-side regular polygon and the arc (segment of the circumference) which this line subtends. If we consider such a relation between line and curve at the horizon, we have an interesting symbol. For we get the figure of a bow, the line of horizon being the arrow shot by an invisible archer. As the line of horizon is a line of self-awareness and intuition, we have a graphic illustration of the eternal effort of man, the archer, shooting at Space—the Universal. His bow is the symbol itself, the taut string of which is the concrete image presented in the symbol, and the curved wood the inner and universal significance of the symbol. The act of shooting is the act of piercing through appearances and reaching the Universal Self, which here becomes *space*, the circle whose center is everywhere and whose circumference is nowhere. This symbol is an ancient one, often found in Hindu philosophy, and embodied also in the symbolism of the zodiacal sign Sagittarius.

In an ordinary birth-chart, if one links by lines the points determined on the ecliptic by the position of the planets, one obtains an irregular polygon with ten sides. This polygon is the "objective form" symbolically characterizing the native's personality—as we use this term. By drawing the radii linking the points of the polygon to the center, the angles are made apparent which separate each planet from the others.* Such a polygon is what we have already called the "planetary pattern." The task of the astrologer is to analyze it and to extract its life-significance.

Theoretically speaking, of course every angular value has its particular significance, just as every degree of the zodiac has its particular significance. As the nature of the relationship between two planets is, in this phase of astrological analysis, characterized by the angle separating the zodiacal positions (longitudes) of the two planets, it is evident that an angular distance of 92 degrees is as significant in itself as one of 90 degrees.

However, just as we divide the Earth's orbit (or magnetic field) into only twelve regions which we call "zodiacal signs," likewise, and for equally valid philosophical reasons, we use only, or mostly, for the purpose of form-analysis, the first

---

* One might ask what a polygon which could not be inscribed in a circle would signify as a particular form. It would be a form which is not "organic;" that is, in which the principle of wholeness (circularness) could not operate and integrate the separate parts. This occurs symbolically in cases of schizophrenia, of multiple personalities, of insanity—and of suicide. The hand of the man who shoots himself is guided by one of the soul-energies which, because of internal disharmony or external compulsion, has bulged, as it were, outside of the circle of wholeness of the psyche. In this sense, every suicide is partially insane. "He" does not kill himself; but one of his "soul-forces" that has burst outside of the sacred circle of the self pulls the trigger. Another word describing the process is, of course, "obsession."

twelve regular polygons and the angles they generate. That is to say, we assume that there are twelve (or even six) basic types of *form-relationship* between life-activities symbolized by the planets; and we symbolize these types by the angles produced by dividing the 360 degrees of the total circumference into three, four, five, six—up to twelve parts. Two planets "aspect each other" when they are separated by an angle measuring to such a value: for instance 120°, 90°, 60°, etc. The list, names and characteristics of these aspects will presently follow.

It is, however, necessary to add at once that with regard to "aspects" we face a situation not unlike that which we found while discussing "cusps." In other words, we must extend the concept of "aspect" so as to make it signify not only an exact angular value (90°) but an "*angular zone*" (such as from 85° to 95°). The exact square-aspect measures to an angular distance of 90°. But two planets are also said to form a square when their angular distance measures to any value between, say, 85° and 95°. This is true of any aspect, especially of the most significant ones.

Yet, for the purpose of a deeper understanding of the factor of planetary relationship or "personality-form," it is obviously necessary to consider not only "angular zones" but each angular value. This, very much for the same reason for which the *substance* of being is not sufficiently analyzed by the twelve-fold differentiation of the zodiac into signs, but often requires further differentiation.

In his course entitled *Pythagorean Astrology*, Marc Edmund Jones approached this problem of how to analyze all possible values of angular relationship between planets in a strikingly original and convincing manner. After studying the basic astrological aspects, he went on to analyze the significance of the degree of exactness (or degree of separation) of aspects. If the angular distance between two planets is 85° or 95°, these two planets form a "square;" but the square is not exact. It is a square *minus* or *plus* five degrees. If the distance between the planets had been 88° or 93°, the aspect would be a square *minus* two or *plus* three degrees.

If, therefore, one should allow for consideration an "angular zone" of, let us say, seven degrees on both sides of exactness of aspect, one would get aspects with a *coefficient of inexactness* varying from o to 7. The value of this coefficient is, according to Marc Jones, most significant, and characterizes the manner in which the aspect itself operates. The matter is too complex to be discussed here; but it was mentioned to show how every angular value can be made significant.

The table of aspects which follows will make the matter clear; for we shall see for instance that a "sextile" represents an angular value of 60°, the "semi-square" of 45°. If one allows a 7-degree zone on each side of the exact values, one will have in fact covered every angular value. For 53° is a sextile "coefficient 7;" and 52° is a semi-square also "coefficient 7." By this method every angular value in whole degrees is given an individual significance.*

NAMES OF ASPECTS	ANGULAR VALUES	CHARACTERISTIC MEANING
Conjunction	0°	**Activity**
Opposition	180°	Awareness
Trine	120°	Creation
Square	90°	Construction
Quintile	72°	Artistry
Sextile	60°	Production
Septile	51° 26′	Fatality

* The reader may notice that the first aspect after the conjunction, considering angular distance, is the semi-sextile–or 30°. Even if we allow ten or more degrees "orb" for a conjunction, there are still several angular values unaccounted for. In subtle analysis the half of semi-quintile (18°), and even semi-sextile (15°), can be taken into consideration. But the main idea is that no aspect of *practical* significance occurs until two planets are separated by a whole zodiacal sign (30°). Actually, if the planets are located in two different signs, there may be "aspects" of less than thirty degrees. But they are ordinarily unnoticed.

Semi-square	45°	Awareness
(and Sesquiquadrate)	(and 135°)	
Nonagen	40°	Creation
Semi-quintile	36°	Union
(and Bi-quintile)	(and 144°)	
One-eleventh	32° 43′	Awareness
Semi-sextile	30°	Creation
(and Quincunx)	(and 150°)	

(Adapted from Marc Jones' *Pythagorean Astrology*)

Of these aspects the most commonly used are: conjunction, opposition, trine, square, sextile. The semi-sextile is usually considered as a sub-division of the sextile; the semi-square, a sub-division of the square. The quintile is—unfortunately— little used, and septile, nonagen and one-eleventh are practically never found in modern astrological text-books.

All these aspects are generated by the inscription within a circle of regular polygons—save the conjunction and opposition, which require some special attention. The conjunction is, essentially, the prototype of all particular manifestation, because it stresses the element of activity in a particular or personal way. We might say that the very fact that a planet is located in a degree means that a conjunction is established between the planet and that degree. The degree, of itself, is one among 360 harmonized and integrated phases of universal being. But when a planet comes to that degree in the chart of a particular man, the degree's quality suddenly becomes vivi- fied, energized, emphasized. The harmonious sequence of the 360 degrees becomes therefore disturbed. One of the degrees acquires an *accent*. Particularity of being is the result of a *pattern of accents*; whereas in universal being there are no permanent accents, no structure-making points of emphasis. It is this fact which has been miscontrued as meaning "form- lessness."

In any chart, planets are points of emphasis, accents, re- leases of energy, sources of activity. The significant quality of the energy released is determined by the symbol of the degree; the type of activity, by the planet. It is this element of activity which becomes the raw material of personality. Activity means stress, tension, disequilibrium. Therefore every planet represents a state of disequilibrium of zodiacal wholeness; just as, to use Goethe's phrase, "colors are the sufferings and joys of the light." The zodiac is the equilibrated cycle of wholeness. Planets introduce disequilibrium, differentiation, sufferings and joys—which mean accents up or accents down.

One planet located within the span of one degree creates an accent. Two planets in this same location may either stress further the accent or blur the directness of the release of energy implied by accentuation. Everything depends: 1) upon the nature of the planets in conjunction; 2) upon the "coefficient of inexactness" of the conjunction. For instance, if two planets of opposite polarities, like Mars and Venus, are conjunct in exactly the same degree, a sort of psychological short-circuit is indicated. A curious kind of self-centeredness and emotional inertia is shown—which can produce an accentuated type of narcissism. But if these two planets are several degrees apart, then, while there is a peculiar sense of self-reliance and often a sort of psychological "hermaphroditism," this contributes to emotional self-control of the type which is found, for instance, in occultists. There is, however, always the suspicion of a "complex" lurking back of every such conjunction of masculine-feminine planets; it lies, in fact, *back of every conjunction*, especially multiple conjunctions, or "stellium." But it is often through "complexes" of some sort that strong releases of psychic energy are induced; perhaps always so.

A conjunction is a symbol of particular stress which releases activity—at times explosively, as in the case of conjunctions of Mars and Saturn, Uranus and Saturn, etc. It stresses the uniqueness of the particular being, or of the particular activity

397

implied. It does not make for spiritual equilibrium; but it generates momentum of one sort or another. It is a concentrated massing of energy. Whether that energy will be released constructively or destructively, whether even it will be released at all, depends on the nature of the planets, and on the actual distance between the planets said to be "in conjunction."

The aspect of opposition is the opposite of, and the antidote to, the conjunction. Two planets in opposition are located, in terms of zodiacal longitude, exactly in opposite directions from the point of view of the Earth-observer. The latter is therefore, as it were, subjected to two contrary pulls. He may be actually "pulled apart" by the opposition. But also, if the two opposed planets are considered as two poles of a battery, he may be *illumined* by the spark flowing from pole to pole. This is especially so where the two planets are basically of opposite polarities.

In order to understand oppositions, one has to grasp fully the meaning of polarity. The Ascendant and Descendant, the Zenith and Nadir, in every chart, are points in zodiacal opposition. Consciousness, which is integrated awareness, is the result of such basic oppositions. Again, all depends on whether or not the individual has the power to "reconcile the opposites;" whether he will pull together or be pulled apart. If the former, then his consciousness will expand and objectify itself; if the latter, he will experience psychological confusion and will not be able to know which way to go. And so he will sit and suffer, torn by doubt.

In the opposition, we witness the more or less simultaneous operation of accent and counter-accent. If the aspect is not exact, a quick rhythm is established which can lead to intense objectivity of consciousness, almost absolute awareness. But if the aspect is exact, or if the native has a very slow "speed of reaction," the counter-accent neutralizes the accent. It may mean *nirvana*—the absorbtion of the particular in the universal—and the Buddha is said to have reached *nirvana* at the full moon of May (Sun-Moon opposition). But it may mean also disintegration, schizophrenia and the like, thus the often nefarious meaning of a lunar eclipse.

Conjunction and opposition can hardly be said to create form; rather, as we have seen, they produce accentuation and counter-accentuation, which are the basic phenomena of the life of the personality. The other aspects will, as it were, *distribute* the idea of accent or emphasis; and will thus convey the idea of purpose. There will be accentuation or counter-accentuation, *tending toward this or that purpose*. The purpose itself will be fulfilled if the aspects involve the completion of the polygonal form which is the foundation of the aspect; that is to say, if configurations named "Grand trine" and "Great Cross"—or the very rare "Great quintile" and "Grand sextile"—are formed, as we shall see later on.

What is meant will be easily grasped if we realize that the polygonal forms with which we ordinarily deal in astrology are based either on the triangle or on the square. Trine, sextile, semi-sextile (and quincunx) are essentially triangular; square and semi-square (and sesquiquadrate) are quadrangular. The first series is usually considered "fortunate;" the second "unfortunate." But such an ethical valuation, which finds its full meaning in "horary astrology," is almost out of place in the type of astrology which we are more particularly studying. In its stead we shall use another classification of meanings, and say that the triangular series deals with the various stages of *creative ideation* (in-"formation"), while the quadrangular series deals with the *insubstantiation of forms*.

These terms may sound formidable, but they are simple enough. The trine is an aspect of "vision" and "perspective." It refers to the birth of ideas or viewpoints, to the initial phase of a new plan and a new purpose. The conjunction is emphasis. As this emphasis begins to operate it takes form as an idea, a project, a new interest for the personality to flow into creatively. At a further stage, the sextile brings forth the

399

project or idea to a point where it is seen actually at work within the warp and woof of personality. Still further, the semi-sextile shows the idea decomposed into its polar elements and correlated with the routine of everyday activity.

If we now consider the quadrangular series, we see in the square the power that forces the abstract idea to become a concrete body. It is the power of incarnation, of birthing. It is indeed crucifixion, from the spirit's viewpoint. From the point of view of substance, it means getting the stones out of the quarry and building them into the perpendicular walls of the future building. The general keynote is mobilization. The semi-square symbolizes the first realization of the self after its being encased in substance. It can be a very depressing realization; but it can also be the first realization of power, for power necessitates some kind of insubstantiation. The semi-square is thus an aspect of power for the soul who understands the laws of life and of power. But it is an aspect of despair and great loneliness for the soul which regrets its spiritual "freedom." If the square signifies "mobilization," the semi-square has the meaning of "action" in the military sense of this term. The individual is in the service of collective purposes.

There is, however, another series which is also important: the series of quintile, semi-quintile and semi-semi-quintile (18 degrees). This series deals with the operation of the individual factor *per se*; and as such is very little understood. It is based on a five-fold differentiation, and integrates, as it were, the two preceding series. When two planets are in quintile aspect, the relation between these two planets is seen to release a particular value of individual significance. From quintiles the *genius* of an individual can be to some extent determined. In between the square (90°) and the sextile (60°), the quintile (72°) shows the creative freedom of the individual in molding materials into forms that are true to the idea they are meant to express. There is found the "individual touch" of the genius which transforms a routine action into an inspiring, significance-releasing performance. The semi-quintile refers more particularly to the *technique* of the performance. Its half (18°) suggests the point where mere accentuation (conjunction) orients itself toward significant performance: the imponderable factors of talent.

The septile is significant only in a planetary sense. It is, we may remember, the division of the "Great Polar Cycle." Through the septile we may see, in rare instances, an overshadowing of planetary purpose—truly, as Marc Jones says, fatality at work. As for the nonagen, its importance may be revealed in an age in which the number 9 is coming to increased significance—as evidenced by the fact that it is the sacred number of Bahaism, and the number on which Bahai temples are to be founded. We spoke before of the meaning of the number 40. The relationship between two planets forty degrees apart *may* indicate spiritual birth or initiation in the realm to which the planets refer. It signifies "birth out of captivity."

All these aspects have been taken, as it were, from the point of conjunction. But some of them can be taken also from the opposition. That is to say, a sesquiquadrate aspect (135°) is an opposition (180°) less a semi-square (45°). A quincunx (150°) is an opposition less a semi-sextile (30°), etc. In those secondary aspects we see the operation of "counter-accent." They indicate, in subtle analysis, the reaction to personal activity: the residua of activity. They may also refer to the "turning back" of activity upon its source: inner sublimation, spiritual transmutation. The so-called bi-quintile (144°) can also be considered as an opposition less a semi-quintile (36°). Here may be seen at work the technique of creative introversion. But, negatively speaking, this may also suggest certain types of obsessions, a "complex" creating its hallucinations.

Again let us repeat that no aspect is fortunate or unfortunate. Each may be seen as a positive or a negative phase of the personality.* What is more important still, no single aspect is of any real significance unless it be seen as an integral part of the total planetary pattern. We have to analyze, first, each aspect separately, in order to get our basic elements for synthetic realization. But this is merely the preliminary phase of the acquisition of a technique of interpretation. The true interpreter reads the planetary pattern as a reader reads a word or a sentence. Only the beginner keeps spelling the letters one by one.

B. THE PLANETARY PATTERN AS A WHOLE

Here we deal not only with the elementary relationship between two planets but with relationships that involve the whole personality, that *focus the meaning of the whole personality*. When a person is met for the first time, the intuitive individual gets at once a general, synthetic "feeling" from such a meeting. The wholeness of him reacts to the wholeness of the other person. This is what we previously called "holistic perception." If such a perception is very keen, it will often single out one or two basic characteristics which, as it were, focalize the "feeling" aroused by the person. Some of the features of this person's total personality will stand out as *centers of significance*. Significance will organize itself around these centers. Through the latter the person will be classified into one of a few general types, and such a classification will center and clarify the general "feeling."

The determination of centers of significance, of what Marc Jones calls "focal determinators," is the first and most impor-

---

* In horary astrology, or in the matter of casting charts from lunations, ingresses, etc., for general prognostications, "personality" becomes "the particular situation and problem considered." These, not being actual organisms, do not react to or compensate for special stresses or accents. In such cases, the quadrangular series of aspects means a breaking down of factors, while the triangular series is an integrating of values. Thus one is considered good, the other evil. But where there is true organic being, these ethical terms become subservient to the purposes of the whole organism.

tant factor in the interpretation of a birth-chart, if such an interpretation is to reveal truly the wholeness, the *livingness*, of the personality—and not be merely pieced-together fragmentary information about the behavior of the person. It is not only the most important but the most difficult factor. Each individual interpreter must more or less develop his own technique of "focal determination"—according to the genius which his own chart may reveal. Besides, only he who is (relatively) whole can have correct holistic perceptions; and in order to determine centers of significance one must needs be also a center of significance.

There are, however, a few general principles of "focal determination" which can be stated, for they are after all only extensions of well-known astrological factors upon which the very symbolism of zodiac, houses and aspects is founded. To understand these is to understand "form," or "*Gestalt*"—in terms of modern psychology; it is to grasp the genius of "groupings" and of "patterns of behavior." Just as, according to new methods of learning how to read, the child is no longer taught to spell letter after letter, but instead to recognize at once groups of letters and word-formations, so also the astrologer who seeks to learn how to fathom the livingness of the personality which the chart symbolizes should train himself in the instantaneous recognition of basic planetary and zodiacal formations. Tabulation of factors is helpful in checking results and getting to a finer degree of analysis. But holistic perception draws the whole and its parts to a center of significance and of livingness. It reveals the "soul" of the situation, the power that animates the whole—the wholeness of the whole, the spirit-energy within the form.

The first and simplest determination of the total meaning of the planetary pattern is made when the planets are distributed in specific ways through the four quarters of the chart; that is, in relation to the "axes of selfhood"—horizon and meridian. For the sake of simplicity and brevity, we shall enunciate, one after the other, the general (very general!) meaning to be attributed to the basic configurations which one may encounter.

All planets above the horizon: "The native necessarily lives out in life" or "finds the focus of his own inner consciousness wholly in external events." (Marc Jones.) A tendency to extraversion and to adopt an objective—often materialistic—viewpoint. (Cf. Queen Victoria's and Mussolini's charts.)

All planets below the horizon: "The native lives within himself or in more subjective realms" or "finds the focus of his own inner consciousness within internal reactions." (Marc Jones.) A tendency to introversion. An intuitive type.

All planets East or West of the meridian: "The zenith meridian divides the universe (all experience) into realms of rising things (East) and setting things (West). . . . If all planets are East the native is called upon to make his own choice in every issue, and to create the issue at will; whereas if West he must accept the choices and issues of life as these are placed before him." (Marc Jones.) This is a division of "outer volition." Usually an exclusively Eastern preponderance indicates an accent on thinking—for thought is the element of (relative) free-will; while an exclusively Western preponderance indicates a feeling-emphasis, for feelings are almost purely determined by the external conditioning of the relation between subject and subject, or between subject and object.

Moreover, all planets may be found in one of the four quarters. This is rare, but produces a still more absolute emphasis on one of the four functions of individual selfhood: intuition (North-east quarter), feeling (North-west quarter), sensation or relationship (South-west quarter), thinking (South-east quarter).

In considering such matters two important ideas must be held in mind. The first one is that no definite conclusions can be drawn from the fact that no planets are found in a house. The absence of accentuation does not mean a negative emphasis. Wholeness is always to be understood as the basis of

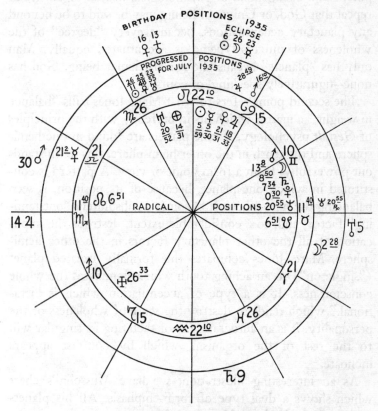

BENITO MUSSOLINI
Born at Doria (Prov. of Forli), Italy, July 29, 1883, 1.19 P.M.

any organic being; therefore it is always implied in the absence of any particular emphasis. This absence of emphasis may mean the previous fulfillment of the quality represented by the non-emphasized house or sign; or it may mean a virgin state of non-differentiation. It always refers to an unconscious state, rather than to a conscious one. But health is unconscious, until it is experienced by the sick person as the absence of illness. Likewise unconsciousness may be most potent as a background of psychological health. Again let us repeat that God, or Universal Being, may be said to be beyond any planetary accentuations, because every "degree" of the wholeness of universal being is accentuated equally. Man only has "planets" because he is a particular being. God has none—figuratively speaking, of course.

The second point refers to what Marc Jones calls "balance in weight," a matter which fits in perfectly with the principles of *Gestalt* psychology. If nine planets are found in one hemisphere and the tenth in the other hemisphere, this tenth stands out powerfully, from a form point of view. A pattern is constituted in which one planet, because of its position, is seen balancing the nine others. It becomes an absolutely "outstanding" factor; and, to a considerable extent, destroys the implication of all the other planetary factors in the other hemisphere. Marc Jones compares this formally isolated planet ("singleton") to an aching tooth which dominates the whole consciousness. It is a type of accentuation which is "irrational," which tends to destroy the sense of wholeness of the personality. It is an autocratic factor dictating its singular will to the rest of the organism, which by contrast appears inchoate.

As an interesting illustration, we have Mussolini's chart which shows a dual type of form-emphasis. All his planets are above the horizon. Moreover, Uranus stands alone in the eastern hemisphere—more precisely, in the South-east quarter. The mass-emphasis is in the section of the chart which deals with human relationship and denotes self-realization through human contacts and objective being. He is seen to accept the choices and issues of life as these are placed before him: a man ruled by his objective destiny. But, while this is true in a fundamental sense, Uranus, accentuated as a "singleton by house position," indicates that there is a powerful and insistent release of unconscious factors operating as subjective volition (Eastern hemisphere), and moreover, that the operation is through a mechanism of sudden thinking (South-east quarter). The latter fact is corroborated by: 1) a planetary concentration in zodiacal signs of concrete thinking (Gemini and Virgo) or of vivid image-making power (Venus-Jupiter conjunction in Cancer, in the house of "vision"); 2) the fact that the Moon's North Node is in the twelfth house, implying power released through meditation or subjective introspection.

This last fact, and the power of unconscious racial factors in Mussolini's life, are further emphasized by the massing of all the planets inside of an exact trine of Neptune and Uranus (planets of the unconscious). The total configuration is balanced, as it were, each side of the Jupiter-Venus conjunction which is sextile to both Uranus and Neptune. This, however, belongs to another type of emphasis to which we shall come presently. At present, we have yet to stress the point of the placing of all the planets in the southern hemisphere. This is a basic accentuation of collective or objective factors— so that however much Uranus might suggest the operation of an interior self-conditioned will or power, yet this will is seen operating solely in terms of collective factors. Even while his "part of imaging" (his release of genius) is located below the horizon, yet it is in the second house referring to racial inheritance and atavistic possessions—a collective factor, though within the individual realm.

Another type of emphasis is produced by the placing of all planets in the four basic divisions of the zodiac.

All planets between Aries and Libra (in the order of the signs): This indicates that the "principal responsibility of the life is spiritual" (Marc Jones)—or, we would rather say, it refers to the projection of ideas and archetypes into objective manifestation. Mussolini is an amazingly strong example of this type of emphasis—whether one likes, or does not, the type of ideas which he projects.

All planets between Libra and Aries: This indicates that "the principal responsibility of the life is material" (Marc Jones)—or rather, it refers to the development of faculties which are the outcome of previous spiritual activity and the matrix of future manifestations.

All planets in signs of long ascension (from Cancer up to Capricorn): "The inner life is lived to make itself manifest to the outer life." (Marc Jones.) This is the period when the Sun moves southward. What has been gained during the other half of the year is brought out into objectivity. The soul comes into manifestation.

All planets in signs of short ascension (from Capricorn up to Cancer): "The inner life is lived to make outer life manifest to itself." (Marc Jones.) This is the period when the Sun moves northward: traditionally, a period of spiritual growth and inner realizations. The fruits of objective experience are garnered and there is an inward maturing process, the growth of significance.

Here also one could apply the principle of singleton emphasis, a planet in one section of the zodiac balancing all others in the opposite section. We should add, moreover, that by changing the words "all planets" into "most planets" one could still get at a less strong, yet noticeable, preponderance of values.

Whether the circle of houses or that of zodiacal signs is considered, what is done actually is a quartering of the whole cycle by establishing two axes at right angles to each other. Such an operation is related to the determination of square aspects. It deals with the establishment of a structure of manifestation, the prototype of which is, of course, the "four seasons of the year." One could attempt the same thing with any one of the axes provided by astrological symbolism—

especially with the *nodal axes* of the planets. We saw previously that the Moon's nodal axis could be considered as establishing a "line of Destiny" between the past and the future (the *karma* and *dharma*) of an individual. Thus the hemisphere counted from the North Node (counter-clockwise) refers to the power of developing new spiritual faculties, whereas the hemisphere counted from the South Node refers to the working out of past tendencies.

In Mussolini's chart, all planets are in the hemisphere counted from the South Node, which gives a striking testimony—which might astonish many. The Italian dictator is shown as doing in this life what he presumably had done in several preceding lives—or, to state it differently, as being the last of a long ancestral line of similar figures. In this sense, he may be said to be a replica of the Caesar-image: a restatement of an old racial formula, which thus adds nothing spiritually new, but is a culmination of racial karma—of individual karma also, according to the theory of reincarnation.

This same procedure could be followed by considering the nodal axes of the planets; but the results require too subtle an interpretation to be of practical importance. Mussolini's chart again offers interesting possibilities of interpretation along the line of planetary nodes' analysis, as at least five of his planets are situated on the North Nodes of other planets. This would tend to show that his personality is a pattern drawn according to an inner super-personal plan. We might call him a "racial avatar," with tremendous psychic race-forces back of him. This is suggested by the symbol of the Sun-degree.

Another type of zodiacal emphasis is provided by the unequal distribution of planets: 1) in fire, air, water, earth signs; 2) in cardinal, fixed or mutable signs. This is a type of emphasis very often found in modern astrological practice. It seems to have little significance, however, unless the inequality of distribution is very great. A most definite preponderance of planets in one type of zodiacal signs is needed, if significant conclusions are to be arrived at. We must refer to our analysis of the meaning of zodiacal categories. A planetary emphasis in any category will bring out the meaning and power of that category in the life of the native.

So far we have studied planetary formations which were determined by reference: 1) to the circle of houses; 2) to the circle of zodiacal signs. The first refers basically to the individual's character and destiny; the second, to the collective factors of his being. By considering the "patterns of aspects" made by the planets, we have another type of form-determination which refers mostly to the personality itself. What we are dealing with now is an extension of the principle of "aspect." The following are aspects involving several planets; in other words, planetary groupings. Their names and a brief description follows:

Stellium. This is a multiple conjunction; a complex accentuation which involves more than two planets located in a small area. There is a stellium by house, when a mass of planets (at least four or five) are found inside of one house; a stellium by sign, when the same number are located in one sign, or in half of a sign. Here, as in the simple conjunction, much depends on what the planets are, and how distant they are from each other. The result is often confusion and personal involvement in the qualities represented by house or sign. The planetary accents blur each other. What stands out is the quality represented by house or sign, rather than the activity symbolized by the several planets.

Fan-handle. This magnified type of opposition occurs when a singleton opposes a stellium; that is, when one planet, alone in a hemisphere, opposes all other planets in the opposite hemisphere. According to Marc Jones, "the singleton contributes to the stellium and throws the emphasis back into the hemisphere containing the other planets. The stellium emphasis becomes a psychological or inner burden of manifes-

tation. It indicates a soul with a more-than-physical problem." The meaning of the emphasized sign (rather than
house) becomes the outstanding factor. The twentieth century opened with a most characteristic stellium, opposing
Neptune to all other (then known) planets. To add to the
meaning of this configuration, it was balanced exactly on the
Moon's nodes axis. Placing Pluto on the map detracts from
the *one-pointedness* of the configuration, as this planet was
close to Neptune. Yet, as Neptune and Pluto both refer to
universalistic factors, and as the configuration is so striking,
it can still profitably be considered as a fan—with a forked
handle!

Grand Trine. In this and the following multiple aspects
we are confronted with the perfect manifestation of single
aspects. We saw that a trine was produced by inscribing an
equilateral triangle in the circumference; a square, by inscribing a square, etc. We are now considering configurations
in which a planet (or several planets) are found located at
each of the angles of the inscribed polygon.

A Grand Trine is thus a figure in which three planets are
mutually related by 120° angles. Some astrologers have considered such a configuration very favorable, others unfavorable. That it should be deemed unfavorable when the trine is
always taken as the most harmonious aspect does not seem
very logical. Yet there is some truth in the assertion, when
we are confronted with an *exact* triangular formation; for
when some of the most important activities of the personality are symbolically so related, they are so well equilibrated
or "formed" that there is very little incentive for outward
manifestation and creation. The Grand Trine is thus, especially when a very exact formation, a symbol of, at least
relative spiritual inertia. If, however, one of the planets (or
groups of planets) entering into this configuration forms a
square aspect to another planet, then this square acts as a

"channel of release" for the energies locked in the Grand Trine.

Usually the Grand Trine produces an emphasis on one of the four zodiacal qualities (fire, air, water, earth) as it links normally the three signs referring to the same quality. Yet this need not be so, if the planets are located near the cusps. Therefore the Grand Trine cannot be said to have any particular significance because of that. If it *does* link, let us say, three fire signs, then the implication is that the "fire" quality ("motion toward objective manifestation" or "emanation") is thoroughly *formed* within the native's being.

Great (or Cosmic) Cross. This configuration is established by four planets (or groups of planets) in mutual 90° relationship. It is to be considered as establishing the "perfect cube," or "perfect stone" of Masonic lore. It symbolizes the total em-bodiment of the idea, or purpose, or self, in other words, fulfillment in objective and concrete existence. In a negative sense, what is meant is crystallization and spiritual bondage in matter.

The most usual way in which a multiple square is found is, however, as a T configuration. The square figure is not complete. Instead of the four-armed cross, we have an Egyptian *Tau*, or by implication, an ansated cross—which, of course, is the hieroglyph of a man with arms horizontally stretched out. In a birth-chart with such a configuration there is an empty house (or sign) where the man's head would be. What is indicated is the utmost release of spirit or purpose toward material existence. This is a highly dynamic configuration. The three arms of the cross throw a dynamic emphasis into the empty house, which often is, as it were, occupied by a whirlpool. In the phase of individual selfhood and destiny represented by the empty house the native finds himself usually helpless, torn by raging conflicts. Only the very strong and conscious ego is able to master such a *dissonant* release of power. If he does, then an amazing amount of creative energy is his.

The perfection of more complex polygonal formations, like the quintile and the sextile, is a rare phenomenon. But sometimes three planets are in mutual quintile aspect—or rather three of them constitute two quintiles, and the outer two are related by tri-quintile aspect (216°)—a very creative linkage between the three types of activities symbolized by the planets, with the suggestion that what is being created is a spiritual faculty, which very likely may not be evident in the outer life.

A complete hexagonal formation (Grand Sextile) is even rarer; but often three planets are in correlated sextile—the outermost constituting a trine equally divided by the middle one. This is what is seen so strikingly in Mussolini's chart, with the added emphasis due to the fact that all planets are located within the trine of Uranus and Neptune (bisected by the conjunction Venus-Jupiter). This particular configuration tends to show that the entire personality is a "formation of the race's unconscious," governed by the conscious. The Jupiter-Venus conjunction at the center of the configuration indicates the point of emergence of the formative power of the collective unconscious in terms of consciousness. Being in the ninth house, this power is not only formative but expansive. The conjunction Jupiter-Venus shows it to be of an idealistic order. Being in Cancer, the ideal will project itself with clearly imaged outlines. Jupiter is situated in a degree (Cancer 19°) which symbolizes "the inner adjustment of values by the unconscious processes of nature, taking the best of the old for the inspiration of the new." (Marc Jones)

A complete hexagonal configuration occurred on July 15, 1935, with Uranus in Taurus; Mercury, Sun and Pluto in Cancer; Venus and Neptune in Virgo; Jupiter in Scorpio; Moon in Capricorn; and Saturn in Pisces—linking all "feminine" signs of the zodiac. This was a configuration highly productive for work and especially for *detailed planning* in terms of practical sustained activity. Children born at such a time should prove to be skillful organizers—especially as the square of Sun and Mars was at the same time releasing the power which otherwise might have remained in a static condition of self-enjoyment and esthetical self-indulgence.

A configuration of the same type is that in which four planets constitute alternately sextiles and trines. A rectangle is formed whose geometrical proportions suggest a mystical significance. In the chart of the wife of one of the greatest living painters Uranus in Virgo 8°, Moon in Scorpio 6°, Jupiter in Pisces 4°, Neptune in Taurus 12° constitute such a configuration. Uranus is sextile to the Moon and trine Neptune, which is sextile to Jupiter in trine to the Moon. This is an interesting combination of trines, sextiles—and of course, two oppositions. A good symbol of "practical mysticism." This person has been a remarkable force of sustainment to her husband, in inner as well as in outer ways, combining spiritual awareness, outer productivity and purposeful planning.

In all such definite planetary patterning we may always suspect equally definite problems in the sphere of personality. Either these problems are the manifestation of psychological complexes which tend to make the personality "different" and often socially unadapted, or else the personality carries a burden of super-personal (planetary) responsibility demanding a strict focalization and particularization of viewpoint. Mussolini's chart is the most typical of the latter case which has come to our attention. It is an over-focalized chart. The man is alive solely to serve a racial purpose and will die in that purpose.

On the other hand, a chart without any outstanding focalization may mean either a scattered personality or a being whose destiny it is to link, to harmonize, and to be a symbol of wholeness of being. This of course is the mark of a true individual—one approximating the likeness of the perfect Individual that is God, the equally all-accentuated Being. A Mussolini is not an individual, but is a racial purpose made personality. He is a most particularized or specialized being: the man of a collective work. This is made clear by every possible factor in his chart, even to the position of the South Node (karma point) in the sixth house (of service, work and discipleship to ideal or personality) and on a degree "of real capitalization upon tradition and established value." *(The woman of Samaria comes to draw from Jacob's well.)*

Selfhood and Destiny

IT IS said that on the portal of the temple of Delphi in
ancient Greece one could see inscribed these words:
KNOW THYSELF. These words were truly indeed the
keynote of an age and a civilization which, for the first time
in human history, sought to raise the focus of man's consciousness to the intellectual level. The great life-problem for
Greek civilization—and for most of the European culture
which unfolded from the seed sowed by the Greeks—was
the *problem of knowledge*: the nature, limitations and extension of knowledge. This led to a study of the process of
development of the conscious and rational sphere of the ego;
then, by complementary reaction, with Christianity, to the
development of a system of devotional ethics—which in turn
modified itself into a system of rational ethics.

We claim that a new basic life-problem is confronting the
"New World" of the West—by which we mean, not only
the races living on the American continent, but all men who
are willing to emerge from the typical patterns of classical
Europeanism and into a new realm of being. We believe that
the American continent is the symbol of this new realm of
being, but not the exclusive habitat of men that are born
therein. The new life-problem for such men—individually—
and for the American continent—in a planetary sense—is the
problem of fulfillment. And thus we present the future builders of the temple of American "mysteries" with a key-utter-
ance, not new in itself, of course, but new as a focal point
for the collective consciousness: FULFILL THYSELF.

The Birth-Chart and the Progressions

Knowledge and *Fulfillment*: two words of tremendous importance when used as focal terms for whole civilizations! In a sense, at least, they can be seen to correspond respectively to two other mighty words: Space and Time. Knowledge is spatial in its essence because it is derived from the establishment of relationships of extension and contrast. Intellectual knowledge is based on analysis and objectivity, on the isolation of factors and elements studied apart from the whole to which they belonged, and from which they had been removed for analytical, experimental or even esthetical purposes.

On the other hand, fulfillment is durational and cyclic—holistic—in its essence. It is a *process* which unfolds at the very core of duration, and is conditioned by the general laws of cyclic becoming. It is not analytical or ethical; not even rational or predominantly conscious. It cannot be charted by *exact* formula. It cannot be defined accurately so as to fit all particular or individual cases, even though it follows a well-definable rhythm with computable climaxes and critical phases. Moreover, this process of fulfillment does not deal with the parts of an organism or with the elements of a situation, as detachable factors. It must always be referred to wholes. The fulfillment of parts is bound to the fulfillment of the whole of which they are parts. There can be no isolated fulfillment of a part. It can be only a relative or illusory consummation.

Yet as each part is a whole, just as each whole can be considered a part of some vaster whole, there are relative moments of fulfillment: "life-transitions" during which wholeness operates within any fulfilled whole. After this occurs, this whole realizes itself as part of a greater whole—and duration and its cycles of fulfillment go on, ever and ever more. But every fulfillment, though we may analyze it spatially and intellectually as purely relative—in terms of some greater whole—is, after all, an absolute. It is absolute inasmuch as wholeness is operating absolutely through every fulfilled whole, small or large. In fact, smallness or greatness are spatial, "knowledge" valuations. In terms of fulfillment, every fulfilled whole is actually and absolutely God. This is the realization often symbolized by the term "eternal now." We may call it a "mystical" realization. What it is called matters little. Experienced fulfillment has no need of intellectual definition. It is a subjective totalistic experience; and this experience is "one-with" the moment *within which* it occurs. Such a moment is what we previously called a "seed-moment"—what the modern Theosophist expresses (and materializes) in a planetary sense as a "Seed-Manu."

We have already stated such ideas in the chapters: "Astrology Faces Modern Thought" and "Individual, Collective, Creative," etc. But it was necessary to re-formulate them in a somewhat altered fashion, for this fundamental dualism of knowledge and fulfillment, space and time, is the key to the most important distinction which we encounter as we come to consider the practical applicability and utility of astrology. On one hand, we have what is called the *radical birth-chart* which gives us the symbolical pattern, or hieroglyph, of the individual being—a spatial figure. On the other hand, we have what are called *progressions* or *directions*, which aim at determining the unfoldment of the individual being throughout the span of his Earthly life—a time element.

The confused state in which astrological theory, as well as practice, is found today is due largely to the common lack of understanding of the relationship existing between these two realms of astrological determination: spatial and durational. Moreover, system after system of progressions or directions are propounded—each apparently most satisfactory in many cases, most unsatisfactory in just as many others. Hardly ever is an attempt made to give a philosophical, coherent interpretation of what "progressions" really mean and of why they operate at all—when they do. This and the next chapter will be devoted to the suggestion of such an interpretation, in the hope, at least, of elucidating several basic points and of offering solutions for confusing problems.

The birth-chart of an individual, indicating the pattern made by celestial bodies surrounding the Earth, in reference to horizon and meridian and in terms of zodiacal longitudes, is called also the *radical* chart, being considered as the root-factor in all astrological interpretation. The term "root" is somewhat inaccurate, and "seed" would be a much better word; for it is in the seed and not in the root that the "archetypal form" of the plant-to-be is focused. But the distinction is a purely philosophical one, with no practical bearing on the matters which we are now considering.

A birth-chart is the symbolical macrocosmic representation of the potential fullness of the perfected microcosm. It is the "blue-print" of the complete man. It is therefore *nothing but* a set of potentialities; and it defines by implication *everything that could possibly be found* in the perfected man. Because it refers only to potentialities, it is entirely abstract. Because it is a representation formed by macrocosmic factors (planets, horizon, etc.), it is purely symbolical. It indicates nothing factual; nothing concrete; nothing precisely "fated." It outlines what would be if the personality matured into the full likeness of the archetype, if actuality accurately matched potentiality. There is not one single precise event of a man's life to be found as such in his birth-chart. What can be traced are more or less definite types of potential eventualities, with varying degrees of "actualizability" at certain more or less accurately determinable times of his life.

In other words, the birth-chart is a set of spatial factors which determine the archetypal structure, or form, of the whole man—if he ever becomes whole. Nothing can indicate *absolutely* whether the man *will* become whole, or remain—like most people—a vague sketch, with ill-defined outlines largely absorbed by the collective racial background. However, from the whole chart there arises often an imponderable significance which gives to the astrologer with developed holistic perception (or with inherited "psychic" gifts) a clue as to the ultimate status of the native at the end of his life; in other words, how much of his life will be a success, how much a failure. But failure and success mean only this: Whether or not the actual life-performance has been true to the "score" of the individual selfhood and destiny; whether or not, speaking in terms of Hindu philosophy, the man has fulfilled his *dharma*.

Selfhood and *Destiny*. These two terms can be referred respectively to the radical chart, and to the progressions derived therefrom; also to space and time, knowledge and fulfillment. The self is to be known: Destiny is to be fulfilled. Both are abstractly identical in form. Yet the life of a man may be a mere caricature of his Destiny, or a mere sketch with blurred outlines. Destiny, as we understand the term, carries no meaning of absolute and factual determinism. It is a schedule of unfoldment for the purpose of manifesting concretely the blue-print which selfhood represents. We have already emphasized this point, but it needs repeated emphasis. Selfhood is a set of potentialities; at the most, a small architect's model of the finished building. But while the architect draws the blue-print and sets the schedule of operation and of delivery of building materials, he cannot tell whether an earthquake, a strike, a war or any such *collective factor*, transcending both architect and plans, will disturb the schedule. Yet if the building is completed, it will have to be an actual embodiment of the plans—unless a spiritual tragedy occurs, such as the death of the architect.

Selfhood is a space-factor. *Abstractly*, this refers to the interior space of pure being, a factor of pure relationship containing as many "dimensions of space" as there are related elements. *Concretely*, this refers to the outer structure of the body—that is to say, essentially, to the skeleton (the Saturn factor) and to the individual appearance, the Ascendant.

The Birth-Chart and the Progressions

Being a space-factor, selfhood is susceptible of being *known*, through form-analysis and significance-releasing synthesis. It is the seed-factor of manifested being. The monad—the unit of energy, or life—is the root-power. Destiny is the schedule of growth of the plant. It is the process whereby selfhood is made manifest. It is therefore conditioned *primarily* by the form of the self (seed-form: viz., the birth-chart); but also *secondarily* by the nature of the social and cosmic environment in the midst of which growth takes place.

In other words, while Destiny is essentially the individual schedule of growth, it is also subject to modifications which are not determined by the individual (his form or his past), but which are the results of the Destiny of the greater whole (race, planet, cosmos) of which the individual is a part. The *basic* internal relationship of this greater whole to the individual is indicated by various factors in the individual's birth-chart; but the *transitory* external pressure of the collectivity upon the individual is another factor belonging to the becoming (not to the being) of the greater whole. This is seen in what astrology calls "transits."

Destiny is selfhood in the becoming. Fulfillment is knowledge demonstrated and made operative through the whole of the knower's physiological and psychological organism. Thus fulfillment is dependent upon knowledge. The completeness of fulfillment is a function of the depth and extension of knowledge. Thus knowledge symbolically represents the East, fulfillment, the West. All knowledge comes from the East, but fulfillment occurs in the West. This is so, not only symbolically and astrologically speaking, but concretely as well. In every unit of civilization knowledge arises in the East, fulfillment is reached in the West. India was the source of the knowledge that was fulfilled in the East-Mediterranean world. Greek knowledge in turn was fulfilled in French integration. European knowledge is being fulfilled in America. Atlantic knowledge reaches Pacific fulfillment. All that is needed to complete the picture is to add that spiritual and regenerative power comes from the North and takes form as religion in the South, as is shown in the fact that all effete civilizations so far have been overcome and regenerated by the invasions of "barbarians" (regenerative men who are pure power without formed consciousness) from the North—in India, in Europe, in Mexico. Moreover, most established religions find their permanent center in the South and propagate northward: witness Buddhism spreading from India to China and Japan; Catholicism established in Rome; Islam moving from Arabia to Persia, Northern India and Spain, etc.

The foregoing may thus explain the reason why we consider the birth-chart as the symbol of the knowledge and power (selfhood) of the individual, while progressions refer to the fulfillment, the re-ligion (etymologically, that which "binds back") of his life. To interpret the birth-chart is relatively (most relatively!) simple because we are there dealing with a *self-contained structure*. Certain factors in the chart truly refer to the outside world and the collective inheritance and environment; but the reference is always to be considered in terms of the individual person. What is shown is not the state of the collective environment (as in transits and birthday charts) pressing upon the individual person, but the knowledge and power of adaptation of this individual to the collective within his total being.

In other words, everything found in the natal or radical chart refers to the native's total being; that is, to the sum total of potentialities this being contains. And we may here add that these potentialities, while they are *definite as to their structure*, are practically *infinite as to the depth of their connections*. That is to say, the *form* of my being—my individual selfhood—is basic; and change or development here means only an increasingly closer approximation of the outer "body" (or bodies) to the archetypal seed-form, which is changeless throughout an entire planetary cycle. But the *contents* of my being—the sum of the connections I have established with the universe, the total of my assimilations—are relatively unlimited. The limits are drawn only by the fact that the human person, being a part of the greater whole that we called the "planetary Individual," is conditioned by the harmonious development of this "planetary Individual." This refers to what the occultist calls the "Ring-Pass-Not."

Scientifically speaking, we would say that, the number of brain and nerve-cells not being infinite, the sum total of their possible connections and correlations is therefore not infinite. But the ordinary man of today operates relatively so few of these possible connections that the possibilities of expansion of the contents of his being are practically unlimited—even though the form of his individual selfhood remains a constant factor. Likewise, the skeleton is an almost constant factor in the human race, approximating ever more closely by very slow and cyclic progress (which includes regressive periods) what we would call the Archetypal Form of Man. Yet man may change the contents of his body by eating one kind of food or another (within the limits of what the Earth produces), by overeating or by starving himself, etc.

On the other hand, in "progressions" we are dealing with a very complex proposition, because we are dealing with the process of life itself. And this means perpetual change and thus, theoretically at least, *imprevisibility*. The process of life is the constant flux of the birth, fulfillment and breaking away of relationship. And it can never be absolutely and accurately charted. It contains necessarily, unavoidably, a *coefficient of indeterminacy*, which in numerical symbolism is the fractional value by which π (3.14159...) is greater than 3, and in astrological Earth-symbolism the value of the fraction 365 (or 366¼) divided by 360.

Selfhood and Relationship are the two polarities of being, corresponding in astrological symbolism to the Eastern and

Western horizons. The former constitutes the form of being; the latter refers to the contents of the manifested "body"—at all levels—of the being. Selfhood *per se* is changeless (throughout a cycle of the greater Whole in which it occurs). Relationship is in a constant state of flux; and is fundamentally imprevisible from the point of view of the self which is one of the multiple factors constituting this multitudinous stream of relations. The Eastern world has emphasized the element of selfhood; the Western world that of relationship—two opposite viewpoints which can never be *rationally* reconciled, though they can be integrated in the creative behavior of personality.

This fact constitutes the *general* principle of indeterminacy which extends Heisenberg's *special* principle of indeterminacy stating that one can never accurately determine at the same time the location and the speed of a sub-atomic particle. Location here symbolizes selfhood, and speed symbolizes process: space and time, once more. In astrology, we have likewise to concentrate either on selfhood-determination or on prognostications. Each factor requires a special type of emphasis, and a special type of astrologer.

Birth-chart and relatively unchartable progressions. To some extent at least we must choose our polarization and allegiance. The highly individualized person will be usually more at ease with the determination of selfhood through natal symbolism; while the person largely influenced by, and an expression of, collective and racial factors will be more naturally attracted toward and more successful in prognostication, "horary astrology" and fortune-telling. The two points of view can, of course, be integrated in a highly gifted personality, but an emphasis of either one or the other will be always noticeable. The situation, in this respect, is similar to that referring to psychological introversion and extraversion. There is always an accentuation one way or the other; but the determination of the nature of the accentuation is at times made very difficult because "in every pronounced type there exists a special *tendency towards compensation for the one-sidedness of his type*, a tendency which is biologically ex-pedient since it is a constant effort to maintain psychic equilibrium."[*]

The same is true in relation to the accuracy of a person's actual response to indications contained either in the natal chart or in the calculation of progressions and transits. Some lives will be most accurately charted by implications found in the birth-chart and in those "directions" which merely spread out in time the structure of the birth-chart. Others will seem accurately governed by transits, "secondary progressions," birth-day charts, and will not seem to "fit in" very closely with a birth-chart interpretation.

The natural conclusion would be that introverts and highly individualized persons live true to their birth-chart and not so exactly to their progressions; while the opposite applies to extraverts and collectively influenced persons. But it is not always so. For a strongly introverted person, by virtue of his or her lack of ease of functioning in society, may be at the mercy of society—helplessly conditioned outwardly by de-mands made by others, the more he or she withdraws in-wardly and tries to be strictly an "individual." On the other hand, a typical extravert may be unconsciously pulled toward "spiritual" subjects to compensate for his extraversion, and he or she may be utterly helpless and· compelled by whatever occurs in his inner self, and in his or her attempts to be "individual" and "different." Thus transits are often cruel to introverts, and "primary" or "radix directions" shattering to extraverts. The problem is as complex as life itself. Not to see why it should be so, and to depreciate astrology because it is so, are symptoms of poor judgment and of a total lack of understanding of the nature and function of astrology.

---

[*] Cf. C. G. Jung: *Psychological Types*, p. 10.

In order to understand thoroughly the way in which astrological interpretation can be built out of the various materials made available by the operation of astrological symbolism, we have to pursue a course which is not at first readily followed, but it seems the only way of bringing the conflicting factors of radical positions, of progressions, directions, transits, into some sort of integrated picture. If the reader will thus bear with us and follow us into the maze of usually unrelated concepts, we shall be able to summon before his mind a vision of the total operation of a birth-chart and of its consequences, in space and time—a vision which undoubtedly is not easily held in mind, yet which, if referred to consistently and constantly, will bring order and significance where, presumably, there was before but chaos or vagueness.

Steps in the Interpretation of a Birth-chart

A birth-chart can (and should) be regarded as a complex geometrical formula establishing relations between a number of points determined by astronomical observations. Fundamentally, there are ten "planets" (including Sun and Moon), twelve cusps and the Moon's nodes—viz., twenty-four factors. A birth-chart is thus a formula relating these twenty-four primary factors in terms of their zodiacal longitude (to which declination—distance North or South of the Celestial Equator—is also sometimes added to determine what are called "parallels of declination"). To interpret a birth-chart is to extract out of these twenty-four factors all the significance which they contain, or rather, which the astrologer is able to perceive. This extraction of significance is done by means of a series of analyses, each analysis being theoretically complete in itself as it covers a whole field of being, yet all these analyses constituting only the raw materials out of which the final synthesis is built. As already said, astrology depends mostly, insofar as a life-interpretation is concerned, upon synthetic "holistic perception." But the latter is a purely individual factor; and in writing about chart-interpretation one must needs emphasize the analytical processes, which are necessary: 1) as a training for the development of basic knowledge; 2) as a means of checking up on the results of "holistic perception;" that is, of a direct perception of the total interrelationships linking the twenty-four primary elements of the birth-chart and any other secondary factors that may be derived therefrom.

These several analyses to which the birth-chart is subjected can be made in varying order, such an order being a purely individual matter. We shall indicate what they are, giving them in a sequence which is derived from the logic of the situation, as we have studied it in this book. But let us always keep in mind that our first task is to study the twenty-four primary factors above-mentioned (planets, cusps, Moon nodes). These factors are significant in terms of:

1) Their sign position.
2) Their house position (this does not apply to cusps).
3) Their degree position (symbols of the degree; also relation to planetary nodes).

This first stage of interpretation is an analysis of position in which each factor is considered independently of any other, and is followed by an analysis of relationships between these factors, thus:

4) The planetary pattern as a whole.
5) The aspects between every two isolated factors.

Then comes another type of analysis, which may or may not be made use of. Two factors are being related to a third factor, which is ordinarily (but not necessarily) either the line of horizon or the meridian. This is a higher degree of analysis of relationship, and it reveals significance of a complex sort—such as is related to man's social nature and to the processes whereby his own society of cells and nerves become ever more closely integrated toward the formation of a "spiritual body." This refers to the Parts.

In this last type of analysis we no longer deal solely with the human personality as it is archetypally or in "blueprint." We deal with the *use* to which this personality or any group of factors within the total personality can be put. We are now considering not only "being" and its structure, but also "purpose" and its axes of crystallization.

One step further, and we shall be studying not only axes of crystallization, (or sensitive nexi of relationship), but we shall visualize the very crystallization of potential relationship into actual personality-occurrences. How shall we do so? By considering these same angular relationships between the twenty-four factors—and more simply the arcs (distances) separating them, but considering them in terms of potential *phases of maturation*. In other words, we shall simply convert spatial values into time values. But we shall do so *without having recourse to anything outside of our twenty-four factors*; simply by a refinement of analysis such as to bring in a fourth-dimensional value of mathematical time, where before we had only three-dimensional spatial relationship.

To put it simply, we shall interpret our birth-chart in such a way that, by transposing our point of view of analysis, we shall obtain time-values (phases of the life-process) where before we had considered space-values.

In order to accomplish this result we have to cease considering the 360 degrees of the zodiac as indices to structural relationship of being, and to begin to regard them as symbols of *phases of life-unfoldment*. We have to transpose our analysis from the plane of geometrical measurements to that of clock-measurements. By doing this we are evidently entering the realm of progressions and more particularly of "directions." But there is a great difference between the ordinary progressions or directions and the procedure just stated—even if the difference appears on the surface to be more theoretical than practical.

We shall be able to evaluate this difference more accurately as we presently study the foundation on which the complex weaving of progressions, directions and transits is built. But we must take one step at a time, lest we become hopelessly entangled in concepts which have grown in the field of modern astrological thought more like wild flowers than like cultivated productions. Our next step will consist in studying briefly what might be called the "time-analysis of the birth-chart."

Time-analysis of the Birth-chart

The procedure is a simple one. Consider Mussolini's chart. The Moon is placed on Gemini 8° 50'; Jupiter, on Cancer 18° 33'. The distance (or "arc") between them is therefore 39° 43'. Let us translate a one-degree arc into a year of the life-process. In this case the relationship Moon-Jupiter, instead of being expressed by a 39° 43' arc (a spatial value), will be stated as a 39-year and less than 9-months' relationship. What is meant thereby is that the *rapport* between Moon (referring to the relation to the public, to the past ancestry, the feelings, etc.) and Jupiter (referring to the point of emergence of the Self, to authority, power, etc.), which exists, potentially and archetypally in the birth-chart, will be actualized at a time of the life which we postulated as 39 years and 9 months after birth. The Fascists' march on Rome, which gave Mussolini dictatorial power, occurred when Mussolini was 39 years and 3 months old. Other aspects made it occur somewhat ahead of the time above calculated.

The birth-relationship Mars to Sun can be expressed likewise by saying either that it is a 52° 51' relation of arc, or a 52 years and about 10 months relation of period. In terms of aspect the relationship is balanced between an 8 degree-*plus* semi-square and a 7 degree-*minus* sextile. Does it mean "fate is hanging in the balance" for Mussolini in June 1936? Other indications might corroborate the possibility of that month being one of expansion (Sun in ninth house) and traveling involving aggressiveness and danger. But as Mars and Sun are the two so-called "rulers" of the chart (a point the meaning of which we shall discuss briefly later), there is a chance that the relationship may actualize itself as extreme increase of power; though it is undoubtedly a dangerous chance, considering the fact that an eclipse fell on his Sun July 29, 1935; a "transit" indication. At any rate, it will mark a turning point in Mussolini's destiny.*

The arc between Saturn and Jupiter equals 41°. The age 41 was a very critical time for Mussolini, as the result of the Matteotti murder in which prominent Fascists were implicated. Yet he rode through the storm roused by the opposition; perhaps because Saturn was, at his birth, sextile Sun. So what might have been his doom fortified, instead, his position.

Mussolini's planets being placed in relatively close grouping, the result is that nearly all of them can be mutually related by this "time-analysis" method. This indicates that the whole of the nature will be drawn out into actual and positive operation. Instead of calculating the arcs separating the planets, one could calculate arcs separating a planet from an aspect of opposition to another planet. The period so revealed would show a linking of the two planets, not in terms of activity (conjunction aspect) as previously, but in terms of awareness (opposition aspect). In Mussolini's chart this could probably occur only between Neptune and Uranus, at the age of 60. This would mark—if he reaches that age—a moment of great realization of the fundamental and spiritual significance of his mission and Destiny—not in terms of something to be done, but of the meaning of something that has been done.

---

* This was written in 1935. The proclamation of the new "Roman Empire" came in May 1936.

Linking through squares, trines, sextiles, may also be attempted. For instance, Mussolini's Sun and Mercury are separated from a square to Moon (in Virgo 8° 50′) by 32° 51′ and 33° 20′. This brings out time-values of about 33 years and 33 years and one-half. He was seriously wounded in the war at the age of 33 years and 6 months.

These examples will have sufficed to give an idea of the procedure followed. It remains, however, for us to explain why the operation of translating space-values into time-values was based upon the equivalence of degrees of zodiacal arcs to years of the life. This much-discussed question will be dealt with from another angle when we study the theory of progressions and directions; but we may say now that the degree is the most *convenient* point of departure for such a translation of space-values into time-values, for, after all, it is the unit of zodiacal measurement, and the entire fabric of astrological symbolism rests more or less upon the degree.

As we already said, the degree is, as it were, a translation of time-value into space-value, for it is theoretically the orbital space which the Earth covers during the period of time it accomplishes a total rotation around its axis, viz., a (sidereal) day. Thus the degree is a day, in terms of spatial measurement along the Earth's orbit. From the day, we pass now to a year, saying, a day equals a year—and thus a degree equals a year. Marc Jones states the matter most ably in his course *Directional Astrology*, as follows:

"The theory . . . is that movement upon any circle of celestial motion has an affinity with the movement in any other related circle of the same scheme, and that the expression of this relationship in any one of the circles creates in that circle an entity which has correspondence with the whole circle in terms of units. Thus, since there are two circles of the heavens used for the measurement of motion of the planets . . . the circles in which the diurnal (daily) and annual (yearly) motions of the earth are measured, it is said at the outset that a day corresponds to a year; and this is a correspondence familiar to symbolism of every sort (as a year becoming a day in the eyes of God). This means that a degree on the circle in one instance equals the whole of the other circle . . . and from this fact, by extension, the degrees upon either circle correspond to a year of life."

What complicates matters, where progressions and directions are concerned, is the fact that there are "more days than degrees" and that actually the day does not correspond to a whole degree but on an average to 59′ 8″. We have discussed this point in our chapter on the Degrees of the Zodiac, and stated that with the degree, considered as the symbol of a fundamental release of creative significance, we are dealing with an archetypal value; and that the discrepancy between the 365 or 366 days and the 360 degrees is an expression of the fundamental "coefficient of indeterminacy" which dominates in one way or another any attempt to translate factors belonging to one level or sphere of being into factors belonging to another level or sphere.

When dealing with phenomenal facts and concrete events —as does the ordinary astrologer using directions or progressions—there is a real justification in using the ever-changing value of the space covered by the Sun in one day (it varies from 0° 57′ to 1° 1′), because, as we shall see, the idea back of these methods is that *birth is a progressive event*. But in the case of the "time-analysis of a birth-chart" the fact of birth (or rather of the beginning of independent existence with the first breath) is held to be altogether sufficient and definite. The birth-chart is the "seed-form" of the individual selfhood. Thus it is considered strictly *as an archetypal pattern* which is unchanging and entirely self-contained. It refers to "being," not to "becoming." Therefore all its values and all the analytical operations related to it should be considered from the archetypal level. The degree is thus to be used for time-analysis because it is a permanent archetypal value; and

not the ever-changing factor of the daily motion of the Sun—
or any such factor—which belongs to the phenomenal world.

The reader may now ask: If the birth-chart does not refer
to "becoming," what is then the meaning of this "time-analysis"? Here again we are confronted with a somewhat metaphysical problem. It can, however, be made clear by referring
once more to the illustration of the building of a temple. The
birth-chart is the "blue-print" which gives the seed-form of
the temple. Any architect looking at this blueprint will
know without a doubt that, *if* the temple is actually to be
built, the foundations will first have to be dug; that a certain
class of working-men will have to be hired first, another
later; that a certain type of material will have to be delivered
on the grounds early in the operations, another later. If he
knows the exact condition of the business world, he will be
able even to give an approximate date as that of the completion of the building.

All these things he will know merely by analyzing the
blue-prints and by studying the requirements for the actualization of the structure, which he beholds *in potentiality*. He
may not know them with the utmost exactness, of course, for
much will depend on the ability of the human materials used
(engineers, foremen, workers, etc.) and on the general social
conditions which may seriously affect the building operations.
But he will know enough to get a rather accurate picture of
the various stages of operations and of the time each stage
will last.

This is exactly what we mean by a "time-analysis" of the
birth-chart. It does not deal with "real becoming" (or with
what Bergson calls "duration") because it merely spreads out
into a schedule of work seed-potentialities, which makes the
process relate to "mathematical time," but not to "creative
duration." As a matter of fact, such a "creative duration" is
by essence *imprevisible*. Each moment is new and wells up

from an ocean of infinite potentialities as unforetellable actuality.

What, then, is the astrologer to do? All he can do is to deal with probabilities and with statistical averages—insofar as forecasting is concerned. He takes so many probable views of the unknown future process, from so many angles, that there will be little room left for the creative unknowable. But to sum up all these probable views will be a prodigious task; and even if the actual events are correctly foreseen, there will always remain a mysterious unforeseeable value: the value of significance. Granted that one knows every step of the future destiny of an individual, what significance will that individual have extracted from his whole life as he lies near death? No one can tell. God, even, cannot know. For God is made out of such "summing-ups of significance." This is God's becoming—pure and creative duration: the unfathomable Mystery that is Life itself.

All that our "time-analysis" can do is to see the mile-stones on the road to personality-fulfillment. In some cases of supreme importance in the individual's destiny—as in the case of the march on Rome in Mussolini's life—the mile-stones mark a definite occurrence which of itself, objectively, is a crucial turning-point. But such cases are not many; and why should they be? In other cases, other types of factors which serve to determine the whole "life-process" may be more potent in precipitating actual events. The factors produced by the time-analysis of the birth-chart (and this time-analysis is susceptible of much more complex developments than have been indicated in this brief sketch) refer to the archetypal Destiny, to that which is individual selfhood in operation: operative wholeness. They deal with the self-contained manifestation of potential being. They are the most abstract, and yet the most powerful, in a life dominated by the seed-form of individual selfhood.

Before we come to investigate progressions and directions proper, one more point is to be stressed. It is called to our mind by the fact that some English astrologers are using this method of time-analysis, in various ways, under the name of "symbolical directions." This qualification, "symbolical," is most misleading, for it tends to make one believe that the usual progressions and directions are *not* symbolical. This is a grievous error. *All progressions and directions are purely symbolical;* and this fact should be well understood, for it is on this fact that the theory of planetary influences breaks utterly—when the term "influence" is taken to mean the emanating of rays or waves which act physically or psychologically upon *a particular individual.*

Every word of this last sentence should be considered carefully, and no wrong or premature conclusion should be arrived at. All progressions and directions are symbolical, because the equivalence of a year to a day or to a four-minute period (in the primary directions) is purely symbolical. How one could fail to recognize the truth of this assertion is hard to understand. It is true that we may say that the individual man (*microcosmos*) is an image or correspondence of the solar system (*macrocosmos*), and that cycles of motion in the one cause analogical responses in the other. But if such a statement means anything at all, it means that the solar system is assumed to be the symbol of the individual man; and that the cyclic motions of the celestial bodies around the Earth *correspond* to cyclic processes of the life-force in any living organisms on Earth. Obviously, there is no difference between saying "correspond to" or "are symbols of." If anyone sees a difference between these two phrases, it is a proof either that he has not understood the vital reality of symbols—especially of collectively valid symbols such as the "primordial images" or "archetypes" of which Jung speaks—or that he uses the term "correspondence" without entering into the real meaning of such a term, often so loosely used by students of occult philosophy.

All progressions and directions are symbolical; and that is why any system "works" so well for the astrologer who has identified himself with it (who *believes* thoroughly in it), and not so well for one who is not used to the "feel" of it. In medical practice, likewise, a drug cures much more readily a patient who has "faith" in it than one who takes it half-heartedly—and by "faith," I do not mean merely a *conscious* belief that the medicine will cure, but rather an *unconscious* yearning to be healed which fastens upon the medicine as upon a *symbol of salvation*. The same is true also with regard to spiritual healing, religious conversion and all instances of profound "life-metamorphosis." They occur because the deep powers of the inner life (call it "unconscious" or whatever you will!) have become concentrated around a "symbol," an image of salvation or of self-renewal. Not an *abstract* idea, let us well understand, but a concrete, visualizable, sensorially evident *image*. Thus the validity of the "personal God" idea, or of the *guru* or "spiritual teachers"—all images and symbols of operative wholeness, viz., of healing and salvation.

Trouble begins when the symbol is taken as a material reality, because then the person begins to believe that *an external entity is influencing him* from some outside basis of tangibility. "Saturn is crucifying me!" clamors the astrological devotee. "A black magician is persecuting me!" sobs the frightened would-be occultist. And fear creeps in and *disintegrates the personality*. Neither Saturn nor the black magician has any meaning for any person, save as a symbol of a phase of the life-process through which every human being must pass, at this or that level of being.

In other words, the frightening "square of Saturn to Sun" or the "black magician" are happenings that have reality *within the sphere of the personality*. That is why sane books on occultism say that the "black master" is not incarnate, but functions on the mental plane. This is a way of saying—according to the peculiar terminology of occult philosophy—that such a nefarious Power is a symbol (or archetype) which, at certain periods in the process of individuation, is activated within the psyche. Likewise, at a certain period of the worm's life its outer skin hardens, and, within what has then become a chrysalis, a process of utter organic disintegration occurs, until the chrysalis is only a hard skin filled with a jellied substance. But out of this apparently inchoate jelly the butterfly will soon form the glory of wings.

Such is the symbolical story of the soul, as known to millennia of human endeavors toward the spiritual state. The worm might well say: "O horrible fate! Saturn conjoins my Sun, and see how my soft skin hardens!" And a little later might cry in utter anguish: "Help me! My progressed Sun is coming to Neptune, and see, all of me is dissolving into a jelly!" Indeed Saturn and Neptune would be adequate "figures of speech," valid symbols of what is happening. Chemical symbols might just as effectively be used to describe the occurrence; or a symphonic sequence in which the normal tonal structure would give place to an atonal and dissonant development. All are symbols—symbols of the rhythm of the life-process which brings alike to galaxies, to worms or to human psyches calculable periods of transformation. Astrological progressions or directions are symbolical means of calculating the time of occurrence, and the duration, of such periods; and as such are extremely valuable for the man who wishes to live *in terms of conscious significance.* They are utterly or spiritually valueless for any other purpose. Nothing is to be done about them, or with them, save to understand and to be more conscious. All else is illusion.

The Formation of Progressions, Directions and Transits

Progressions and directions are based on an analysis of the actual motion of planets or cusps *after* the moment of birth. They are based on the idea that birth is not a *final* gesture and that the act of birthing prolongs itself in time, spreads over a period of hours (primary directions) or days (secondary progressions), and in doing so affords a means to foretell the actual occurrences that will become objectivized during the whole life-span.

This is a most important point, not usually understood. All progressions or directions involving the study of actual planetary motion after birth (first-breath moment) imply that the individual is not yet a complete personality by virtue of his first breath. Individuation is not completed then. And it takes some time more, *more breathing*, before it is completed. Thus living is seen as a process of fulfillment. This process, from a cosmic or spiritual point of view, reaches as perfect a completion as the individual can reach in the body just beginning to live as an independent organism, in a few hours after birth, and in a few weeks after birth—this according as we put ourselves at the level of the individual factor or at the level of the collective factor.

This may seem a difficult point to understand; yet it is very simple, if only we realize that man as a personality (body plus psyche) is the result of the interaction of individual and collective factors. These factors can be considered separately, for each class operates at a certain level of being; or, let us say, *has its own rhythm of being*. Now the rhythm of being of the individual factors is related to, and symbolized in astrology by, the axial rotation of the Earth: the day-and-night rhythm. On the other hand, the rhythm of being of the collective factors is related to and symbolized by the orbital revolution of the Earth: the rhythm of the seasons.

Thus we start with the idea: The first breath is not sufficient to establish fulfillment of personality. Next point: When will this personality reach relative fulfillment? In order to answer this we have to analyze personality into its component factors; and we shall answer:

1) The individual factor will reach relative fulfillment in a few minutes or hours.

2) The collective factor will reach relative fulfillment in a few days or weeks.

3) And the organism, in and through which these two factors are related as actual behavior in the midst of the larger whole of human society, will operate as an organism (i.e., as body and psyche) for so many years or decades.

Fulfillment in the individual factor seems fastest because it is related to the axial rotation of the Earth, and not (as is the collective factor) with the orbital revolution of the Earth. But let us not forget that we said, a few pages back, that fulfillment is relatively absolute and does not depend upon values such as big or small, short or long. If you place yourself looking at the horizon or at the meridian, you will see *all the zodiac* pass before your eyes within 24 hours; and astrologically speaking, that means that you have reached total fulfillment—for the zodiac symbolizes the *circle of perfect wholeness.*

But, from the point of view of orbital revolution and of the rhythm of the seasons, you will see the whole zodiac pass in the line of the relationship Earth-to-Sun (which symbolizes the collective, organic and vital factor) only after one year's time. Thus you will reach perfect wholeness only after a whole year. But wholeness is wholeness irrespective of the size or duration of the whole in which it manifests. So, from the point of view of wholeness, a complete cycle of axial rotation (a sidereal day) and a complete cycle of orbital revolution (a solar year) are analogical—because they both represent *the experience of the whole zodiac.*

To experience the whole zodiac, for the individual self, is to progress through 24 hours of "in-breathing" after birth. It is to breathe-in the whole zodiac as seen from the point of view of the Earth's rotation.

To experience the whole zodiac for the collective-organic

being is to progress through a complete cycle of solar and seasonal changes, a full year. It is to experience the full cycle of vegetable life—for this collective, organic being in us is, archetypally speaking, a plant or a tree; a point the discussion of which is outside of the scope of this book.

We can carry the analogy further and consider the cycle of gyration of the Earth's axis, the Great Polar Cycle (precessional cycle) of 25,868 years. This, too, constitutes a whole "cycle of experience," and it is "zodiacal" at least in the sense that every meridian of our planet during that cycle comes, by precession, in conjunction with every degree of the zodiac in turn. (This is the same as saying that the vernal point comes in contact successively with every meridian.)

We have thus three cycles, each of which represents *a fullness of zodiacal experience*; each of which can be said to be symbolically equal or analogical to the others: the sidereal day, the solar year, and the Great Polar Cycle. They refer respectively to the individual factor, the collective factor and the planetary factor. But we saw previously that when speaking of the planetary factor we referred to the life of the "Planetary Individual" whose "I am-ness" is symbolized by the axis of rotation of the earth: the polar axis. Thus a whole Great Polar Cycle is the cycle of fulfillment of the individual factor in the Planetary Being, whom we may call the "Planetary Logos" or "God." And here we are confronted with a very interesting, if rather puzzling situation. If the reader refers to our study of the Great Polar Cycle (p. 193), he will see that we produced two alternatives of subdivision for this cycle. If we divide it according to the vibratory periods referred to as "nutation" we have a division of the whole cycle into, let us say, 70 periods of 370 solar years (20 cycles of the Moon's nodes). But if we follow what H. P. Blavatsky claims to be the "esoteric calculation" (presumably substantiated by the quotation from the Kabbala), we have instead a division into 370 periods of 70 years.

This is most interesting in reference to our present problem; for we have there two values (370 and 70) which can be taken as the archetypal lengths of the human personality-cycle. Both are true, only they refer to different things. Seventy years (three-score and ten) constitute the karmic period of *individual* manifestation in personality (i.e., the cycle of our individual relationship to the Planetary Individual). Three hundred and seventy years constitute the period of manifestation of archetypal personality: personality as a spiritual organism, as a perfected permanent structure ready to become *a cell of the Planetary Being.*

The subject cannot here be discussed fully, but we had to bring it up inasmuch as it leads to the recognition of this "esoteric" cycle of 370 years which is the true cycle of fulfillment of the personality. Obviously, no ordinary personality (since the time of the Patriarchs) reaches such a length of manifestation in the body; but this is the very reason why no ordinary personality, *at this stage of planetary evolution,* reaches fulfillment as a personality.

And this is just what astrological progressions point out; for by their traditional equating of "a day after birth, or 4 minutes after birth, for a year of the life-process" it is seen at once that no cycle of progressions or directions is ever fulfilled. In other words, the *individual* factor in man does not experience the whole zodiac, but only, let us say, 70 degrees of it measured on the cycle of the Earth's axial rotation. The *collective* factor, likewise, experiences 70 degrees of the zodiac—measured on the circle of the Earth's orbital revolution. And the *personality* can "keep body and soul together" for only 70 years—out of a cycle of total fulfillment of 370 years.

We have, in other words, three cycles of fulfillment: the sidereal day, the solar year and the personality-fulfillment cycle of 370 years. These can be considered as analogical (or "equal") in terms of fulfillment. A unit in one cycle corresponds to a unit in the other cycles. The unit of the sidereal day (axial rotation) is a 4-minute period during which the meridian moves the space of one zodiacal degree. The unit of the solar year (orbital revolution) is the solar day, during which the Sun appears to move on an average of 59° 8′. And these two units are said to correspond to a year of the personality-life.*

The "day equals a year" calculation is backed up by the fact, often mentioned already, that for the "polar axis"—which symbolizes the planetary "I AM"—a year is like unto a day (6-months daylight and 6-months darkness, theoretically). So if four minutes are analogous to a day, and a day is equal to a year, therefore four minutes correspond also to a year—as is understood in "primary directions."

The main points to grasp in such a complex problem are: 1) that "primary directions" refer to the cycle of axial rotation of the Earth and to the individual factor in man; 2) that "secondary progressions" refer to the cycle of orbital revolution and to the collective factor in man; 3) that both are related expressions of the fact that birth does not mean the fulfillment of personality, and that therefore birth is a *continuing process* which goes on at three levels: individual, collective and organic (personality); 4) that each of these three levels, or factors of being, has its own rhythm of development, which relates it respectively to a cycle of fulfillment. Thus the phases of development of the individual factor can be determined from planetary positions, after birth, along the cycle of axial rotation. The phases of development of the collective factor can be determined from planetary positions, after birth, along the cycle of orbital revolution. And the phases of development of the personality, insofar as it is determinable by social and planetary environment, can be computed from the positions of the celestial bodies year after

---

* In another sense, they correspond to a 70-year period of the Great Polar Cycle, during which the equinoxes move about the space of one degree. Every human life and its 70-year life-span is thus seen as a "unit of action" in function of the Planetary Being: a brief cellular gesture!

year—i.e., along its 370-year cycle of fulfillment. Such posi.-tions are what are called "transits."

This, then, gives us three basic methods of determining the phases of the life-process which continues, prolongs and leads to the relative fulfillment of the human being, the structural pattern of which is shown in the birth-chart: Primary directions, secondary progressions, transits.

In these three cases the same procedure is used, generally speaking; planetary positions are calculated for any period of time desired, and the new positions thus obtained (progressed, directed, transiting positions) are compared to the radical or birth positions; or, in some cases, are considered in their new mutual relationships. "Aspects" are thus determined which define or characterize the life-process or the general life-conditioning in a given year, month or day of the life. In every case *new* planetary factors are generated by the use of these methods, which either supersede, or more ordinarily modify, the significance of the twenty-four original factors constituting the birth-chart; whereas in the previously studied method of the "time-analysis of the birth-chart," the only factors used are these twenty-four primary factors, or else secondary factors produced by the combination of the primary factors.

From what has been said throughout this chapter, a more or less definite understanding of the value and the relative meaning of the basic methods used in astrology to express the factor of time and of becoming has presumably been acquired. We shall, however, return to this complex question as we sum up our discussion concerning the use and interpretation of birth-chart and progressions (generally speaking) in relation to the great goal of the integration and fulfillment of personality. But before we reach this point it seems necessary to give some more attention to the technique of progressions, directions and transits, so that the reader may become more familiar with them and with their relative importance and significance.

XIII. *The Technique of Progressions, Directions and Transits*

Secondary Progressions

THESE progressions are the most generally used today, and will be found explained in any good astrological text book. Their technique is quite simple, and all the factors required are found in an ordinary astrological ephemeris. What they measure primarily are changes in the relation Earth-to-Sun; that is, in the relation of organism to organizing life-principle. This relation evolves constantly through the life-process. It is different in youth, in mature life, and in old age. An index to the significance and mode of operation of this constantly changing Earth-to-Sun relationship is found in the "progressed Sun"—its degree, sign and house position, also in the aspects it makes to other planets.

Secondary progressions are calculated with reference to the apparent motion of the Sun, and the solar day—from noon to noon—is the basic unit. One such unit is said to equal one year of life. As the daily motion of the Sun is not a constant, its exact value has to be found in the ephemeris. The position of the Sun each day after the day of birth gives the position of the "progressed Sun" during each year after birth.

Secondary progressions refer to the orbital motion of the Earth, thus to the apparent motion of the Sun on the ecliptic. The solar factor therefore completely dominates these progressions. It is a factor of integration, as the Sun stands for the vital principle in the body, or for the Self within the total personality.

444

What is shown in the "progressed Sun" is the manner in which the process of personality-integration is carried on after birth; how the substance of collective being, in the midst of which the individual grows, is being "assimilated" by the individual—a process leading to the maturity and completion of a full personality. Solar progressions deal therefore with the development of the Self-in-manifestation. They deal with the various stages of embodiment of the integrative monadic Will; also with the modifications of the life-principle as it controls the processes of the physiological organism. From the standpoint of personality-fulfillment they are the most important progressions—more so than as prognostications of concrete events. Secondary progressions are above all *solar* in implication, and nothing can really be obtained from them which does not somewhat partake of the quality of the solar factor in action. As the Sun represents the factor of integration, it is easy to see that "secondary progressions" are the most significant in relation to the psychological-alchemical Great Work.

Most valuable testimonies can also be obtained from the positions of the planets and the Moon—provided those are always considered as somewhat subservient to the solar factor. Progressed planets indicate how the types of activity which they represent *co-operate in the general solar process of fulfillment*. Progressions of Mercury reveal the attitude of the mind and the mental faculties in the "Great Work" of the solar Alchemist within. Progressions of Venus refer to emotional reactions and esthetic responses; those of Mars, to the power of initiative and spontaneous impulsion; of Jupiter, to the compensatory soul-revealing activities of the psyche; of Saturn, to the slow transformations of the very structure of the field of the conscious; of Uranus, to the downflow of transforming, regenerative forces from the hidden world within; of Neptune, to the dissolving of limitations and the

445

birth of universal consciousness (metamorphosis); of Pluto, theoretically, to the possibility of a second birth.

As for the progressed Moon, it is that which, of all progressed planetary factors, most specifically refers to concrete events. It indicates outer changes, the working out of cycles of past karma, the opening, closing and culmination of the outer phases of the life-process. As it passes over the cusps of houses (this is also true to a lesser extent of all progressed planets) it measures definite changes in the concrete emphases of life. This is especially marked as the Moon crosses the four angles, and most of all, the Ascendant.

But even the most powerful and most factual of all such progressions, Moon conjunction Ascendant, does not *always* refer to a concrete change. Often the time of the decision which leads to the change is that which is indicated. At times the change is most potent, yet outwardly unrecognized by the native—especially if he belongs to the introvert type. This is so because, even in the case of the Moon (a solar reflector, in a sense) the meaning of the occurrence has to be related to the progressed Sun. The symbol of the degree of this progressed Sun gives one of the best—if sometimes elusive —indications of the *spiritual significance* of the approximate twelve months to which a full degree of solar progression corresponds.

Before we leave this type of "secondary progressions"—the detailed study of which would require a small book—an important point needs be mentioned. We have not so far made clear the actual procedure by means of which such a phrase as "progression of Venus" can be given factual meaning. How shall we discover the nature of the progressions of Venus? By reference to what? Two possibilities are evident. The progressed Venus is considered either as making aspects with the other progressed planets of the same progressed day-period, or as coming to form definite relations with the planets at their original (radical) places in the birth-chart. For instance, if the native is born on January 1, 1935, his radical Sun is in Capricorn 10 and Jupiter in Scorpio 16° 56'. By the time he is seven (in 1942) his progressed Sun will have reached the Sun's position marked in the ephemeris for January 8 as Capricorn 17. At this same date the progressed Jupiter will be in Scorpio 18° 5'. Now a sextile has been formed early, January 8, between the *progressed* Sun and the *radical* Jupiter (between Capricorn 16° 56' and Scorpio 16° 56'). This is seen to take place in the "life-process" in 1942.

If, however, we wish to consider the sextile of progressed Sun and progressed Jupiter, then we shall have to wait until January 9—when these two planets are found located respectively on Capricorn 18° 13' and Scorpio 18° 13'. This postpones the actualization or fulfillment of the natal Sun-sextile-Jupiter in the native's life to the year 1943. If, instead of Jupiter, which moves slowly, we had taken a fast moving planet, the discrepancy between the dates of consummation of progressed-to-radical-planet and progressed-to-progressed-planet aspects would have been greater. The question is then: Which type of aspect should we select; and if, as is commonly done, both types are considered, should there be a difference between the two?

Here—as on many other occasions!—astrologers differ. Most of them recognize the validity of both procedures, but some think one type is more effective, others, the other type. As always, we shall try to look logically and philosophically into the matter. If we calculate aspects between progressed and radical planetary positions, what we do is to conceive the radical chart as a permanent pattern so indelibly imprinted in the personality that it creates psychically and physiologically sensitive points significant enough to stand as foci of distribution of energy. As the progressed planets strike these points (by conjunction, opposition, square, etc.) a significance is released in terms of the planetary activity. In other words, the radical planets are seen as permanent centers of energy which become activated, stirred, aroused (in one way or another) as progressed planets come into definite aspect to them.

Thus a significant relationship is established between a value of knowledge, being, space, individual selfhood (radical places) and a value of fulfillment, time, becoming, life-flux (progressed planet). If, on the other hand, two progressed planets are related by aspect, then the relationship is between two values of the latter type. Therefore by considering such progressed-to-progressed-planet aspects we are navigating wholly in the boundless flux of "becoming," without any anchorage to the seed-form of "being." We are apt to scatter our interpretation, to lose the *sense of purposefulness* which is the keynote of a proper approach to the secondary progressions.

In the secondary progressions we see the purpose of "being" at work through the "becoming." The various positions of the "progressed Sun" on each successive degree of the zodiac after the day of birth show the evolution of the purpose of the life-activities in the midst of change: purpose as it slowly perfects and refines itself throughout the life. The time-analysis of the birth-chart also revealed such a purpose, but in a more archetypal, subjective and abstract sense. In the secondary progressions we see the purpose of being unfolding itself by actual steps; thus the discrepancy between calculations obtained by following both methods.

Each degree of progression of the Sun strikes a new aspect of this life-purpose (symbolized in the degree of the radical Sun—and, in another sense, in that of the Ascendant); and as this occurs the radical "planetary pattern" slowly changes its form, to fit in, as it were, with this new purpose. If the original seed-form of being (birth-chart) actually dominates the whole development of personality—as it does for instance in men completely overshadowed by a super-personal mission—then progressed positions must be referred almost solely to the radical places of the planets; for the original purpose is absolutely constant and ever active. But if, in the course of the life-time, the personality experiences profound changes of purpose, real metamorphoses of being, then aspects of progressed-to-radical-planets are less valid, and aspects of progressed-to-progressed-planets more significant of actual changes.

Primary Directions

These directions have been presented by astrological text-books in so many different ways, and they involve, as usually taught, such an array of mathematical computations, that the student of astrology may well find himself baffled by the labor of calculating them. The scope of this book does not permit a detailed or precise presentation of these primary directions. But a few points may be brought out to indicate how they fit into the larger scheme of astrological interpretation.

Primary directions, generally speaking, refer to the factor of individual selfhood, because they are calculated along the cycle of axial rotation of the Earth. They refer to the process of fulfillment of this individual factor. In this process, a degree of motion is again equated to a year of the life. But the moving factor is no longer the Sun, the index of the orbital revolution of the Earth (as it was in the Secondary progressions), but instead, the meridian (or Mid-Heaven point in the chart). The meridian moves at a rate of one degree per 4-minute period, completing a circuit in 24 sidereal hours. Thus this 4-minute period is assumed to correspond to a year of the life.

During such a period, obviously, the motion of the planets in their orbits is practically *nil*. Thus, in some systems, they are considered to be absolutely fixed, insofar as their zodiacal positions are concerned. Their motion is produced by the rotation of the Earth, which, as it were, lifts up the whole planetary pattern and turns it around as one would turn a radio dial. We might say that every four minutes a small one-

449

degree motion is given to the whole pattern. As a result, the whole pattern occupies new positions in terms of zodiacal degrees. These new positions are related to the original positions and aspects calculated between original (radical) and new (directed) positions. Thus Saturn by directed position may become square to Sun by radical position after ten little one-degree turns of the dial. And this would mean that ten years after birth the individual factor in the native's personality will experience a crisis of fulfillment expressible in terms of Saturn square Sun.

If this were actually the whole mechanism of primary directions it would be identical in operation (if not in principle) with the technique of our time-analysis of the birth-chart. But matters are much more complex. First of all, because directions are formed actually along the circle of the Earth's axial rotation *which is the equator*, the positions of the apparently moving planets have to be calculated in reference to the equatorial circle, and not to the ecliptic (the path of the apparent motion of the Sun). This means that the positions of the planets must be expressed in terms of Right Ascension (distance from the vernal equinox on the equator), and not in terms of longitude (distance from the vernal equinox on the ecliptic).

Therefore the radical positions of the planets must be recalculated—by the use of special tables, taking also in consideration the latitude of the planets—and they will be found on new degrees of the zodiac. The new positions, by directional motion, will also be expressed in terms of Right Ascension. The aspects will thus be computed between the two Right-Ascensional positions, radical and directed. Such a type of computation offers the simplest type of primary directions. Symbolically speaking, they are the creation of the regular motion of the meridian, and thus carry, as it were, the significance of the Mid-Heaven. They deal with the unfolding of the individual factor in a spiritual or archetypal way, in relation to thinking and to the flow of the power of the being.

But there are much more complex types of directions, which take into consideration the actual motions of the planets, their declination, and above all, the factor of latitude of the birth-place. Latitude is a factor which relates to the horizon and to the Ascendant—because the latitude of the birth-place must be known in order to determine the degree of the Ascendant. Thus we have a type of primary directions which carry, symbolically, the general significance of the Ascendant. They deal with the unfolding of the individual factor in a personal and most particular way. They reveal the uniqueness of individual destiny, the unique inner realization of the individual's own essence.

In such a system of "mundane" directions, changes of residence have also to be taken in consideration; for here is seen the most particular interweaving of individual with planetary factors: man's close relationship to the Earth, either in a trivial and environmental sense, or in terms of spiritual contact with the great Nature-forces of the planet.

Radix Directions

In order to make the first type of primary directions simpler and more easily determinable with the use of the ordinary astrological ephemeris, a system of directions has been devised (by Sepharial and later by Vivian Robson) which is called the "Radix System." In this system the "arcs of directions" between planets are calculated on the ecliptic (that is, in terms of longitude) rather than on the equator (that is, in terms of Right Ascension). If at birth the Sun is in Aries 10 and Venus in Aries 29, the arc of direction between these planets is 19°.

According to Sepharial, and according to most astrologers using this simplest of all systems, a year of life is not calculated as corresponding to one degree, but to 59′ 8″—which is the mean daily motion of the Sun (the result of dividing 365¼ solar days into 360 degrees). In such a system all points of the birth-chart, planets and cusps, are moved at this rate of 59′ 8″ *per* year; and the relationship between these successive positions (yearly and monthly) and the radical positions is analyzed in terms of aspects.

This rate of direction is not the only one considered. Just as the mean daily motion of the Sun provides the astrologer with a coefficient of direction, so the mean daily motion of the Moon (13° 10′) is used for the same purpose, a year of the life corresponding to a directional advance of 13° 10′. This last procedure is called "minor directions," while the former carries the name of "major directions," the minor being always subservient to the major, which give the most basic informations.

Thus, if we consider the birth-chart distance between Sun and Venus (19°), we shall see that such an arc can be interpreted as bringing about a Sun-Venus conjunction primarily at the age of 19⅓ (major directions), and also secondarily at the ages of 18 months, 28 years and two months, 56 years and one month, 83 years and five months (minor directions). A table of exact equivalence of arcs and periods is given at the end of Vivian Robson's book, *The Radix System,* which details the technique of such directions.

Such a system is outwardly very close to the time-analysis method previously studied; but the use of the solar and lunar mean daily motions gives it a flavor of "secondary progressions." There seems in fact very little reason for adopting such coefficients of translation of spatial into durational values, for either the actual daily motion of Sun and Moon should be considered, or the archetypal value of one degree. The Radix System is obviously a compromise aiming at ease of calculation and simplification. But once the principle of the time-analysis of the birth-chart is fully understood, it seems a much more valid foundation for getting at the basic phases of operation of the essential destiny of the individual.

Transits

According to the concepts formulated in our last chapter, transits do not differ fundamentally from progressions or directions. They are constituted by planetary motion along the 370-year cycle of personality-fulfillment. In such motion, a day of progression corresponds to a day of the life, a year to a year. For the rest, they have to be treated exactly like secondary progressions. The aspects may be calculated "progressed-to-progressed" or "progressed-to-radical." "Progressed" here means the actual positions of the planets as seen in the ephemeris for the year of the life considered. The point to remember is always that such positions and the aspects formed refer to the realm of personality; that is, to that manifested synthesis of behavior, feelings and thoughts which is the "concrete man," the man attempting to actualize and to demonstrate in an earth-organism (physiological and psychological) the totality of his being.

An illustration will elucidate completely this point. Let us take again Mussolini's chart. He was born July 29, 1883. Now let us consider the conditions of "transits" for the time of the "march on Rome"; that is, *39 years and 3 months* after his birth: October 30, 1922. We look in the ephemeris for that date and mark down the positions of the planets (by longitude). These positions give us the "transiting positions" of the planets.

If, on the other hand, we had desired the "progressed positions" for that same date, we should have had to look in the ephemeris for September 6, 1883 (that is, *39 days and 6 hours* after birth). And if we had searched by "primary directions" for the positions for this "march on Rome," we should have had to consider the state of the Earth's rotation 157 minutes (that is, *39 times 4 minutes, plus 1 minute*) after the exact moment of Mussolini's first breath. The same process is used in all three cases, save that in the case of "primary directions" the factors considered are of a somewhat different nature, and thus their consideration requires more involved calculations.

Coming back now to the "transiting positions" for the "march on Rome," we find that, just as in the interpretation of secondary progressions, there are two methods possible. The first method is to study the "transiting-to-transiting" aspects; the second, to analyze the aspects formed between transiting and radical positions. The first method refers obviously to the most transitory factors of the situation, to the pure flux of circumstances, having no particular reference to Mussolini as an individual, but characterizing the condition of the general feelings and dispositions of everything on the surface of the Earth that day.

Now we find that on October 30, 1922, the Moon was in conjunction with Uranus, just before noon, in the 10th degree of Pisces; that Neptune in Leo was in sextile to Mercury and Saturn in Libra; Jupiter in distant conjunction to the Sun in Scorpio; Mars in trine to the North Node and in approaching square to Jupiter. On the whole, the set-up was a most favorable one for public regeneration and the display of power. The Sun's symbol that day was "Divers of the deep sea," indicating a fearless plunging into experience, or, as Marc Jones interprets it, "of purposeful venturing." The Moon-Uranus conjunction occurred on a degree symbolized by "An aviator in high altitude flight, master of the skies," which is interpreted as indicating "the transcendence of normal problems to the point of gaining celestial responsibilities" and the "coronation" of human endeavors. All of which is most significant indeed!

But it does not refer to Mussolini as an individual, only to the quality of world-happenings on that day. In order to see how these "planetary positions" refer to Mussolini as an individual, we have to compare them with his radical birth-chart, the seed-form of his destiny. One feature emerges at once, vividly: The "transiting Sun" was in exact conjunction with Mussolini's North Node at the very end of the day. At the end of the day he reached Rome, summoned by the King to assume full power. In other words, as the North Node is a point of future destiny and influx of power, October 30 was the *one day of the year* when, the "transiting Sun" vitalizing it, it would operate with a maximum of power—in reference to Mussolini's *personality*. Obviously, in such an event what was involved more than anything else was the power of personality.

At the same time the Moon-Uranus transiting conjunction occurred in Mussolini's "fourth house"—a change of domicile and of concrete selfhood—in opposition to his radical Part of Fortune—an awareness (opposition) of public responsibility (tenth house); in a sense, opposing his personal happiness (Part of Fortune). This conjunction was square to his radical Saturn-Moon-Mars conjunction, striking squarely the Moon and indicating the incorporation (square) of a public (Moon) destiny. Transiting Neptune was very close to the Mid-Heaven in Leo, showing that the power of the racial collectivity was being focused upon Mussolini's point of public activity and spiritual power. Finally, the transiting North Node was upon the cusp of his "eleventh house," about to enter by natural retrogression his house of public activity—indicating the power of friends and associates in a common cause. We might further add that transiting Mercury and Saturn were in his "third house," close to an opposition to his radical Jupiter and Venus. This was a most valuable restraining influence, bringing common sense, moderation, and attention to near objectives (third house)—as balanced against far and grandiose plans (ninth house). Mussolini's Jupiter-Venus conjunction in the "ninth house" is a danger for him; and this may be particularly evident in the near future, as his "progressed Mars" is adding fuel to an over-expansive and imperialistic configuration.

This reference to a progressed planet leads us to state that at the time of this march on Rome, Mussolini's "progressed Moon" was approximately crossing his radical Ascendant—the strongest indication for a significant change of surroundings and an equally important repolarization of the outer personal life. The most important aspect by "primary direction" is the conjunction of Mars to Jupiter, which shows expansion—this time in reference to the individual factor. Thus an increase of individual assurance and authority, a mobilization of soul-energies for expansive action.

To study in detail all the complex set-up of progressions, directions and transits for this most significant event in Mussolini's life is far beyond the scope of this book; but we trust enough has been said to indicate the general procedure and to show how these three basic methods can be operated in relation to each other.

Transits can be worked out in many ways, but a few points must always be considered when transiting planets are referred to the birth-chart. First of all, fast moving planets, such as Mercury, Mars and Venus, make so many and such frequent aspects to the radical planets that the importance of these aspects is very slight. In such cases the passage of a transiting planet through a radical house is usually the most valuable factor of determination; especially as any transiting planet crosses the "angles" of the radical chart, thus enhancing temporarily in the personality-life the function symbolized by each of the angles, in terms of the type of activity represented by the planet.

The patterns made by the slow moving planets (Uranus, Neptune and Pluto) are, however, of great importance, for through the aspects these transiting planets make to the radical planets (and through their passage through the radical houses) the influence of human collectivities, and of society in general, upon the development of personality can be accurately charted. Transits of Uranus release the individual's genius (or "madness") and make it socially effective. Transits of Neptune refer, on the contrary, to the pressure of collective or group factors upon the individual fighting for his right to be an individual. Transits of Pluto bring out (when effective) the call of a new order to the personality. They force the personality into alignment with new ideals and new social forms. They may cause destiny-affecting deaths in the sphere of the personality; also destiny-affecting partnerships.

The transits of Jupiter and Saturn refer more especially to the manner in which man's ego functions outwardly; to inhibitive and formative phases of development in the case of Saturn; to expansive and compensatory types of soul-release in the case of Jupiter. Saturn's 29-year cycle and Jupiter's 12-year cycle are important factors in the life-process, especially with regard to what might be called the "soul factor."

The influence of transiting planets is much emphasized when a conjunction or opposition of such planets strikes an important point of the radical chart. Thus, every lunation (conjunction—and opposition—of Sun and Moon) has significance for the personality if it occurs in strong aspect to a strong radical planet (or angles). This significance is much enhanced in the case of eclipses. For instance, the eclipse of July 29, 1935,* on Mussolini's Sun may prove to be of quite a striking significance. A massing of planets transiting a strong radical point is, of course, of still greater importance.

Another and most valuable way of using transits is found in the erection of a birth-day chart. Such a chart is made for every birth-day, and shows in a usually most accurate way the type of personality-occurrences to be expected during that particular year of the native's life (i.e., from birthday to birthday). But here again, there are at least two basic methods of erecting such a chart:

* Written in 1934.

1) The birth-day chart is calculated for the original time of birth at the place of residence (not the place of birth).

2) The birth-day chart is calculated for the moment at which the "transiting Sun" returns to the exact zodiacal position it occupied at birth. This moment may not fall on the same day as the day of birth. Therefore such a chart is called, instead of "birth-day chart," a "solar revolution chart." It may be erected either for the latitude of the place of birth or for that of the place of residence. The former is preferable; for this type of chart is definitely correlated to the birth-chart through identity of solar factors—thus to the latitude of birth as well.

In both of these cases the pattern of houses is usually different from that of the birth-chart, unless, in case No. 1, the native resides at his place of birth. If one wishes to retain the birth-pattern of houses, then the birth-day chart must be calculated for the place of birth; in other words, the transiting positions of the planets are marked within the radical frame-work of houses. This is the general way in which transits are calculated.

Thus we have seen briefly how the various types of progressions, directions and transits operate. If we are careful to constantly keep in view the whole picture which such systems make, and if we have thoroughly grasped the psychological division of the whole human being into individual, collective and personality factors, we should have no difficulty in getting hold of a complex situation. The main point we wish to emphasize—and we believe it has never been so emphasized before—is that there is no basic difference between progressions, directions and transits. In these three systems we establish a correspondence between units of three cycles: the day-cycle (individual factor), the year-cycle (collective factor), and the 370-year cycle (personality factor); and we read the actual state of the heavens after birth in terms of such cyclic units, equating them in any way we wish.

Such readings of post-natal positions are in most cases to be referred to the birth-chart, because the latter represents the seed-form of being; and because "becoming" cannot have *significance* save in terms of "being." Pure values of "becoming" may be ascertained usefully in many cases, as in "progressed-to-progressed" and "transiting-to-transiting" planetary aspects. But one obtains thereby information relating, in the case of progressions only, to the flux of "personality-becoming," and in the case of transits only, to the condition of the general environment. As our main preoccupation is with the process following which the individual, after successive assimilation of collective values, reaches fulfillment as a creative personality, it is evident that we can bring significance into this process only by referring all factors of "becoming" to the seed-form of individual "being."

The great difficulty in working with several systems of time-computation is that the time of maturation of the same aspect is different in each system. If, therefore, prognostications of events are attempted, it is very hard indeed to know which time-indication to select for the event. Sometimes, by analyzing the basic import of the type of event considered, one can know whether it is more likely to fall in with the indications given by the individual-factor system or by the collective-factor system, etc. But this is always an uncertain matter.

The point is that no *event* can accurately be foretold by natal astrology. Psychic types of fortune-telling, and to a very considerable extent "horary astrology," can in a way produce better evidences of forecasting accuracy. They *locate* events better perhaps; but they cannot *give significance* to the life-process of which these events are mere outside pointers. Here again we find a psychological type of "principle of indeterminacy" at work. No one can normally give accurately the location of an event and the significance of that event at the same time. Each factor requires a special type of mental or spiritual polarization which, at least to some extent, excludes the other.

Besides, why should events be foretold accurately? The coefficient of inaccuracy is the coefficient of freedom. From a strict astrological viewpoint, the latter is seen to consist in the very fact that there *are* various possible ways of progressing, directing or "transiting" a chart. This fact refers to the basic three-fold constitution of man: the mental principle (individual), the feeling principle (collective) and the behavior principle (personality). Thoughts, feelings, and actions have each a quasi-independent existence in man—as occult philosophy has shown since or before Plato. *Freedom resides in the creative interplay of these three factors.*

Thus the creative factor in progressions and the like is the very element of inaccuracy—the despair of astrologers! Freedom, as we already saw in relation to our analysis of "cusps" (Cf. p. 386), is the "in neutral" element in life. Between the archetypal plane and the realm of actual behavior there is a mysteriously elusive world, which is the world of the human psyche (the much misunderstood *kama-manasic* realm of Theosophists—the *Sukshma* realm of the Hindu philosopher). It is the world of freedom and of illusion; the world of creativeness and of deceit; the world where archetypal realities are seen not as they *are*, but blurred by the motion of becoming—just as a landscape is seen blurred through the closed windows of a fast moving train, especially if motion makes the traveler train-sick! It is the world of personality, the world of relativity—from which the Hindu philosopher is so eager to become disentangled. But what is disentanglement? To us, it is a mere fallacy, unless it mean first of all *fulfillment*. *Freedom is won only through fulfillment.* And to be free means always somewhat *not to know*; it is the coefficient of inaccuracy. It is based on the courage to go forth while not knowing the future.

That is why spiritual teachers or "Masters"—whatever they be—*never* compel, *never* show the exact future of any action undertaken. For to do so would be to rob man of his creative freedom and his creative initiative. What man can do is so to understand the past, so to grasp the full significance of the seed-form of his being and destiny (birth-chart), that he is fully prepared to meet any future—to meet it significantly, with courage, with understanding and from such a "formed" view-point that all events are seen as beautiful. This is the creative and the radiant life of fulfillment.

Rectification of the Birth-chart

We cannot close this chapter without mentioning, in the briefest possible manner, a matter of supreme importance, one which is really the most aggravating factor in any practical astrological work. This factor is the almost universal uncertainty as to the exact moment at which a person breathed his or her first breath. If the reader has followed us understandingly through our presentation of the fundamentals of astrology, it will be evident to him that *all* the factors in a birth-chart which refer to the axial rotation of the Earth are absolutely dependent upon the strictly exact moment of birth (first breath). For a difference of four minutes in birth-time changes the degrees of all cusps, of all astrological Parts, and therefore alters all calculations based on primary directions.

This means, of course, that where there is such an uncertainty of birth-time there must in the same proportion be an incertitude concerning the individual factors within the native's personality and destiny. This is of capital importance for any type of interpretation in which the symbolic factor of degrees is stressed, and in general for any type of psychological and creative interpretation. As an error of four minutes in birth-time is almost unavoidable, considering the haphazard

461

manner in which birth-time is recorded by attending nurses, and considering the variable memory of the mother and relatives—the problem is indeed a most serious one. It actually tends to make the vast majority of astrological interpretations quite unreliable in many ways, especially when the inner nature and the spiritual-creative factors in the process of individuation are analyzed.

To obviate such a handicap, the astrologer has recourse to a procedure called "rectification." It is an attempt at discovering, by one of several methods in use, what the exact birthmoment was. The various bases of these methods of rectification can be generally stated as follows:

1) *Tracing the rising sign by the native's features.* This is based on the fact that the Ascendant refers to the structure of individual being—or rather to the features thereof. Structure, in the sense of the bone-structure, is a matter depending more upon Saturn and the Moon. But "features" refer not only to the general body-structure, but even more to the general expression of the body, and especially of the face. The Sun-sign gives more the vital radiation of the personality as a whole; Saturn and the Moon, the frame of the body and the rhythm of the life of feelings, which is largely conditioned by this body-framework. The Ascendant refers to the individual's expression through the body, to the unique factor of being, to the manner in which the individual lives his life in a material structure. That is why the Ascendant-type becomes usually more evident after the age of 35; for then the individual as such has become more fully "in-corporated," and his mark or signature more clearly visible.

Twelve basic Ascendant-types of features being determined, the astrologer is then able, by looking at the native, to determine his "rising sign"—theoretically! Practically speaking, such a determination is always more or less uncertain, as it is difficult to separate the Ascendant-factor from other factors which influence the bodily appearance. Moreover, this method determines only the nature of the sign rising—which, as an average, means a two-hour period during which the person may have been born. This is, however, a very valuable procedure, always to be used when the person does not know even the hour of his or her birth.

2) *Rectifying by past events.* The principle of this procedure is that, as it is possible to foretell future events from an accurately known birth-moment, so it is possible to deduce the exact birth-moment from accurately known past events. This is, properly speaking, "rectifying" a doubtful birth-time from the knowledge of the native's life-history. Obviously, the procedure is a most hazardous one except when the incertitude as to the birth-moment is confined within narrow time-limits—say, fifteen minutes or half an hour. Nevertheless, it is much easier to find the correct astrological aspect that is an expression of a certain life-event than to predict a precise event as a result of a coming aspect. This, because past destiny is crystallized life—life *minus* the uncertainty of human freedom.

To put it differently: No event occurs in a life to which an astrological aspect cannot be symbolically related, giving to that event an adequate meaning. But it does not follow that a definite aspect will always produce a definite occurrence. An aspect is *necessary* for an event to take place, but it is not *sufficient* testimony for foretelling accurately the coming of a definite event. An important point which one should never forget!

The difficulty is to isolate the particular past occurrence which is truly corresponding to, or signified by, a particular aspect that matured at a particular time. An aspect by secondary progression and an aspect by primary direction may appear to refer, let us say, to an important journey; yet they figure to dates a year or two apart. The problem of rectification is: Which aspect is the one from which to figure back to the unknown birth-moment? Two or more aspects by secondary progressions may also be taken, indifferently, it may seem, to signify one definite event. If calculations are made backward from those several aspects, several putative birth-moments may be found.

Thus rectification involves a very complex series of checks and counter-checks, of figuring backward and forward, which means—even when the life of the native presents sharp turning points (the best case for the purpose of rectification)—spending much time on it and much ingenuity. A real psychological grasp of human life and human reactions is absolutely necessary if the astrologer is to determine which aspect is the most likely symbol of some past event; also the ability to elicit from the native information which he himself may have forgotten, or the importance of which he does not realize. Such an ability is not as frequent as might seem, and every psychoanalyst will be well aware of this fact. Very few persons, indeed, realize which events of their past have really been significant; neither do people usually grasp the true significance of these events. The greatest value of astrology is probably to be found in the aid it gives man in discovering the significance of what has already happened. Only as every factor of his life-history stands out with clear meaning in terms of the whole life-destiny—only then is man really prepared to face his future with intelligence and understanding; in other words, in function of his true individual selfhood.

After considering most of the important astrological factors mentioned as the most telling for the purpose of rectification, we believe that those which Marc Jones mentions in his course *Directional Astrology* are probably the best; at any rate, they are by far the simplest. These are:

1) The passage of the progressed Moon over the angles of the birth-chart—which enables one to compute these angles accurately. The passage over the Ascendant is in almost every case an index to some basic change in destiny or in self-realization. It usually marks a significant change of residence

or environment; in many cases, however, a change of "interior environment," a new approach to self-realization, are the only things traceable in the life—especially in the case of typical introverts.

2) The aspects of Mars or Saturn to the zenith meridian, i.e., to Mid-Heaven or the Nadir point, which often refers to the death of the parents. Such aspects can be calculated according to the simplest type of primary directions; but from our standpoint, what they refer to is what we called the time-analysis of the birth-chart. The death of a parent—especially the first death—marks a definite psychological liberation of the individual factor in almost every life. It is such a basic occurrence that it should be noticed in the very seed-form of destiny, in the blue-prints of the individual structure of being. Such a death is normally accompanied by a release of psychic or soul forces from the deceased parent into the native; and the significance thereof is usually paramount. There are cases, however, in which the clear-cut estrangement of the native from the parents amounts to a "psychological death" of the parents; and it is to this event that the above-mentioned aspect refers, rather than to actual physical death.

The death-aspects to be considered are conjunction, square and semi-square of either Mars or Saturn to Mid-Heaven or Nadir point. If Mars is ten degrees apart from the Mid-Heaven, the death of a parent *may* occur at the age of ten. But it may also occur at the age of 35 (by semi-square aspect). Again, such aspects do not indicate the *necessity* of a death; but if a death *did* happen at the age of 10, and Mars is shown to be 11 degrees away from the Mid-Heaven, then the logical conclusion is that the position of the Mid-Heaven is not correct, and should be moved one degree so as to make the arc between Mars and Mid-Heaven equal 10 degrees. This is what is meant by "rectifying" a chart.

3) Rectifying through the prenatal epoch, or by the mother's birthday are two methods of unequal importance

and widely differing in technique. They are put in one category because both are attempts to define the emergence of the individual factor in a new life-cycle (first breath) in function of its maternal ancestry. The idea is that certain periods affecting the formation of the bodily substance of the being through the mother led in a measurable way to the beginning of the period of individual existence.

Much has been said for and against making a chart for the time of conception. We may merely point out that conception is a moment in the mother's life and *not* in the life of an individual person who can in no way be called an individual until he has acted as an independent and relatively self-sustained entity: viz., until he has breathed. Conception in a sense is no more important for the life of the future individual child than the time when his future mother and father met. It pertains to the cycle antedating his own individual cycle. It is the last of a series of events, stretching as far back as the beginning of the solar system, which conditions that out of which the individual emerges. It sums up heredity. But heredity is merely one of the basic aspects of the collective factor of being; the other aspect is the environment. It does not determine the individual factor. It only conditions that through which this individual factor has to express itself.

In the calculation of the chart of the "pre-natal epoch" (which, besides, does not seem to refer to the exact and actual moment of physiological conception), a relation is established between the Ascendant at birth and the Moon at the approximate time of conception. This is to say symbolically that there is a moment in the mother's life, about the time of conception, when she foreshadows in her creative imagination what the individual self of her future child will be.

The "mother birth-day" calculation, featured by Paul Clancy, goes one step further, and establishes a definite correlation between the Sun's position in the mother's chart and the Ascendant (individual selfhood) of the child. As the Sun in a woman's chart is usually seen to relate to the "husband image," psychologically speaking, one can see a further connection; because the mother often tries to exteriorize psychologically the "ideal husband image" in her child. Moreover child-birth for a woman is normally—at the physiological race level—the equivalent of "individuation" at the psycho-mental level. The "Initiate" is said to give birth to the Christ-child within, etc. As the Sun represents the integrating and individuating power in man, it is also, in the mother, the power of "imaging forth" a child. Thus the importance of the mother's Sun in relation to the individuality of the child.

Both of these methods are somewhat involved, especially the calculation of the "pre-natal epoch," and while they undoubtedly are valuable in many cases, we cannot discuss their technique here. The "mother birth day" calculation can be attempted when no more precise information than the day of birth is available. It seems to give generally approximate results.

We might conclude by saying, as previously, that the reason why it is so difficult to ascertain exactly the cusps of the houses and all elements referring to the axial rotation of the Earth is that they symbolize the true individual factor in man. And this individual factor is indeed sacred. It is well, therefore, that it be hidden from the scrutiny of the indiscreet and the curious. The exact degree of the Ascendant is the key to man's uniqueness of being and destiny. In a world where the individual is scorned and so often crucified by collective stupidity, we should perhaps rejoice in the fact that the Ascendant, and all the cusps, which are the gateways to man's innermost creative selfhood and to his creative freedom, are usually veiled in mystery.

The "Building of the Temple" and the Point of Self

As we close this part of our study, which deals with the factor of time-evolution in astrology, we wish to come back to a matter which we have previously mentioned, but which we are now in a much better position to understand. We opened our discussion of progressions and the like by considering what we called the "time-analysis of the birth-chart." But another type of time-analysis of the birth-chart has been studied in our chapter "The Dial of Houses" (Cf. pp. 231, 239). If we mention it again now, it is because to our mind both these types of time-analysis go deeper into the matter of ascertaining the real values of "becoming" than any other more usual methods which bring in planetary factors produced after birth.

All these methods (progressions, directions, transits) fail to consider the individual as a whole, susceptible of perfection. They break the singleness, uniqueness and unity of astrological symbolization. They spread out birth into an indefinite period of minutes, days, or years; and they show man beginning cycles of development which he cannot normally complete in the present state of human destiny. They show him with the three parts of his nature evolving according to rhythms which do not exactly match. In this, it is true, lies freedom—but also unfulfillment.

In the procedure explained in "The Dial of Houses" we deal with cyclic fulfillment. Man is seen as able to complete the building of his temple of immortality within the span of 84 years (three 28-year cycles). He is seen as the experiencer of whole cycles of experience, through which all his planets, and all their mutual relationships of any conceivable type (Parts, aspects, etc.), are successively energized and expressed. Here, indeed, is a positive, constructive view of Man, a God in the making; whereas in progressions, directions and transits we are made to witness the spectacle of a runner starting on a threefold race which he cannot possibly hope to finish. His "progressed Sun" will never complete the zodiacal race. His "directional Mid-Heaven" will never know a complete day of activity. The transiting Sun will never set upon a personality fulfilled through the "370 leaps" of the Great Serpent of Eternity, of which the Kabbala and H. P. Blavatsky speak (Cf. p. 192).

What, then, is the use of being born, if the individual is fated to be defeated by the race karma and cannot hope to reach the goal of wholeness? Is there no man who, within the normal compass of our present Earth-life, does ever reach fulfillment? If fulfillment is possible for the individual, in spite of the racial environment—if not as an outer personality, at least as an individual self—then progressions, directions and transits alike tell only one part of the story of the life-process. They may deal with the tangible Earth-body and the racial personality; but there is a realm which they do not consider— the only realm, it seems, in which the individual may reach completion, and thus—*immortality*.

The time analysis which we presented in the last chapter does not attempt to chart the wholeness of any cycle of development. It sets no particular limits, refers to no particular cycle. It merely gives information concerning certain critical moments in the process of working out in actuality the implications contained in the birth-chart. But such critical moments could be theoretically repeated *ad infinitum*. Even the equation "one degree equals a year" is not a necessary factor of such a "time analysis." For, as we conceive this method, it is only a matter of abstract relationship between twenty-four *set* factors. What it really intends to show is not the exact *time* of an occurrence as much as the *sequence* of the operations involved in the process of actualizing the potentialities shown in the birth-chart. In other words, the building operations may be speeded up, but the roof will not be placed before the walls are built, nor will the walls be built before the foundations are dug. What the time-analysis reveals, therefore, is a sequence of operations; and the one-degree-a-year equation is only a coefficient which appears to be the most nearly accurate at the present rate of human endeavor.

In some personalities a faster coefficient might be more effective; for instance a 2½-degrees-for-a-year equation has been suggested by Carter (the twelfth part of a zodiacal sign), and in many cases it gives very significant results.

When we detailed the method by which the individual's progress through three 28-year cycles could be charted, we also wrote that this was a way to determine the schedule of operations in the building of the temple of Man. But by the very nature of this type of time-analysis of the birth-chart we deal with *closed cycles*. We deal with very definite—archetypal—time-limits with reference to one life-span. What is not done when it should have been done is left forever undone. But the terms "done" or "undone" do not refer to personality-behavior as much as to individual realizations. Here is an unveiling of the depths of being, a solemn probing into the sanctuary of the individual soul—into the realm of pure significance.

This is particularly evident as we compare the cycle of progressions of the Moon which occurs in over 27 years, closely approximating the 28-year cycle of what we called the Point of Self; also the cycle of transiting Saturn, which covers a somewhat longer period. Whereas the progressed Moon indicates mostly phases of outer being, and the transiting Saturn the slow deepening or crystallization of the ego-factor, the Point of Self refers to values that are purely interior, but which shed light upon the most secret determination of the individual, and his ability or inability to give meaning to life.

In closing, let us warn the student of the cyclic motions of the Point of Self, lest he forget that this point is not really a mere point, but a cross. The four angles of the chart (the two axes of individual selfhood, horizon and meridian) must be seen rotating through the 28-year cycle. Subtle changes of focalization occur, emphasizing in some cases the horizon-factor, in others the meridian-factor. It is only as those are carefully studied, in function of indications given by the birth-chart as a whole, that this method brings forth a really valid, because complete, picture of the inner life of the individual. Through it we can see, outlining itself dimly or vividly against the background of the more obvious and concrete progressions and transits, the slowly unfolding pattern of individual fulfillment. Here man may be discerned, a success or a failure—in terms, not of what he does, but of the significance and the beauty with which he invests every life-incident on his path toward god-hood—or annihilation.

XIV. *Principles of Astrological Interpretation*

INTERPRETATION, in order to be fully significant and creative, must needs be individual. No man, therefore, should tell another man how to interpret his experience or any life-structure and event with which he is confronted. All that can be done is to establish a few general principles of interpretation which are universally valid, and which may serve as milestones in the process of interpretation, which should be determined, for each individual, by the manner in which he has succeeded in interpreting the basic fact of his experience: himself.

The interpretation of a birth-chart is no different from the interpretation of any life-situation, nor from the interpretation of a work of art or of a personality which one meets for the first time. Granted that, in order to interpret an astrological birth-chart, one should first of all be thoroughly cognizant of the general significance of astrological facts, or rather symbols; granted that a knowledge of the contents of the preceding chapters of this book is a prerequisite to an interpretation which would be true at least to the attitude to astrology which we uphold—it still remains that in astrological interpretation there is nothing either more mysterious or less mysterious than in any other instance of life-interpretation. Universal principles have been stated, defining the general character of the symbols used. It is for the individual to let these symbols *organize themselves into wholes of significance* within his own particular structure of understanding.

472

It sounds very simple, and yet, evidently, it may be very difficult. The beginner will "not know how to start." He will stare at the chart in dumb bewilderment, and nothing will happen. Or else he will tabulate every factor he can think of and look in text-books for what each factor is said to mean. And if he tries to add these separate meanings, he will—barring exceptional cases—find a hopelessly confusing situation, in which many factors will negate as many others. Establishing an average will prove of very little use, as human beings are not so conveniently simple as that procedure would suggest them to be. Especially, they are not sum totals of separate factors, but rather an *organic relationship of relations between factors.* Shall one therefore start with the "factors," or with the "relations between factors," or even with the "organic relationship between relations"?

Every potential interpreter must decide for himself—according to the nature of his own understanding. Some will go from the whole to the parts, then to relations between parts, and again will reconsider the whole as an organism of relations. Others will just as wisely analyze parts, then relations between parts, and will sum up by centering the meanings already determined around some center of significance, or "focal determinator."

There is, however, a primary operation, not mentioned so far, which is really the foundation—though ordinarily an unconscious one—of the subsequent process of interpretation. Such an operation is implied in the very first look which one casts at an astrological chart; for every man, looking at a chart to be interpreted, will have or should have determined, clearly or not, as a background for further investigation, *what he is looking for.* By this rather blunt statement we mean his *a priori* attitude toward whatever data are included in the chart. Some interpreters will have decided beforehand, unconsciously if not deliberately, that they are looking for good and evil planets, benefics and malefics, good and bad aspects, fortunate and unfortunate signs and stars. They will scan progressions for fortunate and unfortunate events. Other interpreters will look for the picture of a human being and a destiny, and will interpret this and that planet or sign as an etcher deals with black and white values, a painter with *chiaroscuro*.

In other words, two basic attitudes toward interpretation are possible—and many secondary blends of these two, besides: the *ethical* and the *esthetical* attitudes. We have already defined in general these two approaches to an evaluation and understanding of life in our chapter "Astrology and Analytical Psychology." What remains to be done is briefly to show how the esthetical attitude operates precisely in the field of chart-interpretation. The working of the "ethical" attitude hardly needs to be discussed, as every text-book of postmedieval and even modern astrology, and the ordinary type of astrological practice, are sufficient exemplifications of the ethical method and of its dualistic valuations: good and evil. But the "esthetical" approach is still a mystery for an overwhelming majority of astrological students.

The reason why this is so is undoubtedly that any interpretation and evaluation of life and of its two basic elements—such as male and female, the Chinese *Yang* and *Yin*, light and darkness, positive and negative—have thus far been established at the *physiological-natural* level of consciousness. In other words, man's vital attitude has thus far been based on his instincts, and colored by the result of *instinctual activities*. Light and summer were good because life was safer and easier when both were in the ascendancy; but darkness and winter were bad because life was more unsafe and harder when they held sway. In a similar way, there was an ethical undervaluation of woman and an over-valuation of man; for a man was better able to work for his life in the "jungle," and a woman was weighed down by physiological difficulties.

Until recently mankind has been in the strictly *physiologi-*

cal stage of its development—as we saw in the first chapter of this book. The Hindu *Puranas* speak of this stage as that of "hand and sex power." A most interesting characterization! "Hand power" refers to muscular activity, and in terms thereof the passive-woman pole is seen as inferior. As for "sex power," it all depends upon the way sex is considered. As the manifestation of the creative force and of life, sex makes of the woman, *as mother*, the positive: thus matriarchy. But as a mode of "activity" (muscular and otherwise), it makes of man the positive. The type of environment in which human tribes lived had undoubtedly much to do in determining which attitude was held. As a result, we have the conflict between the matriarchal and the patriarchal systems.

All realms of human relationship, from family life to tribal and national social organizations, have been pervaded by the more or less conscious physiological type of valuation. Moreover, all that has seemed valid for the vast majority of men has been the effort to perpetuate at all cost the physical organism in a condition of relative physiological health and psychological happiness. Thus everything that tended to disrupt—even temporarily—health and happiness (plus prosperity) has been evaluated as evil; while that which consolidated or established health, happiness and prosperity has been considered good. Everything that gave rise to a sense of pressure or weight, to any disturbances from the happy normality of home, religion, and traditional behavior, has been labelled "bad." Thus Saturn and Mars are malefics. Squares are bad aspects. Oppositions, and the doubts they generate (as necessary stimulations to further efforts of understanding) are also bad. But the expansive Jupiter and the home-building Venus are benefics; and trines which bring in new perspectives and new plans are good aspects.

As, however, man's consciousness begins to establish itself at the psycho-mental level, and to conceive its relation to a greater Whole, the power of which it may deliberately focalize as the foundation for super-personal yet conscious activity, the matter of maintenance of the physical organism, the problem of health-happiness-prosperity, and the instinctive fear of that which might break the comfort of blood-relationships and earth-born traditions—all these take on different valuations. At a transitional stage the "good-bad" consideration seems for a time strenuously emphasized, though there is a transference of the focus of discrimination—as we can see in Christian ethics; but later still, life begins to be considered truly "beyond good and evil"—and even beyond happiness. It begins to be seen from the point of view of the creative artist, who knows well that "blacks" are just as necessary and just as significant as "whites" in a black-and-white drawing; that without both there could be no form and *therefore* no significance. Then the esthetical attitude toward life is born—the attitude of "operative wholeness," the goal of "release of power through significant form." For such an attitude there are neither "good" nor "bad," but only degrees of actualization of meaning through forms conveying more or less purely and precisely such meaning. Every life is a work of art which either successfully conveys the meaning that prompted it into being, or turns out as a formless, inexpressive, unconvincing, trite, "wishy-washy" conglomeration of inchoate efforts that have led nowhere—or else as an almost blank sheet of substance but vaguely suggesting commonplace, utterly non-individual, and meaningless shapes.

The following statements—in a somewhat negative way—may serve as postulates of the esthetical attitude toward astrological interpretation:

A. There is no bad planet. Every planet has a definite function. Every function is necessary to the achievement of organic wholeness. Elimination is as valuable as assimilation. The boil which frees the system from poisons is as valuable as the flesh which rounds up the angles of the bones.

B. There is no bad aspect. Involution is as necessary as evolution. The destruction of forms that have become dead shells and the release of the power they held are as valuable as the building of new forms. Tensions are as valuable as ease, and more creative.

C. Each zodiacal sign is as good to be born in as any other. There is no better birth-month or birth-day. What matters only is to fulfill the life-function or "quality" revealed by the sign or degree-symbol.

D. No birth-chart is better than any other. One is always better for some one purpose. But as all purposes are equally valuable and necessary in the economy of the greater Whole, each man's chart is better for the purposes of his life than is anybody else's.

If there is any "evil," it lies in the absolute identification of the consciousness and of the "I" with only one particular phase of one's totality, instead of with the wholeness of being. Evil is thus over-emphasis; or rather, it is the fact of the "I" being bound to and biased by such an over-emphasis. Any planet, in that sense, is "bad" where it flares up into a prominence which negates the compensatory operation of its polar opposite. Any element of a chart, when it is seen to dominate utterly and to pull to itself the nearly total energy of the field of consciousness, becomes "bad." Sooner or later its domination must be broken, if the man is to achieve wholeness.

This does not invalidate "focalization." But to focalize the totality of one's energy for the fulfillment of an individual— and even more, of a super-personal—purpose, is one thing; to identify one's "I" with one single part of the wholeness of the being, so that all other parts become thwarted in their development, is another thing. Only the latter can be called "bad," if one insists on using such an unfortunate qualification! And even such a "badness" may easily be a purely temporary matter, which turns out to be a valuable phase of a development which proceeds by sharp contrasts. Thus we must be careful lest we transfer the ethical valuation of "good" and "bad" to the new level, and call the whole "good" and the parts "bad." Where there is at least relative evil is not in the part being a part, but in the wholeness of the whole abdicating to a part which claims to be or to rule the whole. In that sense, evil is to become what one is not; and good, to fulfill what one is. The law of life, the good law, is the law of fulfillment of *dharma*, that is, of that which one inherently and archetypally is.

And thus we are led in thought back to the great Hindu book, the *Bhagavad Gita*, which says, in the third chapter:

> "Therefore perform thou that which thou hast to do, at all times unmindful of the event; for the man who doeth that which he hath to do, without attachment to the result, obtaineth the Supreme . . . It is better to do one's own duty (*dharma*), even though it be devoid of excellence, than to perform another's duty well. It is better to perish in the performance of one's own duty; the duty of another is full of danger."

To become what one is; to become the fullness of what one is; in other words, to live whole—even if this wholeness is subsequently to be focalized utterly upon one task, to the performance of which every element of the being contributes by deliberate transference and psychic substitution—such is the ageless and universal ideal for the individual. It means the perfect correlation of *all* values within the personality on its way toward full individuation. It means the perfect correlation of individual and collective factors in the creative, ceaselessly operating. The collective provides the substantial elements; the individual provides a form of organization, or structure—which is the exteriorization of the monadic "quality," which in turn is the spiritual identity of the creative.

478

And out of this ever-active, ever-sounding *chord of being and becoming*—of *becoming* operating in and through *being*, of *being* substantialized and made operative in and through *becoming*—emerges the creative wholeness of the organic whole.

Astrology illustrates, exemplifies, provides applications for all these correlations. But it too must be understood whole. It too must be integrated in and through an esthetic approach which alone can reveal a totality of meaning. We have seen previously how this correlation of *being* and *becoming* can be perceived in and through the interaction of birth-chart, progressions, directions and transits. Here again we can point to the fallacy, evident in so much present-day astrological practice, of considering birth-chart and progressions apart from each other. An aspect between progressed planets means little, unless it be related to the birth-chart, to its radical planets, and to the houses in which the aspect operates. Day-by-day aspects are still less significant to an individual, unless they are seen as "transits" proper—that is, referred to the natal chart. Everywhere the genius of astrology is to be found in correlations, in groupings, in balancing lights against shadows, blacks against whites, formative against destructive agencies—accepting all of them equally as functions of the organic wholeness of the whole, discriminating against none—yet, let us not forget, accepting every element of being as valid *only* when such an element is in its proper place at the proper time.

Perhaps a musical analogy will help focalize our meaning. We spoke of the birth-chart as the "chord of individual being;" and, at least by implication and together with our previously studied time-analysis, as the score of the symphony in which *being* and *becoming* interplay for the purpose of ever fuller and more manifest wholeness. What the astrologer should discover is the "tonality" of chord and symphony. It is this tonality of which we spoke a moment ago as "the

The Astrology of Personality

organic relationship of relations between parts." Only he who can uncover this individual tonality of a personality and a destiny may be called a real astrologer. For thus only can he prove that he has the power of "holistic perception" which reveals to him the wholeness of every whole.

Concerning the Procedure of Interpretation

From the point of view of the analytical phase of interpretation—and there should *always* be such a phase, were it only in order to check up on what is revealed by "holistic" perception—very little needs to be added to what has been already said in previous chapters. The two fundamental steps of the analysis refer respectively to the "subjective form," constituted by the relation of the dial of houses to the signs of the zodiac (viz., the zodiacal positions of the cusps, intercepted signs, etc.), and to the "objective form," constituted by the zodiacal positions (signs and degrees) and house positions of the planets, singly and as a group. These two steps in the analysis are to be followed by a third one, as the result of which secondary "factors of relation" between planets, planetary orbits and cusps will be determined: Nodes and Parts.

Then comes what we have called the "time-analysis of the birth-chart," establishing a general "structure of becoming" as an expression of the fundamental individuality of the native. This should be followed and modified by a study of the periods determined or suggested by the progressed motions of all the radical planets, and by the transiting motions of the slower planets (Pluto, Neptune, Uranus, Saturn, Jupiter) through the expected span of the native's life.

We purposely said "a study of the *periods*" of these progressed and transiting planets; for what is valuable at this stage of the process of interpretation is to determine the general form of the becoming of the personality, and a general formula showing the cycles during which the outer world (the collective—society—planetary conditions) will further,

480

and those during which it will hinder (or deepen through opposition and strain), the development of the personality as a whole and in relation to its several basic functions.

The periods of planetary progressions are the component factors in this "form of becoming of the personality"—and not any particular aspect between two progressed planets. A particular aspect situated in a particular sign and house (or usually in two particular signs and houses) may have significance in terms of a particular type of event or trend of events. But this significance is so intermingled with the meaning of a dozen other factors, there are so many possible ways of interpreting its probable operation and of locating it, either in the physiological or in the psychological realm—either in terms of emphasis through *lack* of something, or emphasis through *too much* of that thing—that an absolutely accurate prognostication of events through progressions, directions or transits is practically impossible. It is possible and startlingly accurate in *some* cases; but woefully inaccurate, either in the time element or in the manner of its actualization, in just as many other cases. When, therefore, one realizes the great influence, psychologically speaking, that a prediction may exert upon a sensitive person—and we all are subject to influence, some unconsciously, others consciously—one should also realize how nefarious a wrong prediction may be.

The value of astrology does not depend upon its predictive accuracy, for then it would have relatively little value, save in the hands of spectacularly gifted astrologers, able, through a combination of "horary" and "natal" astrology, to "hit the mark" in an amazingly great proportion of cases. It depends rather upon the fact that it provides us with "formulas" of being (birth-chart) and of becoming (time-analysis, progressions, etc.) which enable us to extract the most significance out of what *is* happening or what *has* happened. If we assimilate that significance thoroughly, we are then able to face whatever *will* happen: 1) with an integrated, unified front; 2) as a bestower of creative significance. By so doing we shall be able to "transfigure" the future; not changing the "form" of our being or becoming, but making that form glow with meaning, harmony and light—as Jesus glowed on the Mount of Transfiguration. He shone with Christ-light, with the power of universal energies and contents—yet He remained in form and individuality, Jesus: Jesus who had become "Christed."

To go back, however, to the periods of progressions. If we see in Mussolini's chart that at the age of 46 his progressed Sun will conjoin Uranus and trine Neptune, that may not give us so much direct information as to events then likely to occur. In fact, as far as can be gleaned from his outer life, relatively little has corresponded at that age to a progressed aspect which should be capital in Mussolini's life, inasmuch as the trine Uranus to Neptune encompasses all his planets and thus plays a most basic part in his being and destiny. It is true that the agreement with the Pope was signed (February 11, 1929) around the time of maturation of the progressed aspects; but granted that this is the correlation wanted, how could an astrologer studying the chart, say in 1900, have predicted such a concrete event? Moreover, why should this Lateran treaty be of such significance astrologically in Mussolini's destiny? However, we may approach the above-mentioned solar progressions in another way.

We can determine the aspects made by the progressed Sun ever since birth. To begin with the later ones: In 1916 the progressed Sun squares the radical Saturn; in 1917 the radical Moon, in 1922 the radical Mars; in 1923 it comes to conjunction Part of Fortune; in 1927 to sextile Jupiter; then in 1929 to trine Neptune and conjunction Uranus; and in 1930 to sextile Venus. Then *periods* of progressions are determined by considering the time elapsing between two aspects. The period of Sun-Moon square operates from 1916 to 1917; the period of Sun-Mars square ends in 1922. Finally, the Sun-

Part of Fortune conjunction period begins witnessing the "march upon Rome" and Mussolini's accession to personal power.

The periods before this last one are all based on square aspects—ever since the square of progressed Sun to Neptune in 1898 (age 15); and before this series of squares, there were only sextiles (to Moon and Mars). This at once establishes—from the point of view of the basic solar progressions—several well-marked life cycles. Up to the age of 15, a period of sextiles—the routine of growth through maternal influence (Moon) and paternal influence (Mars). Then from 1898 to the early spring of 1922 we have a period of struggle to bring down into manifestation an ideal, the struggle to be born as a figure of destiny: all squares, symbols of incarnation and involution.

The year 1922 is dominated by a new type of aspect: the first solar conjunction—with the Part of Fortune. This now means "emphasis." Emphasis on what? On what the Part of Fortune represents. The Part of Fortune is the "Ascendant" of the Moon. It "distributes" and focalizes the Moon's power. Moon represents the life of the personality as an element of becoming; it represents also "the public," the collective confronting the individual. Thus the period of emphasis or accentuation shown by the conjunction Sun-Part of Fortune focalized the power of the collective upon Mussolini's individuality, accentuated the power of his own personality. In the tenth house it emphasized authority and public activity; in Virgo, a cleansing process (even symbolized by the Fascists' using castor oil on unwilling politicians).

It would be futile, however, to find a day or month when this conjunction specifically operates. What is to be understood is rather the general meaning of a period. Likewise, when we speak of the sextile progressed Sun-Jupiter, we refer to the period of 1923-1927, a period of establishment (sextile) of authority (Jupiter). Then from 1927 to 1929 we come to the period progressed Sun-trine-Neptune and conjunction Uranus. Obviously, we have then a period during which the power of the collective unconscious is predominant. All Mussolini's planets are enclosed within the trine Neptune-to-Uranus. As the Sun comes to conjunction Uranus it obviously ends a period of *personal* emphasis and reaches beyond into the unknown, as it were; into that which is unaccentuated and not brought out by planetary activities. Mussolini reaches then beyond what he is as a personality; but before he does that he has rounded up his personal life by taking steps which close one period and open another. This is the meaning of the Lateran Treaty—a ubiquitous, subtle, Neptunian meaning; and of the definite establishment of the Italian "corporate State" which, though outlined during the Jupiter period (1926-1927), becomes implanted into the mind of the nation and its collective unconscious only after 1927.

The period of the sextile Sun to Venus is also a very short one. It presumably refers to Mussolini's emotional life; yet adds conscious individual meaning to that which at first referred to great unconscious factors (under the Sun to Uranus-Neptune aspects). After this, a new period begins, characterized by the coming trine of progressed Sun to Pluto, then to Saturn, Moon and Mars. These periods are expansional. They refer to the formation of new ideals, of new relationships, new alliances. The future will show whether they are to be interpreted positively or negatively. In 1939 the progressed Sun is scheduled to enter Libra; Mussolini will be then 56. A period of his life which began in 1908, when he went to Trento, will then end.

A similar analysis could be worked out by considering not only the progressed Sun, but all progressed planets; again by studying the periods constituted by the motions of the slow planets, after birth, as they transit over important places in the radical chart. Here we have, of course, a very complex and multifarious series of aspects, and the greatest care has to be exerted in order to isolate the most significant factors. But the idea that periods are more significant than the exact aspects marking their boundaries is also valid—especially as with slow-transiting planets these are periods during which, because of alternation of direct and retrograde motion, they pass back and forth over sensitive points of the charts. Periods determined by the transiting motion of a slow planet through a whole house are particularly significant. They show the way in which circumstances and collective forces basically affect the various phases of individual being and destiny—phases symbolized by the houses.

Then there are also to be considered the 28-year and 7-year cycles of the axes of the chart, especially what we called the cyclic motion of the Point of Self. These cycles can be studied in terms of their beginning, their mid-point and their conclusion. They show the inner workings of the process of individuation at its three successive levels—sometimes referring to concrete happenings, but then only insofar as they focalize critical transitions in the general process.

Finally, the primary directions and certain precise transits (as eclipses and multiple conjunctions) can be studied to sharpen the contours of the picture already drawn. There is a school of astrologers who lay the basic emphasis upon primary directions, and who therefore would very much object to our relegating them to the end of the process of interpretation; but they must not forget that our "time-analysis of the birth-chart," which we placed first in the study of *becoming*, gives general indications similar to or almost identical with those found through the simplest method of directing (or through the Radix directions). These, we believe, are not only as effective as the main primary directions, but because of their smaller number are much more valuable to a structural grasp of destiny as an individually determined and significant whole of *becoming*. The other types of directions may be very significant in a detailed analysis, or whenever a close study of the total correlations of astrological factors related to a known event or period of the life is required; and in such cases all the transits have also to be considered. But, for the psychological purposes of personality-integration and life-interpretation, which are the main motivations of our approach to astrology, primary directions of the complex type not only demand too much time and too many calculations, but their very multiplicity almost defeats their purpose; for where you have so much to choose from and to organize in order to determine events or meanings, the attention easily becomes scattered and essentials fade out, obnubilated by the pageant of non-essentials.

Focalization Through Chart-rulership

Before we conclude this chapter, one more point needs to be mentioned, as it occupies an important place in the practice of medieval and modern astrology: the matter of *planetary rulership*.

The principle of planetary rulership rests upon the idea that the basic modes of biological and psychological activity (planets) have various types of "affinity" for the basic types of life-substance (signs of the zodiac). Affinity of such kinds have been determined in traditional astrology, for reasons not always clear or philosophically evident. Thus a planet is said to "rule" one, or usually two, zodiacal signs, which are considered as the planet's "houses." It is said to be "exalted" in another sign. To these positive valuations are added negative ones. In the sign opposite from the sign of its rulership the planet is in its "detriment;" in that opposite from the sign of its exaltation it is said to be in its "fall." Positive valuations are named "dignities;" negative valuations, "debilities." The above-mentioned are the most important among dignities and debilities, they are "essential" dignities or debilities. To these, however, are added a series of "accidental" dignities or debilities, such as arise from the planet being in an angle and well aspected or not afflicted, from its being swift in motion, increasing in light, etc.

The value of such qualifications is obvious. It enables the astrologer to give *quantitative* valuations to the planets and thus to ascertain their relative importance and relative weight in a particular situation or in the make-up of a particular personality. Thus a "weak" Saturn will not be able to neutralize a "strong" Jupiter, and in all aspects between these planets the Jupiterian quality will have the greater weight. Thus a kind of third-dimensional perspective will emerge out of the recognition of this quantitative factor. Some planets will stand out like stars of first magnitude; others will recede into the background as stars of lesser magnitudes. Thus also a certain type of "focal determination" will become possible, as in the case of a most dignified planet among weak brothers or sisters.

Where the difficulty comes is in the philosophical or "holistic" justification of the traditional valuations. Because of such a difficulty, new systems of "rulership" are every so often devised, usually in an attempt to remedy two of the apparent weaknesses of the system: The fact that Sun and Moon rule only one sign each, while the other planets, up to and including Saturn, rule two signs each; and the other fact, i.e., that the newly discovered planets (Uranus, Neptune, Pluto) rule no definite sign; or if signs are attributed to them (as Aquarius to Uranus, and Pisces to Neptune), then two of the "older" planets are each left with only one sign to rule. The confusion, however, looks worse than it actually is, and we may be able to clear up much of the apparent difficulty.

First of all, we shall set down the traditional scheme of rulerships, as follows—adding at the outset that positive signs (every other sign beginning with Aries) are called the "day houses" of the planets, the negative signs the "night houses."

CHART A

POSITIVE SIGNS *(Day Houses)*	RULING PLANET	NEGATIVE SIGNS *(Night Houses)*
Leo ←	SUN – MOON	→ Cancer
Gemini ←	MERCURY	→ Virgo
Libra ←	VENUS	→ Taurus
Aries ←	MARS	→ Scorpio
Sagittarius ←	JUPITER	→ Pisces
Aquarius ←	SATURN	→ Capricorn

This at once shows that Sun and Moon are considered as a unit, in terms of rulership. They always have been put in a special category as: the "lights"—a valuation which is, as we often said, an expression of the old geocentric astrology interpreting celestial phenomena *as seen*, and not in terms of such a scientific intellectual knowledge as that which today constitutes heliocentric astronomy.

Now, we may repeat the same table, but this time giving to the three newly discovered planets the sign to rule which has seemed appropriate to most contemporary astrologers:

CHART B

+		—
Leo ←	SUN – MOON	→ Cancer
Gemini ←	MERCURY	→ Virgo
Libra ←	VENUS	→ Taurus
Aries ←	MARS – PLUTO	→ Scorpio
Sagittarius ←	JUPITER – NEPTUNE	→ Pisces
Aquarius ←	URANUS – SATURN	→ Capricorn

It is easy to see that what is happening is that, *following the example of the pair Sun-Moon*, each of the traditional planets is being given a "mate" to which one of the planet's two original "houses" is delegated as a domain over which to rule. From this a new type of planetary pairing is to be deduced. In a previous chapter we studied the traditional coupling of Saturn and Moon, Jupiter and Mercury, and Mars and Venus. We modified such an arrangement so that the Earth became consistently the center or hinge of the coupling of "inner" and "outer" planets: Mars-Venus, Jupiter-Mercury, Saturn-Solar photosphere;—and the three "planets of the unconscious"—Heart of the Sun. In this latter scheme, deduced from the structure of the solar system as known to modern astronomy, the Moon—as a satellite of the Earth—becomes the factor of linkage between the intra-orbital and the extra-orbital planets.

And now we see another type of coupling emerging from *Chart B.* Because Sun and Moon were respectively the "light of day" and the "light of night," the Sun logically rules a positive (day) sign, and the Moon a negative (night) sign. From this can be derived a general explanation of the emergent process of polarization of *all* planetary rulerships.

Let us reconsider *Chart A,* and imagine that the Moon is not included, and that the Sun has its day and its night houses (Leo and Cancer), as all the other planets have. We have then the series of planets in their actual order, beginning with Sun and ending with Saturn (not, of course, counting our Earth). If, on the other hand, we correlate that series with the series of zodiacal signs *beginning with Leo*, we have a very orderly arrangement, into which the newly discovered planets fit well—except that Pluto is made to rule Aries and not Scorpio:

SUN	Leo	URANUS	Aquarius
MERCURY	Virgo	NEPTUNE	Pisces
VENUS	Libra	PLUTO	Aries
MARS	Scorpio	?	Taurus
JUPITER	Sagittarius	?	Gemini
SATURN	Capricorn	(MOON)	Cancer

We believe that such an arrangement is most significant, but only in terms of Man-the-Individual; or of consciousness. The first six terms of both series refer to the conscious. Starting in Leo on the path to *individualization* with great solar spontaneity, Man reaches in Capricorn full and concrete individualization as an "I am"—in a personal or a planetary sense. Then he begins to assimilate the beyond, the contents of the collective unconscious—and this is the path to *individuation*. Through Uranus, universals pour into the particular ego; through Neptune, the walls of the ego become translucent to the beyond (or they dissolve altogether, most unfortunately); through Pluto, a new beginning is made: the universal Order is born at the core of the transfigured particular. The Moon, at the end of this incomplete series, obviously stands for that principle of *universal relationship* which marks the end of the path to individuation; just as Saturn stood for the principle of relationship-within-a-set-form which marks the end of the path to individualization. Obviously, the Moon is actually only the negative aspect of that principle of *universal relationship*. She symbolizes only physiological motherhood and the integration of elemental life-agencies; whereas whatever shall take her place at the end of the series that begins with Aquarius should represent spiritual Motherhood and the integration of universal Life-forces and Ideas at the psycho-mental or spiritual level—thus perhaps the Galaxy (Milky Way).

Looking at *Chart B* from another angle (and now reversing the places of Mars and Pluto), we can also say that Saturn is to Uranus, Neptune to Jupiter, and Mars to Pluto as the Moon is to the Sun. Stated in such a manner, the situation is also quite clear and significant. Uranus is the breath of the creative "I am" of which the merely conscious ego is but a sort of night-reflection; just as the Moon reflects in a pale way the integrative fire of the Sun. Likewise, Pluto represents cosmic beginnings in a way which Mars and its impulses, limited by physiological conditioning, reflect only faintly and in a personal way. As for the pair Jupiter-Neptune, it may be seen that the function of form-dissolution symbolized by Neptune has to be considered as a negative (or night-pole) of the Jupiterian function of expansion of the life-contents of the form.

However this may be, the above interpretation—while probably not acceptable to all—does at least give a coherent picture worth studying in all its implications. Other students of astrology may prefer Marc Jones' position, refusing to attribute any rulership to Uranus and Neptune or to any trans-Saturnian planets that may be discovered, because the very idea of rulership is not consistent with the meaning of such planets. Rulership is the symbol of organic relationship between activity and the organized substance involved in such activity; and where planets refer to the *trans-organic* (that which is beyond the limits of an organic whole) there can be no question of rulership. The answer to this, however, is that a super-physiological organism is forming in individuals who have reached a certain point in their development, and that the trans-Saturnian planets are trans-organic only insofar as the physiological organism is concerned, but are the very formative agencies which are building, in all men attuned to their positive-creative nature, a psycho-mental organism.*

The difficulty attending a coherent interpretation of planetary rulership is even more evident where the "exaltation" of planets in certain zodiacal signs, and their "ecstasy" on a

---

* It seems valuable to quote the explanation of planetary rulership which Marc Jones gives in his course *Temple Astrology* (Lesson XXV):

"What is here brought out is the existence of astrological domains, or boundaries of character which might be described as race character limits in and through which individual character is to be defined. Aries must always have some of the extension of Mars, and Pisces always some of the expansion of Jupiter, not through any necessity of astrology or the celestial scheme, but because the race has established itself in this fashion. The dignities of the planets involving a permanent relationship with the signs (for a 25,000-year cycle at least) are known as essential dignities, and when the planets are placed in positions of strength or weakness in terms of dignity the native is shown as tending towards or away from the racial norm upon which his well-being and proper growth is largely dependent. This modifies the interpretation of the known facts of his life as these are bent upon the problem of his horoscope, but of course the actual planetary significations remain absolute, with or without dignity."

certain degree of such signs, are concerned. So we shall pass on and discuss only briefly the main uses to which the theory of rulership has been put. It dominates completely the divinatory branch of astrology called "horary astrology"—and perhaps it is from horary astrology that it has come to "natal astrology," the only kind of astrology studied in this work. In natal astrology, the theory of planetary relationship not only creates a sort of linkage between planets and signs—which is very valuable theoretically and logically—but, as we saw, it serves as a means to invest some planets with the characteristics of "focal determinator." As such it has been used consistently in two manners; the first, very much in use today; the second, very seldom taken into consideration.

The first way of singling out a planet, to make it serve as a center of significance, is to find what is called the "ruling planet" or "ruler of the chart." This is usually determined by the sign of the Ascendant. The planet ruling this sign becomes the ruler of the whole chart. The *rationale* of this method is clear. The Ascendant represents the factor of individual selfhood, the monad, the fountainhead of the life and destiny which the chart as a whole symbolizes. Therefore the planet functionally dominating this Ascendant becomes naturally the dominant life-function of the personality. However, in the case of planets rising close to the Ascendant, or when a planet, wherever situated in the chart, "disposes" of all or most other planets,* then two or more planets may divide the honors of chart-rulership.

The second way of singling out a planet as a focal point of the interpretation is the determination of the *Almuten*. The

---

* A planet "disposes" of any other which may be found in the sign which it rules or in which it is exalted. In Mussolini's chart the Sun is in its own "house" Leo and disposes of Mercury, also in Leo. But Mercury "disposes" of Pluto, Saturn, Moon and Mars in Gemini (ruled by Mercury) and of Uranus in Virgo (also ruled by Mercury). Then the Moon disposes of Jupiter and Venus which are in Cancer; and Venus disposes of Neptune in Taurus. Thus directly or indirectly the Sun is seen to dispose of all planets in the chart. It is co-ruler with Mars, ruler of the Ascendant.

Almuten is found by tabulating the essential and accidental dignities and debilities of each planet according to a set of quantitative valuations (5 points for this dignity, 3 points for that), subtracting the sum total of debilities from that of dignities (or vice versa), and thus discovering what planet has received the highest number. That planet is the strongest in the chart. It is said to determine the "temperament" of the native. The method is very similar to that for the determination of an I.Q.—and perhaps it works just as well—whatever that means in the reader's estimation! Mussolini's Almuten seems to be Saturn; with Jupiter a close second. This throws an interesting light on his personal character; in contradistinction to the character he has made himself as the vehicle for a super-personal, racial Idea.

While such types of "chart-rulership" are indeed susceptible of releasing a great deal of significance, we would rather stress the type of "focal determination" discussed in the chapter "Form and the Pattern of Planetary Aspects"—that is, a type which singles out some group-features of the chart as a whole, and considers that feature as the focal point of the interpretation. For instance, we would say that, in Mussolini's chart, the facts that all the planets are contained within a trine of Uranus to Neptune, and that all of them, save Uranus, are located in the South-West quarter, constitute the most significant "focal determination." These facts center the multifarious meanings of the many astrological elements around one primordial significance; and from that, a kind of interpretative perspective emerges which seems to us more valid or more revealing—at least in view of our approach to astrology—than that which would result from giving quantitative valuations of strength or weakness to every separate planet.

Conclusion

With this brief study of some of the main principles upon which a technique of astrological interpretation can be built, which would be consistent with our approach to astrology, we must bring to a close this section consecrated to a reformulation and reinterpretation of the fundamental elements of astrological symbolism. Astrology, defined as an algebra of life, is absolutely protean in its manifestation, and multifarious in the wide diversity of its approaches to particular phases of interpretation. Wherefore we feel most acutely how incomplete has been the reformulation presented in the chapters of this second section. Nevertheless we trust that fundamentals have been established on a coherent basis of both symbolical-logical and psychological understanding; and we may be able in some not too distant future to study at much greater length, and in relation to many more practical instances, some of the astrological factors the meaning of which we have here outlined.

Here again, however, we may add—as a final restatement—that astrology *in its essence* is not bound to any particular application or field of application; that its truths are not empirical in character nor dependent for their success on one realm of life or another. Physicists may conceivably find that their approach to the problem of determining the nature of the atom or of distant galaxies is all wrong, and that their experiments have been so devised as to leave out the main factor in intra-atomic or in cosmic behavior. Yet such a discovery would in no way invalidate group-algebra or any of the mathematical symbols which have been used to establish present-day interpretations, and could be used to build new theories. The number 10 remains a valid symbol even if the ten apples grouped by it into numerical relationship turn out to be peaches. Likewise consider a square of Jupiter to Saturn; we may now say that it refers to "spiritual testing and tribulations," but such a saying has validity only in terms of what we call "tests and tribulations" in our understanding of human psychology. Modify this psychology, and the meaning of the square will change.

And lastly, astrology does not offer interpretations as clear-cut and objective as does modern physics. The ideal of modern science is anonymity and objectivity—that is, the total suppression of the individual element. This does not mean, however, that modern science does not give us "interpretation;" for so-called "scientific laws" are, after all, generalized interpretations of processes and congeries of facts. But such generalized interpretations—arrived at by way of mathematical symbolization—are not considered really valid until there is left no known individual exception, and until a relatively absolute assurance that the future processes will always work out in terms of the laws is made possible *for every one concerned.*

As a result, modern science is obliged to ignore the individualness of every living entity. It reduces every such entity to its generic type, and ignores or denies the individual factor and its uniqueness. And what is unique in any living whole? At first, in the evolutionary process which leads from amoeba to man, it is only the most infinitesimal detail of organic disposition. Then, as evolution proceeds on its course toward greater differentiation, the small individual detail of super-structure is magnified until an organic system becomes adequately developed for individual differentiation. The individualistic super-structure not only coalesces with the generic structure, but more and more influences it.

Then in man we find, within his total organic structure, a generic under-structure (the Great Sympathetic system) and an individual super-structure (the cerebro-spinal system); and the latter is seen increasingly to dominate the former. Then we say that "mind rules matter;" which means mostly that the individual rules the generic or collective, especially when we refer to "mind" as "Universal Mind," which is merely the *operative* wholeness of the "Greater Individual" emerging slowly out of the planetary evolutionary process as a "Greater Person,"—the God-of-the-end of the planetary cycle.

Astrology, as we understand it, complements modern science, insofar as it deals essentially with the individual super-structure rather than with the generic-collective under-structure. Through the study of the "first moment" of the life-cycle it reaches individual being and individual form; and because it does so it is able also to unveil the mystery of significance, which is a purely individual factor. What it is able to grasp of the life-process of becoming itself, is principally in terms of *structural periods of destiny* rather than in terms of set concrete events. Nay more, astrology can only really know the way this process of becoming appears to the individual being. It does not know events in themselves so much as crises in the curve of an individual destiny. In other words, by this knowledge of *form* it reveals the individual to the individuating; and leads the individuating to a perception of the individual significance of individuation as a process.

This is what "life-interpretation" means. It is the perception of individual form and of individual significance by an evolving or individuating personality. This personality is a composite, an aggregation of factors and elements. As these become harmonized by such a "life-interpretation," revealing their potential individual form and significance, the fulfilled and integrated Living Person emerges. Again let us repeat that it is the emergence of this Living Person which constitutes the goal of astrology—or at least of that astrology which we called "Harmonic Astrology." Some further facts related to such an emergence will be discussed in the following "Epilogue."

EPILOGUE

The Use of Astrology in the Processes of Individuation and Civilization

W E HOPE that, throughout the whole of our discussion and reformulation of the philosophy, the symbolism and the technique of astrology, one thing has been made to stand out in clear relief: The fact that the validity and power of astrology depend primarily on the manner in which it is made to serve the universal goal of "more wholeness"—the goal of individuation for the particular man, and the goal of Living Civilization for humanity as a whole. As a system of coherent symbolism, astrology is a most fascinating intellectual study; as a system of divination, it is a remarkable tool for scrutinizing the fringe of future events; as an historical phenomenon it is unique in allowing us to fathom the mentality of more or less distant cultures—in space as well as in time. And yet, unless astrology is *put to use* as a revealer of vital significances and of patterns of organic (or generally, *holistic*) relationships, as a means of probing the secret formulas of all beginnings with the view to leading us to a better consummation—in other words, as a technique of personality-integration—it remains a merely intellectual speculation (as would be an algebra which could not be applied to any group of empirical data)—or else a dangerous game of fortune-telling.

In many ways and in many places we have expressed this view. On the basis of it we have stressed the connection between astrology and psychology—and, had we had the space for it, we might have discussed the relations between astrology and all the arts of physical healing; or else we could have studied the place which astrology might occupy in other arts, which all together constitute the foundation of "culture"— from agriculture to the fine arts. We say here purposely "arts" and not "sciences." For applied astrology, being an art of interpretation based upon: 1) scientific data; 2) a logic of symbolism—it deals essentially with the artistic approach to life, rather than with the scientific. There is no real "science" of living. Medicine, for instance, is not a science, properly speaking, but an art based on the interpretation of data scientifically determined. Analytical psychology is not a science, but an art of interpretation of empirical facts scientifically collected and analyzed. The term "science" should be reserved for so-called "exact sciences," such as physics, mechanics and astronomy, on one hand, and on the other, for "abstract sciences," such as logic and mathematics. Every *applied* science becomes an art whenever the element of individual interpretation enters in. The more predominant it is, the more truly it is an art—an interpretative art.

Be this as it may, the fact is that astrology, as we have studied it in the second part of this book, is essentially related to psychology, and its main purpose is to contribute to the successful completion of the Great Work of man—that by which man reaches fulfillment and operative wholeness, and as a result becomes an organic function or cell within a greater Whole—the "Greater Individual" or the "Planetary Individual," or the Seed-Manu, or the Logos, or God—as one may wish to name this next greater Whole of which the spiritually *perfected* human personality becomes a part. In this concluding section we shall define, more completely than before, the relation between astrology and psychology, especially in terms of the complementary manner in which both may serve toward the above-defined goal. Then we shall outline more specifically astrology's contribution to the achievement of that goal: 1) for the human personality treading the path to individuation; 2) in reference to the new civilization in the making, and to the process of group-formation which is to play so important a part in it.

The Astrological and Psychological Viewpoints Correlated

We refer the reader, first of all, to the chapter: "Individual, Collective, Creative," etc., in which the basis for a correlation between astrology and analytical psychology is established; also to the preceding chapter in which the basic elements of Jung's psychology are briefly stated. In the former we produced a formula which defines the various phases of any and all life-cycles, and we isolated the three basic terms of the Cycle: *beginning, middle* and *end*, corresponding to the One-that-is-in-the-beginning—the process of becoming—the seed-synthesis (Cf. especially page 161 "Summing up"). Without attempting to repeat our statements, we shall now say that the main difference between the astrological and the psychological approaches is that while the latter sees nothing but the "process of becoming whole" as it unfolds in Bergsonian duration through myriads of transformations, the former claims that the ultimate wholeness reached at the end of the process is already there at the very beginning of the process, but *only* as an abstract ideal and a mere potentiality.

If we refer to the trinity of elements which we then defined (Cf. p. 143)—*quality, structure* and *substance*—we shall realize that quality or monad at the beginning relates to, or is projected into, substantial elements which slowly organize themselves as organic bodies through an evolutionary process. This process lasts throughout the cycle and ends, *if successful*, in the perfecting of a body (at the physiological level) and a Soul (at the psycho-mental level) which are the very exteriorization and manifestation of the initial monad, now operating as the Self. Thus the beginning and the end are identical as far as the quality is concerned; but in the end this quality is fully manifest in a substantial body, while in the beginning it is only an abstract potentiality.

From the point of view of spirit (unity), the purpose of the process is to give to the monad a new creative experience and to fulfill relationships unfulfilled in the past cycle or cycles. From the point of view of substance (multiplicity), the purpose of the process is to organize the many elements that constituted the residua of past cycles into a perfect body built in the likeness of God-the-monad. From the point of view of structure, or form, or mind, the process is an esthetical experience of beauty and rhythm.

Analytical psychology takes the point of view of substance, as all empirical sciences do. It deals with the ever-changing process of relationship between individual and collective. All psychological conflicts, repressions, sublimations and assimilations are results of the working out of this process; all evolution likewise. But the initial quality, which antedates the process, does not fundamentally change. The individual structure exteriorizing this quality does not change during the span of the cycle. The wholeness of the end is latent in the monad of the beginning. It is not only latent. It actually is at work within the very heart of the process as the central power of individuation. The energy of the One operates at the core of every one of the Many issued from this One— even though the Many know it not. Thus, in a definite sense, the wholeness of the future whole is acting upon the progressive building of this whole. Past and Future *as one* operate within the present. The finished end of the process is latent in the beginning; *but only provided the process is successful.* And no one can tell whether or not it will be successful in a particular cycle.

The last statements have an essential bearing on the nature and value of astrology. More than that, they are the key to a reconciliation of the old enemies: free will and determinism. They are implied in the philosphy of Time which we sketched out in the first part of this work.

We wrote that every monad is the creative projection of a

moment, the initial moment of this monad's cycle. The potency of the moment exteriorizes itself in the monads which at that very moment begin their individual cycles of becoming. It is as if Time held a bag of seeds, from which at every moment seeds would drop which would be formed in the likeness of the nature of that moment. Each seed is a dynamic and structural potentiality of being. Each drops, as an individual unit (monad), into the soil of the collective; just as moments drop into the past. All these seeds are acted upon by a multitude of influences, which either help or hinder the process of their development from potentiality to actuality, from seed to fulfilled and blossoming plant.

Myriads of seeds never develop. Myriads of seeds begin to develop whose growth is stunted, thwarted or ended by the unsuccessful working out of the relation between their individual selfhood and the collective. That is to say, the personalities are stunted, thwarted or destroyed. In the personality there is a certain amount of free will, insofar as the monad (which is pure, free and spontaneous creative activity) is active—that is, insofar as the individual factor dominates the collective.

If the seed develops into a complete plant, then there is no way for the plant to be anything else in actuality save what the seed was in potentiality—even though the plant may be either more or less sturdy and perfect in its proportions. There is no outside agency or God to determine beforehand: 1) whether there will actually be a full-grown plant; 2) how perfect this full-grown plant will be, if it is at all. But the seed determines the organic structure and characteristics of the finished plant.

The acorn is not free to become an apple tree; and the seed of the oak is absolutely certain to be an acorn. But no one can tell whether a particular acorn will become an oak. It may not even matter. What seems to matter is that a certain number of acorns will keep the oak species manifest, perhaps in a definite numerical strength. Likewise prophetic books, for instance, are wont to say that one-third of the men will be saved, two-thirds lost. It does not seem to matter who in particular will be saved or lost—at least not to the whole of the species. It matters very much, of course, to the individual who is free to choose—free to choose *whether he will become what he is potentially*, or will not. No one is ever free to become successfully what one *is not*. To become what one is not always means to fail to be at all. Either fulfillment of potentialities or failure is inherent in the monad (therefore in the birth-moment). These potentialities inherent in the monad and in the birth-moment can be found symbolized in the birth-chart.

Most people have an "individualistic" but not an "individuated" conception of "freedom."* Freedom is the inherent capacity of fulfilling the potential characteristics of one's individual selfhood. It is not the power to do what it may please one to do. For "pleasing" here refers merely to the ego at its stage of rebellion against any life-contents. Such rebellion means often the desire to do the most silly, meaningless things. This is not freedom, but the result of that phase of "individualization" which is purely negative and separative. "I shall not have anything to do with collective values," says the budding individual. But the mature individual says, on the other hand: "I shall bring the collective to the focalization of my own selfhood, and give it my own significance."

The birth-chart of an individual is the symbol of his freedom, because it is the symbol of *what he is*. The more free an individual, the more perfectly and sharply (sharp, as to outlines) he is what he is, the more clear-cut the form of his individual selfhood, and thus of his behavior. The collective always tends to blur the outlines of any individual selfhood. Therefore it works against the freedom of the individual

---

* For a distinction between "individualization" and "individuation" read again p. 108 in the chapter "Astrology and Analytical Psychology."

unless the individual can "assimilate" the collective contents of his surroundings and his ancestry—that is, unless he can make them "similar to" what he, essentially and archetypally, *is*: a tremendous task in our *Dark Ages*, or as the Hindu has it, *Kali Yuga*; a task the nature and magnitude of which are hardly ever recognized, yet which conditions the entire spiritual development of the personality and the success of the individual in being at the same time true to his structural pattern of selfhood and rich with living contents—all of which had to be assimilated.

These considerations determine the scope of astrology. The birth-chart reveals the *potential structure of the monad*; that is the purely individual element in the native; hence the element of freedom and significance, which is the *spiritual* endowment of every human being. But the birth-chart will not tell whether this potentiality will ever become an actuality, whether or not the process of individuation will be successful. Nevertheless, as we have already written in the chapters on "Progressions," the birth-chart will tell what will be the form and quality of the Soul, *if* it comes to be; also what will be the general cycles of unfoldment of the personality and its crises of growth. But it can never tell, from purely astrological factors, and barring the use of prophetic faculties, whether the crises will be successfully met, and if they are met, what will be the psychic residua accumulating in the personal unconscious as a result of the stress and strain.

What astrology cannot tell on purely astrological grounds analytical psychology can often infer from the data it investigates. The analyst deals directly with the personality, as it becomes and has become. And if the personality has reached a certain age, and if its individual selfhood has been little active, the analyst can quite accurately deduce what the rest of the life will be. The astrologer could tell the analyst *when* the next crises will come; but cannot tell him, from the birth-chart and progressions only, *how* the personality will meet these crises. The analyst cannot say when the crises will come, but can surmise how the personality will meet certain inevitable crises. In other words, the astrologer and the analyst look at two different aspects of the total human being. *Their points of view complete each other*. And they complete each other in the same way in which empirical science and religion (or occultism) complete each other.

Such a statement does not invalidate the conclusions of earlier chapters as to the analogy existing between the relation of mathematics to physics, and the relation of astrology to analytical psychology. Both mathematics (or logic) and astrology deal with "pure form," which exists only "in the beginning" as the abstract structure exteriorizing the quality-monad which is the nucleus of the future life-process. On the other hand, physics and analytical psychology deal with the realm of phenomena and becoming, with the constantly changing formations of the life-process. Abstract "form" does not become; but evolutionary "formations" and bodies do constantly change—and thus, from the point of view of spirit (Hindu philosophy), they are the result of the deterioration of primordial being and truth—thus they are false and illusory. But from the point of view of substance, "abstract form" is merely an intellectual idea, a product of the will to stability and preservation which is inherent in man and which leads so often to a shrinking from reality. Reality, for substance, is the changing world-process. But reality, for spirit, is the changeless (changeless insofar as the whole cycle is concerned) monadic structure.

This duality of point of view is an expression of the eternal ineradicable dualism of all living. In *Psychological Types*, C. G. Jung studies critically many aspects of this basic dualism—as for instance realism and nominalism in medieval philosophy. He points out that they are two basically irreconcilable attitudes which are the outcome of two fundamental psychological types: introvert and extravert.

In other words, he attempts to effect a kind of reconciliation between opposites of thought by referring them to differences in psychological types. Then he tries to show how the basic impulses motivating each type can be integrated within the personality through the operation of a "transcendent function," through "creative phantasy." This fits in well with our trinity of *individual, collective, creative.* The introvert is a personality in whom the balance of forces shows an emphasis upon the process of individuation. The extravert is a personality in whom collectivation is the dominant process. But in the true "creative act" individual and collective join hands. The collective ideas of the past become focalized and individuated within the psycho-mental womb of the creator, and at the same time are released creatively as new collective elements, as the "stuff of civilization," thus becoming eventually the very substance of the ultimate synthesis of Man-the-whole. In the introvert, life operates inward; in the extravert, outward. But in the creator, it operates *"in and through."* The creator, at his highest, is what Hindu wisdom names an "avatar." The avatar is not only the "hypostasis" of a "greater Individual." It is the answer to a collective need; it is the answer, through an individual, to a collective need which the individual focalized within himself—a need, *by fulfilling which, he overcame.*

Speaking, now, strictly in terms of practical method, we claim that astrology could be most helpful to the psychoanalyst, to the psychiatrist, and as well, of course, to the educator, who, if successful, must be, first of all—intuitively if not intellectually—a psychologist. It would give them something *objective* to depend upon, and with which to check upon subjective data, such as dreams and the details of a person's life-story. It would coordinate all these subjective data in terms of structural tendencies of the psyche; tendencies, the cycle of manifestation of which would become objectively apparent, with their waxing and waning movements and their critical moments. It is true that fore-knowledge of psychological or physiological crises may be very dangerous and disintegrating to the person in whom they are to occur—dangerous in proportion as he is not an individual, and therefore is neither free nor creative of meanings; but it would be of vast significance to the analyst or "life-counsellor" who, in this century, is taking the place of priest-confessor or *guru*. Even if such "guides" are to be endowed *a priori* with a keen intuition—if they be true "guides"! —yet the birth-chart and progressions of those they attempt to lead toward fulfillment would in most cases be invaluable adjuncts to and checks on their intuitive perceptions.

This may be even more obvious in the case of the "child-psychologist;" for here there are practically no subjective data to go by, except those given by the parents. The charts of the parents, when correlated with that of the child, would reveal matters that only a thorough "analysis" of the parents would uncover. We shall again discuss this matter of correlations between two or more individual charts; but we can see at once how conjugal problems could be solved much more easily if the psychologist could compare the charts of husband and wife. In many cases, the knowledge obtained by the psychologist through astrological means—and generally speaking by any type of "healer"—would not be discussed as such with the patient; but it would add *a new dimension*, as it were, to the understanding which the analyst gains of his patient. In other cases, with patients convinced of the validity of astrology, reference to definite astrological factors would probably "bring a point home" in a more impressive way than do the usual suggestions.

In such cases, however, it should be clear that *whenever a person feels that planets are entities that influence him and cause things to happen, good or bad,—such a person is psychologically hurt by such a belief.* The same injury, psychologically speaking, would be caused were the person to believe that a "black magician" is pursuing him or her, or that a "white brother" is providing him with soul-salvation or other boons of one type or another. All such beliefs in *outside powers* influencing, or (as is usually the case) compelling, the personality in this or that manner constitute deteriorations of individual selfhood; they lead to psychological slavery through fear or through transference of the power of initiative, or colloquially speaking, through "passing the buck" to some entity outside of the self.

If Mars as a tangible planet is influencing or compelling you to be angry, what is there you can do about it? Can you fight a planet? Can you hide from it? Perhaps you will do as did a Brahmin who thought of escaping a death-dealing planetary aspect by remaining immersed under water during the exact moment of the aspect's maturation, because water is supposed to insulate from certain planetary magnetic influences—and was drowned in the process. Perhaps you will try to "buy" protection from some spiritual agency, church or what-not. And all the time the *fear* will be there, working in you subconsciously, if not consciously—causing the very things that are feared. The more a baneful astrological factor is made into a definite entity, the greater will be the fear of it. For there may seem to be no recourse against such an entity—even though one might repeat a hundred times: "The wise man rules his stars!" Can you "rule" a tornado or an earthquake? Can you forbid an eclipse to occur on your birthday? Can you "rule" cosmic emanations, waves and the like, that sweep from the Sun and "hit" this or that sensitive center in your charts—if those are actual, concrete, measurable forces?

There is indeed no logic in the concept—unless it be taken to mean what Paracelsus said it meant in an excerpt quoted in our first chapter (p. 32): "The stars force nothing into us that we are not willing to take . . . They are free for themselves and we are free for ourselves . . ." In that sense, what is established by astrology is merely a holistic correspondence and a synchronistic relation of process between macrocosm and microcosm, between the universal Person that some call "God" and the particular personality that is man. The life-process, in other words, runs through the universal at the same time as it does through the myriads of particulars. Both are geared, as it were, to the creative moment, of which the spirit in man is the very expression. The moment operates through man's monad and through man's essential archetypal structure (which is his *karma*). That moment *contains* in potency the whole of the celestial pattern of planetary and spatial relationships. When we read the "chart of the Heavens" we merely read the symbolic structure of the moment—and therefore of our own spirit, if the moment considered happens to be our first moment of independent existence, i.e., the beginning of the cycle of our individual selfhood as an organism integrating Earth-materials.

In other words, what "influences" us is only the *moment*, and above all our *first* moment of selfhood. We can read the characteristics of this moment by interpreting the pattern constituted by the celestial bodies surrounding the place of our birth; this pattern represents the visible structural projection of the universal Whole, insofar as this Whole—of which we are a part—concerns us. But no material celestial body affects us *as an individual*. What acts upon our personality—body and psyche—is the creative power of the moment. And this creative power of the moment of birth is our very monad.

Of course there are myriads of moments that follow for us this first moment of selfhood. Such moments are parts of our "life-process" of development, and must be differentiated from the birth-moment which is our individual monad; and also from the death-moment which is a recapitulation and a synthesis. They add *contents* to our personality; but they do not basically alter the archetypal *structure* of our individual selfhood.

These moments of the life-process are symbolized in astrology by the transits. And transits do not affect the structure of our individual selfhood; they symbolize the power which every successive moment of the life-process after our birth has to modify the contents of our personality. Such a "power of modification" is not *fate!* No more than is the fact that each season and geographical location offers to you its own foodstuffs for eating and assimilation. Out of a variety of foodstuffs you can extract by digestion the same basic chemicals which your body needs in order to preserve its organic structure intact. True, some foods may fatten you, others cause you physiological ills—and in that sense you, as a psycho-physiological organism, are affected by the foodstuffs which season and geographical location provide. But *if* your organism is originally healthy, it will have the power to maintain itself and to function creatively on almost any kind of food and in almost any kind of climate; for the healthy organism can extract what it needs from the food provided, and if necessary can transform what it gets to suit its organic purpose. For instance, Arctic explorers have lived exclusively on animal food for over a year, their organism transforming chemically the animal protein into chemicals which normally are derived from starchy foods.

The same applies to any astrological transit—because it applies to what any moment of our life, as it were, projects into our psycho-physiological personality. Each moment provides us with "psychic foodstuffs" (or more generally, experiences), the nature of which we can ascertain from a study of the pattern of celestial bodies at that moment. Some of them may "agree" with us better than others. Some usually tend to cause indigestion; others, we seem unable to assimilate or perhaps even to ingest. And so life is made more or less satisfying to our personal tastes.

Yet this does not mean fate; for in proportion as we are originally whole (healthy), so shall we be able to extract from the food of every experience the psychological elements which we need in order to complete the process of life-fulfillment and individuation. And therefore, to that extent, we are unaffected by and free from the power of moments—and of their symbols, the stars. To the extent to which we are whole as "lesser individuals"—to that extent shall we be unaffected by and free from the conditioning imposed upon us by our position in the organism of the "Greater Individual" of whom we are a part.

But what if we are not whole and originally healthy? This then refers to our monad and its *karma*; and *karma* is nothing more mysterious than the archetypal structure exteriorizing the particular quality of this monad, which quality in turn is an expression of the first moment of individual selfhood— the One-that-is-in-the-beginning. This, then, is our "fatality": that we are what we are. Obviously, the term fatality in this sense is rather meaningless. Spiritually speaking, I cannot *realize* myself as what I am not. I can, of course, make *intellectual* pictures of my *personality* being different from what this personality actually is. But *I* am making these pictures; and I am not going out of myself by making them. I am merely playing with colored phantasms, building castles in the air; "compensating" for certain psychological conditions which are integral parts of what I am. Therefore the "compensation," as well as all my dreams, are integral parts of what I am. My sense of being oppressed by fate is part of what I am. It is merely the reaction of some parts of my total being to other parts with which they are in discordant or dissonant relation.

In another sense, this is the same situation which Bergson discusses at the end of his *Creative Evolution*, when he proves that we cannot really conceive "chaos." Chaos is to us always the absence of a particular order, and a type of order which compensates for all the types of order which we normally expect. Likewise all the things "we should like to be" are merely reactions of certain parts of our total being to other parts thereof; and these reactions themselves are thus parts of our total being.

In other words, selfhood and destiny are two aspects of the same whole, which, to use modern terms, is a time-space continuum within the greater time-space continuum which is the universe. These two continua interact at every point; just as whole and parts always interact at every point of the organism. If a part is originally weak, it will tend to break down easily under the pressure of the demands made upon it by the whole. On the other hand, because of that, the whole will tend to protect more carefully that part which is the weak link in the chain of its organic relationships, and is thus a dangerous point, an "Achilles' heel." Therefore, as already said, an "easy" birth-chart means little release of power from the greater Whole in which we are parts; a "difficult" birth-chart, a great release of such spiritual power. The principle of compensatory action—which is basic in the consideration of any organic whole—is here exemplified.

The sense of fate is thus merely the reaction of a part of the whole being to a situation which involves *a priori* this very sense of fate. It is merely a sense of internal pressure: just as the sense of freedom is a sense of external release. It is an organic sense—usually both at the psychological and at the physiological level, but at times with an emphasis upon one or other of them. The fact remains that—I am what I am. But, let us not forget, this I-am-ness refers to the *form* of self, not to the *contents* of personality. This form may be so universal and adaptable that it may give room to a vast multiplicity of contents—so that the personality may seem truly all-encompassing and all-understanding in its universality. But *a form it must be*; and that form is the structural conditioning of the wholeness that is the fully developed I-am-ness. That form is the exteriorization of the quality which emanated from the moment which was the initial point of the cycle of that I-am.

Why, then, can a Christ-like person and an unprepossessing human being be born at the same moment—or about the same moment? Because in the first case, the structure of selfhood focalizes and releases universal energies from the "Greater Individual;" whereas in the second case, such a structure is a heavy armature, which does not allow any adaptation to universal conditioning, and practically no assimilation of life-contents. There may be a relative identity of structure (many scoundrels look just like Christs, as far as the structure of the head goes); but in the first case that structure is filled in with glorious light; in the second case it is empty and burdened with its own weight. Can astrology ever determine from a birth-chart whether the personality it symbolizes is glowing with universal contents or is empty and dark? *Astrology cannot*. Any more than astrology alone and unaided can say whether a given chart refers to the birth of a cow or of a human being.

Astrology does not deal primarily with life-contents, but only with the structure of individual selfhood. It is, strictly speaking, as *formal* a system of knowledge as algebra. Its formulas apply to any contents—*therefore they do not embody fate*. For this reason, astrology needs psychological analysis, which deals with empirically determined personal contents. Astrology is the male element: that which gives the formula. Psychology is the female element: that which gives the substantial contents. Thus they complement each other in the determination of, and for the purpose of serving the integration of, the whole man: the Living Person.

Astrology and the Process of Individuation

The formulation of a technique by means of which astrology could serve as an essential factor in the process of individuation is outside the scope of this book. It is even doubtful whether mankind at large is prepared to make a constructive use of such a potential technique of integration. As in the case of all so-called "esoteric" techniques of spiritual development or personality integration which are featured in Theosophical, or Rosicrucian or, in general, "occult" groups, it seems necessary for those who would use such a technique to go about it in a steady and careful way, which requires some sort of personal guidance, or at least someone to answer questions and to check up results—physiological as well as psychological. This does not mean that techniques of integration are mysterious or veiled in glamor. They are, on the contrary, very matter-of-fact procedures; but relatively speaking, they are forced psychological processes depending, for the most part, on the use of creative imagination—and they may as easily "go wrong" as any type of psychoanalysis. Unless those who attempt them are either already integrated in their very depths, or are ready to go persistently and steadily "all the way," it would be much better that they did not begin at all.

This is quite evident even where the mere use of astrological symbolism and the casual reading of birth-charts and progressions are concerned. A little astrological knowledge is one of the worst things that can come to one who is not altogether solidly established in his own selfhood. The usual beginner in astrology often gets the queerest notions. He has not, as yet, digested the fundamentals of astrology—how few people really have!—and he is handling promiscuously, at home and in the company of his friends, psychological acids and explosives. That more harm is not done is due only to the fact that even those who read about or vaguely study astrology do not usually believe in it in any vital sense. They are therefore protected by their relative unbelief.

Any deliberate use of astrological symbols, and of one's birth-chart and progressions, for deep and vital purposes, would involve even more psychological danger. It should never be attempted unless one is thoroughly grounded in and convinced of the validity of the attitude which we have developed—much too briefly—in this book: the symbolical attitude. For this reason we cannot present in these pages a very coherent, and still less a complete picture of the way in which astrology could be used deliberately as a technique of individuation. However, various suggestions and leading points can be offered; and the following excerpts from some pamphlets of ours on *Harmonic Astrology* and *Harmonic Psychology* may prove valuable:

"We live in a world of symbols. Every object that surrounds us, every form of Intelligence, every soul, is a symbol. The Creative Principle perpetually produces living forms, forms which are truly works of art, which are symbolic representations of one or the other of the infinitely varied aspects of universal, all-encompassing Being.

"Contemporary psychology deals essentially with the interpretation of symbols. It attempts to free the psyche of man from the depressing and perverted images of the race subconscious, that is, from wrong interpretations of the essential symbols of human life—be it individual or collective—created by the past.

"In order to release in every individual the capacity for the unhindered interpretation of the symbols of his own living, in order therefore to give back to man the freedom to interpret life spontaneously in terms of his own creative center of living, the new psychology reaches to dreams and other symbolical representations of the unconscious; for in those may be found the striking images, the self-revealing pictures which will establish a contact between the confused, inhibited personality and its creative source. As this contact occurs, as this revelation of the submerged creative activities of the inner life-center stirs the soul into realizing its own god-like identity, a process is started which burns up the refuse and the crystallizations of the past, and which releases the creative energies of free selfhood. This is liberation.

"Man's consciousness, enslaved by fetishes of all sorts, can be liberated only by the power perpetually and spontaneously to create symbols, and thus to give meaning and nobility to life. This is the secret of the Art of Living. It is the foundation of true psychology. Only the creator is free; because he alone need not depend upon the symbolism of the past, but is able to live in the act of creating ever new symbols.

"This process of liberation can be started by breaking down the hypnosis of the past and freeing the individual from his hypnotizer, the race's subconscious; or by revealing to him the all-compelling Image of his own selfhood: the seed-Image of his destiny. The first method can be pursued by the use of music and vibrations of a certain character, which re-establish the circulation of the spiritual life-force by burning away obstructions, and so bring back the tone of the psyche to its fundamental harmony or diapason. The second method has been used in the past in the Mysteries, where the symbolic Image of the candidate's Soul was evoked to his outer consciousness by the Hierophant's magical power. But such a procedure does not belong to the field of generalized public application.

"However, what can be accomplished along this line is to interpret to the individual in words this living Symbol of his own Soul-being. This symbol occupies in relation to the sequence of varied events which constitute a person's destiny the place which the tonality of a musical work does to the many notes of the composition, or the place which the seed holds in relation to the plant and the multiplicity of its organs. Thus the term 'Harmonic Psychology,' or as we might also say: 'Seed-Psychology.'

"While psycho-analysis deals analytically and empirically with the many elements that together constitute the human psyche, harmonic psychology operates by synthetic perception, establishing itself at a point whence the soul and destiny of man are seen integrated into a fundamental Chord of life-forces, a seed-form, an organic symbol of selfhood. Thus we substitute the vision of the unity of a life-process for the psychological vivisection of man into symbolic fragments.

"Such a synthetizing perception can be reached by using astrological data as symbolic materials. The astrological birth-chart can be considered as determining the morphology of the soul. It is the signature of the birth-moment, the form taken by universal Life according to a particular set of time-space values. It pictures the seed and general structural plan of growth of the human being: his destiny. It defines the basic relationships which determine man's identity and character, the harmony (consonant or dissonant) which in its wholeness is heard as the tone of the soul.

"The difference between such a use of astrological references and the ordinary fortune-telling variety of astrology is just as great as that between the dream-interpretations of the soothsayer and the use of dream symbolism in the most scientific psycho-analysis. The symbolic use of astrology is just as legitimate as the symbolic use of dreams. The former is a much more scientific and impersonal tool for the synthetic appreciation of a man's essential nature than the latter, colored as dreams are by the patient's superficial reactions—and also necessarily fragmentary.

"Astrology has been debased as fortune-telling and usually deals only with concrete events. But events in themselves are not important. What matters is the significance we bestow upon them. It is only by giving to events the meaning centered in our own Soul, that we make them real. There is no reality except that which we create by the very activity of continuous living. Thus events do not happen, we happen to them; we make them constructive or destructive. We must, therefore, know what we are, rather than what events might be. Harmonic Astrology deals with the integral Form of Man, with the symbols of his wholeness of being, with the archetype of his destiny on earth. It is the means whereby the Image of the soul can be interpreted, outlined and made manifest to the outer personal consciousness. It is thus able to start the creative process of inner combustion and repolarization which—if the individual is really intent upon the task of regeneration—leads to liberation. It will lead to liberation not by virtue of something external entering into the individual, but by means of the power which the true form of the soul possesses to compel the blurred image of the personality to shape itself in the likeness of its archetype, once the latter is brought out of the Unconscious into the Conscious where it begins to operate as a creative reality."

The foregoing approach to the subject is completed by the point of view described in the following paragraphs, which state in a concise manner ideas which can be found scattered through this book:

"Harmonic Astrology deals entirely with the problem of form. It is thus a secure foundation for the 'art of living.' It deals with form not as a merely esthetic element, but as a vessel of integration for evolving forces. The philosophy of astrology is thus the philosophy of form. No one can approach the findings of astrology in a completely integrating way who does not understand the purpose of form in life, and the results accomplished by life in the building, maintenance and disintegration of forms. Everything in astrology may be said to revolve around this three-fold operation.

"What is a human body? It is a relatively permanent form in which biological forces are brought to a focus and made to serve a single purpose. Circulation, digestion, breathing, reproduction, are functional processes resulting from the harmonization and integration of many vital forces. When disintegration sets in and the harmony of the forces operating in the body is disturbed, disease occurs and ultimately death.

"Ages of terrestrial, collective evolution have brought the human body to a point of relative perfection as an organic whole. But the evolution of the psycho-mental organism, or Soul, of man is very far from having reached such a point, generically speaking. Man should be the builder of this psycho-mental organism. It is built by harmonizing and integrating collective elements, 'soul-forces,' all that we inherit at birth or assimilate throughout life—so that these elements become an organic 'web of energies' properly differentiated and inter-related: a living whole, the wholeness of which is the Self (in Jung's sense of the term).

"Man should be the harmonizer of the forces of his Destiny, the builder of his own 'Temple of Solomon.' But how can he do so permanently unless he knows: 1) the nature of the energies he has to deal with, and the laws of their cyclic activities; 2) the plan of the building? If he does not know the former he is likely to be wrecked by the unexpected rush of energies; if he has not seen the plan of the building, how can he know where to fit the materials he has assimilated? He is likely to build a wall where a pillar should stand; and dig caves under columns destined to bear the weight of cupolas.

"Astrology helps us to see—at least intellectually—the vision of our archetypal Form. It tells us what to do with the energies which work in us through our days; not how to destroy or even 'rule' them with an iron hand, but how to balance the one against the other; especially it teaches us that these energies have no right to usurp the prerogatives of our selfhood and proclaim themselves as 'I'—for they are parts and not the whole, and 'I'—when truly understood and operating—is the wholeness of the whole. The real 'I,' however, is the wholeness not so much of the *contents* of our total being, as of the archetypal *form* of this total being. In that sense it is a relatively changeless 'I'. It is in fact the monad, the abstract quality that we are, as particular manifestations of universal life. This 'I'—the essence of our Archetypal Form—is not however *actual*, until this archetypal Form is made into a substantial organism—both at the physical and at the psycho-mental level."

Much of the foregoing may have to be understood in a purely symbolical sense; but one idea ought to emerge clearly, and that is the idea that the birth-chart of an individual is the "signature" of the cyclic identity, the Form or Image of his essential divinity. *Considered as a whole*, that is esthetically, it is the symbol of that which he must strive to become. It is therefore his "magic talisman." He, as a fluctuating and evolving personality, must identify himself with the wholeness of this birth-chart. But—and this is essential—the birth-chart is never to be regarded as indicating life-contents, but only a structure of selfhood. No planet should ever be regarded as an entity or a thing in itself, representing particular life-contents; for to identify oneself with *one* planet, would destroy—or at least tend to destroy—the wholeness of the personality. Identification can refer only to the whole Pattern of the chart.

This distinction is absolutely essential; for all (temporary) evil in a life arises from the fact that one type of energy in the personality has grown so strong as to impose its will upon the whole personality. Thus we say: "I hate"—"I am angry"— "I love," which shows identification of the "I" with *one* function or energy of the psyche. The man who is integrated is no longer subject to such accidents or catastrophes. He can say: "There is hate, or anger, or love rising within me. But I—the essence of the archetypal Form—see and watch this onsurge; and I shall pit against it the combined weight of the other functions which are operating within me; and so the total harmony of the whole of which I am the wholeness will not be disturbed; there will have been only an inner re-adjustment of equilibrium of forces—and such readjustments are fruitful, for they help to avoid the crystallization of a particular internal set-up of energies or functions. If I am a strong intellectual type I shall welcome a strong emotional surge; for it will give to my intellectual function something to do besides thinking intellectual thoughts about this or that. It will force them to combine with long unused forces of my depths, to balance the rise of the strong emotion; and that will vitalize my intellect."

To balance—never to destroy. The strong emotion means power. It summons vital contents from the living organic depths. These contents are needed for the completion of personality. Everything there is is needed—but *in its proper place and with proper emphasis in relation to the purpose of the whole*. A man *minus* anything cannot become a "god." Neither can he do so with too much of anything. The fulfilled personality is an organism: that is, a balanced, operative whole.

There may be, there *are* other paths toward stages of being that may be said to transcend man, as we know him. If we postulate the principle that any whole is eventually to find itself a part in a greater Whole, then man's destiny is to operate as a part in the "Greater Individual"—however we may choose to define and circumscribe the latter. If this be true, then there might be various "paths," following which, this identification of the "lesser individual," as such, with the function that he may, or should, fill within the "Greater

Individual," can be effected. Thus occultism mentions several "paths" of spiritual development, several *margas* or *yogas*, following which man may reach more nearly to a cosmic level of functioning within the "Greater Individual."

However this may be, the approach which we are stressing in this book—and which, we believe, is the typical and natural approach from the standpoint of astrology—can be summed up by the words: harmonization, integration, fulfillment. It is based on an understanding of form, equilibrium, balanced operation and synthesis. It is crowned and made significant by the operation of the creative, through which alone the conflict between individual and collective is solved—solved by significant, symbolic, creative, power-releasing action. It involves the use of creative imagination. It involves an esthetic, as against an ethical, approach. It demands of the individual that he have the courage to stand as an individual, to assume conscious responsibility, to face the future as a father—and (mystically speaking) as a sacrifice to the cycle that will be ushered in by his creative act. It demands, moreover, understanding—and beauty: intuition and self-culture. Being a creative whole, he should know how to face, as a whole, whole situations: which means intuition and that understanding which passes intellection. Being a projector of his own image, he should fulfill the duty that every person has to reveal, and image forth in his own life the maximum of beauty—of body, soul and mind—of which his inheritance has made him capable.

This is the path of personality-integration, the path of creative significance, the path of release of power through Form. The occult quality of this path may be looked for in the numbers 1—4—7; which, by kabbalistic addition, add—as we already saw—to 28. Symbols again. But by using such symbols intuition is developed. Intuition leads to true "seership"—and the seer is he who sees in every thing of Life a living significance. All things reveal to him their archetypal form, their essential "birth-charts." All things are known by their vital "names." And this alone gives to a man power; for to name correctly is to have power over the thing or process named—and it is also to understand with that "creative understanding" which alone, as Keyserling so beautifully reveals, can give birth to the "new world" for which all men of understanding and nobility and spiritual vision not only yearn, but *work*.

Astrology and the Process of Civilization

Living civilization is a process; not a thing. It is the process of the gestation of Man—the seed-condition of perfected mankind. A fallacious theory, product of the earth-bent European mind, has made of civilization a death of living values. But the seed is not dead. Civilization is not to be referred to the crystallized, straw-like stalk of a plant as the fall begins. Such a civilization is not the true, living civilization; it is merely the end of the cultural cycle.

Culture is the equivalent of the process of change—of the personality, which is an ever unstable balance of individual and collective factors. It originates in a spiritual-monadic Impulse; which is the One-that-is-in-the-beginning, the "Avatar," the great Universal Person who, as it were, winds up the spring of the cycle-to-be—because He is a direct agent, an embodied act-of-will of the "Greater Individual," the Planetary Being. Then culture develops through endless vicissitudes and transformations; just as germ, stem and root, leaves, and finally flower and fruit grow—grow from the earth, bound to the earth and its physiological, positive-negative energies.

At last the seed forms itself within the fruit; and as this occurs the seasonal plant already begins to die. The stem hardens. Culture becomes a set of stereotyped formulas of thinking, feeling and behavior. Presently the seed falls to the ground. Already the leaves have begun to disintegrate earthward, to become later on the manure which releases chemical substance—collective elements—to feed the new plant which will rise at the call of the new Spring. But the seed does not disintegrate. It lives; and this life is one of concentrated and relatively permanent wholeness; for in the seed is contained in potency the whole sum of the characteristics and the power of the species.

Living civilization is the seed of Man; but it is also the process that calls the seed into being—the process of individuation; and the process in which the seed dies as a seed that the new plant may be—the process of sacrifice. Living civilization is the creative principle operating through the human race as a whole. It is especially manifest in the "last moment" of the cycle, when all that is living and true to the archetypal pattern that is in the beginning is gathered together into a seed-synthesis which will be food to a humanity as yet to come. According to prophetic symbolism, two-thirds will be lost— that is, they will disintegrate as leaves and stalk, and even as fruit. But one-third will be saved. These will constitute the seed—the *Shistas*: those in and through whom the creative principle will play a new symphony of being as Spring rings the call and leads the performance.

These performers who, as a group, constitute the seed, the orchestra, are those that have become "separate;" those that have experienced a "second birth"—birth out of the realm of decaying leaves into that of the consecrated seed. These individuals are trained eventually to perform their group-work. They are trained individually and as a group. They are not to be soloists, but players in an orchestra. They must give up something of their "personality" (in the usual sense of the term) in order that a "group-personality" may be born: the orchestra. They have to do so, if they are to remain in the orchestra, because the orchestra is *some day* to perform a symphonic score.

A score is a formula of relationship, a pattern of symbolic entities, called "notes of music." A score is the *raison d'être* and purpose of the performance, and of the orchestra. The score is the abstract entity which is the form of the group-personality which is the orchestra. We may imagine that the orchestra is gathered and trained to perform only one symphonic score. If so, then this score is the structural archetype of the orchestral group-personality. For it is the score that will determine what instruments are needed, and where and when each shall have to sound out, to play the part reserved to it.

True, there may develop personal relationships (friendship, dislike, etc.) between the players as emotional human beings; but such relationships must ever be subservient to the one goal of the orchestral group-personality: the performance of the score. The basic and permanent set of relationships between the performers is one determined by the score to be played. It is an archetypal relationship of work and of purpose—a creative relationship; and not a personal or individual-collective relationship of feelings, dependent largely on moods and on the ever-changing influence of natural or momentary conditions.

Such an illustration—which is accurate enough—shows very clearly the part that astrology can play in the process of living civilization, and especially in the process of gathering-in, in the future, performers who in turn will have to become "individuated" into a group-personality: the orchestra. Astrology reveals the score of the symphony, and the place which each performer has to occupy in the orchestra.

The kind of astrology which can reveal the score of a coming civilization is not yet known, at least to ordinary men of the present generation. Whether some "Adepts" are proficient in it or not, is not for us to say. We have touched, however, upon the subject of such a planetary astrology referring to the "planetary creative," in our chapters: "The Key to Astrological Symbolism" and "A Classification of Astrological Viewpoints." It is doubtful whether much more can be stated at present, though there may be—there are, if we believe Blavatsky's *Secret Doctrine*—men who at all times have been trained in the knowledge of the intricacies of planetary and cosmic cycles. The Great Polar Cycle and its so-called "zodiacal Ages"—such as the Piscean and Aquarian Ages—indicate very broadly the characteristics of great civilizations, as they wax and wane on continents which are their *physical* bodies. Most interesting attempts at correlating the precessional Ages and past civilizations, and at relating the zodiacal signs to zones of geographical longitudes, have recently been made. But claims are conflicting, and the final key may not yet have been discovered. It may depend upon a consideration of the seven-fold or seventy-fold division of the Great Polar Cycle itself, as we have already suggested, rather than on that of the twelvefold precessional motion of the equinoxes along the zodiacal-equatorial belt; or better still, on a correlation of both of these points of view.

But there are other planetary cycles which are just as important as the one created by the gyration of the Earth's polar axis in about 25,868 years. A 10,000-year cycle, which might be called symbolically that of the Buddha, because it deals with the planetary process of, let us say, "cosmic individuation"—again, a symbol!—has been hinted at in theosophical literature during the life of H. P. Blavatsky (Cf. *The Mahatma Letters*). It presumably refers to the same thing—at a planetary level—with which our previously studied 28-year cycle dealt at the level of the human personality. And there is the same difference between three 10,000-year cycles and the 25,868 Polar Cycle as there is between three 28-year cycles and the "three score and ten" traditional measure of man's life-span.

Five thousand years have elapsed since what the Brahmins call "the beginning of *Kali Yuga*" (3102 B.C.). Twenty-five hundred years have passed since the coming of the Buddha (around 602 B.C.). And the year 1898 (or the period 1891-1898, which witnessed the death of H. P. Blavatsky as well as that of Baha'u'llah) has been said to mark the beginning of a new era—an era which can be conceived as the period of spiritual gestation or perhaps early babyhood of a new type of human Individual-hood at the psycho-mental level. The diagram below will interpret such a cycle in terms of the conventional astrological figure, and may be of interest to minds interested in such cosmic symbolism. A new spiritual history of mankind may, some day, be attempted on the basis of such

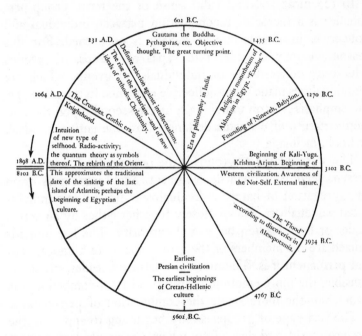

planetary cycles. But our knowledge thereof is obviously too incomplete at present.

The Integration of Group-personality

However, what is of a much more practical significance in our present-day human lives is the use to which astrology may be put in bringing about real and harmonious group-personality. This subject is particularly timely, as there is so much emphasis laid in so many quarters upon the factor of the "group." As a complete theme for discussion it is far beyond the scope of this book; and therefore we cannot attempt to evaluate the significance, importance and validity of this modern trend toward group-behavior and ultimate group-personality. This trend, however, is a fact, and astrology has much to say on the problem of devising a technique for the gathering, harmonizing and integrating of such groups.

In the most real and valid sense of the term, group-personality is a factor of reconciliation between individual and collective, insofar as human society is concerned. For this reason we may consider two types of groups: 1) groups which are collectivities of individuals; 2) groups which are individualities made up of collective elements. In the first type, the emphasis is upon individuals; in the second, upon the collective nature of elements dominated by one entity, or ideal, or book, or image.

The second type of groups is the one usually found at this present stage of human development. Such a group is often an aggregation of barely individualized and still less individuated personalities, drawn closely together either by an actual leader or by a leading belief and authority. The less individualized are the members of the group, the more homogeneous and permanent it is. The more powerful the leader, visible or invisible, the more emotion-arousing and faith-compelling the leadership—the more stable the combination of personalities.

The first type of groups is only beginning to appear in the modern world, and that, often, where one would least suspect it. Here, the group is really an association (or companionship, or cooperative comradeship) of differentiated and self-reliant individuals brought together for a common work and in order to further a common purpose and demonstrate an ideal held valid by all. The group is held together by a common realization, and, in a sense, a common "quality" of being, rather than by a common belief. It has very little to do with personal feelings—in the ordinary sense of the term. It admits of no compulsion, save that of the common purpose and of the need of the jointly undertaken work. Its basic postulate is that every individual should be free to work out his own destiny in a natural and individual manner; that he should do what he can best do, and that group-operation is not only not to hinder the play of the individually creative, but on the contrary is meant to stimulate and enhance it, to give it more significance, more power, a greater scope and permanency of action.

The difficulty is, obviously, that unless one individual's free creative actions *fit in* with other individuals' free creative actions, unless all these actions work into each other harmoniously, in time and space relationship, without sacrificing the essential value of spontaneity and ease—there is bound to be conflict and struggle. Briefly speaking, unless the individuals composing the group fit together *structurally*, as do the pieces of a jig-saw puzzle, such a type of group cannot operate satisfactorily for any length of time. For if there were to be real cooperation (working together) of individuals 'not fitting together structurally and *a priori*, then some of these individuals would necessarily have to alter their creative rhythm, and in this become *what they are not*—granted of course that they actually *were* what they archetypally *are*, *before* they met to constitute a group.

This last sentence emphasizes the two-fold problem: First, the individuals who are to constitute such a group are most often not actually individuated. They are not completely true to their own monad and archetype. They are as yet incompletely formed and unintegrated personalities. Because of that, there is no definiteness and unadulterability in their behavior and their creative processes. They are neither solid nor steady. They follow moods, feelings, and all sorts of un-formed imperatives. They are unknowns—to themselves as well as to their associates. To constitute a real group with such persons is like playing a symphony with musicians who are not sure what note will actually sound when they perform on their own instruments.

The other difficulty (in case of the associates being very definite and fully individuated personalities) is how to find a number of such individuals who will structurally fit together —at least insofar as their creative relationship to the common goal is concerned. Short of some super-normal intuitive and direct perception of the structural characteristics of all the individuals from whom those who are to constitute the group could be selected, astrology is the only solution to the problem.

Here we are dealing with the complex problem of establishing and correctly interpreting valid relationships between the birth-charts of two and more than two individuals. To study how this can be done is also beyond the scope of this book. All that we wish to state now is that, theoretically at least, it can be satisfactorily done. In practice there are numerous difficulties to reckon with.

The first one is to ascertain the exact nature of the contemplated relationship. We have often seen two persons coming with both their charts, for advice as to whether they should or should not marry. Our answer to this is always: What do you want to marry for? What kind of marriage-relationship are you contemplating? For what purpose? Not all people marry for the purpose, consciously or unconsciously, of making a home, raising children, and all that goes with that. Marriage can be regenerative. It can produce spiritual repolarization. It can free both partners from complexes and inhibitions. All of which may not include home, children or even the usual kind of happiness. Marriage can be a dissonant harmony, or a consonant harmony. It may be meant to be permanent; or only for a period. It can include deep conflicts and oppositions of attitudes—and yet be the very salvation, the very need of both partners. Who, then, shall wish to take the responsibility of advising two persons not to marry because strong conflicts and contrasts are shown by comparing the two birth-charts?

This is one difficulty. Another is the usual uncertainty about the exact birth-moment of an individual—even more so of a dozen or two persons. There are still other difficulties which are related to the fact that the psychology of the kind of group we are now considering is very little understood; that in such groups secondary relationships are almost necessarily formed, and those at various levels. Yet, in spite of it all, one can say that astrology, by comparing birth-charts, can define the *kind* of relationship to be expected between the individuals symbolized by these charts. Various other astrological methods, too intricate to detail, can also be used in dealing with this matter of relationship.

The result is that one might be able to select, by studying their charts' relationships, let us say, twelve fully developed individuals, who would be able to cooperate toward the furtherance of a common purpose overshadowing them all, in such a way that the activities of each would remain exactly true to his or her individual selfhood and destiny, and yet in such a way that all these activities would fit together—just as the individual performances of musicians composing an orchestra fit together in the orchestral rendition of a symphony. In this orchestral analogy, to be a first violin or a second French horn or a first bassoon would correspond to the *generic* selfhood of the personalities composing the group (their racial type, their background—occultly speaking their "Ray" of development); while the *individual* selfhood would be symbolized by the written musical part which the player is to perform and which is the "signature" of his function in the group.

Astrology cannot tell much, if anything, as to the generic selfhood; but it can deal satisfactorily with the "score" or the "blue-print" of the individual selfhood. In the case of the formation of a group-personality, the unknown factor is the "score" of this group-personality itself; but even there astrology might interpret significantly the birth-chart of the group, taking as the moment of birth either that at which the first move toward the formation of the group was made, or that at which the first concrete manifestation of group-activity or group-relationship occurred.

If we carry on the illustration of the orchestra, shall we have to say that the orchestra needs a leader? It needs obviously a leading factor, or principle, or purpose; but not necessarily a leading personality. Conductorless orchestras have proven successful. But the point is really beside our present discussion, and could be discussed only by considering what relation there can be between human personalities and the "Greater Individual" at the planetary level.

What counts for us now is the fact that astrology may solve the basic dilemma in the constitution of groups, or of any relationship between two or more personalities. If the persons related are by nature followers, believers and devotees, astrology is of small service. The relationship will be strong and enduring if there is a strong power dominating the relationship. In the typical marriage of physiologically-emotionally centered beings, this power is sex: the race-purpose and social purpose dominate the relationship. In the ordinary groups—whether they be called "occult," religious or political, or even, at the limit, a gang—a leader, visible or invisible, dominates with his strong individual-personal power an aggregation of followers. Such groups, as well as the emotional marriage, are parts of the karmic pattern which rules men who are not yet individuated, just as biological urges and instincts rule the animal and the plant. All these relations and combinations of desires, impulses, loves, hatred—all this birthing, dying and re-birth, belong to the collective, to the vast ebb and flow of the life-process—to that infinite, incommensurable sea of *becoming* which goes on and on.

Astrology can do little in relation to such collective factors.

The Use of Astrology

It may reveal the unavoidable future crises and end of the relationship. But of what good is it to tell someone who is helpless, because he is not really a *one*, that he will be shot in so many days! Where there is no freedom—and there is little freedom, indeed, in relationships controlled by biological urges or by the blind psychic force of belief—astrology is usually more destructive than constructive. And freedom exists only in function of the individual. Only that which is whole can ever be free.

In terms of groups, only groups of actual individuals have any need of astrology, because in those groups only is there a problem of how to balance inherent individual freedom and the efficiency of the group; how to retain individual form within the group-structure. No group of individuals is possible unless this problem is solved. And to solve this problem does not mean that a leader should select the members of his "orchestra" astrologically; but it should rather mean that individual performers should come together on the basis of such a structural-astrological knowledge of relationship.

We have referred elsewhere to such a significant relationship between creative individuals as an "air-relationship," in contradistinction to "earth-relationship" or "blood-relationship" which binds emotionally and tends to reduce the *relata* to a heavy mass—powerful perhaps, yet neither free nor significant in terms of individuals. We have called for "an aristocracy of Living Persons integrated by a common will to serve Life and Man; a creative aristocracy; an aristocracy of Equals in terms of Soul-equality, not of body similarity or likeness of duty; an aristocracy which would be a *group* by virtue of the unanimous self-consecration of its units to a common purpose *self-evident* to each and all. This group would be dynamic, mobile, always in action—by thought or deed: a web of centers of force and releases of power, radiating the energy of intense living and strenuous interrelationship, shirking no responsibility, ready to serve in utter self-dedication to the Cause, always creating values, individually and in group; always stirring and fecundating minds and souls. Not a static body rooted in self-complacent isolation, but a unanimous Idea operating concretely in utmost diversity through many individual centers acting as foci for the greater Whole in widely different conditions; in all states, countries, classes, religions; ubiquitous, plastic, self-regenerating, unbound by dogma, rooted only in Life and Purpose, universalistic—a moving force of Free Men and Free Women who dare to assume the creative responsibility of a New World. With a somewhat different emphasis, Alice Bailey has been holding before her students, and before the vast number of the readers of her publications, the ideal of a universalistic and spiritually creative "New Group of World Servers;" and modern Theosophists have spoken for over fifty years, with varying degrees of comprehension, of a ubiquitous "White Lodge" of Adepts—which as a group constitutes the *Seed-Being* of the Last Day of our human-planetary cycle.

In these cases, and in others which more or less approach a similar type of group-ideal, the basic emphasis is always to be put upon the creative significance of the individual. Individuals co-operating, co-creating; companions who (etymologically speaking) "eat of the same bread" of significance, "friends" who have made of their personal relations a vast relationship of living friendship—but always individuals, because the "greater Whole" that is the end of human planetary evolution can be formed only by the creative interaction of men who are whole, and thus individuals.

Astrology, when symbolically and structurally interpreted, can guide and give full significance to such a creative interaction of individuals. It becomes, as such, an art of interpretation of symbolic forms of relationship; and it can serve the purpose of the formation of groups, because it itself deals with groupings of symbolic factors, and is a practical method of perception of the meaning of groups in the process of their becoming fully individuated as integral personalities.

Personality, in this sense, appears as the final stage of the life-process; and it can mean either the Christ-like human Personality, or the "Greater Person" whom we may call the Planetary Whole; or, in between the two, any Group-Personality which has cyclically permanent and creative individual characteristics. But it is these individual characteristics which give form and significance to Personality, because in every case Personality is the stage of complete actualization of individual Form. It is the cyclic end which is the fulfillment in a substantial organism of the cyclic beginning. The individual is the potential structure; the fully individuated personality, the actual organism.

Meaning resides in this consummation of the Last Day of the cycle. It is a function of the wholeness of the individuated whole. It resides in the individual pole of being, as against the essential meaninglessness of the vast tides of the collective. In wholeness alone is there intelligence and understanding—for in it only, because it is an end-moment and fulfillment, is there form conscious of itself, and is there beauty. The world-process has no meaning. No event has meaning, save as man gives it meaning; man—or any being, or wholeness of related beings, in whom there is intelligence and form and fulfillment.

The life-process has no meaning, save in terms of the "last moment" of its every cycle; for this protean "last moment" is Meaning itself. Neither has the life-process form, save in terms of the "first moment" of its every cycle; for this "first moment" is Form itself. As for the myriads of events which crowd in serried ranks from beginning to end of innumerable cycles, these are but the "happenings" of collective elements, save for him who is able to relate them to his own "form of destiny," to fit them meaningfully into the structure of his own individual selfhood. This individual selfhood is in the beginning, and it becomes ever more manifest and concrete as integrated Personality, as each moment is related to it and stamped, as it were, with the creative symbol and signature of the "I am."

"In the beginning was the Word"—and the Word is the individual structure of Self. In the beginning was Form. Astrology, as "the science of all beginnings" (Marc Jones), is therefore the one revealer of the "form" of all things that are in process of becoming. Meaning is completed when the potential form, and back of that the quality of the One-that-is-in-the-beginning—the Monad—is actualized as a fulfilled, integrated organism. In integration alone is meaning made real and creative. The process of individuation is that universal process which ends in the realization of meaning. It starts with Form and ends in Significance; and all meaning is born within the innermost of the individual, but of an individual who, after constant assimilations of collective life-contents, has reached a condition of fulfillment as integrated Personality.

There is the individual—and there is Life. And Life is a vast, limitless, formless flux of energies which obeys but one Law: the Law of Equilibrium, of balance—or of compensatory action. Out of this Law, which involves the trinity of motion, space and duration, arises the type of activity which we called "cyclic." All cycles are essentially pendulum-like oscillations —or call them "vibrations." And all these oscillations, infinite in their smallness as in their vastness, are aimless, meaningless. They *are*—and that fact is the substratum of all, and yet means nothing in particular. These oscillations have obviously four basic moments, exemplified by the four cardinal moments of the Sun's yearly journey: solstices, points of farther dis-equilibrium, equinoxes, points of unstable equilibrium. These are the four great symbols of the cycle of change, the cycle of natural, biological energies which wax and wane, mean-inglessly.

But for the man who has become individuated, and who has established individual consciousness at the mental level of being, where Form is revealed and Significance rises out of lives lived in fulfillment, the meaningless Four become the Three, in which there is meaning. This meaning is the realm of beginning-middle-and-end. This is the realm of the *alpha* and the *omega* integrated in the living Christ—the man who is whole and full of seed. As this Christ-state is reached, the Three merge into the eternal One; and the realm of spirit is *born anew*. It is born anew in every Christ-being; for it is not a postulated fact, but a reality that emerges only from within the individual structure of fulfillment, out of the individual bestowing of significance upon every moment, experienced in beauty.

It is this fulfillment in beauty and in the harmony that is peace, which builds spirit ever anew. Spirit is the creative consummation of every moment. Spirit is the integrating of beginning and end in a synthesis that is reborn and made significant at every moment. It is the cycle concentrated into the Now. *It is the Creative Now.*

May the power of this Creative Now illumine our every moment with significance! Indeed there is beauty and meaning in every moment—because in every moment the individual may reach integration and joy that is creative, that fathers forth new cycles and affirms toward the unknown the noble will to destiny. The skies above are no more radiant, the form of constellations no more luminous and revealing, than is the realization within our deepest selfhood that we are whole; that in wholeness which is creative everything that is and ever will be is fulfilled in the Now. Oh! indeed—*NOW*—all is beautiful! The Whole is beautiful.

THE END

This symbol, wrought in silver, was discovered during the summer, 1934, in the mountains of New Mexico—for which I must thank M. R., who brought it forth to be a "Signature" to this book—a true signature indeed, as it reveals in its hieroglyphs the formula of fulfilled Personality.

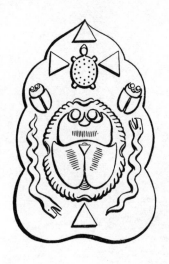